Strategies
of
Qualitative
Inquiry

INTERNATIONAL ADVISORY BOARD

Strategies *of* Qualitative Inquiry

Norman K. Denzin
Yvonna S. Lincoln
Editors

SAGE Publications
International Educational and Professional Publisher
Thousand Oaks London New Delhi

For information:

SAGE Publications, Inc.
2455 Teller Road
Thousand Oaks, California 91320
E-mail@sagepub.com

SAGE Publications Ltd.
6 Bonhill Street
London EC2A 4PU
United Kingdom

SAGE Publications India Pvt. Ltd.
M-32 Market
Greater Kailash I
New Delhi 110048 India

Printed in the United States of America

Library of Congress Cataloging-in-Publication Data

Main entry under title:

Strategies of qualitative inquiry / edited by Norman K.
Denzin and Yvonna S. Lincoln.
   p. cm.
Includes bibliographical references and index.
ISBN 0-7619-1435-8 (pbk.: acid-free paper)
   1. Social sciences—Methodology. 2. Social
sciences—Research—Methodology. I. Denzin, Norman K. II. Lincoln,
Yvonna S.
H61.S8823 1998
300'.7'2—dc21   98-8894

99 00 01 02 03 04 8 7 6 5 4 3

Acquiring Editor:	Peter Labella
Production Editor:	Astrid Virding
Production Assistant:	Karen Wiley
Typesetter/Designer:	Danielle Dillahunt
Indexer:	Juniee Oneida
Cover Designer:	Ravi Balasuriya
Print Buyer:	Anna Chin

Contents

Preface

For more than two decades, a quiet methodological revolution has been taking place in the social sciences. A blurring of disciplinary boundaries has occurred. The social sciences and humanities have drawn closer together in a mutual focus on an interpretive, qualitative approach to research and theory. Although these trends are not new, the extent to which the "qualitative revolution" has overtaken the social sciences and related professional fields has been nothing short of amazing.

Reflecting this revolution, a host of textbooks, journals, research monographs, and readers have been published in recent years. In 1994, we published the *Handbook of Qualitative Research* in an attempt to represent the field in its entirety, to take stock of how far it had come and how far it might yet go. Although it became abundantly clear that the "field" of qualitative research is defined primarily by tensions, contradictions, and hesitations—and that they exist in a less-than-unified arena—we believed that the handbook could be valuable for solidifying, interpreting, and organizing the field in spite of the essential differences that characterize it.

Putting together the *Handbook* was a massive undertaking that was carried out over several years, the full story of which can be found in the preface to the *Handbook* (which can also be found on the Web site for the *Handbook*: http://www.sagepub.com/sagepage/denzin_lincoln.htm).

We have been enormously gratified and heartened by the response to the *Handbook* since its publication. Especially gratifying has been that it has been used and adapted by such a wide variety of scholars and graduate students in precisely the way we had hoped: as a starting point, a springboard for new thought and new work.

◆ The Paperback Project

There was one constituency we did not focus on centrally as we developed the plan for the *Handbook*: students in the classroom. The sheer size of the *Handbook,* with its corresponding expense, seemed to make the book a difficult one to assign in courses. Yet within a year of publication, it became clear that the material contained in the *Handbook* was deemed sufficiently valuable to override some considerations of size and expense.

Despite the reception the *Handbook* received in the classroom, students and teachers alike have urged us to publish the book in a less expensive, paperback iteration. We and our publisher, Sage Publications, decided to figure out a plan to do this.

Peter Labella, our editor at Sage, canvassed more than 50 scholars and students about the way the *Handbook* works in the classroom setting. Through a series of phone interviews and e-mail surveys—which themselves led to an ongoing conversation—a plan to do the book as a series of paperbacks began to emerge. The three-volume plan was codified at a series of meetings in the spring of 1997.

It was decided that the part structure of the *Handbook* could serve as a useful point of departure for the organization of the paperbacks. Thus Volume 1, titled *The Landscape of Qualitative Research: Theories and Issues,* takes a look at the field from a broadly theoretical perspective, and is composed of the *Handbook*'s Parts I ("Locating the Field"), II ("Major Paradigms and Perspectives"), and VI ("The Future of Qualitative Research." Volume 2, titled *Strategies of Qualitative Inquiry,* focuses on just that, and consists of Part III of the *Handbook.* Volume 3, titled *Collecting and Interpreting Qualitative Materials,* considers the tasks of collecting, analyzing, and interpreting empirical materials, and comprises the *Handbook*'s Parts IV ("Methods of Collecting and Analyzing Empirical Materials") and V ("The Art of Interpretation, Evaluation, and Presentation").

We decided that nothing should be cut from the original *Handbook.* Nearly everyone we spoke to who used the *Handbook* had his or her own way of using it, leaning heavily on certain chapters and skipping others altogether. But there was great consensus that this reorganization made a great deal of sense both pedagogically and economically. We and Sage are committed to making this iteration of the *Handbook* accessible for class-room use. This commitment is reflected in the size, organization, and price of the paperbacks, as well as in the addition of end-of-book bibliographies.

It also became clear in our conversations with colleagues who used the *Handbook* that the single-volume, hard-cover version has a distinct place and value, and Sage will keep the original version available until a revised edition is published.

◆ Organization of This Volume

Strategies of Qualitative Inquiry isolates the major strategies—historically, the research methods—that researchers can use in conducting concrete qualitative studies. The question of methods begins with the design of the qualitative research project. This always begins with a socially situated researcher who moves from a research question to a paradigm or perspec-tive, and then to the empirical world. So located, the researcher then addresses the range of methods that can be employed in any study. The history and uses of these strategies are explored extensively in this volume.

◆ Acknowledgments

Of course, this book would not exist without its authors or the editorial board members for the *Handbook* on which it is based. These individuals were able to offer both long-term, sustained commitments to the project and short-term emergency assistance.

In addition, we would like to thank the following individuals and institutions for their assistance, support, insights, and patience: our respec-tive universities and departments, as well as Jack Bratich and Rob Leffel, our respective graduate students. Without them, we could never have kept this project on course. There are also several people to thank at Sage Publications. We thank Peter Labella, our new editor; this three-volume version of the *Handbook* would not have been possible without Peter's wisdom, support, humor, and grasp of the field in all its current diversity. Peter had the vision to understand how a three-volume set could be better suited to the classroom and to the needs of students than the original format of the *Handbook*.

As always, we appreciate the efforts of Lenny Friedman, the director of marketing at Sage, along with his staff, for their indefatigable efforts in getting the word out about the *Handbook* to teachers, researchers, and methodologists around the world. Astrid Virding was essential in moving this project through production; we are also grateful to the copy editor, Judy Selhorst, and to those whose proofreading and indexing skills were so central to the publication of the *Handbook* on which these volumes are based. Finally, as ever, we thank our spouses, Katherine Ryan and Egon Guba, for their forbearance and constant support.

The idea for this three-volume paperback version of the *Handbook* did not arise in a vacuum, and we are grateful for the feedback we received from countless teachers and students, both informally and in response to our formal survey. We wish especially to thank the following individuals: Jim Barott, University of Utah; Joanne Cooper, University of Hawaii; Fran Crawford, Curtin University; Morten Ender, University of North Dakota; Rich Hoffman, Miami University of Ohio; Patti Lather, Ohio State University; Michael Lissack, Henley-on-Thames; Martha MacLeod, University of Northern British Columbia; Suzanne Miller, University of Buffalo; Peggy Rios, University of Miami; Cynthia Russell, University of Tennessee, Memphis; Diane Schnelker, University of Northern Colorado; Coleen Shannon, University of Texas at Arlington; Barry Shealy, University of Buffalo; Ewart Skinner, Bowling Green State University; Jack Spencer, Purdue University; and Carol Tishelman, Karolinska Institute.

NORMAN K. DENZIN
University of Illinois at Urbana-Champaign

YVONNA S. LINCOLN
Texas A&M University

Introduction to
This Volume

◆ Qualitative researchers think historically, interactionally, and structurally. They attempt to identify the varieties of men and women who prevail in a given historical period (Mills, 1959, p. 7). Such scholars seek to examine the major public and private issues and personal troubles that define a particular historical moment. Qualitative researchers self-consciously draw upon their own experiences as a resource in their inquiries. They always think reflectively, historically, and biographically. They seek strategies of empirical inquiry that will allow them to make connections among lived experience, larger social and cultural structures, and the here and now. These connections are forged out the empirical materials that are gathered in any given investigation.

Empirical inquiry, of course, is shaped by paradigm commitments and by the recurring questions that any given paradigm, or interpretive perspective, asks about human experience. Critical theorists, for example examine the material conditions and systems of ideology that reproduce class structures. Ethnic and feminist researchers examine the stereotypes, prejudices, and injustices connected to race, ethnicity, and gender.

The researcher-as-*bricoleur* is always already in the empirical world of experience. Still, this world is confronted, in part, through the lens that the scholar's paradigm, or interpretive perspective, provides. In turn, the world so conceived ratifies the individual's commitment to the paradigm in question. However, as specific investigations are planned and carried out, two issues must be confronted immediately: research design and choice of strategy of inquiry.[1] We take them up in order. Each resolves into a variety of related questions and issues that must also be addressed.

◆ Research Design

The research design, as analyzed by Valerie Janesick, situates the investigator in the empirical world.[2] Four basic questions structure the issue of design: (a) How will the design connect to the paradigm being used? That is, how will empirical materials be informed by and interact with the paradigm in question? (b) Who or what will be studied? (c) What strategies of inquiry will be used? (d) What methods or research tools will be used for collecting and analyzing empirical materials?

Paradigm, Perspective, and Metaphor

The positivist, postpositivist, constructionist, and critical paradigms dictate, with varying degrees of freedom, the design of a qualitative research investigation. This can be looked at as a continuum, with rigorous design principles on one end and emergent, less well-structured directives on the other. Positivist research designs place a premium on the early identification and development of a research question and a set of hypotheses, choice of a research site, and establishment of sampling strategies, as well as a specification of the research strategies and methods of analysis that will be employed. A research proposal may be written that lays out the stages and phases of the study. These phases may be conceptualized in terms of those outlined by Janice Morse in this volume (reflection, planning, entry, data collection, withdrawal from the field, analysis, and write-up). This proposal may also include a budget, a review of the relevant literature, a statement concerning protection of human subjects, a copy of consent forms, interview schedules, and a timeline. Positivist designs attempt to anticipate all of the problems that may arise in a qualitative study. Such designs provide rather well-defined road maps for the researcher. The scholar working in this tradition hopes to produce a work that finds its place in the literature on the topic being studied.

In contrast, much greater ambiguity is associated with postpositivist and nonpositivist designs—those based, for example, on the constructivist or critical theory paradigms or the ethnic, feminist, or cultural studies perspectives. In studies shaped by these paradigms and perspectives there is less emphasis on formal grant proposals, well-formulated hypotheses, tightly defined sampling frames, structured interview schedules, and predetermined research strategies and methods and forms of analysis. The researcher follows a path of discovery, using as a model qualitative works that have achieved the status of classics in the field. Enchanted, perhaps, by the myth of the Lone Ethnographer, the scholar hopes to produce a work that has the characteristics of a study done by one of the giants of the past (Malinowski, Mead, Bateson, Goffman, Becker, Strauss, Wolcott).

The Dance of Design

Janesick presents a fluid view of the design process. Influenced by Martha Graham, Elliot Eisner, and John Dewey, she approaches the problem of research design from an aesthetic, artistic, and metaphoric perspective. With Dewey and Eisner, she sees research design as a work of art: as an event, a process, with phases connected to different forms of problematic experience, and their interpretation and representation. Art molds and fashions experience. In its dance form, art becomes a choreographed production, with distinct phases: warming up, exercises and design decisions, cooling down, interpretation, evaluation, and criticism.

Qualitative research design decisions parallel the warm-up, exercise, and cool-down periods of dance. Just as dance mirrors and creates life, so too do research designs adapt, change, and mold the very phenomena they are intended to examine. Janesick fits traditional design questions (research questions, research sites, timelines, research strategies) into this framework. She then addresses the problems involved in pilot studies, interdisciplinary triangulation, and alternative views of validity, reliability, and generalizability, criticizing the "methodolatry" (preoccupation with method) of many traditional, positivist approaches to these topics.

Thus do paradigms shape the interpretive imaginations of qualitative researchers.

Who and What Will Be Studied?

The who and what of qualitative studies involve cases, or instances of phenomena and/or social processes. Three generic approaches may be taken to the question of who or what will be studied. First, a single case, or single process, may be studied, what Robert Stake calls the intrinsic case study. Here the researcher examines in detail a single case or instance of the phenomenon in question—for example, a classroom, or the process of death and dying as given in the single case of a dying patient (see Glaser & Strauss, 1967). Fiske's discussion of his study of the weekly media viewing patterns of a group of college students living in the same house is another example of the single-case, single-process approach. His research design took him to a site and told him what questions to ask and what methods to use in answering them. This is what any research design does.

Second, the researcher may focus on a number of cases, in what Stake calls the collective case approach. These cases are then analyzed in terms of their specific and generic properties. Third, the researcher can examine multiple instances of a process as that process is displayed in a variety of different cases. For instance, Denzin's (1987) study of relapse in the careers of recovering alcoholics examined types of relapses across several different types of recovering careers. This process approach is then grounded or anchored in specific cases.

Research designs vary, of course, depending on the needs of multifocus or single-focus case and process inquiries. Different sampling issues arise in each situation. These needs and issues also vary according to the paradigm being employed.

Every instance of a case or process bears the stamp of the general class of phenomena it belongs to. However, any given instance is likely to be particular and unique. Thus, for example, any given classroom is like all classrooms, but no two classrooms are the same.

For these reasons, many postpositivist, constructionist, and critical theory qualitative researchers employ theoretical or purposive, and not random, sampling models (Glaser & Strauss, 1967, pp. 62-65). They seek out groups, settings, and individuals where (and for whom) the processes being studied are most likely to occur. At the same time, a process of constant comparison (Glaser & Strauss, 1967, pp. 101-115) among groups, concepts, and observations is necessary, as the researcher seeks to develop an understanding that encompasses all instances of the process, or case, under investigation. A focus on negative cases is a key feature of this process.

These sampling and selection issues would be addressed differently by a postmodern ethnographer in the cultural studies tradition. This investigator would be likely to place greater stress on the intensive analysis of a small body of empirical materials (cases and processes), arguing, after Sartre (1981, p. ix) that no individual or case is ever just an individual or a case. He or she must be studied as a single instance of more universal social experiences and social processes. The person, Sartre (1981) states, is "summed up and for this reason universalized by his epoch, he in turn resumes it by reproducing himself in it as a singularity" (p. ix). Thus to study the particular is to study the general. For this reason, any case will necessarily bear the traces of the universal; consequently, there is less interest in the traditional positivist and postpositivist concerns with negative cases, generalizations, and case selection. The researcher assumes that readers will be able, as Robert Stake argues, to generalize subjectively (or "naturalistically") from the case in question to their own personal experiences.

◆ Strategies of Inquiry

The *strategy of inquiry* comprises the skills, assumptions, and practices used by the researcher-as-*bricoleur* when moving from a paradigm and a research design to the collection of empirical materials. Strategies of inquiry connect researchers to specific approaches and methods for collecting and analyzing empirical materials. The case study, for example, relies on interviewing, observing, and document analysis. Research strategies locate paradigms in specific empirical sites and in specific methodological practices—for example, making a case an object of study.

We turn now to a brief review of the strategies discussed in this work. Each is connected to a complex literature with its own history, its own exemplary works, and its own set of preferred ways for putting the strategy into motion. Each strategy also has its own set of problems involving the positivist, postpositivist, and postmodern legacies.

The Case Study

Stake argues that not all case studies are qualitative, although many are. Focusing on those that are attached to the naturalistic, holistic, cultural, and phenomenological paradigms, he contends that the case study is not a methodological choice, but a choice of object to be studied, such as a child or a classroom (for other views of this method, see the essays in Feagin, Orum, & Sjoberg, 1991; for arguments over what a case is, see the chapters in Ragin & Becker, 1992).[3]

Ultimately, the researcher is interested in a process, or a population of cases, not an individual case. Stake, as noted above, identifies several types of case studies (intrinsic, instrumental, collective) and outlines the uses, varieties, and problems (bias, theory, triangulation, telling the story, case selection, ethics) of each. He notes that case researchers routinely provide information on such topics as the nature of the case, its historical background, and its relation to contexts and other cases, as well as on their informants.

Ethnography and Participant Observation

Ethnography is perhaps the most hotly contested site in qualitative research today. Traditionalists (positivists), postpositivists, and postmodernists compete over the definitions of this field, the criteria that are applied to its texts, and the reflexive place of the researcher in the interpretive process (see Bruner, 1993). Many argue that the ethnographic text is a fiction fashioned out of the researcher's engagement with the world studied. Accordingly, such texts can be evaluated only in terms of their ability to create a sense of verisimilitude for the reader. Others set forth rigorous criteria for the production and evaluation of ethnographic texts (several chapters in this volume and in Volume 3 of this series take up these issues).

Paul Atkinson and Martyn Hammersley steer a careful course down the middle of these several controversies. They argue that ethnographic methods rely chiefly on participant observation. Such methods are characterized by the collection of relatively unstructured empirical materials, a small number of cases, and a writing and style of analysis that are primarily interpretive, involving descriptions of phenomena. Atkinson and Hammersley sketch the history of this method, from Malinowski to the present. They also outline contemporary problems surrounding ethnography, including the so-called science of ethnography, how ethnographic texts represent lived experience, ethnographic authority, the ethical issues involved in studying the "Other," and the literary turn in recent anthropological work (see also Atkinson, 1992; Hammersley, 1992).

Noting the literary turn in ethnography, Atkinson and Hammersley caution against a wholesale relativism that treats all texts as fiction. In turn, they reject a naive realism that says texts easily represent reality. At the same time, they reject many postpositivist criteria for evaluating texts, arguing that these criteria often fail to make clear distinctions between the means and the procedures for establishing the goals of reliability and validity. Although they do not fully develop it in their contribution to this volume, Atkinson and Hammersley have in other work articulated a subtle realism that sets forth two criteria: validity, which asks how truthful, plausible, and credible an account is; and relevance, or whether an account has relevance for theory or social policy (see, e.g., Hammersley, 1992, pp. 69-78).

Phenomenology, Ethnomethodology, and Interpretive Practice

James Holstein and Jaber Gubrium examine that family of qualitative research approaches concerned with reality-constituting interpretive practices (phenomenology, ethnomethodology). These approaches examine how human beings construct and give meaning to their actions in concrete social situations. Many researchers in this tradition use participant observation and interviewing as ways of studying the interpretive practices persons use in their daily lives. Other scholars, those more firmly rooted in the ethnomethodological tradition, criticize the use of any method as a tool, seeing methods instead as practices that produce verifiable findings for any given paradigm.

Holstein and Gubrium draw attention to the interpretive procedures and practices that give structure and meaning to everyday life. These practices are both the topic of and the resources for qualitative inquiry. All knowledge is always local, situated in a local culture and embedded in organizational sites. This local culture embodies cultural stereotypes and ideologies, including understandings about race, class, and gender, and is part of what Dorothy Smith (1993) calls the ruling apparatuses and relations of ruling of society. Holstein and Gubrium show how Smith's project concretely articulates a critical theory of discourse and social structure. Smith's feminist standpoint epistemology connects the ethnomethodological project to critical, feminist, Marxist theory.

The emphasis on interpretive resources, local cultures, and the artful production of meaning connects ethnomethodology, Holstein and Gubrium argue, to deconstructionism and the postmodern context. Such a connection also enlivens the reflexive and reflective turn in qualitative research, calling attention, again and again, to the situated practices that constitute and define this project.

Grounded Theory

Anselm Strauss and Juliet Corbin give an overview of the origins, purposes, and uses of grounded theory, which is a general methodology for developing theory that is grounded in data systematically gathered and analyzed. Grounded theory may be the most widely employed interpretive strategy in the social sciences today. It gives the researcher a specific set of steps to follow that are closely aligned with the canons of "good science." Strauss and Corbin compare this methodology with other approaches to qualitative research, noting that a major difference lies in the explicit commitment to theory development and theory verification. (This methodology can be used in both qualitative and quantitative studies.) Basic strategies include theoretical sampling, systematic coding, and guidelines for achieving conceptual density, variation, and integration. A conditional matrix is used to connect and specify the place of micro and macro conditions and consequences in a resulting theory.

Critics have argued that grounded theory has yet to feel the direct influence of the newer, feminist, postmodern arguments, although Strauss and Corbin disagree. Some critics have suggested that the authors remain vague on how verification is accomplished, and many have questioned the status of data and the actor's perspective within the theory. Others have commented on the perceived tendency of researchers to impose their own order on empirical materials (see Glaser, 1992). As presented by Strauss and Corbin, grounded theory methodology remains firmly entrenched within the modernist, postpositivist tradition.

The Biographical Method

Louis Smith reminds us that every text is biographical, as he outlines the biographical method, which seeks to report on and document the history of a person's life. All methods are biographical in the sense that they work outward and inward from the personal histories of the researcher and those studied. Smith shows how the biographical method cuts across all social science disciplines, creating its own subject matter as it goes along. Writers, that is, create the lives they write about. This method takes many different forms: objective, historical, artistic, narrative, personal, collective, institutional, fictional. The method is filled with problems when put into use, including the factual status of the materials utilized; how these materials are retrieved, organized, and then used; the conventions that structure the genre itself; and how and where the biographer is located in the biographical text.

Every qualitative study involves the intersection of public and private lives and biographies. Many researchers study problems anchored in their personal biographies. How these biographical materials can become part of the research process is a topic more fully explored in Volume 3 of this series.

The Historical Method

Gaye Tuchman, echoing Smith, argues that social phenomena must be studied in their historical context. This involves the use of historical documents and written records of the past, including diaries, letters, newspapers, census tract data, novels and other popular literature, and popular culture documents. To understand historical documents one must have an interpretive point of view, and this point of view in turn shapes how one gathers, reads, and analyzes historical materials. Tuchman outlines several interpretive approaches to historical materials (functional, cliometric, Marxist, feminist), showing that a historian's account of the past is a social text that constructs and reconstructs the realities of the past.

Couched within the postmodern perspective, Tuchman argues that history is always the story of lived experience. The stories that tell history are always biased; none can ever document "the truth." Together, they present a revealing montage that should speak to us today. But how history speaks reveals the politics of power, for history is not purely referential; it is constructed by the historian. Thus, as Tuchman argues, quoting Joan Scott (1989), written history both reflects and creates relations of power. Today's struggles are, then, about how we shall know the past, and how the past will be constituted in the present. Every historical method thus implies a different way of telling these stories.

Applied and Action Research

Peter Reason moves participatory research and action inquiry, perhaps the most humanistic of the traditions considered, up against the postmodern and poststructural perspectives. Work in this tradition attempts to make qualitative research more humanistic, holistic, and relevant to the lives of human beings. This worldview sees human beings as cocreating their reality through participation, experience, and action. This participative worldview is present in three action research traditions: cooperative inquiry, participatory action research, and action inquiry. Reason examines each of these traditions, showing their humanistic commonalities and differences.

It is this humanistic emphasis that Reason sees clashing with the postmodern point of view. He correctly reads these positions as saying that raw, lived experience can be accessed only through text-mediated discourse. However, he then argues that any attempt at experiential knowing is rendered impossible from the start. This carries the implication, he contends, of silencing the voices of people already oppressed.

We share Reason's commitment to lived experience and its expression. However, we disagree with this interpretation of the postmodern position. In destabilizing all privileged positions, the postmodern sensibility creates the spaces for those voices Reason wishes to be heard. Although this is not an infrequent criticism of the postmodern position, we regard it as essentially incorrect. It is our hope that there will be a closer alignment between these two perspectives in the fifth moment of qualitative research.

Clinical Models

Applied and action research has a natural affinity with clinical methods. Each tradition reflects a commitment to change, although clinical research displays a greater concern with diagnosis and treatment than with large-scale social change per se. Historically, the positivist and postpositivist paradigms have dominated clinical, medical research. William Miller and Benjamin Crabtree present a qualitative alternative approach that locates clinical research in the tradition of postpositivist applied anthropology. They outline an experience-based, interpretive view of clinical practice, a view that makes the clinical practitioner and the patient coparticipants in the realities of medical treatment. On this point they are quite close to the arguments advanced by Reason. Their perspective stresses research design; experimental, survey, documentary, and field methods; and the uses of grounded theory, personal experience methods, clinical interviews, and participant observation. They rely heavily on the data management methods and techniques developed by Tesch and by Miles and Huberman, offering an innovative model of rigorous analysis for qualitative materials.

The multimethod approach that Miller and Crabtree advocate represents an attempt to bring about radical change in biomedical culture, which historically has been very quantitative and critical of nonquantitative research. They, like Reason, speak to the politics of qualitative research. In the clinical as in other areas of qualitative research, the multimethod approach is often the only avenue to a more interpretive conception of the research process.

More is going on here in the chapters by Reason and Miller and Crabtree. It involves using research and the social text to effect social change. That is, can social texts, or text-mediated systems of discourse, to use Dorothy Smith's phrase, change social situations? Reason says no, preferring to develop a model that links research directly to political action. Miller and Crabtree want to change consciousness in the medical setting by changing the language and the paradigm that physicians now use. The tools that these authors advocate are powerful agents for social change, and they can be easily supplemented with the discourse, or text-mediated, position. Modifying Smith (1993), it can be argued that qualitative research is discourse and practice. Our business as qualitative researchers is to write the ongoing activities and experiences of people "into the texts of that discourse" (p. 183). With Smith, we understand that there is a place for people outside the text, but that our project is to find a place for them in the texts that are written. Thus the "notion of a standpoint outside discourse holds a place in discourse for she who has not yet spoken, not yet declared herself, not yet disinterred her buried life" (p. 183).

There are matters that need to be written that discourse has not yet addressed, matters such as those discussed by Olesen, Reason, and Miller and Crabtree in this volume. But once they are heard, and then written, voices that were previously silenced can speak as agents of social change and personal destiny. In such texts research is connected to political action, systems of language and meaning are changed, and paradigms are challenged.

◆ Notes

1. We include two chapters on design in this volume. Janice Morse presents a treatment of this topic that is directly fitted to the needs of those researchers who write grant proposals for traditional funding agencies. Valerie Janesick presents another version of the design process that is less geared to such audiences.

2. Mitch Allen's comments have significantly shaped our treatment of the relationship between paradigms and research designs.

3. Ragin (1992, p. 9) offers a framework for distinguishing four fundamentally different approaches to case-based research. This framework involves two dichotomies: Is the case considered to be a theoretical or empirical unit? and Is it an example of general or specific phenomena? Thus a case as an empirical unit can be found (invisible communities) or treated as an object, or ongoing event (a family), whereas a case as a theoretical unit can be constructed (modern tyranny) or treated as a convention (gang).

◆ References

Atkinson, P. (1992). *Understanding ethnographic texts*. Newbury Park, CA: Sage.

Bruner, E. M. (1993). Introduction: The ethnographic self and the personal self. In P. Benson (Ed.), *Anthropology and literature* (pp. 1-26). Urbana: University of Illinois Press.

Denzin, N. K. (1987). *The recovering alcoholic*. Newbury Park, CA: Sage.

Feagin, J. R., Orum, A. M., & Sjoberg, G. (1991). *A case for the case study*. Chapel Hill: University of North Carolina Press.

Glaser, B. G. (1992). *Basics of grounded theory*. Mill Valley, CA: Sociology Press.

Glaser, B. G., & Strauss, A. L. (1967). *The discovery of grounded theory: Strategies for qualitative research*. Chicago: Aldine.

Hammersley, M. (1992). *What's wrong with ethnography? Methodological explorations*. London: Routledge.

Mills, C. W. (1959). *The sociological imagination*. New York: Oxford University Press.

Ragin, C. C. (1992). Introduction: Cases of "What is a case?" In C. C. Ragin & H. S. Becker (Eds.), *What is a case?* New York: Cambridge University Press.

Ragin, C. C., & Becker, H. S. (Eds.). (1992). *What is a case?* New York: Cambridge University Press.

Sartre, J.-P. (1981). *The family idiot: Gustave Flaubert, 1821-1857* (Vol. 1). Chicago: University of Chicago Press.

Smith, D. E. (1993). High noon in Textland: A critique of Clough. *Sociological Quarterly, 34,* 183-192.

NORMAN K. DENZIN
University of Illinois at Urbana-Champaign

YVONNA S. LINCOLN
Texas A&M University

1
Introduction

Entering the Field
of Qualitative Research

Norman K. Denzin & Yvonna S. Lincoln

◆ Qualitative research has a long and distinguished history in the human disciplines. In sociology the work of the "Chicago school" in the 1920s and 1930s established the importance of qualitative research for the study of human group life. In anthropology, during the same period, the pathbreaking studies of Boas, Mead, Benedict, Bateson, Evans-Pritchard, Radcliffe-Brown, and Malinowski charted the outlines of the fieldwork method, wherein the observer went to a foreign setting to study the customs and habits of another society and culture (for a critique of this tradition, see Rosaldo, 1989, pp. 25-45). Soon qualitative research would be employed in other social science disciplines, including education, social work, and communications. The opening chapter in Part I, Volume 1, by Vidich and Lyman, charts key features of this history.

In this introductory chapter we will briefly define the field of qualitative research, then review the history of qualitative research in the human disciplines, so that this volume and its contents may be located in their proper historical moment. A conceptual framework for reading the qualitative

AUTHORS' NOTE: We are grateful to the many people who have helped with this chapter, including Mitch Allen, Katherine E. Ryan, and Harry Wolcott.

1

research act as a multicultural, gendered process will be presented. We will then provide a brief introduction to the chapters that follow.

◆ Definitional Issues

Qualitative research is a field of inquiry in its own right. It crosscuts disciplines, fields, and subject matter.[1] A complex, interconnected family of terms, concepts, and assumptions surround the term *qualitative research*. These include the traditions associated with positivism, poststructuralism, and the many qualitative research perspectives, or methods, connected to cultural and interpretive studies (the chapters in Part II of Volume 1 take up these paradigms). There are separate and detailed literatures on the many methods and approaches that fall under the category of qualitative research, such as interviewing, participant observation, and visual methods.

Qualitative research operates in a complex historical field that crosscuts five historical moments (we discuss these in detail below). These five moments simultaneously operate in the present. We describe them as the traditional (1900-1950), the modernist or golden age (1950-1970), blurred genres (1970-1986), the crisis of representation (1986-1990), and postmodern or present moments (1990-present). The present moment is defined, Laurel Richardson (1991) argues, by a new sensibility, the core of which "is doubt that any discourse has a privileged place, any method or theory a universal and general claim to authoritative knowledge" (p. 173).

Successive waves of epistemological theorizing move across these five moments. The traditional period is associated with the positivist paradigm. The modernist or golden age and blurred genres moments are connected to the appearance of postpositivist arguments. At the same time, a variety of new interpretive, qualitative perspectives made their presence felt, including hermeneutics, structuralism, semiotics, phenomenology, cultural studies, and feminism.[2] In the blurred genres phase the humanities became central resources for critical, interpretive theory, and the qualitative research project was broadly conceived. The blurred genres phase produced the next stage, the crisis of representation, where researchers struggled with how to locate themselves and their subjects in reflexive texts. The postmodern moment is characterized by a new sensibility that doubts all previous paradigms.

2

Any description of what constitutes qualitative research must work within this complex historical field. *Qualitative research* means different things in each of these moments. Nonetheless, an initial, generic definition can be offered: Qualitative research is multimethod in focus, involving an interpretive, naturalistic approach to its subject matter. This means that qualitative researchers study things in their natural settings, attempting to make sense of, or interpret, phenomena in terms of the meanings people bring to them. Qualitative research involves the studied use and collection of a variety of empirical materials—case study, personal experience, intro-spective, life story, interview, observational, historical, interactional, and visual texts—that describe routine and problematic moments and meanings in individuals' lives. Accordingly, qualitative researchers deploy a wide range of interconnected methods, hoping always to get a better fix on the subject matter at hand.

The Qualitative Researcher as *Bricoleur*

The multiple methodologies of qualitative research may be viewed as a bricolage, and the researcher as *bricoleur.* Nelson, Treichler, and Grossberg (1992, p. 2), Lévi-Strauss (1966, p. 17), and Weinstein and Weinstein (1991, p. 161) clarify the meaning of these two terms.[3] A *bricoleur* is a "Jack of all trades or a kind of professional do-it-yourself person" (Lévi-Strauss, 1966, p. 17). The *bricoleur* produces a bricolage, that is, a pieced-together, close-knit set of practices that provide solutions to a problem in a concrete situation. "The solution (bricolage) which is the result of the *bricoleur's* method is an [emergent] construction" (Weinstein & Weinstein, 1991, p. 161) that changes and takes new forms as different tools, methods, and techniques are added to the puzzle. Nelson et al. (1992) describe the methodology of cultural studies "as a bricolage. Its choice of practice, that is, is pragmatic, strategic and self-reflexive" (p. 2). This understanding can be applied equally to qualitative research.

The qualitative researcher-as-*bricoleur* uses the tools of his or her methodological trade, deploying whatever strategies, methods, or empiri-cal materials as are at hand (Becker, 1989). If new tools have to be invented, or pieced together, then the researcher will do this. The choice of which tools to use, which research practices to employ, is not set in advance. The "choice of research practices depends upon the questions that are asked, and the questions depend on their context" (Nelson et al., 1992, p. 2), what is available in the context, and what the researcher can do in that setting.

Qualitative research is inherently multimethod in focus (Brewer & Hunter, 1989). However, the use of multiple methods, or triangulation, reflects an attempt to secure an in-depth understanding of the phenomenon in question. Objective reality can never be captured. Triangulation is not a tool or a strategy of validation, but an alternative to validation (Denzin, 1989a, 1989b, p. 244; Fielding & Fielding, 1986, p. 33; Flick, 1992, p. 194). The combination of multiple methods, empirical materials, perspectives and observers in a single study is best understood, then, as a strategy that adds rigor, breadth, and depth to any investigation (see Flick, 1992, p. 194).

The *bricoleur* is adept at performing a large number of diverse tasks, ranging from interviewing to observing, to interpreting personal and historical documents, to intensive self-reflection and introspection. The *bricoleur* reads widely and is knowledgeable about the many interpretive paradigms (feminism, Marxism, cultural studies, constructivism) that can be brought to any particular problem. He or she may not, however, feel that paradigms can be mingled, or synthesized. That is, paradigms as overarching philosophical systems denoting particular ontologies, epistemologies, and methodologies cannot be easily moved between. They represent belief systems that attach the user to a particular worldview. Perspectives, in contrast, are less well developed systems, and can be more easily moved between. The researcher-as-*bricoleur*-theorist works between and within competing and overlapping perspectives and paradigms.

The *bricoleur* understands that research is an interactive process shaped by his or her personal history, biography, gender, social class, race, and ethnicity, and those of the people in the setting. The *bricoleur* knows that science is power, for all research findings have political implications. There is no value-free science. The *bricoleur* also knows that researchers all tell stories about the worlds they have studied. Thus the narratives, or stories, scientists tell are accounts couched and framed within specific storytelling traditions, often defined as paradigms (e.g., positivism, postpositivism, constructivism).

The product of the *bricoleur*'s labor is a bricolage, a complex, dense, reflexive, collagelike creation that represents the researcher's images, understandings, and interpretations of the world or phenomenon under analysis. This bricolage will, as in the case of a social theorist such as Simmel, connect the parts to the whole, stressing the meaningful relation-

4

ships that operate in the situations and social worlds studied (Weinstein & Weinstein, 1991, p. 164).

Qualitative Research as a Site of Multiple Methodologies and Research Practices

Qualitative research, as a set of interpretive practices, privileges no single methodology over any other. As a site of discussion, or discourse, qualitative research is difficult to define clearly. It has no theory, or paradigm, that is distinctly its own. As Part II of this volume reveals, multiple theoretical paradigms claim use of qualitative research methods and strategies, from constructivism to cultural studies, feminism, Marxism, and ethnic models of study. Qualitative research is used in many separate disciplines, as we will discuss below. It does not belong to a single discipline.

Nor does qualitative research have a distinct set of methods that are entirely its own. Qualitative researchers use semiotics, narrative, content, discourse, archival, and phonemic analysis, even statistics. They also draw upon and utilize the approaches, methods, and techniques of ethnomethodology, phenomenology, hermeneutics, feminism, rhizomatics, deconstructionism, ethnographies, interviews, psychoanalysis, cultural studies, survey research, and participant observation, among others (see Nelson et al., 1992, p. 2).[4] All of these research practices "can provide important insights and knowledge" (Nelson et al., 1992, p. 2). No specific method or practice can be privileged over any other, and none can be "eliminated out of hand" (p. 2).

Many of these methods, or research practices, are also used in other contexts in the human disciplines. Each bears the traces of its own disciplinary history. Thus there is an extensive history of the uses and meanings of ethnography and ethnology in education (Hymes, 1980; LeCompte & Preissle, 1992); participant observation and ethnography in anthropology (Marcus, Volume 1, Chapter 12), sociology (Atkinson & Hammersley, Volume 2, Chapter 5), and cultural studies (Fiske, Volume 1, Chapter 11); textual, hermeneutic, feminist, psychoanalytic, semiotic, and narrative analysis in cinema and literary studies (Lentricchia & McLaughlin, 1990; Nichols, 1985; see also Manning & Cullum-Swan, Volume 3, Chapter 9); archival, material culture, historical, and document analysis in history, biography, and archaeology (Hodder, Volume 3, Chapter 4; Smith, Volume 2, Chapter 8; Tuchman, Volume 2, Chapter 9); and discourse and conversational analysis in communications and education (Holstein & Gubrium, Volume 2, Chapter 6).

The many histories that surround each method or research strategy reveal how multiple uses and meanings are brought to each practice. Textual analysis in literary studies, for example, often treat texts as self-contained systems. On the other hand, a researcher employing a cultural studies or feminist perspective would read a text in terms of its location within a historical moment marked by a particular gender, race, or class ideology. A cultural studies use of ethnography would bring a set of understandings from postmodernism and poststructuralism to the project. These understandings would likely not be shared by mainstream postpositivist sociologists (see Atkinson & Hammersley, Volume 2, Chapter 5; Altheide & Johnson, Volume 3, Chapter 10). Similarly, postpositivist and poststructural historians bring different understandings and uses to the methods and findings of historical research (see Tuchman, Volume 2, Chapter 9). These tensions and contradictions are all evident in the chapters presented here.

These separate and multiple uses and meanings of the methods of qualitative research make it difficult for researchers to agree on any essential definition of the field, for it is never just one thing.[5] Still, a definition must be established for use here. We borrow from, and paraphrase, Nelson et al.'s (1992, p. 4) attempt to define cultural studies:

> Qualitative research is an interdisciplinary, transdisciplinary, and sometimes counterdisciplinary field. It crosscuts the humanities and the social and physical sciences. Qualitative research is many things at the same time. It is multiparadigmatic in focus. Its practitioners are sensitive to the value of the multimethod approach. They are committed to the naturalistic perspective, and to the interpretive understanding of human experience. At the same time, the field is inherently political and shaped by multiple ethical and political positions.
>
> Qualitative research embraces two tensions at the same time. On the one hand, it is drawn to a broad, interpretive, postmodern, feminist, and critical sensibility. On the other hand, it is drawn to more narrowly defined positivist, postpositivist, humanistic, and naturalistic conceptions of human experience and its analysis.

This rather awkward statement means that qualitative research, as a set of practices, embraces within its own multiple disciplinary histories constant tensions and contradictions over the project itself, including its methods and the forms its findings and interpretations take. The field

6

sprawls between and crosscuts all of the human disciplines, even including, in some cases, the physical sciences. Its practitioners are variously committed to modern and postmodern sensibilities and the approaches to social research that these sensibilities imply.

Resistances to Qualitative Studies

The academic and disciplinary resistances to qualitative research illustrate the politics embedded in this field of discourse. The challenges to qualitative research are many. Qualitative researchers are called journalists, or soft scientists. Their work is termed unscientific, or only exploratory, or entirely personal and full of bias. It is called criticism and not theory, or it is interpreted politically, as a disguised version of Marxism, or humanism.

These resistances reflect an uneasy awareness that the traditions of qualitative research commit the researcher to a critique of the positivist project. But the positivist resistance to qualitative research goes beyond the "ever-present desire to maintain a distinction between hard science and soft scholarship" (Carey, 1989, p. 99). The positive sciences (physics, chemistry, economics, and psychology, for example) are often seen as the crowning achievements of Western civilization, and in their practices it is assumed that "truth" can transcend opinion and personal bias (Carey, 1989, p. 99). Qualitative research is seen as an assault on this tradition, whose adherents often retreat into a "value-free objectivist science" (Carey, 1989, p. 104) model to defend their position. They seldom attempt to make explicit, or to critique, the "moral and political commitments in their own contingent work" (Carey, 1989, p. 104). The opposition to positive science by the postpositivists (see below) and the poststructuralists is seen, then, as an attack on reason and truth. At the same time, the positive science attack on qualitative research is regarded as an attempt to legislate one version of truth over another.

This political terrain defines the many traditions and strands of qualitative research: the British tradition and its presence in other national contexts; the American pragmatic, naturalistic, and interpretive traditions in sociology, anthropology, communications, and education; the German and French phenomenological, hermeneutic, semiotic, Marxist, structural, and poststructural perspectives; feminist, African American studies, Latino studies, gay and lesbian studies, and studies of indigenous and aboriginal cultures (Nelson et al., 1992, p. 15). The politics of qualitative research creates a tension that informs each of the above traditions. This tension itself is constantly being reexamined and interrogated, as qualitative research confronts a changing historical world, new intellectual positions, and its own institutional and academic conditions.

To summarize: Qualitative research is many things to many people. Its essence is twofold: a commitment to some version of the naturalistic, interpretive approach to its subject matter, and an ongoing critique of the politics and methods of positivism. We turn now to a brief discussion of the major differences between qualitative and quantitative approaches to research.

Qualitative Versus Quantitative Research

The word *qualitative* implies an emphasis on processes and meanings that are not rigorously examined, or measured (if measured at all), in terms of quantity, amount, intensity, or frequency. Qualitative researchers stress the socially constructed nature of reality, the intimate relationship between the researcher and what is studied, and the situational constraints that shape inquiry. Such researchers emphasize the value-laden nature of inquiry. They seek answers to questions that stress how social experience is created and given meaning. In contrast, quantitative studies emphasize the measurement and analysis of causal relationships between variables, not processes. Inquiry is purported to be within a value-free framework.

Research Styles: Doing the Same Things Differently?

Of course, both qualitative and quantitative researchers "think they know something about society worth telling to others, and they use a variety of forms, media and means to communicate their ideas and findings" (Becker, 1986, p. 122). Qualitative research differs from quantitative research in five significant ways (Becker, 1993). These points of difference turn on different ways of addressing the same set of issues. They return always to the politics of research, and who has the power to legislate correct solutions to these problems.

Uses of positivism. First, both perspectives are shaped by the positivist and postpositivist traditions in the physical and social sciences (see the discussion below). These two positive science traditions hold to naive and critical realist positions concerning reality and its perception. In the positivist version it is contended that there is a reality out there to be studied,

8

captured, and understood, whereas postpositivists argue that reality can never be fully apprehended, only approximated (Guba, 1990, p. 22). Postpositivism relies on multiple methods as a way of capturing as much of reality as possible. At the same time, emphasis is placed on the discovery and verification of theories. Traditional evaluation criteria, such as internal and external validity, are stressed, as is the use of qualitative procedures that lend themselves to structured (sometimes statistical) analysis. Computer-assisted methods of analysis that permit frequency counts, tabulations, and low-level statistical analyses may also be employed.

The positivist and postpositivist traditions linger like long shadows over the qualitative research project. Historically, qualitative research was defined within the positivist paradigm, where qualitative researchers attempted to do good positivist research with less rigorous methods and procedures. Some mid-century qualitative researchers (e.g., Becker, Geer, Hughes, & Strauss, 1961) reported participant observation findings in terms of quasi-statistics. As recently as 1990, two leaders of the grounded theory approach to qualitative research attempted to modify the usual canons of good (positivistic) science to fit their own postpositivist conception of rigorous research (Strauss & Corbin, 1990; see also Strauss & Corbin, Volume 2, Chapter 7; but also see Glaser, 1992). Some applied researchers, while claiming to be atheoretical, fit within the positivist or postpositivist framework by default. Spindler and Spindler (1992) summarize their qualitative approach to quantitative materials: "Instrumentation and quantification are simply procedures employed to extend and reinforce certain kinds of data, interpretations and test hypotheses across samples. Both must be kept in their place. One must avoid their premature or overly extensive use as a security mechanism" (p. 69).

Although many qualitative researchers in the postpositivist tradition use statistical measures, methods, and documents as a way of locating a group of subjects within a larger population, they seldom report their findings in terms of the kinds of complex statistical measures or methods to which quantitative researchers are drawn (e.g., path, regression, or log-linear analyses). Much of applied research is also atheoretical.

Acceptance of postmodern sensibilities. The use of quantitative, positivist methods and assumptions has been rejected by a new generation of qualitative researchers who are attached to poststructural, postmodern sensibilities (see below; see also Vidich & Lyman, Volume 1, Chapter 2, and Richardson, Volume 3, Chapter 12). These researchers argue that

9

positivist methods are but one way of telling a story about society or the social world. They may be no better or no worse than any other method; they just tell a different kind of story.

This tolerant view is not shared by everyone. Many members of the critical theory, constructivist, poststructural, and postmodern schools of thought reject positivist and postpositivist criteria when evaluating their own work. They see these criteria as irrelevant to their work, and contend that these criteria reproduce only a certain kind of science, a science that silences too many voices. These researchers seek alternative methods for evaluating their work, including verisimilitude, emotionality, personal responsibility, an ethic of caring, political praxis, multivoiced texts, and dialogues with subjects. In response, positivists and postpositivists argue that what they do is good science, free of individual bias and subjectivity; as noted above, they see postmodernism as an attack on reason and truth.

Capturing the individual's point of view. Both qualitative and quantitative researchers are concerned about the individual's point of view. However, qualitative investigators think they can get closer to the actor's perspective through detailed interviewing and observation. They argue that quantitative researchers seldom are able to capture the subject's perspective because they have to rely on more remote, inferential empirical materials. The empirical materials produced by the softer, interpretive methods are regarded by many quantitative researchers as unreliable, impressionistic, and not objective.

Examining the constraints of everyday life. Qualitative researchers are more likely than quantitative researchers to confront the constraints of the everyday social world. They see this world in action and embed their findings in it. Quantitative researchers abstract from this world and seldom study it directly. They seek a nomothetic or etic science based on probabilities derived from the study of large numbers of randomly selected cases. These kinds of statements stand above and outside the constraints of everyday life. Qualitative researchers are committed to an emic, idiographic, case-based position, which directs their attention to the specifics of particular cases.

Securing rich descriptions. Qualitative researchers believe that rich descriptions of the social world are valuable, whereas quantitative researchers, with their etic, nomothetic commitments, are less concerned with such detail.

The five points of difference described above (uses of positivism, acceptance of postmodern sensibilities, capturing the individual's point of view, examining the constraints of everyday life, and securing rich descriptions) reflect commitments to different styles of research, different epistemologies, and different forms of representation. Each work tradition is governed by a different set of genres; each has its own classics, its own preferred forms of representation, interpretation, and textual evaluation (see Becker, 1986, pp. 134-135). Qualitative researchers use ethnographic prose, historical narratives, first-person accounts, still photographs, life histories, fictionalized facts, and biographical and autobiographical materials, among others. Quantitative researchers use mathematical models, statistical tables, and graphs, and often write about their research in impersonal, third-person prose.

With the differences between these two traditions understood, we will now offer a brief discussion of the history of qualitative research. We can break this into four historical moments, mindful that any history is always somewhat arbitrary.

◆ The History of Qualitative Research

The history of qualitative research reveals, as Vidich and Lyman remind us in Chapter 2 of Volume 1, that the modern social science disciplines have taken as their mission "the analysis and understanding of the patterned conduct and social processes of society." The notion that this task could be carried out presupposed that social scientists had the ability to observe this world objectively. Qualitative methods were a major tool of such observations.[6]

Throughout the history of qualitative research, investigators have always defined their work in terms of hopes and values, "religious faiths, occupational and professional ideologies" (Vidich & Lyman, Volume 1, Chapter 2). Qualitative research (like all research) has always been judged on the "standard of whether the work communicates or 'says' something to us" (Vidich & Lyman, Volume 1, Chapter 2), based on how we conceptualize our reality and our images of the world. *Epistemology* is the word that has historically defined these standards of evaluation. In the contemporary period, as argued above, many received discourses on epistemology have been "disprivileged," or cast into doubt. The history presented by Vidich and Lyman covers the following (somewhat) overlapping stages: early ethnography (to the seventeenth century); colonial ethnography (seventeenth-, eighteenth-, and nineteenth-century explorers); the ethnography of the American Indian as "other" (late nineteenth- and early twentieth-century anthropology); the ethnography of the "civic other," or community studies, and ethnographies of American immigrants (early twentieth century through the 1960s); studies of ethnicity and assimilation (mid-century through the 1980s); and the present, which we call the *fifth moment*.

In each of these eras researchers were and have been influenced by their political hopes and ideologies, discovering findings in their research that confirmed prior theories or beliefs. Early ethnographers confirmed the racial and cultural diversity of peoples throughout the globe and attempted to fit this diversity into a theory about the origin of history, the races, and civilizations. Colonial ethnographers, before the professionalization of ethnography in the twentieth century, fostered a colonial pluralism that left natives on their own as long as their leaders could be co-opted by the colonial administration.

European ethnographers studied Africans and other Third World peoples of color. Early American ethnographers studied the American Indian from the perspective of the conqueror, who saw the life world of the primitive as a window to the prehistoric past. The Calvinist mission to save the Indian was soon transferred to the mission of saving the "hordes" of immigrants who entered the United States with the beginnings of industrialization. Qualitative community studies of the ethnic other proliferated from the early 1900s to the 1960s, and included the work of E. Franklin Frazier, Robert Park, and Robert Redfield and their students, as well as William Foote Whyte, the Lynds, August Hollingshead, Herbert Gans, Stanford Lyman, Arthur Vidich, and Joseph Bensman. The post-1960s' ethnicity studies challenged the "melting pot" hypothesis of Park and his followers and corresponded to the emergence of ethnic studies programs that saw Native Americans, Latinos, Asian Americans, and African Americans attempting to take control over the study of their own peoples.

The postmodern challenge emerged in the mid-1980s. It questioned the assumptions that had organized this earlier history, in each of its colonializing moments. Qualitative research that crosses the "postmodern divide" requires one, Vidich and Lyman argue, to "abandon all established and preconceived values, theories, perspectives, . . . and prejudices as resources for ethnographic study." In this new era the qualitative researcher does more than observe history; he or she plays a part in it. New tales of the field will now be written, and they will reflect the researcher's direct and personal engagement with this historical period.

Vidich and Lyman's analysis covers the full sweep of ethnographic history. Ours, presented below, is confined to the twentieth century and complements many of their divisions. We begin with the early foundational work of the British and French, as well the Chicago, Columbia, Harvard, and Berkeley schools of sociology and anthropology. This early foundational period established the norms of classical qualitative and ethnographic research.

◆ The Five Moments of Qualitative Research

As noted above, we divide our history of qualitative research in this century into five phases, each of which is described in turn below.

The Traditional Period

We call the first moment the traditional period (this covers Vidich and Lyman's second and third phases). It begins in the early 1900s and continues until World War II. In this period, qualitative researchers wrote "objective," colonializing accounts of field experiences that were reflective of the positivist scientist paradigm. They were concerned with offering valid, reliable, and objective interpretations in their writings. The "other" who was studied was alien, foreign, and strange.

Here is Malinowski (1967) discussing his field experiences in New Guinea and the Trobriand Islands in the years 1914-1915 and 1917-1918:

> Nothing whatever draws me to ethnographic studies. . . . On the whole the village struck me rather unfavorably. There is a certain disorganization . . . the rowdiness and persistence of the people who laugh and stare and lie discouraged me somewhat. . . . Went to the village hoping to photograph a few stages of the *bara* dance. I handed out half-sticks of tobacco, then

13

watched a few dances; then took pictures—but results were poor. . . . they would not pose long enough for time exposures. At moments I was furious at them, particularly because after I gave them their portions of tobacco they all went away. (quoted in Geertz, 1988, pp. 73-74)

In another work, this lonely, frustrated, isolated field-worker describes his methods in the following words:

> In the field one has to face a chaos of facts. . . . in this crude form they are not scientific facts at all; they are absolutely elusive, and can only be fixed by interpretation. . . . Only laws and generalizations are scientific facts, and field work consists only and exclusively in the interpretation of the chaotic social reality, in subordinating it to general rules. (Malinowski, 1916/1948, p. 328; quoted in Geertz, 1988, p. 81)

Malinowski's remarks are provocative. On the one hand they disparage fieldwork, but on the other they speak of it within the glorified language of science, with laws and generalizations fashioned out of this selfsame experience.

The field-worker, during this period, was lionized, made into a larger-than-life figure who went into and then returned from the field with stories about strange people. Rosaldo (1989) describes this as the period of the Lone Ethnographer, the story of the man-scientist who went off in search of his native in a distant land. There this figure "encountered the object of his quest . . . [and] underwent his rite of passage by enduring the ultimate ordeal of 'fieldwork' " (p. 30). Returning home with his data, the Lone Ethnographer wrote up an objective account of the culture he studied. These accounts were structured by the norms of classical ethnography. This sacred bundle of terms (Rosaldo, 1989, p. 31) organized ethnographic texts in terms of four beliefs and commitments: a commitment to objectivism, a complicity with imperialism, a belief in monumentalism (the ethnography would create a museumlike picture of the culture studied), and a belief in timelessness (what was studied never changed). This model of the researcher, who could also write complex, dense theories about what was studied, holds to the present day.

The myth of the Lone Ethnographer depicts the birth of classic ethnography. The texts of Malinowski, Radcliffe-Brown, Margaret Mead, and Gregory Bateson are still carefully studied for what they can tell the novice about fieldwork, taking field notes, and writing theory (see the discussion of Bateson and Mead in Harper, Volume 3, Chapter 5). Today this image has been shattered. The works of the classic ethnographers are seen by many as relics of the colonial past (Rosaldo, 1989, p. 44). Although many feel nostalgic about this image, others celebrate its passing. Rosaldo (1989) quotes Cora Du Bois, a retired Harvard anthropology professor, who lamented this passing at a conference in 1980, reflecting on the crisis in anthropology: "[I feel a distance] from the complexity and disarray of what I once found a justifiable and challenging discipline. . . . It has been like moving from a distinguished art museum into a garage sale" (p. 44).

Du Bois regards the classic ethnographies as pieces of timeless artwork, such as those contained in a museum. She detests the chaos of the garage sale, which Rosaldo values: "It [the garage sale] provides a precise image of the postcolonial situation where cultural artifacts flow between unlikely places, and nothing is sacred, permanent, or sealed off. The image of anthropology as a garage sale depicts our present global situation" (p. 44). Old standards no longer hold. Ethnographies do not produce timeless truths. The commitment to objectivism is now in doubt. The complicity with imperialism is openly challenged today, and the belief in monumentalism is a thing of the past.

The legacies of this first period begin at the end of the nineteenth century, when the novel and the social sciences had become distinguished as separate systems of discourse (Clough, 1992, pp. 21-22). However, the Chicago school, with its emphasis on the life story and the "slice-of-life" approach to ethnographic materials, sought to develop an interpretive methodology that maintained the centrality of the narrated life history approach. This led to the production of the texts that gave the researcher-as-author the power to represent the subject's story. Written under the mantle of straightforward, sentiment-free social realism, these texts used the language of ordinary people. They articulated a social science version of literary naturalism, which often produced the sympathetic illusion that a solution to a social problem had been found. Like films about the Depression-era juvenile delinquent and other social problems (Roffman & Purdy, 1981), these accounts romanticized the subject. They turned the deviant into a sociological version of a screen hero. These sociological stories, like their film counterparts, usually had happy endings, as they followed individuals through the three stages of the classic morality tale: existence in a state of grace, seduction by evil and the fall, and finally redemption through suffering.

The Modernist Phase

The modernist phase, or second moment, builds on the canonical works of the traditional period. Social realism, naturalism, and slice-of-life ethnographies are still valued. This phase extended through the postwar years to the 1970s; it is still present in the work of many (see Wolcott, 1992, for a review). In this period many texts attempted to formalize qualitative methods (see, for example, Bogdan & Taylor, 1975; Cicourel, 1964; Filstead, 1970; Glaser & Strauss, 1967; J. Lofland, 1971; Lofland & Lofland, 1984).[7] The modernist ethnographer and sociological participant observer attempted rigorous, qualitative studies of important social processes, including deviance and social control in the classroom and society. This was a moment of creative ferment.

A new generation of graduate students, across the human disciplines, encountered new interpretive theories (ethnomethodology, phenomenology, critical theory, feminism). They were drawn to qualitative research practices that would let them give a voice to society's underclass. Postpositivism functioned as a powerful epistemological paradigm in this moment. Researchers attempted to fit the arguments of Campbell and Stanley (1963) about internal and external validity to constructionist and interactionist models of the research act. They returned to the texts of the Chicago school as sources of inspiration (see Denzin, 1970, 1978).

A canonical text from this moment remains *Boys in White* (Becker et al., 1961). Firmly entrenched in mid-century methodological discourse, this work attempted to make qualitative research as rigorous as its quantitative counterpart. Causal narratives were central to this project. This multitimethod work combined open-ended and quasi-structured interviewing with participant observation and the careful analysis of such materials in standardized, statistical form. In a classic article, "Problems of Inference and Proof in Participant Observation," Howard S. Becker (1958/1970) describes the use of quasi-statistics:

> Participant observations have occasionally been gathered in standardized form capable of being transformed into legitimate statistical data. But the exigencies of the field usually prevent the collection of data in such a form to meet the assumptions of statistical tests, so that the observer deals in what have been called "quasi-statistics." His conclusions, while implicitly numerical, do not require precise quantification. (p. 31)

16

In the analysis of data, Becker notes, the qualitative researcher takes a cue from statistical colleagues. The researcher looks for probabilities or support for arguments concerning the likelihood that, or frequency with which, a conclusion in fact applies in a specific situation. Thus did work in the modernist period clothe itself in the language and rhetoric of positivist and postpositivist discourse.

This was the golden age of rigorous qualitative analysis, bracketed in sociology by *Boys in White* (Becker et al., 1961) at one end and *The Discovery of Grounded Theory* (Glaser & Strauss, 1967) at the other. In education, qualitative research in this period was defined by George and Louise Spindler, Jules Henry, Harry Wolcott, and John Singleton. This form of qualitative research is still present in the work of such persons as Strauss and Corbin (1990) and Miles and Huberman (1993), and is represented in their chapters in this three-volume set.

The "golden age" reinforced a picture of qualitative researchers as cultural romantics. Imbued with Promethean human powers, they valorized villains and outsiders as heroes to mainstream society. They embodied a belief in the contingency of self and society, and held to emancipatory ideals for which "one lives and dies." They put in place a tragic and often ironic view of society and self, and joined a long line of leftist cultural romantics that included Emerson, Marx, James, Dewey, Gramsci, and Martin Luther King, Jr. (West, 1989, chap. 6).

As this moment came to an end, the Vietnam War was everywhere present in American society. In 1969, alongside these political currents, Herbert Blumer and Everett Hughes met with a group of young sociologists called the "Chicago Irregulars" at the American Sociological Association meetings held in San Francisco and shared their memories of the "Chicago years." Lyn Lofland (1980) describes the 1969 meetings as a

> moment of creative ferment—scholarly and political. The San Francisco meetings witnessed not simply the Blumer-Hughes event but a "counterrevolution." . . . a group first came to . . . talk about the problems of being a sociologist and a female. . . . the discipline seemed literally to be bursting with new . . . ideas: labelling theory, ethnomethodology, conflict theory, phenomenology, dramaturgical analysis. (p. 253)

Thus did the modernist phase come to an end.

Blurred Genres

By the beginning of the third stage (1970-1986), which we call the moment of blurred genres, qualitative researchers had a full complement of paradigms, methods, and strategies to employ in their research. Theories ranged from symbolic interactionism to constructivism, naturalistic inquiry, positivism and postpositivism, phenomenology, ethnomethodology, critical (Marxist), semiotics, structuralism, feminism, and various ethnic paradigms. Applied qualitative research was gaining in stature, and the politics and ethics of qualitative research were topics of considerable concern. Research strategies ranged from grounded theory to the case study, to methods of historical, biographical, ethnographic action and clinical research. Diverse ways of collecting and analyzing empirical materials were also available, including qualitative interviewing (open-ended and quasi-structured) and observational, visual, personal experience, and documentary methods. Computers were entering the situation, to be fully developed in the next decade, along with narrative, content, and semiotic methods of reading interviews and cultural texts.

Two books by Geertz, *The Interpretation of Cultures* (1973) and *Local Knowledge* (1983), defined the beginning and end of this moment. In these two works, Geertz argued that the old functional, positivist, behavioral, totalizing approaches to the human disciplines were giving way to a more pluralistic, interpretive, open-ended perspective. This new perspective took cultural representations and their meanings as its point of departure. Calling for "thick description" of particular events, rituals, and customs, Geertz suggested that all anthropological writings were interpretations of interpretations. The observer had no privileged voice in the interpretations that were written. The central task of theory was to make sense out of a local situation.

Geertz went on to propose that the boundaries between the social sciences and the humanities had become blurred. Social scientists were now turning to the humanities for models, theories, and methods of analysis (semiotics, hermeneutics). A form of genre dispersion was occurring: documentaries that read like fiction (Mailer), parables posing as ethnographies (Castañeda), theoretical treatises that look like travelogues (Lévi-Strauss). At the same time, many new approaches were emerging: poststructuralism (Barthes), neopositivism (Philips), neo-Marxism (Althusser), micro-macro descriptivism (Geertz), ritual theories of drama and culture

(V. Turner), deconstructionism (Derrida), ethnomethodology (Garfinkel). The golden age of the social sciences was over, and a new age of blurred, interpretive genres was upon us. The essay as an art form was replacing the scientific article. At issue now is the author's presence in the interpretive text, or how the researcher can speak with authority in an age when there are no longer any firm rules concerning the text, its standards of evaluation, and its subject matter (Geertz, 1988).

The naturalistic, postpositivist, and constructionist paradigms gained power in this period, especially in education in the works of Harry Wolcott, Egon Guba, Yvonna Lincoln, Robert Stake, and Elliot Eisner. By the end of the 1970s several qualitative journals were in place, from *Urban Life* (now *Journal of Contemporary Ethnography*) to *Qualitative Sociology, Symbolic Interaction,* and *Studies in Symbolic Interaction.*

Crisis of Representation

A profound rupture occurred in the mid-1980s. What we call the fourth moment, or the crisis of representation, appeared with *Anthropology as Cultural Critique* (Marcus & Fischer, 1986), *The Anthropology of Experience* (Turner & Bruner, 1986), *Writing Culture* (Clifford & Marcus, 1986), *Works and Lives* (Geertz, 1988), and *The Predicament of Culture* (Clifford, 1988). These works made research and writing more reflexive, and called into question the issues of gender, class, and race. They articulated the consequences of Geertz's "blurred genres" interpretation of the field in the early 1980s.

New models of truth and method were sought (Rosaldo, 1989). The erosion of classic norms in anthropology (objectivism, complicity with colonialism, social life structured by fixed rituals and customs, ethnographies as monuments to a culture) was complete (Rosaldo, 1989, pp. 44-45). Critical and feminist epistemologies and epistemologies of color now compete for attention in this arena. Issues such as validity, reliability, and objectivity, which had been settled in earlier phases, are once more problematic. Interpretive theories, as opposed to grounded theories, are now more common, as writers continue to challenge older models of truth and meaning (Rosaldo, 1989).

Stoller and Olkes (1987) describe how the crisis of representation was felt in their fieldwork among the Songhay of Niger. Stoller observes: "When I began to write anthropological texts, I followed the conventions of my training. I 'gathered data,' and once the 'data' were arranged in neat piles, I 'wrote them up.' In one case I reduced Songhay insults to a series of neat logical formulas" (p. 227). Stoller became dissatisfied with this form of writing, in part because he learned "everyone had lied to me and . . . the data I had so painstakingly collected were worthless. I learned a lesson: Informants routinely lie to their anthropologists" (Stoller & Olkes, 1987, p. 229). This discovery led to a second, that he had, in following the conventions of ethnographic realism, edited himself out of his text. This led Stoller to produce a different type of text, a memoir, in which he became a central character in the story he told. This story, an account of his experiences in the Songhay world, became an analysis of the clash between his world and the world of Songhay sorcery. Thus did Stoller's journey represent an attempt to confront the crisis of representation in the fourth moment.

Clough (1992) elaborates this crisis and criticizes those who would argue that new forms of writing represent a way out of it:

> While many sociologists now commenting on the criticism of ethnography view writing as "downright central to the ethnographic enterprise" [Van Maanen, 1988, p. xi], the problems of writing are still viewed as different from the problems of method or fieldwork itself. Thus the solution usually offered is experiments in writing, that is a self-consciousness about writing. (p. 136)

However, it is this insistence on the difference between writing and fieldwork that must be analyzed.

In writing, the field-worker makes a claim to moral and scientific authority. These claims allow the realist and the experimental ethnographic text to function as sources of validation for an empirical science. They show, that is, that the world of real lived experience can still be captured, if only in the writer's memoirs, fictional experimentations, or dramatic readings. These works have the danger of directing attention away from the ways in which the text constructs sexually situated individuals in a field of social difference. They also perpetuate "empirical science's hegemony" (Clough, 1992, p. 8), for these new writing technologies of the subject become the site "for the production of knowledge/power . . . [aligned] with . . . the capital/state axis" (Aronowitz, 1988, p. 300, quoted in Clough, 1992, p. 8). Such experiments come up against, and then back away from, the difference between empirical science and social criticism. Too often they fail to engage fully a new politics of textuality that would "refuse the identity of empirical science" (Clough, 1992, p. 135). This new social criticism "would intervene in the relationship of information economics, nation-state politics, and technologies of mass communication, especially in terms of the empirical sciences" (Clough, 1992, p. 16). This, of course, is the terrain occupied by cultural studies.

Richardson, in Volume 3, Chapter 12, and Clandinin and Connelly, Volume 3, Chapter 6, develop the above arguments, viewing writing as a method of inquiry that moves through successive stages of self-reflection. As a series of writings, the field-worker's texts flow from the field experience, through intermediate works, to later work, and finally to the research text that is the public presentation of the ethnographic and narrative experience. Thus do fieldwork and writing blur into one another. There is, in the final analysis, no difference between writing and fieldwork. These two perspectives inform each other throughout every chapter in this volume. In these ways the crisis of representation moves qualitative research in new, critical directions.

A Double Crisis

The ethnographer's authority remains under assault today. A double crisis of representation and legitimation confronts qualitative researchers in the social sciences. Embedded in the discourses of poststructuralism and postmodernism (Vidich & Lyman, Volume 1, Chapter 2; Richardson, Volume 3, Chapter 12), these two crises are coded in multiple terms, variously called and associated with the *interpretive, linguistic,* and *rhetorical* turns in social theory. This linguistic turn makes problematic two key assumptions of qualitative research. The first is that qualitative researchers can directly capture lived experience. Such experience, it is now argued, is created in the social text written by the researcher. This is the representational crisis. It confronts the inescapable problem of representation, but does so within a framework that makes the direct link between experience and text problematic.

The second assumption makes the traditional criteria for evaluating and interpreting qualitative research problematic. This is the legitimation crisis. It involves a serious rethinking of such terms as *validity, generalizability,* and *reliability,* terms already retheorized in postpositivist, constructionist-naturalistic (Lincoln & Guba, 1985, p. 36), feminist (Fonow & Cook, 1991, pp. 1-13; Smith, 1992), and interpretive (Atkinson, 1990; Hammersley, 1992; Lather, 1993) discourses. This crisis asks, How are qualitative studies to be evaluated in the poststructural moment? Clearly these two crises blur together, for any representation must now legitimate itself in terms of some set of criteria that allows the author (and the reader) to make connections between the text and the world written about.

The Fifth Moment

The fifth moment is the present, defined and shaped by the dual crises described above. Theories are now read in narrative terms, as "tales of the field" (Van Maanen, 1988). Preoccupations with the representation of the "other" remain. New epistemologies from previously silenced groups emerge to offer solutions to this problem. The concept of the aloof researcher has been abandoned. More action-, activist-oriented research is on the horizon, as are more social criticism and social critique. The search for grand narratives will be replaced by more local, small-scale theories fitted to specific problems and specific situations (Lincoln, 1993).

Reading History

We draw four conclusions from this brief history, noting that it is, like all histories, somewhat arbitrary. First, each of the earlier historical moments is still operating in the present, either as legacy or as a set of practices that researchers still follow or argue against. The multiple, and fractured, histories of qualitative research now make it possible for any given researcher to attach a project to a canonical text from any of the above-described historical moments. Multiple criteria of evaluation now compete for attention in this field. Second, an embarrassment of choices now characterizes the field of qualitative research. There have never been so many paradigms, strategies of inquiry, or methods of analysis to draw upon and utilize. Third, we are in a moment of discovery and rediscovery, as new ways of looking, interpreting, arguing, and writing are debated and discussed. Fourth, the qualitative research act can no longer be viewed from within a neutral, or objective, positivist perspective. Class, race, gender, and ethnicity shape the process of inquiry, making research a multicultural process. It is to this topic that we next turn.

◆ Qualitative Research as Process

Three interconnected, generic activities define the qualitative research process. They go by a variety of different labels, including *theory, method* and *analysis,* and *ontology, epistemology,* and *methodology.* Behind these terms stands the personal biography of the gendered researcher, who speaks from a particular class, racial, cultural, and ethnic community perspective. The gendered, multiculturally situated researcher approaches the world with a set of ideas, a framework (theory, ontology) that specifies a set of questions (epistemology) that are then examined (methodology, analysis) in specific ways. That is, empirical materials bearing on the question are collected and then analyzed and written about. Every researcher speaks from within a distinct interpretive community, which configures, in its special way, the multicultural, gendered components of the research act.

Behind all of these phases of interpretive work stands the biographically situated researcher. This individual enters the research process from inside an interpretive community that incorporates its own historical research traditions into a distinct point of view. This perspective leads the researcher to adopt particular views of the "other" who is studied. At the same time, the politics and the ethics of research must also be considered, for these concerns permeate every phase of the research process.

◆ The Other as Research Subject

From its turn-of-the-century birth in modern, interpretive form, qualitative research has been haunted by a double-faced ghost. On the one hand, qualitative researchers have assumed that qualified, competent observers can with objectivity, clarity, and precision report on their own observations of the social world, including the experiences of others. Second, researchers have held to a belief in a real subject, or real individual, who is present in the world and able, in some form, to report on his or her experiences. So armed, researchers could blend their observations with the observations provided by subjects through interviews and life story, personal experience, case study, and other documents.

These two beliefs have led qualitative researchers across disciplines to seek a method that would allow them to record their own observations accurately while still uncovering the meanings their subjects bring to their

TABLE 1.1 The Research Process

Phase 1: The Researcher as a Multicultural Subject
    history and research traditions
    conceptions of self and the other
    ethics and politics of research
Phase 2: Theoretical Paradigms and Perspectives
    positivism, postpositivism
    constructivism
    feminism(s)
    ethnic models
    Marxist models
    cultural studies models
Phase 3: Research Strategies
    study design
    case study
    ethnography, participant observation
    phenomenology, ethnomethodology
    grounded theory
    biographical method
    historical method
    action and applied research
    clinical research
Phase 4: Methods of Collection and Analysis
    interviewing
    observing
    artifacts, documents, and records
    visual methods
    personal experience methods
    data management methods
    computer-assisted analysis
    textual analysis
Phase 5: The Art of Interpretation and Presentation
    criteria for judging adequacy
    the art and politics of interpretation
    writing as interpretation
    policy analysis
    evaluation traditions
    applied research

life experiences. This method would rely upon the subjective verbal and written expressions of meaning given by the individuals studied, these expressions being windows into the inner life of the person. Since Dilthey (1900/1976), this search for a method has led to a perennial focus in the human disciplines on qualitative, interpretive methods.

Recently, this position and its beliefs have come under attack. Poststructuralists and postmodernists have contributed to the understanding that there is no clear window into the inner life of an individual. Any gaze is always filtered through the lenses of language, gender, social class, race, and ethnicity. There are no objective observations, only observations socially situated in the worlds of the observer and the observed. Subjects, or individuals, are seldom able to give full explanations of their actions or intentions; all they can offer are accounts, or stories, about what they did and why. No single method can grasp the subtle variations in ongoing human experience. As a consequence, as argued above, qualitative researchers deploy a wide range of interconnected interpretive methods, always seeking better ways to make more understandable the worlds of experience that have been studied.

Table 1.1 depicts the relationships we see among the five phases that define the research process. Behind all but one of these phases stands the biographically situated researcher. These five levels of activity, or practice, work their way through the biography of the researcher.

Phase 1: The Researcher

Our remarks above indicate the depth and complexity of the traditional and applied qualitative research perspectives into which a socially situated researcher enters. These traditions locate the researcher in history, both guiding and constraining work that will be done in any specific study. This field has been characterized constantly by diversity and conflict, and these, David Hamilton argues in Volume 1, Chapter 3, are its most enduring traditions. As a carrier of this complex and contradictory history, the researcher must also confront the ethics and politics of research. The age of value-free inquiry for the human disciplines is over, and researchers now struggle to develop situational and transsituational ethics that apply to any given research act.

Phase 2: Interpretive Paradigms

All qualitative researchers are philosophers in that "universal sense in which all human beings . . . are guided by highly abstract principles" (Bateson, 1972, p. 320). These principles combine beliefs about ontology (What kind of being is the human being? What is the nature of reality?), epistemology (What is the relationship between the inquirer and the known?), and methodology (How do we know the world, or gain knowledge of it?) (see Guba, 1990, p. 18; Lincoln & Guba, 1985, pp. 14-15; see also Guba & Lincoln, Volume 1, Chapter 6). These beliefs shape how the qualitative researcher sees the world and acts in it. The researcher is "bound within a net of epistemological and ontological premises which—regardless of ultimate truth or falsity—become partially self-validating" (Bateson, 1972, p. 314).

This net that contains the researcher's epistemological, ontological, and methodological premises may be termed a *paradigm* (Guba, 1990, p. 17), or interpretive framework, a "basic set of beliefs that guides action" (Guba, 1990, p. 17). All research is interpretive, guided by a set of beliefs and feelings about the world and how it should be understood and studied. Some of these beliefs may be taken for granted, only assumed; others are highly problematic and controversial. However, each interpretive paradigm makes particular demands on the researcher, including the questions that are asked and the interpretations that are brought to them.

At the most general level, four major interpretive paradigms structure qualitative research: positivist and postpositivist, constructivist-interpretive, critical (Marxist, emancipatory), and feminist-poststructural. These four abstract paradigms become more complicated at the level of concrete specific interpretive communities. At this level it is possible to identify not only the constructivist, but also multiple versions of feminist (Afrocentric and poststructural)[8] as well as specific ethnic, Marxist, and cultural studies paradigms. These perspectives, or paradigms, are examined in Part II of Volume 1.

The paradigms examined in Volume 1, Part II, work against and alongside (and some within) the positivist and postpositivist models. They all work within relativist ontologies (multiple constructed realities), interpretive epistemologies (the knower and known interact and shape one another), and interpretive, naturalistic methods.

Table 1.2 presents these paradigms and their assumptions, including their criteria for evaluating research, and the typical form that an interpre-

TABLE 1.2 Interpretive Paradigms

Paradigm/Theory	Criteria	Form of Theory	Type of Narration
Positivist/ postpositivist	internal, external validity	logical-deductive, scientific, grounded	scientific report
Constructivist	trustworthiness, credibility, transferability, confirmability	substantive-formal	interpretive case studies, ethnographic fiction
Feminist	Afrocentric, lived experience, dialogue, caring, accountability, race, class, gender, reflexivity, praxis, emotion, concrete grounding	critical, standpoint	essays, stories, experimental writing
Ethnic	Afrocentric, lived experience, dialogue, caring, accountability, race, class, gender	standpoint, critical, historical	essays, fables, dramas
Marxist	emancipatory theory, falsifiable, dialogical, race, class, gender	critical, historical, economic	historical, economic, sociocultural analysis
Cultural studies	cultural practices, praxis, social texts, subjectivities	social criticism	cultural theory as criticism

tive or theoretical statement assumes in the paradigm.[9] Each paradigm is explored in considerable detail in Volume 1, Part II, by Guba and Lincoln (Chapter 6), Schwandt (Chapter 7), Kincheloe and McLaren (Chapter 8), Olesen (Chapter 9), Stanfield (Chapter 10), and Fiske (Chapter 11). The positivist and postpositivist paradigms have been discussed above. They work from within a realist and critical realist ontology and objective epistemologies, and rely upon experimental, quasi-experimental, survey, and rigorously defined qualitative methodologies. In Volume 3, Chapter 7, Huberman and Miles develop elements of this paradigm.

The constructivist paradigm assumes a relativist ontology (there are multiple realities), a subjectivist epistemology (knower and subject create understandings), and a naturalistic (in the natural world) set of methodological procedures. Findings are usually presented in terms of the criteria of grounded theory (see Strauss & Corbin, Volume 2, Chapter 7). Terms such as *credibility, transferability, dependability,* and *confirmability* replace the usual positivist criteria of *internal* and *external validity, reliability,* and *objectivity.*

Feminist, ethnic, Marxist, and cultural studies models privilege a materialist-realist ontology; that is, the real world makes a material difference in terms of race, class, and gender. Subjectivist epistemologies and naturalistic methodologies (usually ethnographies) are also employed. Empirical materials and theoretical arguments are evaluated in terms of their emancipatory implications. Criteria from gender and racial communities (e.g., African American) may be applied (emotionality and feeling, caring, personal accountability, dialogue).

Poststructural feminist theories emphasize problems with the social text, its logic, and its inability ever to represent fully the world of lived experience. Positivist and postpositivist criteria of evaluation are replaced by others, including the reflexive, multivoiced text that is grounded in the experiences of oppressed peoples.

The cultural studies paradigm is multifocused, with many different strands drawing from Marxism, feminism, and the postmodern sensibility. There is a tension between humanistic cultural studies stressing lived experiences and more structural cultural studies projects stressing the structural and material determinants (race, class, gender) of experience. The cultural studies paradigm uses methods strategically, that is, as resources for understanding and for producing resistances to local structures of domination. Cultural studies scholars may do close textual readings and discourse analysis of cultural texts as well as local ethnographies, open-ended interviewing, and participant observation. The focus is on how race, class, and gender are produced and enacted in historically specific situations.

Paradigm and history in hand, focused on a concrete empirical problem to examine, the researcher now moves to the next stage of the research process, namely, working with a specific strategy of inquiry.

Phase 3: Strategies of Inquiry and Interpretive Paradigms

Table 1.1 presents some of the major strategies of inquiry a researcher may use. Phase 3 begins with research design, which, broadly conceived, involves a clear focus on the research question, the purposes of the study, "what information most appropriately will answer specific research questions, and which strategies are most effective for obtaining it" (LeCompte & Preissle, 1993, p. 30). A research design describes a flexible set of guidelines that connects theoretical paradigms to strategies of inquiry and methods for collecting empirical material. A research design situates researchers in the empirical world and connects them to specific sites, persons, groups, institutions, and bodies of relevant interpretive material, including documents and archives. A research design also specifies how the investigator will address the two critical issues of representation and legitimation.

A strategy of inquiry comprises a bundle of skills, assumptions, and practices that researchers employ as they move from their paradigm to the empirical world. Strategies of inquiry put paradigms of interpretation into motion. At the same time, strategies of inquiry connect the researcher to specific methods of collecting and analyzing empirical materials. For example, the case study method relies on interviewing, observing, and document analysis. Research strategies implement and anchor paradigms in specific empirical sites, or in specific methodological practices, such as making a case an object of study. These strategies include the case study, phenomenological and ethnomethodological techniques, as well as the use of grounded theory, the biographical, historical, action, and clinical methods. Each of these strategies is connected to a complex literature; each has a separate history, exemplary works, and preferred ways for putting the strategy into motion.

Phase 4: Methods of Collecting and Analyzing Empirical Materials

The researcher has several methods for collecting empirical materials,[10] ranging from the interview to direct observation, to the analysis of artifacts, documents, and cultural records, to the use of visual materials or personal experience. The researcher may also use a variety of different methods of reading and analyzing interviews or cultural texts, including content, narrative, and semiotic strategies. Faced with large amounts of qualitative materials, the investigator seeks ways of managing and interpreting these documents, and here data management methods and computer-assisted models of analysis may be of use.

Phase 5: The Art of Interpretation

Qualitative research is endlessly creative and interpretive. The researcher does not just leave the field with mountains of empirical materials and then easily write up his or her findings. Qualitative interpretations are constructed. The researcher first creates a field text consisting of field notes and documents from the field, what Roger Sanjek (1990, p. 386) calls "indexing" and David Plath (1990, p. 374) calls "filework." The writer-as-interpreter moves from this text to a research text: notes and interpretations based on the field text. This text is then re-created as a working interpretive document that contains the writer's initial attempts to make sense out of what he or she has learned. Finally, the writer produces the public text that comes to the reader. This final tale of the field may assume several forms: confessional, realist, impressionistic, critical, formal, literary, analytic, grounded theory, and so on (see Van Maanen, 1988).

The interpretive practice of making sense of one's findings is both artful and political. Multiple criteria for evaluating qualitative research now exist, and those we emphasize stress the situated, relational, and textual structures of the ethnographic experience. There is no single interpretive truth. As we argued earlier, there are multiple interpretive communities, each having its own criteria for evaluating an interpretation.

Program evaluation is a major site of qualitative research, and qualitative researchers can influence social policy in important ways. David Hamilton, in Volume 1, Chapter 3, traces the rich history of applied qualitative research in the social sciences. This is the critical site where theory, method, praxis, or action, and policy all come together. Qualitative researchers can isolate target populations, show the immediate effects of certain programs on such groups, and isolate the constraints that operate against policy changes in such settings. Action-oriented and clinically oriented qualitative researchers can also create spaces for those who are studied (the other) to speak. The evaluator becomes the conduit for making such voices heard. Greene, in Volume 3, Chapter 13, and Rist, in Volume 3, Chapter 14, develop these topics.

◆ The Fifth Moment: What Comes Next?

Marcus, in Volume 1, Chapter 12, argues that we are already in the post "post" period—post-poststructuralism, post-postmodernism. What this means for interpretive, ethnographic practices is still not clear, but it is certain that things will never be the same. We are in a new age where messy, uncertain, multivoiced texts, cultural criticism, and new experimental works will become more common, as will more reflexive forms of fieldwork, analysis, and intertextual representation. The subject of our final essay in this volume is this "fifth moment." It is true that, as the poet said, the center cannot hold. We can reflect on what should be at a new center.

Thus we come full circle. The chapters in these volumes take the researcher through every phase of the research act. The contributors examine the relevant histories, controversies, and current practices associated with each paradigm, strategy, and method. They also offer projections for the future—where specific paradigms, strategies, or methods will be 10 years from now.

In reading the chapters that follow, it is important to remember that the field of qualitative research is defined by a series of tensions, contradictions, and hesitations. This tension works back and forth between the broad, doubting postmodern sensibility and the more certain, more traditional positivist, postpositivist, and naturalistic conceptions of this project. All of the chapters that follow are caught in and articulate this tension.

◆ Notes

1. Qualitative research has separate and distinguished histories in education, social work, communications, psychology, history, organizational studies, medical science, anthropology, and sociology.

2. Definitions of some of these terms are in order here. *Positivism* asserts that objective accounts of the world can be given. *Postpositivism* holds that only partially objective accounts of the world can be produced, because all methods are flawed. *Structuralism* asserts that any system is made up of a set of oppositional categories embedded in language. *Semiotics* is the science of signs or sign systems—a structuralist project. According to *poststructuralism*, language is an unstable system of referents, thus it is impossible ever to capture completely the meaning of an action, text, or intention. *Postmodernism* is a contemporary sensibility, developing since World War II, that privileges no single authority, method, or paradigm. *Hermeneutics* is an approach to the analysis of texts that stresses how prior understandings and prejudices shape the interpretive process. *Phenomenology* is a complex system of ideas associated with the works of Husserl, Heidegger, Sartre, Merleau-Ponty, and Alfred Schutz. *Cultural studies* is a complex, interdisciplinary field that merges critical theory, feminism, and poststructuralism.

3. According to Weinstein and Weinstein (1991), "The meaning of *bricoleur* in French popular speech is 'someone who works with his (or her) hands and uses devious means compared to those of the craftsman.' . . . the *bricoleur* is practical and gets the job done" (p. 161). These authors provide a history of this term, connecting it to the works of the German sociologist and social theorist Georg Simmel and, by implication, Baudelaire.

4. Here it is relevant to make a distinction between techniques that are used across disciplines and methods that are used within disciplines. Ethnomethodologists, for example, employ their approach as a method, whereas others selectively borrow that method as a technique for their own applications. Harry Wolcott (personal communication, 1993) suggests this distinction. It is also relevant to make distinctions among topic, method, and resource. Methods can be studied as topics of inquiry—for instance, how a case study gets

done. In this ironic, ethnomethodological sense, method is both a resource and a topic of inquiry.

5. Indeed, any attempt to give an essential definition of qualitative research requires a qualitative analysis of the circumstances that produce such a definition.

6. In this sense all research is qualitative, because "the observer is at the center of the research process" (Vidich & Lyman, Volume 1, Chapter 2).

7. See Lincoln and Guba (1985) for an extension and elaboration of this tradition in the mid-1980s.

8. Olesen (Volume 1, Chapter 9) identifies three strands of feminist research: mainstream empirical, standpoint and cultural studies, and poststructural, postmodern, placing Afrocentric and other models of color under the cultural studies and postmodern categories.

9. These, of course, are our interpretations of these paradigms and interpretive styles.

10. *Empirical materials* is the preferred term for what are traditionally described as data.

◆ References

Aronowitz, S. (1988). *Science as power: Discourse and ideology in modern society*. Minneapolis: University of Minnesota Press.

Atkinson, P. A. (1990). *The ethnographic imagination: Textual constructions of reality*. London: Routledge.

Bateson, G. (1972). *Steps to an ecology of mind*. New York: Ballantine.

Becker, H. S. (1970). Problems of inference and proof in participant observation. In H. S. Becker, *Sociological work*. Chicago: Aldine. (Reprinted from *American Sociological Review, 1958, 23,* 652-660)

Becker, H. S. (1986). *Doing things together*. Evanston, IL: Northwestern University Press.

Becker, H. S. (1989). Tricks of the trade. *Studies in Symbolic Interaction, 10,* 481-490.

Becker, H. S. (1993, June 9). *The epistemology of qualitative research*. Paper presented at the MacArthur Foundation Conference on Ethnographic Approaches to the Study of Human Behavior, Oakland, CA.

Becker, H. S., Geer, B., Hughes, E. C., & Strauss, A. L. (1961). *Boys in white: Student culture in medical school*. Chicago: University of Chicago Press.

Bogdan, R., & Taylor, S. J. (1975). *Introduction to qualitative research methods: A phenomenological approach to the social sciences*. New York: John Wiley.

Brewer, J., & Hunter, A. (1989). *Multimethod research: A synthesis of styles*. Newbury Park, CA: Sage.

Campbell, D. T., & Stanley, J. C. (1963). *Experimental and quasi-experimental designs for research*. Chicago: Rand McNally.

Carey, J. W. (1989). *Communication as culture: Essays on media and society*. Boston: Unwin Hyman.

Cicourel, A. V. (1964). *Method and measurement in sociology*. New York: Free Press.

Clifford, J. (1988). *The predicament of culture: Twentieth-century ethnography, literature, and art*. Cambridge, MA: Harvard University Press.

Clifford, J., & Marcus, G. E. (Eds.). (1986). *Writing culture: The poetics and politics of ethnography*. Berkeley: University of California Press.

Clough, P. T. (1992). *The end(s) of ethnography: From realism to social criticism.* Newbury Park, CA: Sage.

Denzin, N. K. (1970). *The research act.* Chicago: Aldine.

Denzin, N. K. (1978). *The research act* (2nd ed.). New York: McGraw-Hill.

Denzin, N. K. (1989a). *Interpretive interactionism.* Newbury Park, CA: Sage.

Denzin, N. K. (1989b). *The research act* (3rd ed.). Englewood Cliffs, NJ: Prentice Hall.

Dilthey, W. L. (1976). *Selected writings.* Cambridge: Cambridge University Press. (Original work published 1900)

Fielding, N. G., & Fielding, J. L. (1986). *Linking data.* Beverly Hills, CA: Sage.

Filstead, W. J. (Ed.). (1970). *Qualitative methodology.* Chicago: Markham.

Flick, U. (1992). Triangulation revisited: Strategy of validation or alternative? *Journal for the Theory of Social Behaviour, 22,* 175-198.

Fonow, M. M., & Cook, J. A. (1991). Back to the future: A look at the second wave of feminist epistemology and methodology. In M. M. Fonow & J. A. Cook (Eds.), *Beyond methodology: Feminist scholarship as lived research* (pp. 1-15). Bloomington: Indiana University Press.

Geertz, C. (1973). *The interpretation of cultures: Selected essays.* New York: Basic Books.

Geertz, C. (1983). *Local knowledge: Further essays in interpretive anthropology.* New York: Basic Books.

Geertz, C. (1988). *Works and lives: The anthropologist as author.* Stanford, CA: Stanford University Press.

Glaser, B. G. (1992). *Emergence vs. forcing: Basics of grounded theory.* Mill Valley, CA: Sociology Press.

Glaser, B. G., & Strauss, A. L. (1967). *The discovery of grounded theory: Strategies for qualitative research.* Chicago: Aldine.

Guba, E. G. (1990). The alternative paradigm dialog. In E. G. Guba (Ed.), *The paradigm dialog* (pp. 17-30). Newbury Park, CA: Sage.

Hammersley, M. (1992). *What's wrong with ethnography? Methodological explorations.* London: Routledge.

Hymes, D. (1980). Educational ethnology. *Anthropology and Education Quarterly, 11,* 3-8.

Lather, P. (1993). Fertile obsession: Validity after poststructuralism. *Sociological Quarterly, 34,* 673-693.

LeCompte, M. D., & Preissle, J. (1992). Toward an ethnology of student life in schools and classrooms: Synthesizing the qualitative research tradition. In M. D. LeCompte, W. L. Millroy, & J. Preissle (Eds.), *The handbook of qualitative research in education* (pp. 815-859). New York: Academic Press.

LeCompte, M. D., & Preissle, J., with Tesch, R. (1993). *Ethnography and qualitative design in educational research* (2nd ed.). New York: Academic Press.

Lentricchia, F., & McLaughlin, T. (Eds.). (1990). *Critical terms for literary study.* Chicago: University of Chicago Press.

Lévi-Strauss, C. (1966). *The savage mind* (2nd ed.). Chicago: University of Chicago Press.

Lincoln, Y. S. (1993, January 27-28). *Notes toward a fifth generation of evaluation: Lessons from the voiceless, or, Toward a postmodern politics of evaluation.* Paper presented at the Fifth Annual Meeting of the Southeast Evaluation Association, Tallahassee, FL.

Lincoln, Y. S., & Guba, E. G. (1985). *Naturalistic inquiry.* Beverly Hills, CA: Sage.

Lofland, J. (1971). *Analyzing social settings: A guide to qualitative observation and analysis.* Belmont, CA: Wadsworth.

Lofland, J., & Lofland, L. H. (1984). *Analyzing social settings: A guide to qualitative observation and analysis* (2nd ed.). Belmont, CA: Wadsworth.

Lofland, L. (1980). The 1969 Blumer-Hughes talk. *Urban Life, 8,* 248-260.

Malinowski, B. (1948). *Magic, science and religion, and other essays.* New York: Natural History Press. (Original work published 1916)

Malinowski, B. (1967). *A diary in the strict sense of the term.* New York: Harcourt Brace.

Marcus, G., & Fischer, M. (1986). *Anthropology as cultural critique: An experimental moment in the human sciences.* Chicago: University of Chicago Press.

Miles, M. B., & Huberman, A. M. (1993). *Qualitative data analysis: A sourcebook of new methods* (2nd ed.). Newbury Park, CA: Sage.

Nelson, C., Treichler, P. A., & Grossberg, L. (1992). Cultural studies. In L. Grossberg, C. Nelson, & P. A. Treichler (Eds.), *Cultural studies* (pp. 1-16). New York: Routledge.

Nichols, B. (Ed.). (1985). *Movies and methods* (Vol. 2). Berkeley: University of California Press.

Plath, D. (1990). Fieldnotes, filed notes, and the conferring of note. In R. Sanjek (Ed.), *Fieldnotes: The makings of anthropology* (pp. 371-384). Albany: State University of New York Press.

Richardson, L. (1991). Postmodern social theory. *Sociological Theory, 9,* 173-179.

Roffman, P., & Purdy, J. (1981). *The Hollywood social problem film.* Bloomington: Indiana University Press.

Rosaldo, R. (1989). *Culture and truth: The remaking of social analysis.* Boston: Beacon.

Sanjek, R. (Ed.). (1990). *Fieldnotes: The makings of anthropology.* Albany: State University of New York Press.

Smith, D. (1992). Sociology from women's perspective: A reaffirmation. *Sociological Theory, 10,* 88-97.

Spindler, G., & Spindler, L. (1992). Cultural process and ethnography: An anthropological perspective. In M. D. LeCompte, W. L. Millroy, & J. Preissle (Eds.), *The handbook of qualitative research in education* (pp. 53-92). New York: Academic Press.

Stoller, P., & Olkes, C. (1987). *In sorcery's shadow: A memoir of apprenticeship among the Songhay of Niger.* Chicago: University of Chicago Press.

Strauss, A. L., & Corbin, J. (1990). *Basics of qualitative research: Grounded theory procedures and techniques.* Newbury Park, CA: Sage.

Turner, V., & Bruner, E. (Eds.). (1986). *The anthropology of experience.* Urbana: University of Illinois Press.

Van Maanen, J. (1988). *Tales of the field: On writing ethnography.* Chicago: University of Chicago Press.

West, C. (1989). *The American evasion of philosophy.* Madison: University of Wisconsin Press.

Weinstein, D., & Weinstein, M. A. (1991). Georg Simmel: Sociological flaneur bricoleur. *Theory, Culture & Society, 8,* 151-168.

Wolcott, H. F. (1992). Posturing in qualitative research. In M. D. LeCompte, W. L. Millroy, & J. Preissle (Eds.), *The handbook of qualitative research in education* (pp. 3-52). New York: Academic Press.

2
The Dance of Qualitative Research Design

Metaphor, Methodolatry, and Meaning

Valerie J. Janesick

Every dance is to some greater or lesser extent
a kind of fever chart, a graph of the heart.

—Martha Graham

♦ When Martha Graham, the dance world's at once most famous and infamous dancer and dance maker, was asked to describe dance, she said these words to capture the essence of dance. In this chapter, I would like to discuss the essence of qualitative research design. I have selected the metaphor of dance for two reasons. First, dance is the art form to which I am most devoted, having been a dancer and choreographer for more than 25 years. I began dance classes as a child. My mother was a dancer in USO shows, and she had a strong influence on me. I became a choreographer as a natural evolution, following in the footsteps of many of my adored and influential teachers. In dance, a vibrant mentor-protégé system is in place.

I have choreographed modern dance, ballet, ethnic and folk dances, and dances for musicals for the Ann Arbor Civic Theater and for various university and regional dance companies. Because I was a teacher, I also did choreography for various school districts in Michigan and Ohio. I directed my own dance company, in Ann Arbor, East Lansing, and Bowling Green, Ohio. In Ohio, I received grants, along with the Bowling Green University Dancers, from the Ohio Council for the Arts, to bring dance in the schools' programs into Ohio. I spent summers in New York City, studying technique at the schools of Martha Graham, Merce Cunningham, Alvin Ailey, and Erick Hawkins.[1] While studying at Michigan State University, at the Institute for Research on Teaching, I taught all levels of modern dance, choreography, dance history, and anatomy for the dancers at Lansing Community College in addition to my research internship. In fact, it was this simultaneous experience in dance and research studies that prepared me for my academic career as an ethnographic researcher and teacher of qualitative research methods.

A second reason I have selected the metaphor of dance is simply because of its power. Metaphor in general creeps up on you and surprises. It defies the boilerplate approach to a topic. I can only wholeheartedly agree with Eisner (1991) when he discusses metaphor:

> What is ironic is that in the professional socialization of educational researchers, the use of metaphor is regarded as a sign of imprecision; yet, for making public the ineffable, nothing is more precise than the artistic use of language. Metaphoric precision is the central vehicle for revealing the qualitative aspects of life. (p. 227)

Consequently, I invite the reader to embrace this metaphor of dance, often called the mother of the arts. Dance, as a true art form, is a useful reference point for recalling Dewey's (1934/1958) notion that there is no work of art apart from human experience. For Dewey, the work of art is an event. He sees art as engaging and developing experience with a sense of meaning. Even in the art world, meaning can be lost in the event of objectification of the art. For example, the dance world is filled with wheelers and dealers, aestheticians, foot doctors, managers, advertisers, promoters, and charming eccentrics. At any intersection of the work of art with some individuals, the work of art can be decontextualized and objectified. But it is in the Deweyan sense that I speak of dance. Because dance is about lived experience, it seems to me the perfect metaphor for qualitative research design.

In addition, the qualitative researcher is very much like an artist at various stages in the design process, in terms of situating and recontextualizing the research project within the shared experience of the researcher and the participants in the study. Dewey sees art as the bridge between the experience of individuals and the community. In other words, art forces us to think about how human beings are related to each other in their respective worlds. How appropriate to view dance as an expressively dynamic art form that connects the cultural meanings of dancers, choreographer, and community. Like Dewey (1934/1958), who notes that the actual work of art is what the product does with and in experience, the qualitative researcher, as designer of a project, recognizes the potential of design. The design serves as a foundation for the understanding of the participants' worlds and the meaning of shared experience between the researcher and participants in a given social context. Dance is an interpretive art form, and I see qualitative research design as interpretive as well.

◆ Qualitative Research Design as Choreography

All dances make a statement and begin with the question, What do I want to say in this dance? In much the same way, the qualitative researcher begins with a similar question: What do I want to know in this study? This is a critical beginning point. Regardless of point of view, and quite often because of our point of view, we construct and frame a question for inquiry. After this question is clear, we select the most appropriate methodology to proceed with the research project. I am always surprised by doctoral students and colleagues who forthrightly state that they wish to do a qualitative study without any question in mind. They ask about books and references to learn all the steps. They are taken aback when I give them a reading list, because over the past 25 years or so, in education alone, there has been published quite an impressive and lengthy list of methods texts and articles in journals with illustrative studies using qualitative methods. The next question becomes, Yes, but which one tells me exactly what to do, step by step? You see the point. They are not ready to design qualitative projects, for they have no research question from which to choose appropriate methods. Some go even further, saying, I have pages of data from

37

teachers, how do I make this into a qualitative study? Again, there is no question to guide the inquiry. It is difficult to take such an approach seriously.

Qualitative research design begins with a question. Of course, qualitative researchers design a study with real individuals in mind, and with the intent of living in that social setting over time. They study a social setting to understand the meaning of participants' lives in the participants' own terms. I mention this to contrast it to the quantitative paradigm, which is perfectly comfortable with aggregating large numbers of people without communicating with them face to face. So the questions of the qualitative researcher are quite different from those of the quantitative researcher. Elsewhere in the literature, the reader may find information on the kinds of questions suited to qualitative methods (Erickson, 1986; Janesick, 1983). In general, questions that are suited to qualitative inquiry have long been the questions of many curriculum researchers and theorists. For example:

1. questions concerning the quality of a given curriculum, innovation, or program
2. questions regarding meaning or interpretation about some component of curriculum
3. questions that relate to curriculum in terms of its sociolinguistic aspects
4. questions related to the whole system, as in a classroom, school, or school district
5. questions regarding the political, economic, or sociopsychological aspects of schooling
6. questions regarding the hidden curriculum
7. questions pertaining to the social context of schooling
8. questions pertaining to teachers' implicit theories about teaching and curriculum

This list is not meant to be exhaustive; it serves only to illustrate the basic areas where research has been completed in the field of education and has employed qualitative techniques because of, among other things, the suitability of the technique and the question.

Just as the dancer begins with a warm-up of the body, follows through with floor exercises, and then moves to a cool-down period, I like to think of qualitative design as made up of three stages. First there is the warm-up stage, or design decisions made at the beginning of the study; second is the total workout stage, during which design decisions are made throughout the study; and third is the cool-down stage, when design decisions are made at the end of the study. Just as the dancer relies on the spine for the power and coherence of the dance, so the qualitative researcher relies on the design of the study. Both are elastic. Like the dancer who finds her center from the base of the spine and the connection between the spine and the body, the qualitative researcher is centered by a series of design decisions. A dancer who is centered may tilt forward and backward and from side to side, yet always returns to the center, the core of the dancer's strength. If one thinks of the design of the study as the spine and the base of the spine as the beginning of the warm-up in dance, the beginning decisions in a study are very much like the lower-spine warm-up, the beginning warm-up for the dancer.

◆ Warming Up: Design Decisions at the Beginning of the Study

The first set of design decisions have to do with what is studied, under what circumstances, for what duration of time, and with whom. I always start with a question. For example, when I studied deaf culture in Washington, D.C., over a four-year period (Janesick, 1990), my basic question was, How do some deaf adults manage to succeed academically and in the workplace given the stigma of deafness in our society? This basic question informed all my observations and interviews, and led me to use focus groups and oral history techniques later in the study. Both the focus groups and oral histories evolved after I came to know the perspectives on deafness of the twelve individuals in my study. I then used theoretical sampling techniques to select three individuals to participate in an oral history component of the study.[2] I use this example to illustrate the elasticity of qualitative design. Focus groups allowed me to moderate and observe interactions among three of my participants on their perspectives on deafness, something I could not have planned in the first days in the field. Neither could I have realized at the beginning of the study the value of incorporating these techniques. These techniques allowed me to capture a richer interpretation of participants' perspectives on deafness.

Simultaneous with the question that guides the study, the qualitative researcher needs to select a site according to some rationale. Access and entry are sensitive components in qualitative research, and the researcher must establish trust, rapport, and authentic communication patterns with participants. By establishing trust and rapport at the beginning of the study, the researcher is better able to capture the nuance and meaning of each participant's life from the participant's point of view. This also ensures that participants will be more willing to share everything, warts and all, with the researcher. Maintaining trust and rapport continues through the length of the study and long after, in fact. Yet it must begin at the beginning. It would be difficult to imagine establishing trust, say, six months into a study. Any of us who have done fieldwork know how critical initial interactions in the field are as a precursor to establishing trust and rapport.

Once the researcher has a question, a site, a participant or a number of participants, and a reasonable time period to undertake the study, he or she needs to decide on the most appropriate data collection strategies suited to the study. The selection of these strategies is intimately connected to how the researcher views the purpose of the work, that is, how to understand the social setting under study. Most often, qualitative researchers use some combination of participant observation, interviews, and document analysis. The literature on approaches and strategies used in qualitative studies is extensive (e.g., Bogdan & Biklen, 1992; Denzin, 1989; Goetz & LeCompte, 1984; LeCompte, Millroy, & Priessle, 1992; Lincoln & Guba, 1985; Spradley, 1979, 1980; Strauss & Corbin, 1990). For example, in education over the past three decades, case study methods, oral history, including narrative and life history approaches, grounded theory, literary criticism, and ethnographic approaches to research have been discovered and used for their fit with questions in education and human services. This makes sense, as these are the very approaches that allow researchers to deal with individuals.

Summary

The warm-up period, or the period of making decisions at the beginning of the study, includes decisions regarding the following:

1. the questions that guide the study
2. selection of a site and participants
3. access and entry to the site and agreements with participants
4. timeline for the study
5. selection of appropriate research strategies, which may include some of the following (this list is not meant to be inclusive of all possibilities)
   a. ethnography

    b. life history

    c. oral history

    d. ethnomethodology

    e. case study

    f. participant observation

    g. field research or field study

    h. naturalistic study

    i. phenomenological study

    j. ecological descriptive study

    k. descriptive study

    l. symbolic interactionist study

    m. microethnography

    n. interpretive research

    o. action research

    p. narrative research

    q. historiography

    r. literary criticism

6. the place of theory in the study

7. identification of the researcher's own biases and ideology

8. identification of appropriate informed consent procedures and willingness to deal with ethical issues as they present themselves

In terms of the last two items, I would like to point out that qualitative researchers accept the fact that research is ideologically driven. There is no value-free or bias-free design. The qualitative researcher early on identifies his or her biases and articulates the ideology or conceptual frame for the study. By identifying one's biases, one can see easily where the questions that guide the study are crafted. This is a big difference among paradigms. As we try to make sense of our social world and give meaning to what we do as researchers, we continually raise awareness of our own biases. There is no attempt to pretend that research is value free. Likewise, qualitative researchers, because they deal with individual persons face-to-face on a daily basis, are attuned to making decisions regarding ethical concerns, because this is part of life in the field. From the beginning moments of informed consent decisions, to other ethical decisions in the field, to the completion of the study, qualitative researchers need to allow for the possibilities of recurring ethical dilemmas and problems.

In addition to the decisions made at the beginning of the study, it is helpful to consider some characteristics of qualitative design. Again, the following list is not meant to be exhaustive; it is offered merely as a heuristic tool.

1. Qualitative design is holistic. It looks at the larger picture, the whole picture, and begins with a search for understanding of the whole.

2. Qualitative design looks at relationships within a system or culture.

3. Qualitative design refers to the personal, face-to-face, and immediate.

4. Qualitative design is focused on understanding a given social setting, not necessarily on making predictions about that setting.

5. Qualitative design demands that the researcher stay in the setting over time.

6. Qualitative design demands time in analysis equal to the time in the field.

7. Qualitative design demands that the researcher develop a model of what occurred in the social setting.

8. Qualitative design requires the researcher to become the research instrument. This means the researcher must have the ability to observe behavior and must sharpen the skills necessary for observation and face-to-face interview.

9. Qualitative design incorporates informed consent decisions and is responsive to ethical concerns.

10. Qualitative design incorporates room for description of the role of the researcher as well as description of the researcher's own biases and ideological preference.

11. Qualitative design requires ongoing analyses of the data.

Other chapters in this volume discuss many of the above characteristics in depth, and the reader will benefit from those discussions. Once the researcher begins the study and is in the field, another set of decision points emerges.

◆ Exercises: The Pilot Study and Ongoing Design Decisions

Before devoting oneself to the arduous and significant time commitment of a qualitative study, it is a good idea to do a pilot study. Preinterviews with selected key participants and a brief period of observation and document review can assist the researcher in a number of ways. The pilot study allows the researcher to focus on particular areas that may have been unclear previously. In addition, pilot interviews may be used to test certain questions. Still further, this initial time frame allows the researcher to begin

to develop and solidify rapport with participants as well as to establish effective communication patterns. By including some time for the review of records and documents, the researcher may uncover some insight into the shape of the study that previously was not apparent. Again to use an example from my study on deaf culture, prior to my interviews with participants, I spent time in the Gallaudet University archives, reading journals, looking at newspaper clippings, and viewing videotapes, all of which were helpful for my understanding of the historical influences that led to the "Deaf President Now" movement.[3] I saw, in retrospect, common themes and categories in the subsequent interview transcripts that made perfect sense given a series of historical situations in a 125-year period prior to the selection of Gallaudet University's first deaf president. Thus the time invested in a pilot study can be valuable and enriching for later phases in the study.

Other decisions made during the study usually concern effective use of time, participants' issues, and researcher issues. Because working in the field is unpredictable a good deal of the time, the qualitative researcher must be ready to adjust schedules, to be flexible about interview times and about adding or subtracting observations or interviews, to replace participants in the event of trauma or tragedy, and even to rearrange terms of the original agreement. My own experiences in conducting long-term ethnographic studies have led me to refine and readjust the design constantly as I proceed through the study, especially at this phase. Being totally immersed in the immediate and local actions and statements of belief of participants, the researcher must be ready to deal with the substantive focus of the study and with the researcher's own presuppositions. Simply observing and interviewing does not ensure that the research is qualitative, for the qualitative researcher must also interpret the beliefs and behaviors of participants. In a sense, while in the field, the researcher is constantly immersed in a combination of deliberate decisions about hypotheses generated and tested on the one hand and intuitive reactions on the other. The researcher finds in the vast literature of sociology, anthropology, and education common rules of thumb on which most researchers agree:

1. Look for the meaning and perspectives of the participants in the study.
2. Look for relationships regarding the structure, occurrence, and distribution of events over time.
3. Look for points of tension: What does not fit? What are the conflicting points of evidence in the case?

As Erickson (1986) so eloquently reminds us, the use of qualitative techniques does not necessarily mean that the research being conducted is qualitative. What makes the research qualitative is a matter of "substantive focus and intent." Erickson uses the example of narrative description. A quantitative researcher may use this technique and come up with a product that is a very different product from that arrived at by a qualitative researcher in the same setting:

> It is important to emphasize at the outset that the use of continuous narrative description as a technique—what can less formally be called "writing like crazy"—does not necessarily mean that the research being conducted is interpretive or qualitative, in a fundamental sense. What makes such work interpretive or qualitative is a matter of substantive focus and intent, rather than of procedure in data collection, that is, a research *technique* does not constitute a research *method*. The technique of continuous narrative description can be used by researchers with a positivist and behaviorist orientation that deliberately excludes from research interest the immediate meanings of actions from the actors' point of view. Continuous narrative description can also be used by researchers with a nonpositivist, interpretive orientation, in which the immediate (often intuitive) meanings of actions to the actors involved are of central interest. The presuppositions and conclusions of these two types of research are very different, and the content of the narrative description that is written differs as well. If two observers with these differing orientations were placed in the same spot to observe what was ostensibly the "same" behavior performed by the "same" individuals, the observers would write substantively differing accounts of what had happened, choosing differing kinds of verbs, nouns, adverbs, and adjectives to characterize the actions that were described. (pp. 119-120)

Furthermore, he argues that the state of the art in research on teaching, for example, is one of rival theories, rival research programs, and rival uses of techniques. The qualitative researcher needs to come to grips with this in a practical sense at some point during the research project. Erickson (1986) puts it this way:

> The current conflict in research on teaching is not one of competing paradigms, I would argue, not because the competing views do not differ ontologically, but simply because as Lakatos (1978) and others have argued for the natural sciences—and especially for the social sciences—paradigms do not actually compete in scientific discourse. Old paradigms are rarely

44

replaced by falsification. Rather the older and the newer paradigms tend to coexist, as in the survival of Newtonian physics, which can be used for some purposes, despite the competition of the Einsteinian physics, which for other purposes has superseded it. Especially in the social sciences, paradigms don't die; they develop varicose veins and get fitted with cardiac pacemakers. The perspective of standard research on teaching and the interpretive perspective are indeed rival theories—rival research programs—even if it is unlikely that the latter will totally supersede the former. (p. 120)

It is much the same in the dance world. Although the Graham technique represented a paradigm shift from ballet into modern dance, elements of ballet are still used within the idiom of modern dance. Furthermore, modern dance has embraced multiple competing and rival techniques, such as those of Cunningham and Tharp. Basically, the qualitative researcher as designer of the research project will be making decisions at all stages of the project. Warm-up decisions made before entering the field constitute the first set of decisions. Exercises, the second stage of decisions, occur within the period of data collection in the field. The third stage of design decisions consists of those made at the end of the study, after leaving the field—what I call cooling down.

◆ Cooling Down: Design Decisions Made at the End of the Study

Design decisions at the end of the study are similar to the cool-down portion of the dance movement. The researcher must decide when to leave the field setting, often an emotional and traumatic event because of the close rapport that can develop during the course of a study. I usually ease out of the setting much as I would cool down after the exercise of dance. For example, in my study of a teacher's classroom perspective (Janesick, 1982), after observing on a daily basis for six months, I started staggering my observations and interviews in the seventh month of fieldwork from five days per week to three days to once per week and then to meetings with the teacher to go over interview transcripts at his convenience.

Following the process of leaving the field, final data analysis can begin. Of course, the qualitative researcher has been developing categories from the data through constant comparative analysis over the entire time frame of the study.[4] The process of reduction of data into a manageable model constitutes an end goal of qualitative research design. There is a continual reassessment and refining of concepts as the fieldwork proceeds. The researcher purposely seeks negative examples because they may disprove some initial hypothetical constructs. As the analysis proceeds, the researcher develops working models that explain the behavior under study. As the analysis continues, the researcher can identify relationships that connect portions of the description with the explanations offered in the working models. The researcher attempts to determine the significance of the various elements in the working models and to verify these by checking through field notes, interview transcripts, and documents.

Following the construction of a model, the next component of the process is the presentation of the data in narrative form supported by evidence from the statements and behaviors recorded in the notes and interviews. In other words, the researcher makes empirical assertions supported by direct quotations from notes and interviews. The researcher also needs to provide some interpretive commentary framing the key findings in the study. The theoretical discussion should be traceable in the data. In addition, the researcher should describe his or her own role thoroughly, so that the reader understands the relationship between the researcher and participants. This allows the researcher to confront the major assertions in the study with credibility while surveying the full range of evidence. Because qualitative work recognizes early on in the study the perspective of the researcher as it evolves through the study, the description of the role of the researcher is a critical component in the writing of the report of the study.

Triangulation

The researcher often relies on triangulation, or the use of several kinds of methods or data. Denzin (1978) identifies four basic types of triangulation:

1. *data triangulation:* the use of a variety of data sources in a study
2. *investigator triangulation:* the use of several different researchers or evaluators
3. *theory triangulation:* the use of multiple perspectives to interpret a single set of data
4. *methodological triangulation:* the use of multiple methods to study a single problem

I would like to add a fifth type to this list: *interdisciplinary triangulation.* Interdisciplinary triangulation will help to lift us up out of the dominant trench of psychology. In education, at least, psychology has dominated the discourse altogether. Not only is the dominance seen in the quantitative arena, but in fact a good deal of the discourse in qualitative research is heavily influenced by underlying psychometric views of the world. The prevailing myths about aggregating numbers and, more tragically, aggregating individuals into sets of numbers have moved us away from our understanding of lived experience. By using other disciplines, such as art, sociology, history, dance, architecture, and anthropology to inform our research processes, we may broaden our understanding of method and substance.

Triangulation is meant to be a heuristic tool for the researcher. Although the term was originally used by land surveyors to describe the use of three points to locate oneself at particular intersections, it is not to be taken literally, as a student of mine once asked, "Does triangulation mean that you can only use three types of methods or perspectives?" Clearly this limit does not apply in qualitative research. For further elaboration of Denzin's construct, see Patton's (1990) adaptation of it for the evaluation researcher.

◆ Major Considerations in Writing the Narrative

The qualitative researcher uses inductive analysis, which means that categories, themes, and patterns come from the data. The categories that emerge from field notes, documents, and interviews are not imposed prior to data collection. Early on, the researcher will develop a system of coding and categorizing the data. There is no one best system for analysis. The researcher may follow rigorous guidelines described in the literature (see Eisner, 1991; Fetterman, 1989; Goetz & LeCompte, 1984; Lincoln & Guba, 1985; Miles & Huberman, 1984; Patton, 1990), but the ultimate decisions about the narrative reside with the researcher. Like the choreographer, the researcher must find the most effective way to tell the story, to convince the audience. Staying close to the data is the most powerful means of telling the story, just as in dance the story is told through the body itself. As in the quantitative arena, the purpose of conducting a qualitative study is to produce findings. The methods and strategies used are not ends in themselves. There is a danger in becoming so taken up with methods that the substantive findings are obscured.

◆ Methodolatry

I use the term *methodolatry,* a combination of *method* and *idolatry,* to describe a preoccupation with selecting and defending methods to the exclusion of the actual substance of the story being told. Methodolatry is the slavish attachment and devotion to method that so often overtakes the discourse in the education and human services fields. In my lifetime I have witnessed an almost constant obsession with the trinity of validity, reliability, and generalizability. It is always tempting to become overinvolved with method and, in so doing, separate experience from knowing. Methodolatry is another way to move away from understanding the actual experience of participants in the research project. In the final stage of writing up the project, it is probably wise to avoid being overly preoccupied with method. In other words, the qualitative researcher should immediately focus on the substance of the findings. Qualitative research depends on the presentation of solid descriptive data, so that the researcher leads the reader to an understand of the meaning of the experience under study.

In classic terms, sociologists and anthropologists have shown us that finding categories and the relationships and patterns between and among categories leads to completeness in the narrative. Spradley (1980) suggests searching for cultural themes or domains. Denzin (1989) follows Husserl's earlier conception of bracketing, which is to hold the phenomenon up to serious inspection, and suggests the following steps:

1. Locate within the personal experience, or self-story, key phrases and statements that speak directly to the phenomenon in question.
2. Interpret the meanings of these phrases as an informed reader.
3. Obtain the participants' interpretation of these findings, if possible.
4. Inspect these meanings for what they reveal about the essential, recurring features of the phenomenon being studied.
5. Offer a tentative statement or definition of the phenomenon in terms of the essential recurring features identified in Step 4.

So, in the process of bracketing, the researcher has the opportunity to treat the data in all its forms equally. Then the researcher may categorize, group, and cluster the data in order to interpret them. The researcher uses constant comparative analysis to look for statements and indices of behavior that occur over time and in a variety of periods during the study. In addition, bracketing allows the researcher to find points of tension and conflict and what does not fit. After total immersion in the setting, the researcher requires time for analysis and contemplation of the data. By allowing sufficient time to go over the data carefully, the researcher opens up possibilities for uncovering the meaning in participants' lives. I have found Moustakis (1990) helpful in providing a heuristic approach here. He offers room to use inductive analysis through five phases. First, immersion in the setting starts the inductive process. Second, the incubation process allows for thinking, becoming aware of nuance and meaning in the setting, and capturing intuitive insights, to achieve understanding. Third, there is a phase of illumination that allows for expanding awareness. Fourth, and most understandably, there is a phase of explication that includes description and explanation to capture the experience of individuals in the study. Finally, creative synthesis enables one to bring together as a whole the individual's story, including the meaning of the lived experience.

The purposes of these disciplined approaches to analysis are of course to describe and to explain the essence of experience and meaning in participants' lives. Patton (1990) suggests a balance between description and interpretation. Denzin (1989) elaborates further by suggesting that thick description makes thick interpretation possible. Endless description is not useful if the researcher is to present a powerful narrative. Analysis and interpretation effectively balance description.

The Issue of Credibility

The qualitative research literature contains many valuable and useful treatments of the issue of credibility (see, e.g., Eisner, 1991; Lincoln & Guba, 1985; Patton, 1990). Basically, qualitative researchers have been patiently responding to questions, usually formulated from a psychometric perspective. As Patton (1990) puts it, a credible qualitative study addresses three questions:

1. What techniques and methods were used to ensure the integrity, validity, and accuracy of the findings?
2. What does the researcher bring to the study in terms of experience and qualifications?
3. What assumptions undergird the study?

Qualitative researchers may find these questions a useful guide in writing up the narrative.

Validity, Generalizability, and Reliability

In responding to the issues of validity, generalizability, and reliability, I rely on experience and the literature. Description of persons, places, and events has been the cornerstone of qualitative research. I believe it will remain the cornerstone, because this is the qualitative researcher's reason for being. What has happened recently, as Wolcott (1990) reminds us, is that the term *validity*, which is overspecified in one domain, has become confusing because it is reassigned to another. *Validity* in the quantitative arena has a set of technical microdefinitions of which the reader is most likely well aware. Validity in qualitative research has to do with description and explanation, and whether or not a given explanation fits a given description. In other words, is the explanation credible?

By applying the suggestions of Lincoln and Guba (1985) and others, we may cross-check our work through member checks and audit trails. As a rule, in writing up the narrative, the qualitative researcher must decide what form the member check will take. For example, quite often, participants in a study move, leave the area, or request that they omit being part of the member check. The researcher needs to find a way to allow for the participants to review the material one way or another. For years, anthropologists and sociologists have incorporated a kind of member check by having an outsider read their field notes and interview transcripts. This current variation is a good one, for education research is always public, open to the public, and in many cases funded under federal mandates. Implicit in the member check directive, however, is the psychometric assumption that the trinity of validity, generalizability, and reliability, all terms from the quantitative paradigm, are to be adhered to in research. I think it is time to question the trinity.

Wolcott (1990) provides a provocative discussion about seeking and rejecting validity. He argues for understanding the absurdity of validity by developing a case for no single "correct" interpretation. Similarly, Donmoyer (1990) makes an even stronger case for rejecting traditional notions of generalizability for those researchers in education and human services who are concerned with individuals and the meaning in their lives. He argues that traditional ways of thinking about generalizability are

50

inadequate. He does not eschew generalizability altogether, however. Bureaucrats and policy makers, for example, seem to prefer aggregated numbers about certain social conditions, and for their needs generalizability seems to make sense. On the other hand, for those of us interested in questions of meaning and interpretation in individual cases, the kind of research done in education and human services, traditional thinking about generalizability falls short. The traditional view of generalizability limits the ability of the researcher to reconceptualize the role of social science in education and human services. In addition, the whole history of case study research in anthropology, education, sociology, and history stands solidly on its merits. In fact, the value of the case study is its uniqueness; consequently, reliability in the traditional sense of replicability is pointless here. I hope that we can move beyond discussions of this trinity of psychometrica and get on with the discussion of powerful statements from carefully done, rigorous long-term studies that uncover the meanings of events in individuals' lives.

Somehow we have lost the human and passionate element of research. Becoming immersed in a study requires passion: passion for people, passion for communication, and passion for understanding people. This is the contribution of qualitative research, and it can only enhance educational and human services practice. For too long we have allowed psychometrics to rule our research and thus to decontextualize individuals. In depersonalizing the most personal of social events, education, we have lost our way. Now it is time to return to a discourse on the personal, on what it means to be alive.

◆ Meaning and the Dance Metaphor

Isn't it remarkable that the entire history of dance has been characterized by a deep division? What might we learn from this? All arts and sciences draw upon tradition, and a first step in understanding them is to understand their past. Dance and choreography are tied to the past in a peculiar way. Dance and choreography derive from one element of society, the courts of kings and queens. Dance, a type of storytelling, has always fulfilled a basic need in society, expressing happiness, sadness, fears, joy, and wishes. As societies developed and organized, dividing into tribes, nations, and classes, the function of dance became much more complicated. Its language, steps, and movements no longer represented primitive classless tribes. Dance became divided.

One form of this division survives as folk dance from the ancient primitive thread of communal dances. The other emerged from society's ruling class, the court, center of social power. It was not long before ballet became an official lexicon of the court and the court dances a definite class and status symbol. It was not until this century that the ruling influence in dance, ballet, was challenged by a determined, frail woman from Vermont, Martha Graham. The field today in dance is well into a postmodern era, mostly, but not exclusively, owing to Merce Cunningham's artistry. Essentially, Cunningham made the following claims (Banes, 1980, p. 6):

1. Any movement can be material for dance.
2. Any procedure can be valid.
3. Any part or parts of the body can be used, subject to nature's limitation.
4. Music, costume, lighting, and dancing have their own separate logics and identities.
5. Any dancer in a company may be a soloist.
6. Any space may be danced in.
7. Dancing can be about anything, but it is fundamentally and primarily about the human body and its movements, beginning with walking.

Cunningham's dances decentralize space and stretch out time. They do away with what is familiar and easy. They are unpredictable. They sometimes do not even turn out as planned. He may use chance methods, such as tossing coins (Banes, 1980, points out that although this was to be random, the dancers' movements were determined by this chance event). Chance subverts habits and allows for new combinations and interpretations. Cunningham truly makes the word *radical*, returning to the root, come alive. He preserves continuity and a physical logic to his search for meaning in movement and the desire to tell a story. In thinking about dance as a metaphor for qualitative research design, the meaning for me lies in the fact that the substance of dance is the familiar; walking, running, any movement of the body. The qualitative researcher is like the dancer, then, in seeking to describe, explain, and make understandable the familiar in a contextual, personal, and passionate way. As Goethe has told us, "The hardest thing to see is what is in front of your eyes."

◆ Summary and Afterthoughts

The qualitative researcher's design decisions can be thought of as similar to the dancer's three stages of warm-up, exercises, and cool-down. The qualitative researcher makes a series of decisions at the beginning, middle, and end of the study. Qualitative research design has an elastic quality, much like the elasticity of the dancer's spine. Just as dance mirrors and adapts to life, qualitative design is adapted, changed, and redesigned as the study proceeds, because of the social realities of doing research among and with the living. The qualitative researcher focuses on description and explanation, and all design decisions ultimately relate to these acts. Built into qualitative research design is a system of checks and balances that includes staying in a setting over time and capturing and interpreting the meaning in individuals' lives. By staying in a setting over time, the researcher has the opportunity to use data triangulation, investigator triangulation, theory triangulation, methodological triangulation, and interdisciplinary triangulation. This allows for multiple views of framing the problem, selecting research strategies, and extending discourse across several fields of study. This is exactly the opposite of the quantitative approach, which relies on one mind-set, the psychometric, and which prefers to aggregate numbers that are one or more steps removed from social reality. The qualitative researcher is uncomfortable with methodolatry and prefers to capture the lived experience of participants in order to understand their meaning perspectives. Finally, the qualitative researcher is like the choreographer, who creates a dance to make a statement. For the researcher, the story told is the dance in all its complexity, context, originality, and passion.

◆ Notes

1. I went to New York because it is the center of the dance world and all levels and varieties of technique are taught in the various dance schools there. I was originally trained in Graham technique, so I naturally went to that school first. In the first day, first class, I was totally bored. I had outgrown the vocabulary of the method and asked if anyone was questioning this approach. Another student in class told me that Erick Hawkins and Merce Cunningham had resisted, rebelled, and broken away from Graham and started their own schools. I found an opening at the Hawkins school and from that point my life was changed.

From Erick Hawkins I learned that creativity and the body/mind are one, and I was introduced to Eastern thought. There is no need to separate one's creative self from living. He and all his teachers were inspiring and brilliant teachers. I decided that I would perfect both the art and craft of teaching as a dance instructor and an arts educator. From Merce Cunningham and the teachers at Westbeth, I learned to trust the body and to draw upon lived experience in my work as a choreographer. For Cunningham, dance is a chance encounter among movement, sound, and light through space. The viewer makes of it what the viewer will. Cunningham pursues the process of dance Zen-like. He has been called the anarchist of modern dance as well as the beginning point of the postmodern movement in dance. All dances are grounded in some experience, and all stories that are told about that experience rely on the body, that is, the research instrument. The body is the instrument through which life is lived. In dance, the body cannot deny the impulse to express the lived experience. It is virtually impossible for the body to tell a lie or to cover up the truth in the dance. The downside of this, of course, is that the body is bounded by the aging process. There is a place for vicarious experience in the dance world, but it is always secondary to lived experience. Merce Cunningham, for example, is in his 70s and still teaching, but only now is he writing about the process of doing choreography and only recently are his dances being videotaped and/or filmed. For the dancer, one has to dance (see Cunningham, 1985).

2. I first learned of theoretical sampling in my training as an ethnographer of the symbolic interactionist school, by reading Glaser and Strauss (1967). Theoretical sampling is the heart of grounded theory approaches to research. It allows for using the constant comparative method in data collection and analysis. Theoretical sampling allows for direction in the study and allows the researcher to have confidence in his or her categories as they emerge from the data and are constantly and selectively reformulated along the way. The data in any study do not speak for themselves. The researcher must make sense of the data in a meaningful way, and this technique allows the researcher to find an active way of searching the data.

3. Gallaudet University is the only liberal arts college dedicated to educating deaf individuals. Dr. I. King Jordan became Gallaudet's first deaf president after the "Deaf President Now" campaign was realized. This grassroots movement, involving both students and faculty members, closed the institution during deliberations on the selection of a president. Gallaudet University has approximately 2,000 students; all of the undergraduate student population is deaf (about 1,500 students) and, of the 500 graduate students, approximately 100 are deaf. Established in 1864 through the efforts of President Lincoln, Gallaudet had only hearing presidents until Dr. Jordan was inaugurated.

4. Constant comparative analysis allows the researcher to develop grounded theory. A grounded theory is one inductively derived from the study. Data collection, analysis, and theory are related reciprocally. One grounds the theory in the data from statements of belief and behavior of participants in the study. See Glaser and Strauss (1967) and Strauss and Corbin (1990) for a more detailed description of grounded theory. It is basically opposite to the use of theory in the quantitative paradigm. Instead of proving a theory, the qualitative researcher studies a setting over time and develops theory grounded in the data. This is a well-established methodology in social psychology and sociology. Educational researchers are beginning to use grounded theory more and more, because it makes sense given the types of questions we ask.

◆ References

Banes, S. (1980). *Terpsichore in sneakers: Post-modern dance.* Boston: Houghton Mifflin.

Bogdan, R. C., & Biklen, S. K. (1992). *Qualitative research for education: An introduction to theory and methods.* Boston: Allyn & Bacon.

Cunningham, M. (1985). *The dancer and the dance.* New York: Marion Boyars.

Denzin, N. K. (1978). *The research act: A theoretical introduction to sociological methods* (2nd ed.). New York: McGraw-Hill.

Denzin, N. K. (1989). *Interpretive interactionism.* Newbury Park, CA: Sage.

Dewey, J. (1958). *Art as experience.* New York: G. P. Putnam's Sons. (Original work published 1934)

Donmoyer, R. (1990). Generalizability and the single-case study. In E. W. Eisner & A. Peshkin (Eds.), *Qualitative inquiry in education: The continuing debate* (pp. 175-200). New York: Teachers College Press.

Eisner, E. (1991). *The enlightened eye: Qualitative inquiry and the enhancement of educational practices.* New York: Macmillan.

Erickson, F. (1986). Qualitative methods in research on teaching. In M. C. Wittrock (Ed.), *Handbook of research on teaching* (3rd ed., pp. 119-161). New York: Macmillan.

Fetterman, D. M. (1989). *Ethnography: Step by step.* Newbury Park, CA: Sage.

Glaser, B. G., & Strauss, A. L. (1967). *The discovery of grounded theory: Strategies for qualitative research.* Chicago: Aldine.

Goetz, J., & LeCompte, M. D. (1984). *Ethnography and qualitative design in educational research.* New York: Academic Press.

Janesick, V. J. (1982). Of snakes and circles: Making sense of classroom group processes through a case study. *Curriculum Inquiry, 12,* 161-185.

Janesick, V. J. (1983). Reflections on teaching ethnographic research methods. *Anthropology and Education Quarterly, 14,* 198-202.

Janesick, V. J. (1990). *Proud to be deaf: An ethnographic study of deaf culture.* Paper presented at the Qualitative Research in Education Conference, University of Georgia, Athens.

LeCompte, M. D., Millroy, W. L., & Preissle, J. (Eds.). (1992). *The handbook of qualitative research in education.* New York: Academic Press.

Lincoln, Y. S., & Guba, E. G. (1985). *Naturalistic inquiry.* Beverly Hills, CA: Sage.

Miles, M. B., & Huberman, A. M. (1984). *Qualitative data analysis: A sourcebook of new methods.* Beverly Hills, CA: Sage.

Moustakis, C. (1990). *Heuristic research design, methodology, and applications.* Newbury Park, CA: Sage.

Patton, M. Q. (1990). *Qualitative evaluation and research methods* (2nd ed.). Newbury Park, CA: Sage.

Spradley, J. P. (1979). *The ethnographic interview.* New York: Holt, Rinehart & Winston.

Spradley, J. P. (1980). *Participant observation.* New York: Holt, Rinehart & Winston.

Strauss, A. L., & Corbin, J. (1990). *Basics of qualitative research: Grounded theory procedures and techniques.* Newbury Park, CA: Sage.

Wolcott, H. F. (1990). On seeking and rejecting validity in qualitative research. In E. W. Eisner & A. Peshkin (Eds.), *Qualitative inquiry in education: The continuing debate* (pp. 121-152). New York: Teachers College Press.

3

Designing Funded
Qualitative Research

Janice M. Morse

◆   My purposes in this chapter are to identify and describe the major
      design issues in the planning stage of a qualitative project and to
suggest practical ways for the researcher to overcome the paradoxes
inherent in qualitative inquiry. I provide a guide to the planning of
qualitative proposals and include suggestions for avoiding the pitfalls
inherent in the research process. I have chosen to organize the chapter in
the same sequence one would use when planning to conduct a qualitative
project. Therefore, I begin with the stage of reflection, in which the project
is merely a good idea, and proceed to the stage of planning (including
writing the proposal) and the stage of entry, or beginning the fieldwork.
When data collection is going well and is fruitful, the researcher enters the
stage of productive data collection. Next is the stage of withdrawal, which
is followed by the most important stage of all, the stage of writing.

◆ The Stage of Reflection

Identifying the Topic

Recognizing that selection of a topic or research question is a fairly
long-term commitment (and one that will require intensive effort) is often

stressful enough to put student investigators into a state of panic. Students cannot think of researchable topics or think of anything of sufficient interest to make the time commitment required to complete the project. The additional requirement that the research should investigate a relatively new area or innovative question further increases the fear that they will not be able to come up with an original and promising topic.

The key to selecting a qualitative research topic is to identify something that will hold one's interest over time. New investigators can best identify such a topic by reflecting on what is of *real* personal interest to them. Surprisingly, these topics may not be among those on which an individual has already written. Enticing topics may be those that distract a person in the library; they may be topics that preoccupy a person and draw him or her into interesting conversations with others. Identifying such topics often requires some self-reflection and critical self-examination. The topic identified may be an area of interest rather than a more narrowly defined problem or question per se, and, at this stage, it is almost never an elegantly worded research question.

Research questions may also arise from a problem noted in the course of clinical practice, or from a significant experience that occurs in the course of everyday living. Researchable questions may also be "assigned" in consultation with other researchers, or identified in the technical literature (Strauss & Corbin, 1990). Joining a research project and taking responsibility for a "piece" often provides the novice researcher with supportive colleagues who can provide advice and encouragement, and may even provide funding or transcribing services to help with the research. If a research topic arises from suggested recommendations at the end of a published research article, it is wise for the researcher to consult with the author(s) of that article. Considerable time will have elapsed between the completion of the first project and its publication, and the author(s) may have already conducted the particular study that logically extends from the first project. In any case, the author(s) may have important advice about how to proceed with the new investigation.

Finally, researchable questions often become apparent when one reads the literature. For instance, a student interested in breast-feeding may be seeking information to assist mothers coping with breast expression and find that the information in the literature consists entirely of prescriptive accounts on *how* to express the breasts, or maintain lactation. The discovery of a gap, of instances where no information is available, is an exciting indicator that a topic would be good candidate for qualitative study.

Similarly, if the reader has a hunch that the information available is poor or biased, or that the theory is wrong, then a qualitative study may also be indicated.

Having identified a topic, the researcher's next step is to go to the library to read in the general area of the research topic. At this stage, the researcher should become familiar with the literature, with what has been done generally in the area, and with the "state of the art." He or she should develop a comfortable knowledge base without spending an extraordinary amount of time on minute details or chasing obscure references. As qualitative inquiry at this stage is unfocused, and as the researcher has the opportunity to return to the library later in the study, when he or she better understands the direction of inquiry, it is inappropriate to spend too much time in the library at this point. As a reminder of the perils of getting bogged down in the library at this stage, I have students read about the fictitious plight of the young man who spent his entire research career in the library trying to learn all that was known about the evil eye (van Gennep, 1967/1992).

Researchers select topics for various reasons, and it is helpful at this stage for the researcher to recognize why he or she has selected a particular topic for study: Why does it hold his or her interest? Often, one reason a topic is selected is that the researcher has had personal or professional experiences related to the subject and has residual personal unmet needs or strong feelings stemming from these experiences. For example, a student may be interested in the experience of abortion because she herself has experienced one; another may be interested in survivors of suicide because he had a sibling or close friend who died that way. Using such personal experiences as the impetus for a research study is not *wrong*, but it is best if the researcher is aware of his or her possible motives for conducting the study, as such experiences may give the study a particular bias. Of even more concern is the possibility that the researcher, when meeting and interviewing participants who have had the same experience, may have many unresolved feelings emerge and may be emotionally unable to continue with the study.

Identifying Paradigmatic Perspectives

Wolcott (1992) identifies three "postures" underlying qualitative research: theory-driven (for example, cultural theory underlies ethnography), concept-driven (such as focusing on the concept of care in a clinical ethnography), and "reform-focused" or "problem-focused" ideas, in which the underlying purpose of the project is political, with predetermined goals, such as feminist research (Code, 1991; DeVault, 1990; Harding, 1987; Reinharz, 1992) or critical theory (Anderson, 1989; Campbell, 1991; Quantz, 1992). Although the techniques and methods used in these approaches are similar to other qualitative techniques, they differ in their levels of abstraction, their foci, and their outcomes. For instance, feminist research challenges the social science research status quo by claiming that research historically conducted by men portrays only the male perspective, the paternalistic life world, and has virtually—and deliberately—excluded women's perspective and contributions. Using the same techniques as other qualitative research, feminist researchers collect data to ensure that the female perspective has been elicited and analyzed, that the feminist perspective is primarily presented. The feminist research agenda is to fill the void of decades of social science research that has ignored women informants, women's work, women's roles, and women's contribution to society.

It is actually a misnomer to label research theory or concept "driven," for if theory actually guided data collection and analysis, inductive assumptions of qualitative research would be violated. Rather, in qualitative inquiry the theory is used to focus the inquiry and give it boundaries for comparison in facilitating the development of the theoretical or conceptual outcomes. The theory or concept of interest at best may be considered a conceptual template with which to compare and contrast results, rather than to use as a priori categories into which to force the analysis.

At this stage of planning the project, it is also helpful to examine the research questions in light of the expected results, considering the potential audience and aims of the research. For instance, can the study be conducted with the explicit aim of improving *nursing* practice, and will the results be read by nurse educators? Or is the study being conducted to assist patients' families, and the research will reach an essentially lay readership? Keeping in mind the end results or purpose—even before the study question is refined—places the study in the broader picture; by so doing, the researcher will help refine the question, the focus of data collection and analysis, and guide the style of presentation of the final report.

◆ The Stage of Planning

Planning involves many elements, including selection of a site and a research strategy, the investigator's preparation, creation and refinement of the research question, the writing of the proposal, and, if necessary, obtaining clearance from an institutional review board (IRB). These are discussed in turn below.

Selecting a Site

The possible setting in which the study will be conducted must be identified, and the access to and characteristics of possible participants considered. It is foolish for the researcher to put too much work into a study that must be conducted in one particular setting unless he or she can be assured that access will not be denied. The researcher should visit a possible setting and tentatively sound out administrators to determine if the proposed project would be welcomed and if researchers would be tolerated on site. Administrators may, for example, be wary of a project that will essentially evaluate their personnel or institution, if they have no control over the research outcomes, or if they feel that the results may be detrimental to the organization, even if the researcher assures them that the site will not be identified in the final report. Evaluation research is more typically conducted at the request of administration, as contract research.

Considering alternatives. Much research could feasibly be conducted in several settings, such as in one of several schools or hospitals. This does not mean that the investigator necessarily has the opportunity to choose among settings, but rather that he or she must decide which setting to approach. In these instances, it is best for the researcher to visit each institution and put out feelers to see which is most receptive to having the project conducted there. The researcher should talk to the staff and see if, given the opportunity, they would participate. If possible, he or she should talk to other researchers who have previously worked in the institution to see if the environment is receptive and facilitative.

Selecting a research setting is an important step, and as negotiations for entry are often time-consuming (frequently involving human subjects review and administrative review to assess any costs to the institution), it must be done early. The researcher should solicit letters of support from the clinical setting and from the president of the institution to include with his or her proposal. He or she should also meet with the staff in the setting in which data will actually be collected to ensure their cooperation.

Frequently two settings are selected for the distinct purpose of comparing and contrasting the populations. This design is most commonly used in anthropology, where the behaviors or practices of two cultures or subcultures are of interest. At first glance, such a strategy appears to increase the *work* of research. However, as the process of comparing and contrasting may ease the process of data analysis by making significant factors more readily apparent, the duration of the research may not be unduly lengthened, and the product may be much stronger than if only one group is studied.

The last factor in selecting a research setting is the consideration of available resources, which are always limited. Is the study feasible without a research grant, or will the continuation of the project be contingent on the receipt of funding? If funding must be obtained, the researcher needs to identify the possible sources at this time and obtain the organizations' terms of references (and even establish contact with the agencies) to make sure that his or her project is within their areas of interest for funding purposes. The researcher must note the deadlines for applications and draw up a schedule so that he or she can prepare and submit all the necessary approvals on time.

One final word of warning: It is not wise for an investigator to conduct a qualitative study in a setting in which he or she is already employed and has a work role. The dual roles of investigator and employee are incompatible, and they may place the researcher in an untenable position. The expectations of coworkers will make it difficult for the researcher to stop work to do participant observation, to write notes, or to interview. Collecting data may also place the investigator in an awkward position in which the roles of employee and data collector are in conflict; for instance, the researcher may learn confidential information that should be reported by a loyal employee but that should be kept confidential by an ethical researcher.

The flip side of this is the consideration of how the researcher fits into the setting and how those in the setting perceive him or her. These perceptions affect the types of data informants share and even the kinds of information reported to the researcher during interviews. For instance, when a researcher conducts participant observation in a classroom, his or her perceived role will influence the data he or she can collect. If the students, teachers, and parents perceive the researcher *as a teacher,* the information they offer will focus largely on topics they think will most interest and be most helpful to teachers. In a clinical setting, if participants view the observer as a nurse, then the information will focus on the "medical" aspects of care (such as details about treatments and symptoms) rather than the day-to-day coping with illness. Breaking through such perceptual stereotypes takes a great deal of effort on the part of the researcher. Wearing a uniform identifies the researcher as an employee of the institution, and this may also restrict his or her access to some types of information. Another disadvantage is that the researcher may find him- or herself expected to work (rather than to observe), and these expectations, once met, are difficult for the researcher to change; clearly, this will impede data collection. In light of this, it is best for the researcher to dress somewhat ambiguously—for example, to wear a uniform of a different color if a uniform is called for, or to wear both a scrub suit and a lab coat—as a signal to staff that he or she does not really belong in that setting and is there to collect data, and not to act as an employee.

Selecting a Strategy

The research strategy is determined by the nature of the research question (Field & Morse, 1991). Research strategies are merely *tools*; it is the researcher's responsibility to understand the variety available and the different purposes of each strategy, to appreciate in advance the ramifications of selecting one method over another, and to become astute in the selection of one method over another. Each qualitative strategy offers a particular and unique perspective that illuminates certain aspects of reality more easily than others and produces a type of results more suited for some applications than others. Some qualitative strategies are designed for particular types of data; for instance, they facilitate the management of certain types of observations. Finally, the link between the question and the method chosen will determine the types of results obtained and ultimately the *usefulness of the results,* or the pragmatic application of the study findings. Therefore, the competent researcher is versatile enough to view a setting and recognize the restrictions in the types of data that can be collected and the possibilities that will enable the achievement of his or her research aims. A good researcher is not confined methodologically by being trained in—and limited to—a single strategy (for instance, "I only 'do' ethnography"). Such a restriction limits the types of questions the researcher may ask and the types of results he or she can obtain, and restricts the strength of the research.

Table 3.1 links the major types of qualitative research questions with the research strategies and methods used. Although the table is by no means comprehensive, it provides a beginning guide for research planning. Note

TABLE 3.1 Comparison of the Major Types of Qualitative Strategies

Type of Research Questions	Strategy	Paradigm	Method	Other Data Sources	Major References
Meaning questions—eliciting the essence of experiences	phenomenology	philosophy (phenomenology)	audiotaped "conversations"; written anecdotes of personal experiences	phenomenological literature; philosophical reflections; poetry; art	Bergum (1991), Giorgi (1970), van Manen (1984, 1990)
Descriptive questions—of values, beliefs, practices of cultural group	ethnography	anthropology (culture)	unstructured interviews; participant observation; field notes	documents; records; photography; maps; genealogies; social network diagrams	Ellen (1984), Fetterman (1989), Grant & Fine (1992), Hammersley & Atkinson (1983), Hughes (1992), Sanjek (1990), Spradley (1979), Werner & Schoepfle (1987a, 1987b)
"Process" questions—experience over time or change, may have stages or phases	grounded theory	sociology (symbolic interactionism)	interviews (tape-recorded)	participant observation; memoing; diary	Chenitz & Swanson (1986), Glaser (1978, 1992), Glaser & Strauss (1967), Strauss (1987), Strauss & Corbin (1990)
Questions regarding verbal interaction and dialogue	ethnomethodology; discourse analysis	semiotics	dialogue (audio/video recording)	observation; field notes	Atkinson (1992), Benson & Hughes (1983), Denzin (1970, 1989), Douglas (1970), Heritage (1984), Leiter (1980), Rogers (1983)
Behavioral questions					
macro	participant observation	anthropology	observation; field notes	interviews; photography	Jorgensen (1989), Spradley (1980)
micro	qualitative ethology	zoology	observation	videotape; note taking	Eibl-Eibesfeldt (1989), Morse & Bottorff (1990), Scherer & Ekman (1982)

that the qualitative strategy used in the study is largely determined by the purpose of the study, the nature of the research questions, and the skills and resources available to the investigator. For instance, if the research question concerns the *meaning* of a phenomenon, then the method that would best answer the question is phenomenology. If the question concerns the *nature* of the phenomenon, then the answer is best obtained using ethnography. If the question concerns an experience and the phenomenon in question is a process, the method of choice for addressing the question is grounded theory.

Another helpful tactic in proposal writing is to *imagine* what one wants to find out. By projecting the research outcome, the researcher may begin to conceptualize the question, the sample size, the feasibility of the study, the data sources, and so forth. A variation of this exercise may be demonstrated in the classroom: A topic of interest may be suggested and the students walked through steps in the research process examining, in particular, the different results that would be obtained with different questions and different strategies. For instance, consider a mock project with the title "Arrivals and Departures: Patterns of Human Attachment." We could imagine we are studying human attachment at the local airport, watching passengers leave relatives or be greeted by relatives. Then, by listing various questions that would be best asked using different qualitative strategies, we quickly discover the differences in the main types of qualitative strategies. Students can participate in these hypothetical research projects by imagining who would be best to interview as participants in each project, or, if an observational method is selected for discussion, where and when the observations could be conducted. Students can explore issues of sample size and modes of data analysis. Finally, they can clearly see, through the construction of a comparative grid such as that shown in Table 3.2, how qualitative strategies vary and how different types of strategies produce very different results.

This type of "planning" is crucial to the development of a solid and enticing proposal. The mental walk-through that the researcher takes in envisioning research plans may even ease some of the researcher anxiety that is invariably a part of entering the setting.

Methodological Triangulation

Because different "lenses" or perspectives result from the use of different methods, often more than one method may be used within a project so the

TABLE 3.2 A Comparison of Strategies in the Conduct of a Hypothetical Project: "Arrivals and Departures: Patterns of Human Attachment"[a]

Strategy	Research Question/Focus	Participants/Informants[a]	Sample Size[b]	Data Collection Methods	Type of Results
Phenomenology	What is the meaning of arriving home?	travelers arriving home; phenomenological literature; art, poetry, and other descriptions	approximately six participants	in-depth conversations	in-depth reflective description of the experience of "what it feels like to come home"
Ethnography	What is the arrival gate like when an international plane arrives?	travelers, families, others who observe the setting, such as skycaps, rental car personnel, cleaning staff, security guards	approximately 30-50 interviews	interviews; participant observation; other records, such as airport statistics	description of the day-to-day events at the arrival gate of the airport
Grounded theory	Coming home: reuniting the family	travelers, family members	approximately 30-50	in-depth interviews; observations	description of the social psychological process in the experience of returning home
Ethnoscience	What are types of travelers?	those who observe the setting daily—skycaps, rental car personnel, cleaning staff, security guards, and so forth	approximately 30-50	interviews to elicit similarities and differences of travelers; card sorts	taxonomy and description of types and characteristics of travelers
Qualitative ethology	What are the greeting behaviors of travelers and their families?	travelers and their families	units—numbers of greetings—100-200	photography, video; coded	description of the patterns of greeting behaviors

a. Examples only.
b. Number depends on saturation.

researcher can gain a more holistic view of the setting. Two or more qualitative methods may be used sequentially or simultaneously, provided the analysis is kept separate and the methods are not muddled (Stern, 1994). For example, Wilson and Hutchinson (1991) compared the use of grounded theory and Heideggerian hermeneutics to illustrate how the philosophical and methodological features of each method are distinct, yet complementary. The main methods of Heideggerian hermeneutics (thick description, paradigm cases, and exemplars) enable the researcher to elicit and interpret the meaning of lived experience. On the other hand, the technique of grounded theory incorporates other sources of data (such as document review and observational data along with unstructured interviews) and aims to develop a basic social process and a more abstract, mid-range theory.

Qualitative research may also incorporate quantitative methods into the design to answer particular questions. Of most importance to this chapter is the incorporation of quantitative research into a qualitative project (that is, qualitatively *driven*) (see Morse, 1991a). In this case the nature of the qualitative sample (with a small *n* and purposely selected) violates the assumptions of size and random selection of quantitative research and cannot be used for quantitative data collection. However, if the quantitative measure is standardized (i.e., normative results are available), then a quantitative measure may be administered to the qualitative sample and the results compared with the standardized norms. Such procedures provide important additional information. For example, rather than describing the participants in a qualitative sample as "highly anxious," the researcher can describe exactly *how* anxious they are, compared with a normal population. However, if the quantitative measure is not standardized, then sequential triangulation techniques must be employed, with the researcher administering the instrument to a separate, larger and randomly selected, sample following the completion of the qualitative data analysis.

Investigator Preparation

Qualitative research is only as good as the investigator. It is the researcher who, through skill, patience, and wisdom, obtains the information necessary during data collection and fieldwork to produce a rich qualitative study. Good qualitative researchers must be prepared to learn to be trusted in the setting; they must be patient and wait until they are accepted by informants; they must be flexible and resilient; and, as Wax (1971) notes, they must be prepared to "make fools of themselves."

An important quality that will help ensure success is versatility. Experienced researchers are versatile in research methods and know that there is always a best way to obtain the necessary information. They are persistent, recognizing that good fieldwork is often merely a matter of completing one small task after another. Good researchers are meticulous about their documentation, file methodically, and keep notes up-to-date. They are well prepared in their topic, so they can pick up subtle clues in interviews and latch on to, and follow, leads. The ability to follow leads also means that the researcher is well versed in social science theory. The researcher must be able to recognize remnants of other theorists' work, so that when glimpses of interesting leads are present in an interview, these leads may be pursued and verified, or recognized as new and unique phenomena. The good researcher is familiar enough with social science theory that he or she can recognize an appropriate "framework" or paradigm for the study and still work inductively, letting the qualitative assumptions drive the research. For example, the qualitative researcher will recognize the contribution of symbolic interactionist theory in grounded theory or the theoretical base that culture provides for ethnography, using these paradigms as *perspectives* without permitting them to dominate the data. Mature investigators have confidence in their own interpretations of the data and in their own ideas, and are articulate enough to express and defend them.

Information must be verified and cross-checked constantly, on an ongoing basis, and researchers must be constantly reviewing notes and other data collected. They are not stymied by ambiguity. They are not discouraged when progress is slow, nor are they hasty in jumping to conclusions. Good researchers revel in the intellectual work of making sense of their data; they thrive on living with information, on being haunted by the puzzle of their data. They keep working until the study is published. Although the confidence that comes with experience reinforces some of these qualities, it is important for neophyte researchers to know they are not alone in experiencing conceptual confusion in the midst of a qualitative project.

Creating and Refining the Research Question

The wording of the research question determines the focus and scope of the study. As qualitative inquiry is often tenuous in the early stages (in that the investigator does not have extensive knowledge about the setting), the researcher should make the question as broad as possible rather than prematurely delimit the study with a narrow question. Narrowness distracts the researcher from seeing the whole picture. For example, Norris (1991), when studying the experience of mothers with adolescent daughters undergoing abortion, initially focused on the abortion as a discrete event. Later in the study, however, she realized that the abortion was actually part of a larger process of "monitoring . . . daughters' contraceptive behavior." The researcher should state the question so that he or she can later refine it to make it appropriate to maximize the research effort. The researcher can do this as soon he or she begins to understand "what is going on" in the setting and what is possible given the constraints.

Occasionally, when the researcher enters the setting, it becomes evident that the original question is a poor fit or would be poorly answered in the setting, and the question—and sometimes the topic—must be discarded. When this occurs, it is usually necessary for the researcher to notify the IRB and the agencies involved, including the funding agency, that the focus of the study has changed.

In participant observation, familiarity with the setting dulls the researcher's awareness, and the significance and quality of the data are reduced when the researcher does not view the setting "as a stranger" (Agar, 1980). As the researcher gets to know others in the setting and becomes very familiar with the routine—perhaps even becomes bored, with a feeling of having "seen it all"—data may be considered "saturated" and the observer should withdraw from the setting.

Writing the Proposal

The first principle of grantsmanship is to recognize that a good proposal is an argument—a fair and balanced one, but nevertheless an argument—for the researcher's project. The proposal must make a case to the granting agency that the research question is interesting, that the study is important, and, most important, why it should be funded. Thus the proposal must be written persuasively. (This may seem strange advice for novice researchers, who for many years have been taught to write *objectively*, without emotion.) The proposal must be complete, with all major authors listed. It must be clear, interesting to read, technically neat, and professional in appearance. The final version should be printed out on a laser printer, after the researcher has double-checked the budget and the references, and has made sure he or she has followed the agency's guidelines with utmost care. A sloppily prepared proposal will, at best, send a message to the agency that if it funds the proposal, the research may also be sloppy. At worst, the proposal will not even be considered for funding, but will be returned to the investigator because missing information or missing pieces of the proposal prohibit it from being considered.

Granting agencies must have good reasons for funding a study and must be able to justify that funding to their boards of directors, to the press, and to the public. It is the responsibility of the proposal writer to provide these reasons. Apparently trivial research questions are not awarded grant funds. If the study will have clear cost benefits, the researcher should present those figures as expected annual savings, and so forth. If the expected gains from the research are less tangible, such as "improved staff morale," the researcher would be wise to focus on the cost benefits of "reducing staff turnover." If the proposal is for basic research—that is, research that addresses an interesting question but has no clear-cut benefits—the proposal writer needs to make the interesting question fascinating. He or she needs to entice the reviewers into the proposal, so that by the end of the first page they will also be captivated with the problem. The writer should place the problem in context to show, for instance, that "when we understand this, we will be able to work on that." This strategy makes the significance of the problem clear even to reviewers who are outside the researcher's discipline. And because some of the reviewers will be from other disciplines, the proposal writer should assume nothing and explain everything.

Because qualitative research is unstructured, the results unpredictable, and the outcome uncertain, it is difficult to write a WYSIWYG ("what you see is what you get") proposal. It may not be possible for the researcher to project what he or she will find or to promise exciting results; rather, it is a skill to balance both persuasiveness and realism. This problem makes writing the proposal difficult, but if the researcher does not try to "sell" the idea, the proposal will not be funded.

Before the researcher submits a proposal to a granting agency, he or she should have it reviewed by seasoned experts to ensure that the research design is "tight," that the methods are rigorous, and that the tone is balanced. The proposal should also be reviewed by someone outside the field to ensure that it is interesting, clear, and comprehensive. As most review committees consist primarily of quantitative researchers, some qualitative researchers have their proposals reviewed by quantitative researchers so that any anticipated "flaws" in the methods will be addressed before the proposals go to the review committee. These presubmission reviews take time; researchers should allow at least a month in the proposal-preparation timeline for these reviews and subsequent revisions.

The second principle in writing a successful proposal is that one should think and plan *before* starting to write. The researcher should select a topic, a research question, and mentally walk through the steps in the research process, as earlier described. As most writer's block comes from not knowing what to write, this planning process greatly facilitates the process of writing. It also helps the researcher to identify the advantages and disadvantages of various approaches and designs. For instance, the researcher can plan by identifying the types of data sources available. Incorporating observational data and other data sources into the study affects the complexity of the study, which, in turn, directly affects the cost of data collection, data analysis, and the duration of the project. The options of using more than one site, of using a comparative design, of triangulating other data sources, and of conducting a prospective design or a cross-sectional design all have profound ramifications for budgeting and are so costly that it is not usually possible to add such changes to the study design *after* the budget has been approved (without a supplement). Ideally, such options should be calculated into the budget in the submission, and the design justified in the methods section of the proposal. In addition, selecting—and justifying—the method is an essential step in preparing the proposal; the ways to plan this have been discussed above.

Once decisions have been made regarding the research design and the setting, the actual writing of the proposal can begin. Although the components of a proposal vary from funding agency to funding agency, those listed in Table 3.3 are basic requirements. The researcher should read the agency's guidelines carefully for the order of these components, and for any page-length restrictions. In particular, he or she should look for any limits on budget requests. Some agencies, for example, will not fund equipment or travel, and other sources of funding must be identified if essential items are to be obtained elsewhere.

In addition to the stance of the researcher writing a persuasive document, the qualitative researcher may find him- or herself describing the research methods in terms that may be meaningless to researchers who do not use qualitative methods. In 1983, Downs wrote in an editorial that as long as "qualitative researchers refuse to describe how their theory was derived . . . we have a smile without a cat." Although this strong statement

TABLE 3.3 Components of a Qualitative Proposal

Title/signature page
    full title of proposal and running head
    list of investigators (with signature lines), affiliations, phone and fax numbers
    total budget and start and completion dates of project
    names, signature lines, and addresses for the institutional research administration personnel
Abstract page
Body of the proposal
    introduction
    statement of purpose or aims
    review of the literature
        importance of project
        research question
    methods
        description of setting and participants
        data collection
          procedure for data collection
        data analysis
        human subjects protection
        timeline (schedule for plan of work)
References
Appendices
    investigators' vitae
        summary of principal investigator's and other key personnel's vitae
          (limited to two pages per person)
    consent forms
    interview schedules
    publications
        previous publications by investigator pertinent to this project

was targeted toward completed articles, it is also true for the proposal. Tripp-Riemer and Cohen (1991) suggest providing examples of data analysis and theory development by placing paragraphs of fictive text in the data analysis section of the proposal and coding this text to demonstrate how the coding is done. Another suggestion is to select such text carefully so that it provides another piece of information about research in the topic at hand. For instance, although fictive, the text may be used to illustrate the experiences of participants, and thus to help build a case that an important and urgent area for study is addressed in the proposal.

The appendices of the proposal contain the budget pages, IRB approvals, letters of permission from administrators in the agency indicating their support for the project and permission to conduct the study, and letters of agreement to serve from prospective staff. A great deal of attention must be given to the budget to ensure that realistic and adequate funding is requested for the project. Appendix A of this chapter includes suggestions for preparing a budget for a qualitative proposal. IRB clearance must follow the requirements of the researcher's home institution, the host institution, and the funding agency. Federal regulations require that any research that will be conducted on human subjects must be reviewed by a board charged with assessing the risks and benefits of the project. As qualitative research is usually of naturalistic design (i.e., there is no research intervention), and thus the researcher is not disrupting or increasing the risks of *everyday life,* such projects often receive expedited review. However, the researcher should refer to "Protection of Human Subjects," Part 46 of the *Code of Federal Regulations,* Title 45 (revised in 1983) or consult his or her IRB for further information (see Appendix B, which presents the types and levels of human subjects review required for approval of NIH grant applications).

◆ The Stage of Entry

Once the researcher receives funding from the granting agency, the data collection may start. The most difficult part of the entire project is entering the setting for the first time and knowing what to do, or knocking on the first door to solicit the first participant. The researcher may find that practicing explaining the study (in the form of role play) will help him or her overcome this barrier somewhat. Still, the new researcher can expect to feel awkward, useless, uncomfortable, in the way, and a nuisance in the research setting.

During the first period of data collection in an ethnographic study the researcher's observations must remain unfocused. Because feelings of confusion associated with "being new" are extreme, data collection is necessarily unfocused. The researcher should spend the first few days learning who's who; he or she may find it helpful to make an organizational chart of all the participants in the setting and a map of the physical layout. The researcher needs to take this time to learn the routine and the setting's formal and informal rules. He or she should observe for short periods and then retire to record field notes.

72

Sampling

As the researcher learns the roles and relationships among participants, he or she may identify appropriate informants. A good informant is one who has the knowledge and experience the researcher requires, has the ability to reflect, is articulate, has the time to be interviewed, and is willing to participate in the study (Morse, 1986, 1991b). *Primary selection* of participants describes the opportunity for the researcher to sample informants using these criteria. *Secondary selection* of participants takes place if the researcher cannot select participants according to these criteria and obtains participants by some other means, such as through advertising (Morse, 1991b). In this case, it is possible that the researcher may conduct an interview that is of little use to the project. If this happens, he or she should complete the interview but not waste research time and funds having the interview transcribed. The researcher should simply put such interviews aside (not dispose of or erase them), in case the information becomes important at a later date.

Patton (1990) provides guidelines for sampling and suggests that the logic and power behind purposeful selection of informants is that the sample should be *information rich*. First, *extreme* or *deviant case* sampling is used to select participants who exemplify characteristics of interest. For example, if studying the pain experience, the researcher selects participants who have experienced excruciating pain rather than participants with chronic pain. Extreme cases maximize the factors of interest, thus clarifying factors of importance.

Intensity sampling has less emphasis on extremes. With intensity sampling, one selects participants who are experiential experts and who are authorities about a particular experience. For instance, when studying patient-nurse relationships, the researcher would select participants who have been hospitalized over an extended period of time, who have experience in forming relations with many nurses, and who have observed others in such relationships.

Maximum variety sampling is the process of deliberately selecting a heterogeneous sample and observing commonalities in their experiences. It is a most useful methods of sampling when exploring abstract concepts, such as hope, and selecting, for instance, participants from a variety of backgrounds in which hope is evidently of primary importance. Patton (1990) notes that two types of data are obtained using this technique. The first is high-quality case descriptions, useful for documenting uniqueness;

73

second, significant shared patterns of commonalities existing across participants may be identified.

Critical case sampling is the selection of examples that are significant for the identification of critical incidents that may be generalized to other situations. Again, the analysis focuses on instances, attributes, or key factors that contribute significantly to the example. Once analysis is progressing, data are enriched by the purposeful selection of *confirming cases* and *disconfirming* (negative) *cases.*

Interview Techniques

The primary feature of all these methods of sampling is that the situation of the sample is determined according to the needs of the study, and not according to external criteria, such as random selection. Participants are representative of the same experience or knowledge; they are not selected because of their demographic reflection of the general population.

The researcher should keep the first interviews with participants broad, letting the participants "tell their stories." He or she can then use subsequent interviews to obtain more targeted information and to fill gaps left by the earlier interviews. When the researcher no longer feels uncomfortable in the setting and can relax and focus on what is happening, instead of on him- or herself, then the stage of productive data collection begins.

When participants in the setting eventually begin to understand what the study is about and to recognize the special interests of the researcher, they may facilitate the inquiry by offering information. Finally, the researcher has reciprocal obligations to the participants (Reinharz, 1992). Such courtesies as providing cookies and coffee to facilitate focus group interaction can help to smooth data collection (Carey, 1994).

◆ The Stage of Productive Data Collection

Productive data collection is the most exciting phase of qualitative inquiry; during this phase, out of confusion, order and understanding *emerge.* But the emergence of this understanding does not take place without effort. Only with diligent observation and conceptual work on the part of the researcher do the patterns of relationships become apparent. This takes time, determination, persistence, and perseverance. It takes the ability to withstand frustration and discouragement when pieces of the puzzle apparently do not fit. It requires wisdom and contemplation to understand the relationships of seemingly unrelated facts or "negative cases"—informants or behaviors that do not conform to the apparent patterns.

The analysis of data begins shortly after the data collection commences and continues during data collection and beyond. The concurrent processes of data collection and analysis allow the analysis to guide data collection in a process of theoretical sampling, so that excess and unnecessary data are not collected. Thus research costs are kept to a minimum and researcher confusion is reduced. The outcome is that the researcher maintains control rather than "drowning in data."

The use of data management methods during the study is essential for the efficiency of the study. Transcripts and notes must be easily retrieved, easily cross-referenced, and easily separated from and linked with their original sources. In precomputer days, this was achieved by cutting and pasting—literally by cutting the desired passages from the transcript and taping the segments onto separate pieces of paper (for a detailed description of this procedure, see Field & Morse, 1991, pp. 101-102). Researchers may wish to become acquainted with the various qualitative data analysis software tools, applications for which are discussed by Richards and Richards in Chapter 8, Volume 3 of this series. Once the researcher appreciates the basics of analysis, he or she will find it worthwhile to master one of the many computer programs designed to facilitate content analysis (Fielding & Lee, 1991; for a comprehensive review of available programs, see Tesch, 1990, 1991).

Qualitative research does not have to be a "lone ranger" endeavor, with a single researcher struggling alone in a basement with piles of data. Researchers have conducted ethnography in teams, and the team approach has many advantages. For instance, it allows for more complete coverage of the setting and a more rapid period of data collection. Further, a research group may have an exponential effect on the analysis, as the insights of one person trigger new perspectives or insights in other team members. Thus leads may be confirmed or refuted more quickly. However, the team must have several characteristics: Team members must be able to brainstorm together frequently, preferably every day; members must have respect for the contributions of others; and relationships among team members must be excellent and egalitarian. If members of the team are from different disciplines, their implicit disciplinary perspectives may weaken—or may enrich—theoretical development of the research as the different perspectives provide paradigmatic tensions within the group. Members of the research team should also be aware from the outset that it may be more difficult to work within a multidisciplinary team than within a unidisciplinary team. One discipline may be more dominant than another, and different disciplines often use different terms for the same phenomena, making communication difficult. But the advantages that come from insights of such theoretically diverse teams are immense, and productivity can be enhanced many fold over the single-investigator model.

As the study progresses, theoretical insights and linkages between categories increase, making the process exciting as "what is going on" finally becomes clearer and more obvious. Data collection and sampling are dictated by and become directed entirely toward the emergent model. The researcher seeks indices of saturation, such as repetition in the information obtained and confirmation of previously collected data. Using theoretical sampling, he or she looks for negative cases to enrich the emergent model and to explain all variations and diverse patterns.

Ensuring Rigor

There are numerous methods of ensuring rigor in qualitative work, some more appropriate than others. The major methods for ensuring rigor are intricately linked with reliability and validity checks. Descriptions of the main methods follow.

Criteria of adequacy and appropriateness of data. In qualitative research, *adequacy* refers to the amount of data collected, rather than to the number of subjects, as in quantitative research. Adequacy is attained when sufficient data have been collected that saturation occurs and variation is both accounted for and understood. *Appropriateness* refers to selection of information according to the theoretical needs of the study and the emerging model. Sampling occurs purposefully, rather than by some form of random selection from a purposefully chosen population, as in quantitative research. In qualitative research, the investigator samples until repetition from multiple sources is obtained. This provides concurring and confirming data, and ensures saturation. The results of the study must be rich, and sampling strategies such as seeking negative cases also contribute to ensuring the adequacy and appropriateness of the data (Morse, 1986).

The audit trail. Careful documentation of the conceptual development of the project should leave an adequate amount of evidence that interested parties can reconstruct the process by which the investigators reached their conclusion. The audit trail consists of six types of documentation: raw data, data reduction and analysis products, data reconstruction and synthesis products, process notes, materials relating to intentions and dispositions, and instrument development information (this list was developed by Halpern, 1983, and reported in Lincoln & Guba, 1985, pp. 319-320).

Verification of the study with secondary informants. The resulting model may be taken back to the informants and presented to them. Often informants will be able to confirm immediately the accuracy and validity of the study, and may even, at that time, offer additional stories to confirm the model further (Glaser, 1978). However, sometimes the results report on findings that are implicit in the setting; then even the participants are not aware of the findings and must themselves "check out" the results. This occurred in a study on childbirth in Fiji in which the results of an ethnography revealed that Fiji-Indian primipara in labor did not have basic knowledge of the mechanics of delivery and in fact did not know how the baby was "going to get out." The Fiji- Indian nurses had learned such "facts of life" during their nursing education, but values of modesty prevented the nurses from sharing their knowledge with their patients, and thus from recognizing the culturally condoned ignorance of the Fiji-Indian mothers. Therefore, the nurses were surprised and shocked to discover this fact, and needed to confirm and reconfirm this lack of knowledge in their patients in order to satisfy their own sense of discovery (see Morse, 1989).

Multiple raters. Occasionally, a qualitative investigator uses a second investigator to read and code a transcript, or checks the "validity" of a category by asking someone else to affirm that, indeed, he or she is "seeing what is there." This process actually violates the process of induction, because the first investigator has a bank of knowledge from conducting other interviews and from observing that the second researcher does not have.

As the process of inductive qualitative inquiry frequently depends on insight and on the process of linking data (both among categories and with established theory), expecting another investigator to have the same insight from a limited data base is unrealistic.

Furthermore, limiting each step of analysis to small bits of data may even impede inquiry and stunt the development of the model. (I argue elsewhere that the process of synthesizing data is similar to the cognitive process of synthesizing others' articles for a literature review. No one takes a second reader to the library to check that indeed he or she is interpreting the original sources correctly, so why does anyone need a reliability checker for his or her data? See Morse, 1994b.) Thus the quantitative model of ensuring reliability and validity by using external raters is not recommended for qualitative research.

◆ The Stage of Withdrawal

Unfortunately, the productive period of data collection does not last. The assimilation of the researcher into the setting is a constant process, and eventually a point is reached when the researcher is viewed as a *part of the setting*. The researcher eventually becomes a full member of the group. At this stage, two processes impede data collection. First, the researcher loses sensitivity to the day-to-day activities in the setting. As daily activities become predictable and the researcher becomes bored, his or her ability to see and to record details of events becomes dulled and data collection becomes increasingly difficult. Second, the researcher loses objectivity toward the setting and the members of the group. As a fully indoctrinated member of the group, the researcher develops loyalties, becoming aligned with the group and the institution, and the neutral stance of the researcher-as-a-data-collector is lost.

The major sign that the researcher has reached the point of withdrawal is the tendency to "go native." The researcher may suddenly recognize that he or she is putting other goals ahead of the research. For instance, the researcher may suddenly realize that he or she did not record an event in the field notes because it may reflect poorly on the participants, or because it was "everyday" or not special or interesting enough. When this happens, the researcher must realize that it is necessary to withdraw from the setting. However, analysis is not complete, and as it may be necessary to return to the setting to collect confirming data, to fill in gaps, or to observe special cases or events, it is important that he or she not withdraw completely. In leaving, the researcher should try to say something to participants that will allow him or her to return, if necessary, such as "I *think* I have finished, but may I come back if I find that I need to ask some more questions or observe something else?"

Public statements that the main part of data collection is soon to be completed usually bring out many participants who are suddenly determined to have their say, to tell the researcher "exactly how it is." This is a normal part of withdrawal and one that may put new life into the research. However, if the researcher is not learning anything new, he or she may be reasonably certain that data are saturated.

During this time, data analysis should be intense. The model or theory should becoming more refined and the researcher should be quite excited about the results. Explaining the emerging model to colleagues and having them ask questions will refine the results and move the researcher forward in his or her thinking. The more the researcher presents the theory, the easier it will be to write. Links will become obvious and the researcher will become more articulate.

◆ The Stage of Writing

Qualitative writing is different from quantitative writing. Whereas the latter consists of a concise presentation of the methods and the results of the study, the qualitative report must be a convincing argument systematically presenting data to support the researcher's case and to refute alternative explanations (see Morse, 1994a). Two main approaches to qualitative articles are (a) to write the article as though the reader is solving the puzzle with the researcher, and (b) to present a summary of the major finding and then present the findings that supports the conclusion. Researchers should use quotations to illustrate their interpretations of the data, rather than in place of descriptive text.

One question that is frequently asked is, How much editing can be done on a quotation? It is important not to edit the essence of the quotation from the passage, but at the same time it is legitimate to remove the "mmms" and the pauses unless the intonation and expression are important for the meaning. The researcher may also remove irrelevant phrases and sentences, replacing them with ellipses. He or she should pay close attention to the punctuation, checking each passage with the audiotape to ensure that commas and periods (indicating pauses and breaks in the speech) are correctly used to maintain the speaker's expression.

At the beginning of the study (when giving informed consent), the participants were promised anonymity for their participation. The researcher must check carefully that none of the quotations used makes a speaker recognizable through some contextual reference. He or she must ensure that demographic data are presented in aggregates, so that identifiers (such as gender, age, and years of experience) are not linked (making individuals recognizable) and are not consistently associated with the same participant throughout the text, even if a code name is used. This prevents those who know all the participants in the setting from determining who participated in the study and who did not. In addition, the text should not identify which informants provided quotes. Tagging quotations with participant numbers may also place participants at risk of being identified.

If the institution's administrators choose to be acknowledged publicly for their contribution to the project, the researcher should allow them to read a draft of the completed document to ensure that they still wish to be listed in the acknowl- edgments. Administrators forget that they cannot be both publicly thanked for their cooperation and not identified. If they want to be acknowledged, the researcher should request a letter of permission before listing the organization's name in the acknowledgments. One administrator may request such a citation, but someone else, perhaps a board member, may take exception to the citation at a later date.

The organization's and the participants' efforts demand some reciprocal gesture from the researcher. He or she should arrange for the results to be presented to the institution at a future date (before the participants hear about the research at a conference) and prepare a summary of the study to be mailed to all participants and others who are interested. Finally, the researcher should provide the institution with a copy of the completed study and the final report to the funding agency.

Publication is the most important means for disseminating research findings. Qualitative research may not always be "split" into several articles, and many publishers are willing to publish entire studies as monographs. Some studies, however, lend themselves naturally to segmentation, with each portion making a reasonably comprehensive article. Publication in shorter articles has the advantage of increasing citations in serial indexes, which, in turn, lead to speedier dissemination of the work.

◆ Conclusion

In this chapter, I have described techniques for designing and conducting a qualitative project. I have addressed some of the special problems that occur in qualitative research, such as how to present a proposal in a convincing manner—so that the idea will be fundable—while maintaining the flexibility necessary to achieve the qualitative research goals. I have also addressed the issue of how to maintain the freedom necessary to embark on qualitative inquiry without invalidating the study with deductive assumptions and prematurely developed research plans. I have also outlined techniques for preparing a proposal, from idea to submission. Finally, I have described some issues related to the selection of an appropriate methodology and design according to the nature of the research question and the purpose of the study. The remaining chapters in Part III of the *Handbook* address the major qualitative methods used in qualitative inquiry.

APPENDIX A:
HINTS FOR BUDGETING

The following list will assist the researcher in preparing a qualitative budget:

1. *Personnel:* A secretary can do much more to facilitate the project than simply transcribe the interviews. He or she can make appointments for interviews, monitor the budget, catalog tapes, and organize consent forms, articles, and transcribed interviews. To calculate the length of time needed for transcribing, a rule of thumb for a fast typist (i.e., more than 65 words per minute) is four times the length of the tape. If the typist replays the tape to check the transcriptions, change this to six times the length of the recording. Calculate the length of time you expect to complete the work, and then double it. This allows for a more realistic completion of the project, and allows for "disasters" that will inevitably delay the completion of the project. Remember Strauss's (1987) advice that qualitative inquiry cannot be forced or rushed.

2. *Equipment:* Purchase the best tape recorder. Tape recorders wear out, and generally they are not worth repairing. A researcher cannot afford to lose an interview because the tape has tangled. A foot pedal for the tape recorder will be helpful for transcribing or making notes while listening to the tape, as it leaves both hands free. As a clear recording will make for easier transcribing, use an external microphone. A solar-powered microphone is a good investment, as it is not dependent on batteries.

3. *Supplies:* Medium-quality tapes are fine. The cheapest 90-minute tapes should be avoided as they tend to tangle relatively easily. Allow for plenty of photocopying.

APPENDIX B:
LEVEL OF HUMAN SUBJECT REVIEW

The types and levels of approval required for NIH grant applications are listed here. Quoted material is from "Protection of Human Subjects" (Part 46 of *Code of Federal Regulations,* Title 45, revised 1983).

Minimal risk in research is defined as "the probability and magnitude of physical or psychological harm that is normally encountered in daily lives, or in the routine medical, dental, or psychological examination of healthy persons" (p. 14). Three levels of approval exist: exempt review, expedited review, and full review. Definitions of these and types of research of interest to qualitative researchers are as follows:

1. *Exempt review:* Research that is exempt from review is research that is conducted in "established or commonly accepted educational settings, involving normal educational practices; research involving survey or interview procedures, except where the human subjects (i) can be identified directly or through identifiers linked to the subject, and (ii) the subject's responses, if they become known outside the research, could reasonably place the subject at risk of criminal or civil liability or be damaging to the subject's financial standing or employability, and (iii) the research deals with sensitive aspects of the subject's own behavior, such as illegal conduct, or use of alcohol" (p. 5). It also includes observational research of public behavior, when the data are recorded anonymously, as well as research involving the collection or study of publicly available existing data, records, pathological specimens, or diagnostic specimens (p. 5).

2. *Expedite review:* Expedite review is the approval of the research by the chairperson of the IRB (or his or her designate), and is used for research that is on the list of research that contains no more than minimal risk. Included in this list are "voice recordings made for research purposes" and "the study of existing data, documents, records, pathological specimens, or diagnostic specimens" (p. 19).

3. *Full review:* This is the review of the research by the IRB, which considers that the risks to the subject are minimized, that the risks to the subject are reasonable in relation to the anticipated benefits, and the importance of the knowledge that may reasonably be expected to result (p. 8).

◆ References

Agar, M. H. (1980). *The professional stranger: An informal introduction to ethnography.* New York: Academic Press.

Anderson, G. L. (1989). Critical theory in education: Origins, current status, and new directions. *Review of Educational Research, 59,* 240-270.

Atkinson, P. (1992). The ethnography of a medical setting: Reading, writing and rhetoric. *Qualitative Health Research, 2,* 451-474.

Benson, D., & Hughes, J. A. (1983). *The perspective of ethnomethodology.* London: Longman.

Bergum, V. (1991). Being a phenomenological researcher. In J. M. Morse (Ed.), *Qualitative nursing research: A contemporary dialogue* (rev. ed., pp. 55-71). Newbury Park, CA: Sage.

Campbell, J. C. (1991). Voices and paradigms: Perspectives on critical and feminist theory. *Advances in Nursing Science, 13*(3), 1-15.

Carey, M. A. (1994). The group effect in focus groups: Planning, implementing, and interpreting focus group research. In J. M. Morse (Ed.), *Critical issues in qualitative research methods* (pp. 225-241). Newbury Park, CA: Sage.

Chenitz, W. C., & Swanson, J. M. (1986). *From practice to grounded theory.* Menlo Park, CA: Addison-Wesley.

Code, L. (1991). *What can she know? Feminist theory and the construction of knowledge.* Ithaca, NY: Cornell University Press.

Denzin, N. K. (1970). Symbolic interactionism and ethnomethodology. In J. Douglas (Ed.), *Understanding everyday life* (pp. 261-286). Chicago: Aldine.

Denzin, N. K. (1989). *Interpretive interactionism.* Newbury Park, CA: Sage.

DeVault, M. L. (1990). Talking and listening from women's standpoint: Feminist strategies for interviewing and analysis. *Social Problems, 37,* 96-116.

Douglas, J. (Ed.). (1970). *Understanding everyday life.* Chicago: Aldine.

Downs, F. (1983). "One dark and stormy night" [Editorial]. *Nursing Research, 32,* 259.

Eibl-Eibesfeldt, I. (1989). *Human ethology.* New York: Aldine de Gruyter.

Ellen, R. F. (Ed.). (1984). *Ethnographic research.* London: Academic Press.

Fetterman, D. M. (1989). *Ethnography: Step by step.* Newbury Park, CA: Sage.

Field, P. A., & Morse, J. M. (1991). *Nursing research: The application of qualitative approaches.* London: Chapman & Hall.

Fielding, N. G., & Lee, R. M. (Eds.). (1991). *Using computers in qualitative research.* London: Sage.

Giorgi, A. (1970). *Psychology as a human science: A phenomenologically based approach.* New York: Harper & Row.

Glaser, B. G. (1978). *Theoretical sensitivity.* Mill Valley, CA: Sociology Press.

Glaser, B. G. (1992). *Basics of grounded theory analysis.* Mill Valley, CA: Sociology Press.

Glaser, B. G., & Strauss, A. L. (1967). *The discovery of grounded theory: Strategies for qualitative research.* Chicago: Aldine.

Grant, L., & Fine, G. A. (1992). Sociology unleashed: Creative directions in classical ethnography. In M. D. LeCompte, W. L. Millroy, & J. Preissle (Eds.), *The handbook of qualitative research in education* (pp. 405-446). New York: Academic Press.

Halpern, E. S. (1983). *Auditing naturalistic inquiries: The development and application of a model.* Unpublished doctoral dissertation, Indiana University.

Hammersley, M., & Atkinson, P. (1983). *Ethnography: Principles in practice.* London: Tavistock.

Harding, S. (Ed.). (1987). *Feminism and methodology: Social science issues.* Bloomington: Indiana University Press.

Heritage, J. (1984). *Garfinkel and ethnomethodology.* Cambridge: Polity.

Hughes, C. C. (1992). "Ethnography": What's in a word—Process? Product? Promise? *Qualitative Health Research, 2,* 451-474.

Jorgensen, D. L. (1989). *Participant observation: A methodology for human studies.* Newbury Park, CA: Sage.

Leiter, K. (1980). *A primer on ethnomethodology.* New York: Oxford University Press.

Lincoln, Y. S., & Guba, E. G. (1985). *Naturalistic inquiry.* Beverly Hills, CA: Sage.

Morse, J. M. (1986). Qualitative research: Issues in sampling. In P. L. Chinn (Ed.), *Nursing research methodology: Issues and implementation* (pp. 181-193). Rockville, MD: Aspen.

Morse, J. M. (1989). Cultural variation in behavioral response to parturition: Childbirth in Fiji. *Medical Anthropology, 12*(1), 35-54.

Morse, J. M. (1991a). Approaches to qualitative-quantitative methodological triangulation. *Nursing Research, 40,* 120-123.

Morse, J. M. (1991b). Strategies for sampling. In J. M. Morse (Ed.), *Qualitative nursing research: A contemporary dialogue* (rev. ed., pp. 127-145). Newbury Park, CA: Sage.

Morse, J. M. (1994a). Disseminating qualitative research. In E. V. Dunn, P. G. Norton, M. Stewart, F. Tudiver, & M. J. Bass (Eds.), *Disseminating research/changing practice* (pp. 59-75). Newbury Park, CA: Sage.

Morse, J. M. (1994b). "Emerging from the data": The cognitive processes of analysis in qualitative inquiry. In J. M. Morse (Ed.), *Critical issues in qualitative research methods* (pp. 23-43). Newbury Park, CA: Sage.

Morse, J. M., & Bottorff, J. L. (1990). The use of ethology in clinical nursing research. *Advances in Nursing Science, 12*(3), 53-64.

Norris, J. (1991). Mothers' involvement in their adolescent daughters' abortions. In J. M. Morse & J. L. Johnson (Eds.), *The illness experience: Dimensions of suffering* (pp. 201-236). Newbury Park, CA: Sage.

Patton, M. Q. (1990). *Qualitative evaluation and research methods* (2nd ed.). Newbury Park, CA: Sage.

Quantz, R. A. (1992). On critical ethnography (with some postmodern considerations). In M. D. LeCompte, W. L. Millroy, & J. Preissle (Eds.), *The handbook of qualitative research in education* (pp. 447-505). New York: Academic Press.

Reinharz, S. (1992). *Feminist methods in social research.* New York: Oxford University Press.

Rogers, M. F. (1983). *Sociology, ethnomethodology, and experience.* Cambridge: Cambridge University Press.

Sanjek, R. (Ed.). (1990). *Fieldnotes: The makings of anthropology.* Albany: State University of New York Press.

Scherer, K. R., & Ekman, P. (1982). *Handbook of methods in nonverbal behavior research.* Cambridge: Cambridge University Press.

Spradley, J. P. (1979). *The ethnographic interview.* New York: Holt, Rinehart & Winston.

Spradley, J. P. (1980). *Participant observation.* New York: Holt, Rinehart & Winston.

Stern, P. N. (1994). Eroding grounded theory. In J. M. Morse (Ed.), *Critical issues in qualitative research methods* (pp. 212-223). Newbury Park, CA: Sage.

Strauss, A. L. (1987). *Qualitative analysis for social scientists.* New York: Cambridge University Press.

Strauss, A. L., & Corbin, J. (1990). *Basics of qualitative research: Grounded theory procedures and techniques.* Newbury Park, CA: Sage.

Tesch, R. (1990). *Qualitative research: Analysis types and software tools.* New York: Falmer.

Tesch, R. (1991). Computer programs that assist in the analysis of qualitative data: An overview. *Qualitative Health Research, 1,* 309-325.

Tripp-Riemer, T., & Cohen, M. Z. (1991). Funding strategies for qualitative research. In J. M. Morse (Ed.), *Qualitative nursing research: A contemporary dialogue* (rev. ed., pp. 243-256). Newbury Park, CA: Sage.

van Gennep, A. (1992). The research topic: Or, folklore without end. In J. M. Morse (Ed.), *Qualitative health research* (pp. 65-68). Newbury Park, CA: Sage. (Original work published 1967)

van Manen, M. (1984). Practicing phenomenological writing. *Phenomenology + Pedagogy, 2,* 36-69.

van Manen, M. (1990). *Researching the lived experience.* London: University of Western Ontario.

Wax, R. H. (1971). *Doing fieldwork: Warnings and advice.* Chicago: University of Chicago Press.

Werner, O., & Schoepfle, G. M. (1987a). *Systematic fieldwork: Foundations of ethnography and interviewing* (Vol. 1). Newbury Park, CA: Sage.

Werner, O., & Schoepfle, G. M. (1987b). *Systematic fieldwork: Ethnographic analysis and data management* (Vol. 2). Newbury Park, CA: Sage.

Wilson, H., & Hutchinson, S. (1991). Triangulation of qualitative methods: Heideggerian hermeneutics and grounded theory. *Qualitative Health Research, 1,* 263-276.

Wolcott, H. F. (1992). Posturing in qualitative inquiry. In M. D. LeCompte, W. L. Millroy, & J. Preissle (Eds.), *The handbook of qualitative research in education* (pp. 3-52). New York: Academic Press.

4

Case Studies

Robert E. Stake

◆ Some case studies are qualitative studies, some are not. In this chapter
I will concentrate on case studies where qualitative inquiry dominates, with strong naturalistic, holistic, cultural, phenomenological interests. Case study is not a methodological choice, but a choice of object to
be studied. We choose to study the case. We could study it in many ways.
The physician studies the child because the child is ill. The child's symptoms
are both qualitative and quantitative. The physician's record is more
quantitative than qualitative. The social worker studies the child because
the child is neglected. The symptoms of neglect are both qualitative and
quantitative. The formal record the social worker keeps is more qualitative
than quantitative.[1] In many professional and practical fields, cases are
studied and recorded. As a form of research, case study is defined by interest
in individual cases, not by the methods of inquiry used.

Perhaps a majority of researchers doing case studies call their work by
some other name. Howard Becker, for example, when asked at the second
Cambridge Conference (Simons, 1980) what he calls his own studies,
reluctantly said, "Fieldwork," adding that such labels contribute little to
the understanding of what researchers do. The name *case study* is emphasized by some of us because it draws attention to the question of what
specifically can be learned from the single case. That epistemological
question is the driving question of this chapter: What can be learned from
the single case? I will emphasize designing the study to optimize understanding of the case rather than generalization beyond.

◆ Identification of the Case

A case may be simple or complex. It may be a child or a classroom of children or a mobilization of professionals to study a childhood condition. It is one among others. In any given study, we will concentrate on the one. The time we may spend concentrating our inquiry on the one may be long or short, but while we so concentrate, we are engaged in case study.

Custom has it that not everything is a case. A child may be a case. A doctor may be a case—but *his doctoring* lacks the specificity, boundedness, to be called a case.[2] An agency may be a case. The reasons for child neglect or the policies of dealing with neglectful parents would seldom be considered a case. Those topics are generalities rather than specificities. The case is a specific. Even more, the case is a functioning specific. The case, in the words of Louis Smith (1978), is a "bounded system." In the social sciences and human services, it has working parts, it probably is purposive, even having a self. It is an integrated system. The parts do not have to be working well, the purposes may be irrational, but it is a system.

Its behavior is patterned. Consistency and sequentialness are prominent. It is common to recognize that certain features are within the system, within the boundaries of the case, and other features outside. Some are significant as context. William Goode and Paul Hatt (1952) have observed that it is not always easy for the case researcher to say where the child ends and where the environment begins. But the boundedness and the behavior patterns of the system are key factors in understanding the case (Stake, 1988).

Ultimately we may be more interested in a phenomenon or a population of cases than in the individual case. We cannot understand this case without knowing about other cases. But while we are studying it, our meager resources are concentrated on trying to understand its complexities. For the while, we probably will not study comparison cases. We may simultaneously carry on more than one case study, but each case study is a concentrated inquiry into a single case.

The concept of *case* remains subject to debate,[3] and the term *study* is ambiguous (Kemmis, 1980). A case study is both the process of learning about the case and the product of our learning. Lawrence Stenhouse (1984) advocates calling the product a "case record," and occasionally we do, but the practice of calling the final report a "case study" is widely established. Custom is not so strong that researchers (other than graduate students) will get into trouble by calling anything they please a case study.[4] But the more the object of study is a specific, unique, bounded system, the greater the usefulness of the epistemological rationale described in this chapter.

◆ Intrinsic and Instrumental Interest in Cases

Different researchers have different purposes for studying cases. To keep such differences in mind, I find it useful to identify three types of study. In what we may call *intrinsic case study,* study is undertaken because one wants better understanding of this particular case. It is not undertaken primarily because the case represents other cases or because it illustrates a particular trait or problem, but because, in all its particularity and ordinariness, this case itself is of interest. The researcher temporarily subordinates other curiosities so that the case may reveal its story. The purpose is not to come to understand some abstract construct or generic phenomenon, such as literacy or teenage drug use or what a school principal does. The purpose is not theory building—though at other times the researcher may do just that. Study is undertaken because of intrinsic interest in, for example, this particular child, clinic, conference, or curriculum. Some books that illustrate intrinsic case study include the following:

- *Akenfield* (Blythe, 1955/1969)
- *Argonauts of the Western Pacific* (Malinowski, 1922/1984)
- *Bread and Dreams: A Case Study of Bilingual Schooling in the U.S.A.* (MacDonald, Adelman, Kushner, & Walker, 1982)
- *God's Choice* (Peshkin, 1986)

In what we may call *instrumental case study,* a particular case is examined to provide insight into an issue or refinement of theory. The case is of secondary interest; it plays a supportive role, facilitating our understanding of something else. The case is often looked at in depth, its contexts scrutinized, its ordinary activities detailed, but because this helps us pursue the external interest. The case may be seen as typical of other cases or not. (I will discuss the small importance of typicality later.) The choice of case is made because it is expected to advance our understanding of that other interest. Because we simultaneously have several interests, often changing, there is no line distinguishing intrinsic case study from instrumental; rather, a zone of combined purpose separates them. The following books illustrate instrumental case study:

88

- *A Bright and Shining Lie: John Vann and America in Vietnam* (Sheehan, 1988)
- *Boys in White: Student Culture in Medical School* (Becker, Geer, Hughes, & Strauss, 1961)
- *Middletown: A Study in American Culture* (Lynd & Lynd, 1929)
- *La Vida* (Lewis, 1966)

With even less interest in one particular case, researchers may study a number of cases jointly in order to inquire into the phenomenon, population, or general condition. We might call this *collective case study*.[5] It is not the study of a collective but instrumental study extended to several cases. Individual cases in the collection may or may not be known in advance to manifest the common characteristic. They may be similar or dissimilar, redundancy and variety each having voice. They are chosen because it is believed that understanding them will lead to better understanding, perhaps better theorizing, about a still larger collection of cases. Books illustrating collective case study include the following:

- *Children of Crisis* (Coles, 1967)
- *Habits of the Heart: Individualism and Commitment in American Life* (Bellah, Madsen, Sullivan, Swidler, & Tipton, 1985)
- *Innovation Up Close: How School Improvement Works* (Huberman & Miles, 1984)
- *Savage Inequalities* (Kozol, 1991)

Authors and reports seldom fit neatly into such categories, and I see these three as heuristic more than functional. Peshkin responded to my classification of *God's Choice* by saying: "I mean to present my case so that it can be read with interest in the case itself, but I always have another agenda—to learn from the case about some class of things. Some of what that will be remains an emergent matter for a long time." For three years, Peshkin studied a single school, Bethany Baptist Academy. Until the final chapter, he did not tell the reader about the emergent matters of great importance to him and to school people and citizens broadly. The first order of business was to understand the case. The immediate, if not ultimate, interest was intrinsic. The methods Peshkin used centered on the case, not intentionally on his abiding concerns about community, freedom, and survival.

Other types of case study could be acknowledged. There is a common form used in teaching, we could call it the teaching case study. It is used to illustrate a point, a condition, a category, something important for instruction (Kennedy, 1979). For decades, Harvard Law School and School of Business professors have paraded these cases. For staff development and management training, such reports constitute the articles of the *Journal of Case Research,* key publication of the North American Case Research Association. Used for instruction and consultation, they result from instrumental case study.[6]

One could also make a separate category for biography. Louis Smith's contribution to this volume (Chapter 8) is case centered, noting that biography calls for demanding chronological structures and extra attention to procedures for the protection of human subjects. Similarly, television documentaries, many of them easily classifiable as case studies, require their own methods. In law, the case has a special definition: the practice of law itself could be called case study. The work of ethnographers, critical theorists, institutional demographers, and many others has conceptual and stylistic patterns that not only amplify the taxonomy but extend the foundation for case study research in the social sciences and social services. My purpose in categorization here is more limited: To emphasize variation in the concern for and methodological orientation to the case, I have named three types of study—intrinsic, instrumental, and collective.

◆ Study of the Particular

Case researchers seek out both what is common and what is particular about the case, but the end result regularly presents something unique (Stouffer, 1941). Uniqueness is likely to be pervasive, extending to

1. the nature of the case
2. its historical background
3. the physical setting
4. other contexts, including economic, political, legal, and aesthetic
5. other cases through which this case is recognized
6. those informants through whom the case can be known

To study the case, many researchers will gather data on all the above.

Uniqueness, particularity, diversity is not universally loved. Case study methodology has suffered somewhat because it has sometimes been presented by people who have a lesser regard for study of the particular (Denzin, 1989; Glaser & Strauss, 1967; Herriott & Firestone, 1983; Yin, 1984). Many social scientists have written about case study as if intrinsic study of a particular case is not as important as studies to obtain generalizations pertaining to a population of cases. They have emphasized case study as typification of other cases, as exploration leading up to generalization-producing studies, or as an occasional early step in theory building. Thus, by these respected authorities, case study method has been little honored as the intrinsic study of a valued particular, as it is generally in biography, institutional self-study, program evaluation, therapeutic practice, and many lines of work. But insistence on the ultimacy of theory building appears to be diminishing in qualitative social science.

Case study can usefully be seen as a small step toward grand generalization (Campbell, 1975), but generalization should not be emphasized in all research (Feagin, Orum, & Sjoberg, 1991; Simons, 1980). Damage occurs when the commitment to generalize or create theory runs so strong that the researcher's attention is drawn away from features important for understanding the case itself.[7] The case study researcher faces a strategic choice in deciding how much and how long the complexities of the case should be studied. Not everything about the case can be understood—how much needs to be? Each researcher will make up his or her own mind.

Uniqueness of Situations

With its own unique history, the case is a complex entity operating within a number of contexts, including the physical, economic, ethical, and aesthetic. The case is singular, but it has subsections (e.g., production, marketing, sales departments), groups (e.g., students, teachers, parents), occasions (e.g., workdays, holidays, days near holidays), a concatenation of domains—many so complex that at best they can only be sampled.

Holistic case study calls for the examination of these complexities. As Egon Guba and Yvonna Lincoln point out in Chapter 6, Volume 1 of this series, much qualitative research is based on a holistic view that social phenomena, human dilemmas, and the nature of cases are situational and influenced by happenings of many kinds. Qualitative researchers are sometimes disposed toward causal determination of events, but more often tend to perceive, as did Tolstoy in *War and Peace,* events not simply and singly caused. Many find the search for cause of little use, dramatizing, rather, the coincidence of events, seeing some events purposive, some situational, many of them interrelated. They favor inquiry designs seeking data describing diverse operations of the case. To do case studies does not require examination of diverse issues and contexts, but that is the way that most qualitative researchers do them.

Issues

Whether so called or not, the researcher's themes or "abstract dimensions" are often *issues,* problematic circumstances that draw upon the common disciplines of knowledge, such as sociology, economics, ethics, and literary criticism. With broader purview than that of crafters of experiments and testers of hypotheses, qualitative case researchers orient to complexities connecting ordinary practice in natural habitats to the abstractions and concerns of diverse academic disciplines. This broader purview is applied to the single case. Generalization and proof (Becker, 1958) are not without risk.[8]

Even when stated as generalities, the issues are matters for study regarding the specific case. Starting with a topical concern, researchers pose foreshadowed problems,[9] concentrate on issue-related observations, interpret patterns of data that reform the issues as assertions. The transformation I have experienced in my work in program evaluation is illustrated by the sequence in Table 4.1, issues for a hypothetical case study of a music education program.

In choosing issues to organize their study, researchers accentuate one task or another. To treat the case as an exemplar, they ask, Which issues bring out our initial concerns, the dominant theme? To maximize understanding of the case, they ask, Which issues seek out compelling uniquenesses? For an evaluation study, they ask, Which issues help reveal merit and shortcoming? And in general, they ask, Which issues facilitate the planning and activities of inquiry, including inspiring and rehabilitating the researcher? Issues are chosen partly in terms of what can be learned within the opportunities for study. They will be chosen differently depending on the importance of each task, differently by different researchers. One might say a personal contract is drawn between researcher and phenomenon. For all the devotion to science or a client, What is to be learned here that a solitary researcher feels compelled to learn?

The issues used to *organize* the study may or may not be the ones used to report the case to others. Observing is different work from presenting the case report. At the end, it may be the readers' issues that determine what will

TABLE 4.1 An Example of Issue Development in a Study

1. *Topical issue:* The goals of the music education program.
2. *Foreshadowed problem:* The majority of the community supports the present emphasis on band, chorus, and performances, but a few teachers and community leaders want a more intellectual emphasis, such as history, literature, and critical review of music.
3. *Issue under development:* What is the extent of interest of this teaching staff in teaching music courses required of everyone?
4. *Assertion:* This community would not generate the extra funding necessary for providing intellectual learning of music for all secondary school students.

be said. Some researchers choose to serve the readers, even when quite unsure as to who the eventual readers might be and as to the concerns they have.

Telling the Story

It is not uncommon for qualitative case researchers to call for letting the case "tell its own story" (Carter, 1993; Coles, 1989). We cannot be sure that a case telling its own story will tell all or tell well, but the ethnographic ethos of *interpretive* study, seeking out emic meanings held by the people within the case, is strong. The choices of presentation styles are many; John Van Maanen (1988) identifies seven: realistic, impressionistic, confessional, critical, formal, literary, and jointly told. One cannot know at the outset what the issues, the perceptions, the theory will be. Case researchers enter the scene expecting, even knowing, that certain events, problems, relationships will be important, yet discover that some actually are of little consequence (Parlett & Hamilton, 1976; Smith, Chapter 8, this volume). Case content evolves in the act of writing itself.

Even though committed to empathy and multiple realities, it is the researcher who decides what is the case's own story, or at least what of the case's own story he or she will report. More will be pursued than was volunteered. Less will be reported than was learned. Even though the competent researcher will be guided by what the case may indicate is most important, even though patrons and other researchers will advise, what is necessary for an understanding of the case will be decided by the researcher. It may be the case's own story, but it is the researcher's dressing of the case's own story. This is not to dismiss the aim of finding the story that best represents the case, but to remind that the criteria of representation ultimately are decided by the researcher.

Many a researcher would like to tell the whole story but of course cannot; the whole story exceeds anyone's knowing, anyone's telling. Even those inclined to tell all find strong the obligation to winnow and consolidate. A continuum runs from telling lots to telling nothing. The holistic researcher, like the single-issue researcher, must choose. Criteria for selecting content are many (Van Maanen, 1988). Some are set by funding agencies, prospective readers, rhetorical convention, the researcher's career pattern, the prospect of publication. Some criteria are set by a notion of what represents the case most fully, most appreciably for the hospitality received, most comprehensibly. These are subjective choices not unlike those all researchers make in choosing what to study. Some are made while designing the case study, but some continue to be made through the final hours.

◆ Learning From the Particular Case

The researcher is a teacher using at least two pedagogical methods (Eisner, 1985). Teaching *didactically,* the researcher teaches what he or she has learned. Arranging for what educationists call *discovery learning,* the researcher provides material for readers to learn, on their own, things the teacher does not know as well as those he or she does know. What can one learn from a single case? Donald Campbell (1975), David Hamilton (1980), Stephen Kemmis (1980), Robert Yin (1989), and William Firestone (1993) have considered the epistemology of the particular. How we may learn from the singular case ultimately derives from how the case is like and not like other cases—yet, as I claim later, direct comparison diminishes opportunity to learn from it.

From case reports we learn both propositional and experiential knowledge (Geertz, 1983; Polanyi, 1962; Rumelhart & Ortony, 1977; von Wright, 1971). Certain descriptions and assertions are assimilated by readers into memory. When the researcher's narrative provides opportunity for vicarious experience, readers extend their memories of happenings. Naturalistic, ethnographic case materials, to some extent, parallel actual experience, feeding into the most fundamental processes of awareness and understanding. Deborah Trumbull and I have called these processes *naturalistic generalization* (Stake & Trumbull, 1982). The reader comes to know some things told, as if he or she had experienced them.

94

Enduring meanings come from encounter, and are modified and reinforced by repeated encounter.

In life itself, this occurs seldom to the individual alone but in the presence (if not proximity) of others. In a social process, together they bend, spin, consolidate, and enrich their understandings. We come to know what has happened partly in terms of what others reveal as their experience. The case researcher emerges from one social experience, the observation, to choreograph another, the report. Knowledge is socially constructed— we constructivists believe (see Schwandt, Chapter 7, this volume)— and thus case study researchers assist readers in the construction of knowledge.

Knowledge Transfer From Researcher to Reader

Both researcher and reader need conceptual structures, advanced organizers (Ausubel & Fitzgerald, 1961), schemata (Anderson, 1977), scaffolding (Cazden, 1988), an unfolding of realization (Bohm, 1985). They do not have to be aware of this need. Thought itself, conversation surely, and writing especially draw phrases into paragraphs, append labels onto constructs. Attention focuses. Generalization can be an unconscious process.

In private and personal ways, ideas are structured, highlighted, subordinated, connected, embedded *in* contexts, embedded *with* illustration, laced with favor and doubt. However moved to share ideas, however clever and elaborated their writings, case researchers, as others, pass along to readers some of their personal meanings of events and relationships—and fail to pass along others. They know that the reader too will add and subtract, invent and shape—reconstructing the knowledge in ways that leave it differently connected and more likely to be personally useful.

Knowledge of the case faces hazardous passage from writer to reader. The writer needs ways of safeguarding the trip. Even as reading begins, often much earlier, the case assumes a place in the company of previously known cases. Conceptually for the reader, the new case cannot be but some combination of cases already known. A new case without commonality cannot be understood. Yet a new case without distinction will not be noticed. Researchers cannot know well the already-known cases, the peculiarities of mind, of their readers. They seek ways to protect and validate the transfer of knowledge.

The researcher recognizes the need to accommodate to readers' preexisting knowledge. Though everyone deals with this need every day and draws upon a lifetime of experience, we know precious little about how new experience merges with old. According to Spiro, Vispoel, Schmitz, Samarapungavan, and Boerger (1987), most personal experience is "ill-structured," neither pedagogically nor epistemologically neat; it follows that a well-structured, propositional presentation will often not be the better way to "transfer" experiential knowledge. The reader has a certain "cognitive flexibility," the readiness to assemble a situation-relative schema from the knowledge fragments of a new encounter. Spiro et al. contend that

> the best way to learn and instruct in order to attain the goal of cognitive flexibility in knowledge representation for future application is by a method of case-based presentations which treats a content domain as a landscape that is explored by "criss-crossing" it in many directions, by reexamining each case "site" in the varying contexts of different neighboring cases, and by using a variety of abstract dimensions for comparing cases. (p. 178)

Transfer remains difficult to understand. Even less understood is how a small aspect of the case may be found by many readers to modify an existing understanding about cases in general, even when the case is not typical. In a ghetto school, I observed a teacher with one set of rules for classroom decorum, except that for one nearly expelled, indomitable youngster, a more liberal set had to be continuously invented. Reading my account, teachers from very different schools agreed with both. "Yes, you have to be strict with the rules." "Yes, sometimes you have to bend the rules." They recognized in the report an unusual but generalizable circumstance. People find in case reports certain insights into the human condition, even while they are well aware of the atypicality of the case. They may be too quick to accept the insight. The case researcher needs to provide grounds for validating both the observation and generalization.

Triangulation

With reporting and reading "ill-structured" and within an atmosphere of constructivism, it is not surprising to find tolerance for ambiguity and championing of pluralism. Still, most case researchers are concerned about the validity of their communication. Meanings do not transfer intact, but take on some of the conceptual uniqueness of the reader, but there is expectation that the meanings of situation, observation, reporting, and reading will have a certain correspondence. Joseph Maxwell (1992) has written of the need for thinking of validity separately for descriptions, interpretations, theories, generalizations, and evaluative judgments.

To reduce the likelihood of misinterpretation, we employ various procedures, including redundancy of data gathering and procedural challenges to explanations (Denzin, 1989; Goetz & LeCompte, 1984). For qualitative case work, these procedures generally are called *triangulation.* David Altheide and John Johnson discuss them in Volume 3 of this series, as do Michael Huberman and Matthew Miles. Triangulation has been generally considered a process of using multiple perceptions to clarify meaning, verifying the repeatability of an observation or interpretation. But, acknowledging that no observations or interpretations are perfectly repeatable, triangulation serves also to clarify meaning by identifying different ways the phenomenon is being seen (Flick, 1992).

Comparisons

Researchers report their cases as cases that will be compared with others. They differ as to how much they will take responsibility for making comparisons, setting up comparative cases for the reader, or acknowledging reference cases different for each reader. Most naturalistic, ethnographic, phenomenological researchers will concentrate on describing the present case in sufficient detail so that the reader can make good comparisons. Sometimes the researcher will point out comparisons that might be made. More quantitative case researchers will try to provide some comparisons, sometimes by presenting one or more reference cases, sometimes providing statistical norms for reference groups from which a hypothetical reference case can be imagined. Both the quantitative and qualitative approaches provide narrow grounds for strict comparison of cases—even though a tradition of grand comparison exists within comparative anthropology and related disciplines (Firestone, 1993; Ragin, 1987; Tobin, 1989).

I see comparison as an epistemological function competing with learning about and from the particular case. Comparison is a powerful conceptual mechanism, fixing attention upon the few attributes being compared and obscuring other knowledge about the case. Comparative description is the opposite of what Clifford Geertz (1973) calls "thick description." Thick description of the music program might include the staffing, recent program changes, the charisma of the choral director, the working relationship with the Catholic church organist, a critical vote of the school board, and the lack of student interest in taking up the clarinet. Such identify the vitality, trauma, and uniqueness of the case. Comparison might be made on any of these characteristics but tends to be made on more general variables traditionally noted in the organization of music programs, such as staffing, budget, and tour policy. Even with major attention to the bases for comparison, they will be few, with uniquenesses and complexities glossed over. Designed comparison substitutes (a) the *comparison* for (b) the *case* as the focus of the study.

Regardless of the type of case study—intrinsic, instrumental, or collective—readers learn little from researcher-provided cases as the basis for comparison. When there are multiple cases of intrinsic interest, then of course it can be useful to compare them. But usually, for the researcher, there is but one or none of intrinsic interest. Readers with intrinsic interest in the case learn more of it directly from the description, not ignoring comparisons with other cases but not concentrating on comparisons. Readers examining instrumental case studies are shown how the phenomenon exists within a particular case. Seldom is there interest in how a case without the phenomenon is different because there are too many ways to be different.[10] Generalizations from differences between any two cases are much less to be trusted than generalizations from one. Illustration as to how the phenomenon occurs in the circumstances of the particular exemplar can be valued and trustworthy knowledge.

Many are the ways of conceptualizing cases to maximize learning from the case. The case is expected to be something that functions, that operates; the study is the observation of operations. There is something to be described and interpreted. The conceptions of most naturalistic, holistic, ethnographic, phenomenological case studies emphasize objective description and personalistic interpretation, a respect and curiosity for culturally different perceptions of phenomena, and empathic representation of local settings—all blending (perhaps clumped) within a constructivist epistemology.

◆ Methods of Study

Perhaps the simplest rule for method in qualitative case work is this: Place the best brains available into the thick of what is going on. The brain work ostensibly is observational, but more basically, reflective. (I would prefer /to call it *interpretive* to emphasize the production of meanings/but ethnog- raphers have tried to make that term mean "to learn the special views of actors, the local meanings"; see Erickson, 1986.) In being ever reflective, the researcher is committed to pondering the impressions, deliberating recollections and records—but not necessarily following the conceptuali- zations of theorists, actors, or audiences (Carr & Kemmis, 1986). Local meanings are important; foreshadowed meanings are important; and readers' consequential meanings are important. The case researcher teases out meanings of these three kinds and, for whatever reason, works on one kind more than the others. In each case, the work is reflective.[11]

If we typify qualitative casework, we see data sometimes precoded but continuously interpreted, on first sighting and again and again. Records and tabulations are perused not only for classification and pattern recog- nition but for "crisscrossed" reflection (Spiro et al., 1987). Qualitative case study is characterized by the main researcher spending substantial time, on site, personally in contact with activities and operations of the case, reflecting, revising meanings of what is going on.

Naturalistic, ethnographic, phenomenological caseworkers seek to see what is natural in happenings, in settings, in expressions of value. What the researchers are unable to see for themselves is obtained by interviewing people who did see or by finding documents recording it. The contributions to this series by Paul Atkinson and Martyn Hammersley in this volume (Chapter 5) and in Volume 3 by Andrea Fontana and James Frey (Chapter 2), Patricia and Peter Adler (Chapter 3), Ian Hodder (Chapter 4), Douglas Harper (Chapter 5), and D. Jean Clandinin and F. Michael Connelly (Chapter 6) elaborate extensively on the methods of qualitative research. These pertain, of course, to qualitative case study.

Reviewing the literature, I have found case study methods written about largely by people who believe that the research should contribute to scientific generalization. The bulk of case study work, however, is done by people who have *intrinsic* interests in the cases. Their intrinsic case study designs draw the researcher toward understanding of what is important about that case within its own world, not so much the world of researchers and theorists, but developing its issues, contexts, and interpretations. In contrast, the/ methods of instrumental case study draw the researcher toward illustrating how the concerns of researchers and theorists are manifest in the case. Because the critical issues are more likely to be known in advance and following disciplinary expectations, such a design can take greater advantage of already-developed instruments and preconceived coding schemes.

In intrinsic case study, researchers do not avoid generalization—they cannot. Certainly they generalize to happenings of their cases at times yet to come and in other situations. They expect their readers to comprehend their interpretations but to arrive as well at their own. Thus the methods for casework actually used are to learn enough about the case to encapsulate complex meanings into a finite report but to describe the case in sufficient descriptive narrative so that readers can vicariously experience these happenings, and draw their own conclusions.

Case Selection

Perhaps the most unique aspect of case study in the social sciences and human services is the selection of cases to study. Intrinsic casework regularly begins with cases prespecified. The doctor, the social worker, the program evaluator receive their cases; they do not choose them. The cases are of prominent interest before formal study begins. Instrumental and collective casework regularly require cases to be chosen. Understanding the critical phenomena may depend on choosing the case well (Patton, 1990; Yin, 1989). Suppose we are trying to understand the behavior of people who take hostages, and decide to probe the phenomenon using a case study. Hostage taking does not happen often—in the whole world there are few cases to choose. Current options—let us imagine—boil down to a bank robber, an airline hijacker, an estranged father who kidnapped his own child, and a Shi'ite Muslim group. We want to generalize about hostage-taking behavior, yet realize that each of these cases, this sample of one, weakly *represents* the larger group of interest.

When one designs a study in the manner advocated by Miles and Huberman (1984; see also Chapter 7, Volume 3, this series), nothing is more important than making a proper selection of cases. It is a sampling problem. The cases will be selected to represent some population of cases. The phenomenon of interest observable in the case represents the phenomenon generally. For Miles and Huberman, Yin, and Malinowski, the main work is science, an enterprise to gain the best possible explanations of phenomena (von Wright, 1971). In the beginning, phenomena are given; the cases are opportunities to study the phenomena.

The phenomenon on the table is hostage taking. We want to improve our understanding of hostage taking, to fit it into what we know about criminology, conflict resolution, human relations—that is, various "abstract dimensions." [12] We recognize a large population of hypothetical cases, a small subpopulation of accessible cases. We want to generalize about hostage taking without special interest in any of those cases available for study. On representational grounds, the epistemological opportunity seems small, but we are optimistic that we can learn some important things from almost any case. We choose one or a small number of exemplars. Hostages usually are strangers who happen to be available. We might rule out studying a father who takes his own child as hostage. Such kidnappings may actually be more common than other kinds, but we rule out the father. We are more interested in hostage-taking accompanying a criminal act, hostage taking in order to gain refuge. The researcher examines various interests in the phenomenon, selecting a case of some typicality, but leaning toward those cases that seem to offer *opportunity to learn.* My choice would be to take that case from which we feel we can learn the most. [13] That may mean taking the one that we can spend the most time with. Potential for learning is a different and sometimes superior criterion to representativeness. Often it is better to learn a lot from an atypical case than a little from a magnificently typical case.

Another illustration: Suppose we are interested in the attractiveness of interactive (the visitor manipulates, gets feedback) displays in children's museums. We have resources to study four museums, to do a collective study of four cases. It is likely that we would set up a typology, perhaps of (a) museum types, namely, art, science, and history; (b) city types, namely, large and very large; and (c) program types, namely, exhibitory and participative; making a 12-cell matrix. Examples probably cannot be found for all 12 cells, but resources do not allow studying 12 anyway. With four to be studied, we are likely to start out thinking we should have one art, one history, and two science museums (because interactive displays are more common in science museums), two located in large and two in very large cities, and two each of the program types. But when we actually look at existing cases, the logistics, the potential reception, the resources, and additional characteristics of relevance, we move toward choosing four museums to study that offer variety (falling short of structured representation) across the attributes, the four that give us the best opportunities to learn about interactive displays. [14] Any best possible selection of four museums from a balanced design would not give us compelling representation of museums as a whole, and certainly not a statistical basis for generalizing about interactions between interactivity and site characteristics.

Several desirable types usually have to be omitted. Even for collective case studies, selection by sampling of attributes should not be the highest priority. Balance and variety are important; opportunity to learn is of primary importance.

Sampling Within the Case

The same process of selection will occur as part of intrinsic case study. Even though the case is decided in advance (usually), there are subsequent choices to make about persons, places, and events to observe. Here again, training and intuition tell us to seek a good sample. Suppose that we are studying a program for placing computers in the homes of fourth graders for scholastic purposes.[15] The cases—that is, the school sites—have already been selected. Although there is a certain coordination of activity, each participating researcher has one case study to develop. A principal issue has to do with impact on the family, because certain expectations of computer use accompany placement in the home. (The computer should be available for word processing, record keeping, and games by family members, but certain time should be set aside for fourth-grade homework.) At one site, 50 homes now have computers. The researcher can get certain information from every home, but observation in the home can occur in only a small number. Which homes should be selected? Just as in the collective case study, the researcher notes attributes of interest: gender of the fourth grader, siblings, family structure, home discipline, previous use of computers and other technology in the homes, and so on. The researcher discusses these characteristics with informants, gets recommendations, visits several homes, and gets attribute data. The choice is made,[16] assuring variety but not necessarily representativeness, without strong argument for typicality, again weighted by considerations of access and even by hospitality, for the time is short and perhaps too little can be learned from inhospitable parents. Here, too, the primary criterion is opportunity to learn.

Ethics

Ethical considerations for qualitative research are discussed by Maurice Punch in Chapter 5, Volume 1 of this series. Case studies often deal with matters of public interest but for which there is neither public nor scholarly "right to know." Funding, scholarly intent, or a passed preliminary oral does not constitute license to invade the privacy of others. The value of the best research is not likely to outweigh injury to a person exposed. Qualitative researchers are guests in the private spaces of the world. Their manners should be good and their code of ethics strict.

With much qualitative work, case study research shares an intense interest in personal views and circumstances. Those whose lives and expressions are portrayed risk exposure and embarrassment: loss of standing, employment, self-esteem. Issues of observation and reportage should be discussed in advance. Limits of accessibility should be suggested and agreements heeded. It is important but not sufficient for targeted persons to receive drafts of how they are presented, quoted, or interpreted, and for the researcher to listen well for cries of concern. It is imperative that great caution be exercised to minimize the risks. Rules for protection of human subjects should be heeded. The researcher should go beyond those rules, avoiding low-priority probing of sensitive issues, drawing upon others to oversee the protective system.

◆ Summary

As I have discussed above, the major conceptual responsibilities of the qualitative case researcher are as follows:

1. bounding the case, conceptualizing the object of study
2. selecting phenomena, themes, or issues—that is, the research questions—to emphasize
3. seeking patterns of data to develop the issues
4. triangulating key observations and bases for interpretation
5. selecting alternative interpretations to pursue
6. developing assertions or generalizations about the case

Except for the first of these, the steps are similar to those taken by other qualitative researchers. The more the researcher has intrinsic interest in the case, the more the focus of study will usually be on the case's uniqueness, particular context, issues, and story. Some major stylistic options for case researchers include the following:

1. how much to make the report a story
2. how much to compare with other cases
3. how much to formalize generalizations or leave that to readers

4. how much, in the report, to include description of the researcher as participant

5. whether or not and how much to anonymize

Case study is a part of scientific method, but its purpose is not limited to the advance of science. Whereas single or a few cases are poor representation of a population of cases and poor grounds for advancing grand generalization, a single case as negative example can establish limits to grand generalization. For example, we lose confidence in the generalization that a child of separated parents is better off placed with the mother when we find a single instance of resultant injury. Case studies are of value in refining theory and suggesting complexities for further investigation, as well as helping to establish the limits of generalizability.

Case study can also be a disciplined force in public policy setting and reflection on human experience. Vicarious experience is an important basis for refining action options and expectations. Formal epistemology needs further development, but somehow people draw from the description of an individual case implications for other cases, not always correctly, but with a confidence shared by people of dissimilar views.

The purpose of case study is not to represent the world, but to represent the case. Criteria for conducting the kind of research that leads to valid generalization need modification to fit the search for effective particularization. The utility of case research to practitioners and policy makers is in its extension of experience. The methods of qualitative case study are largely the methods of disciplining personal and particularized experience.

◆ Notes

1. Case study can be qualitative or quantitative or a combination of the two. In search of fundamental pursuits common to both qualitative and quantitative research, Robert Yin (1992) analyzed three thoroughly crafted research efforts: a quantitative investigation to resolve disputed authorship of the *Federalist Papers*, a qualitative study of Soviet intent at the time of the Cuban missile crisis, and his own studies of the recognizability of human faces. He found four common commitments: to bring expert knowledge to bear upon the phenomena studied, to round up all the relevant data, to examine rival interpretations, and to ponder and probe the degree to which the findings have implication elsewhere. These commitments are as important in case research as in any other kind of research.

2. The editors have reminded me of the ethnomethodological treatment of topic and method. Ethnomethodologists study methods as topics of inquiry, examining how certain

things get done, and so on (Garfinkel, 1967). Coming to understand a case usually requires extensive examining of how things get done, but the prime referent in case study is the case, not the methods by which cases operate.

3. Definition of the case is not independent of interpretive paradigm or methods of inquiry. Seen from different worldviews and in different situations, the "same" case is different. And however we originally define the case, the working definition changes as we study. And the definition of the case changes in different ways under different methods of study. The case of Theodore Roosevelt was not just differently portrayed but differently defined as biographer Edmund Morris (1979) presented him as "the Dude from New York," "the Dear Old Beloved Brother," "the Snake in the Grass," "the Rough Rider," "the Most Famous Man in America," and so on.

4. The history of case study, like the history of curiosity and common sense, is found throughout the library. Useful briefs are included in Bogdan and Biklen (1982), Delamont (1992), Feagin, Orum, and Sjoberg (1991), Stake (1978), and throughout this volume.

5. Collective case study is essentially what Robert Herriott and William Firestone (1983) call "multisite qualitative research." A number of German sociologists, such as Martin Kohli and Fritz Schutze, have used collective case studies with Strauss's grounded theory approach.

6. Historians and political scientists regularly examine a singular episode or relationship, such as Napoleon's siege of Moscow or the Cuban missile crisis. I choose not to call these case studies because the episode or relationship—however complex, impacting, and bounded—does not have its own purpose and self.

7. In 1922, Bronislaw Malinowski said, "One of the first conditions of acceptable Ethnographic work certainly is that it should deal with the totality of all social, cultural and psychological aspects of the community" (1922/1984, p. xvi). Good spirit there, although totalities defy the acuity of the eye and the longevity of the watch.

8. Generalization from collective case study has been discussed by Herriott and Firestone (1983), Lofland and Lofland (1984), Miles and Huberman (1984), and again by Firestone (1993).

9. Malinowski (1922/1984) claims we can distinguish between arriving with closed minds and arriving with an idea of what to look for: "Good training in theory, and acquaintance with its latest results, is not identical with being burdened with 'preconceived ideas.' If a man sets out on an expedition, determined to prove certain hypotheses, if he is incapable of changing his views constantly and casting them off ungrudgingly under the pressure of evidence, needless to say his work will be worthless. But the more problems he brings with him into the field, the more he is in the habit of moulding his theories according to facts, and of seeing facts in their bearing upon theory, the better he is equipped for the work. Preconceived ideas are pernicious in any scientific work, but *foreshadowed problems* are the main endowment of a scientific thinker, and these problems are first revealed to the observer by his theoretical studies" (p. 9).

10. Evaluation studies comparing the innovative program to a control case regularly fail to make the comparison credible. No matter how well studied, the control case too weakly represents cases already known to the reader. By comprehensively describing the program case, the researcher should help the reader draw naturalistic generalizations.

11. Ethnographic use of the term *reflective* sometimes limits attention to the need for self-challenging the researcher's etic issues, frame of reference, cultural bias (see Atkinson

& Hammersley, Chapter 5, this volume). That challenge is important, but, following Donald Schön (1983), I refer to a general frame of mind when I call qualitative casework reflective.

12. As indicated in a previous section, I call them issues or issue areas. Mary Kennedy (1979) calls them "relevant attributes." Spiro et al. (1987) call them "abstract dimensions." Malinowski (1922/1984) calls them "theories." In our research, these will be our working theories more than the grand theories of the disciplines.

13. My emphasis is on learning the most about both the individual case and the phenomenon, especially the latter if the special circumstances may yield unusual insight into an issue.

14. Firestone (1993) advises maximizing diversity and being "as like the population of interest as possible."

15. This in fact happened with the Buddy Project, a component of the Indiana public school reform effort in 1990-1993 (see Quinn & Quinn, 1992).

16. Patton (1990), Strauss and Corbin (1990), and Firestone (1993) have discussed successive selection of cases over time.

◆ References

Anderson, R. C. (1977). The notion of schema and the educational enterprise. In R. C. Anderson, R. J. Spiro, & W. E. Montague (Eds.), *Schooling and the acquisition of knowledge* (pp. 415-431). Hillsdale, NJ: Lawrence Erlbaum.

Ausubel, D. P., & Fitzgerald, D. (1961). Meaningful learning and retention: Interpersonal cognitive variables. *Review of Educational Research, 31,* 500-510.

Becker, H. S. (1958). Problems of interference and proof in participant observation. *American Sociological Review, 23,* 652-660.

Becker, H. S., Geer, B., Hughes, E. C., & Strauss, A. L. (1961). *Boys in white: Student culture in medical school.* Chicago: University of Chicago Press.

Bellah, R. N., Madsen, R., Sullivan, W. M., Swidler, A., & Tipton, S. M. (1985). *Habits of the heart: Individualism and commitment in American life.* Berkeley: University of California Press.

Blythe, R. (1969). *Akenfield.* London: Penguin. (Original work published 1955)

Bogdan, R. C., & Biklen, S. K. (1982). *Qualitative research for education: An introduction to theory and methods.* Boston: Allyn & Bacon.

Bohm, D. (1985). *Unfolding meaning: A weekend of dialogue with David Bohm.* New York: Routledge.

Campbell, D. T. (1975). Degrees of freedom and case study. *Comparative Political Studies, 8,* 178-193.

Carr, W. L., & Kemmis, S. (1986). *Becoming critical: Education, knowledge and action research.* London: Falmer.

Carter, K. (1993). The place of story in the study of teaching and teacher education. *Educational Researcher, 22,* 5-12.

Cazden, C. B. (1988). *Classroom discourse: The language of teaching and learning.* Portsmouth, NH: Heinemann Educational Books.

Coles, R. (1967). *Children of crisis.* Boston: Little, Brown.

Coles, R. (1989). *The call of stories: Teaching and the moral imagination.* Boston: Houghton Mifflin.

Delamont, S. (1992). *Fieldwork in educational settings: Methods, pitfalls and perspectives.* London: Falmer.

Denzin, N. K. (1989). *The research act* (3rd ed.). Englewood Cliffs, NJ: Prentice Hall.

Eisner, E. (Ed.). (1985). *Learning and teaching the ways of knowing* (84th yearbook of the National Society for the Study of Education). Chicago: University of Chicago Press.

Erickson, F. (1986). Qualitative methods in research on teaching. In M. C. Wittrock (Ed.), *Handbook of research on teaching* (3rd ed., pp. 119-161). New York: Macmillan.

Feagin, J. R., Orum, A. M., & Sjoberg, G. (1991). *A case for the case study.* Chapel Hill: University of North Carolina Press.

Firestone, W. A. (1993). Alternative arguments for generalizing from data as applied to qualitative research. *Educational Researcher, 22*(4), 16-23.

Flick, U. (1992). Triangulation revisited: Strategy of validation or alternative? *Journal for the Theory of Social Behaviour, 22,* 175-198.

Garfinkel, H. (1967). *Studies in ethnomethodology.* New York: Prentice Hall.

Geertz, C. (1973). Thick description: Toward an interpretive theory of culture. In C. Geertz, *The interpretation of cultures* (pp. 3-30). New York: Basic Books.

Geertz, C. (1983). *Local knowledge: Further essays in interpretive anthropology.* New York: Basic Books.

Glaser, B. G., & Strauss, A. L. (1967). *The discovery of grounded theory: Strategies for qualitative research.* Chicago: Aldine.

Goetz, J. P., & LeCompte, M. D. (1984). *Ethnography and qualitative design in educational research.* New York: Academic Press.

Goode, W. J., & Hatt, P. K. (1952). The case study. In W. J. Goode & P. K. Hatt, *Methods of social research* (pp. 330-340). New York: McGraw-Hill.

Hamilton, D. (1980). Some contrasting assumptions about case study research and survey analysis. In H. Simons (Ed.), *Towards a science of the singular* (pp. 76-92). Norwich: University of East Anglia, Centre for Applied Research in Education.

Herriott, R. E., & Firestone, W. A. (1983). Multisite qualitative policy research: Optimizing description and generalizability. *Educational Researcher, 12*(2), 14-19.

Huberman, A. M., & Miles, M. B. (1984). *Innovation up close: How school improvement works.* New York: Plenum.

Kemmis, S. (1980). The imagination of the case and the invention of the study. In H. Simons (Ed.), *Towards a science of the singular* (pp. 93-142). Norwich: University of East Anglia, Centre for Applied Research in Education.

Kennedy, M. M. (1979). Generalizing from single case studies. *Evaluation Quarterly, 3,* 661-678.

Kozol, J. (1991). *Savage inequalities.* New York: Harper.

Lewis, O. (1966). *La vida.* New York: Random House.

Lofland, J., & Lofland, L. H. (1984). *Analyzing social settings: A guide to qualitative observational research.* Belmont, CA: Wadsworth.

Lynd, R. S., & Lynd, H. M. (1929). *Middletown: A study in American culture.* New York: Harcourt, Brace.

MacDonald, B., Adelman, C., Kushner, S., & Walker, R. (1982). *Bread and dreams: A case study of bilingual schooling in the U.S.A.* Norwich: University of East Anglia, Centre for Applied Research in Education.

Malinowski, B. (1984). *Argonauts of the western Pacific.* Prospect Heights, IL: Waveland. (Original work published 1922)

Maxwell, J. A. (1992). Understanding and validity in qualitative research. *Harvard Educational Review, 63,* 279-300.

Miles, M. B., & Huberman, A. M. (1984). *Qualitative data analysis: A sourcebook of new methods.* Beverly Hills, CA: Sage.

Morris, E. (1979). *The rise of Theodore Roosevelt.* New York: Coward, McCann & Geognegan.

Parlett, M., & Hamilton, D. (1976). Evaluation as illumination: A new approach to the study of innovative programmes. In G. V. Glass (Ed.), *Evaluation studies review annual* (Vol. 1, pp. 141-157). Beverly Hills, CA: Sage.

Patton, M. Q. (1990). *Qualitative evaluation and research methods* (2nd ed.). Newbury Park, CA: Sage.

Peshkin, A. (1986). *God's choice.* Chicago: University of Chicago Press.

Polanyi, M. (1962). *Personal knowledge: Towards a post-critical philosophy.* Chicago: University of Chicago Press.

Quinn, W., & Quinn, N. (1992). *Buddy evaluation.* Oakbrook, IL: North Central Regional Educational Laboratory.

Ragin, C. C. (1987). *The comparative method.* Berkeley: University of California Press.

Rumelhart, D. E., & Ortony, A. (1977). The representation of knowledge in memory. In R. C. Anderson, R. J. Spiro, & W. E. Montague (Eds.), *Schooling and the acquisition of knowledge* (pp. 99-135). Hillsdale, NJ: Lawrence Erlbaum.

Schön, D. (1983). *The reflective practitioner: How professionals think in action.* New York: Basic Books.

Sheehan, N. (1988). *A bright and shining lie: John Vann and America in Vietnam.* New York: Random House.

Simons, H. (Ed.). (1980). *Towards a science of the singular.* Norwich: University of East Anglia, Centre for Applied Research in Education.

Smith, L. M. (1978). An evolving logic of participant observation, educational ethnography and other case studies. In L. Shuman (Ed.), *Review of research in education* (Vol. 6, pp. 316-377). Itasca, IL: Peacock.

Spiro, R. J., Vispoel, W. P., Schmitz, J. G., Samarapungavan, A., & Boerger, A. E. (1987). Knowledge acquisition for application: Cognitive flexibility and transfer in complex content domains. In B. C. Britton (Ed.), *Executive control processes* (pp. 177-199). Hillsdale, NJ: Lawrence Erlbaum.

Stake, R. E. (1978). The case study method of social inquiry. *Educational Researcher, 7*(2), 5-8.

Stake, R. E. (1988). Case study methods in educational research: Seeking sweet water. In R. M. Jaeger (Ed.), *Complementary methods for research in education* (pp. 253-278). Washington, DC: American Educational Research Association.

Stake, R. E., & Trumbull, D. J. (1982). Naturalistic generalizations. *Review Journal of Philosophy and Social Science, 7,* 1-12.

Stenhouse, L. (1984). Library access, library use and user education in academic sixth forms: An autobiographical account. In R. G. Burgess (Ed.), *The research process in educational settings: Ten case studies* (pp. 211-234). London: Falmer.

Stouffer, S. A. (1941). Notes on the case-study and the unique case. *Sociometry, 4,* 349-357.

Strauss, A. L., & Corbin, J. (1990). *Basics of qualitative research: Grounded theory procedures and techniques.* Newbury Park, CA: Sage.

Tobin, J. (1989). *Preschool in three cultures.* New Haven, CT: Yale University Press.

Van Maanen, J. (1988). *Tales of the field: On writing ethnography.* Chicago: University of Chicago Press.

von Wright, G. H. (1971). *Explanation and understanding.* London: Routledge & Kegan Paul.

Yin, R. K. (1984). *Case study research: Design and methods.* Beverly Hills, CA: Sage.

Yin, R. K. (1989). *Case study research: Design and methods* (2nd ed.). Newbury Park, CA: Sage.

Yin, R. K. (1992, November). *Evaluation: A singular craft.* Paper presented at the annual meeting of the American Evaluation Association, Seattle.

5

Ethnography and Participant Observation

Paul Atkinson & Martyn Hammersley

◆ Ethnographic methods, relying substantially or partly on "participant observation," have a long if somewhat checkered career in the social sciences. They have been employed, in various guises, by scholars identified with a variety of disciplines. In this chapter we shall not attempt a comprehensive review of the historical and contemporary methodological literature. Rather, we shall focus on several complementary themes that relate to some of the sources and dimensions of diversity and difference in ethnographic research, the recurrent tensions within the broad ethnographic tradition, and contemporary responses to these.

Definition of the term *ethnography* has been subject to controversy. For some it refers to a philosophical paradigm to which one makes a total commitment, for others it designates a method that one uses as and when appropriate. And, of course, there are positions between these extremes. In practical terms, *ethnography* usually refers to forms of social research having a substantial number of the following features:

- ◆ a strong emphasis on exploring the nature of particular social phenomena, rather than setting out to test hypotheses about them

- ◆ a tendency to work primarily with "unstructured" data, that is, data that have not been coded at the point of data collection in terms of a closed set of analytic categories

- investigation of a small number of cases, perhaps just one case, in detail
- analysis of data that involves explicit interpretation of the meanings and functions of human actions, the product of which mainly takes the form of verbal descriptions and explanations, with quantification and statistical analysis playing a subordinate role at most

The definition of *participant observation* has been less controversial, but its meaning is no easier to pin down. A distinction is sometimes drawn between participant and nonparticipant observation, the former referring to observation carried out when the researcher is playing an established participant role in the scene studied. However, although it is important to recognize the variation to be found in the roles adopted by observers, this simple dichotomy is not very useful, not least because it seems to imply that the nonparticipant observer plays no recognized role at all. This can be the case, but it need not be. More subtle is the widely used fourfold typology: complete observer, observer as participant, participant as observer, and complete participant (Gold, 1958; Junker, 1960). Even this tends to run together several dimensions of variation, such as the following:

- whether the researcher is known to be a researcher by all those being studied, or only by some, or by none
- how much, and what, is known about the research by whom
- what sorts of activities are and are not engaged in by the researcher in the field, and how this locates her or him in relation to the various conceptions of category and group membership used by participants
- what the orientation of the researcher is; how completely he or she consciously adopts the orientation of insider or outsider[1]

Moreover, it has been argued that in a sense *all* social research is a form of participant observation, because we cannot study the social world without being part of it (Hammersley & Atkinson, 1983). From this point of view participant observation is not a particular research technique but a mode of being-in-the-world characteristic of researchers.

Both ethnography and participant observation have been claimed to represent a uniquely humanistic, interpretive approach, as opposed to supposedly "scientific" and "positivist" positions. At the same time, within the ethnographic tradition there are authors espousing a "scientific" stance, as opposed to those who explicitly reject this in favor of an engaged advocacy and a critical stance. The philosophical, ethical, and methodological strands intertwine. They meet and coalesce to form particular "schools" or subtypes of ethnography; they engage with different theoretical movements and fashions (structural functionalism, symbolic interactionism, cultural and cognitive anthropology, feminism, Marxism, ethnomethodology, critical theory, cultural studies, postmodernism, and so on). There is never an orthodoxy. Rather, there is a constant process of oppositions, of successive heterodoxies and heresies. Just as the ethnographer in the field often cultivates the position of the "marginal native" (Freilich, 1970), so ethnographers collectively seek to distance themselves repeatedly from versions of "mainstream" orthodoxy. These are enshrined in the creation myths of ethnography itself. They are carried through into contemporary debates and differences over methodology. The particular focus for methodological or epistemological controversy changes, of course. Earlier debates concerned the problems of data collection, inference, and topic. In the later sections of this chapter we examine more recent controversies, including those concerning the textual character of ethnography and the problems of representation and authority associated with that. The fashionable preoccupations of poststructuralism and postmodernism have both stimulated interest in these new issues and provided a new slant on older themes. They have given a new critical edge to the recurrent methodological issues: the tensions between disinterested observation and political advocacy, between the "scientific" and the "humane," between the "objective" and the "aesthetic." Ethnography has, perhaps, never been so popular within the social sciences. At the same time, its rationales have never been more subject to critical scrutiny and revision.

◆ A Historical Sketch

The beginnings of modern forms of ethnographic fieldwork are usually identified with the shift by social and cultural anthropologists in the late nineteenth and early twentieth centuries toward collecting data firsthand. Often regarded as of most significance here is Malinowski's (1922) fieldwork in the Trobriand Islands, the distinctiveness of which lay in his concern to document the everyday social life of the islanders (Burgess, 1982, pp. 2-4; Kaberry, 1957; Richards, 1939; Young, 1979). However, there are no simple and uncontroversial beginnings in history, and some commentators have taken a longer view, tracing elements of the ethnographic orientation back to eighteenth- and nineteenth-century German philosophy (Hammersley, 1989), to the Renaissance (Rowe, 1965), and even to the writings of the ancients, for example, Herodotus (Wax, 1971).

Although in its particular style and substance ethnography is a twentieth-century phenomenon, its earlier history can be illuminating. It has certainly been shaped by its association with Western interest in the character of non-Western societies and the various motives underlying that interest (Asad, 1973; Clifford, 1988; Marcus & Fischer, 1986). Equally, however, it reflects the influence of historicism, an orientation stemming in large part from the Renaissance, but developed theoretically in the nineteenth century as hermeneutics, the study of the principles of understanding historical texts. At the heart of this was a recognition that people of the past were different in culture from those of today—indeed, that those who lived in different periods in Western history inhabited different cultural worlds. This is not just a matter of the *recognition* of differences but also the judgment that these differences cannot be properly understood by seeing them in terms of deplorable deviation from the norms of the observer's here and now or as signs of cultural backwardness. And it was not long before this recognition of cultural differences was also applied by Westerners to societies contemporaneous with their own, especially to the newly discovered cultures of South America and the East. Most important of all, historicism posed the methodological problem of whether and how other cultures could be understood, a problem that still lies at the heart of modern ethnography.

Perhaps the most distinctive feature of the twentieth century in this respect is the increasing recognition that the problem of understanding is not restricted to the study of past times and other societies—it applies to the study of one's own social surroundings too. The application of ethnographic method by Western anthropologists and sociologists to the investigation of their own societies has been a central feature of twentieth-century social science (Cole, 1977). Furthermore, this is not just a matter of the discovery of pockets of "traditional" culture on the peripheries of these societies (for example, see Arensberg & Kimball, 1940), it also involves the recognition that diverse cultures are to be found in their metropolitan centers (e.g., Hannerz, 1969; Suttles, 1968; Whyte, 1955, 1981).[2]

Running alongside and influencing these developments was the institutionalization of the social sciences in Western universities, a process displaying recurrent crises, most of which centered on the possibility, character, and desirability of a science of social life. In the nineteenth century the conflict was drawn between those attempting to apply an empiricist conception of natural science method to the study of human behavior and those who saw a different model of scientific scholarship as appropriate to the humanities and social sciences. For those influenced by hermeneutics, social research was distinct from physical science because in seeking to understand human actions and institutions we could draw on our own experience and cultural knowledge, and through that reach understanding based on what we share with other human beings, despite cultural differences. Others placed emphasis on the difference between the concern of the natural sciences with the discovery of universal laws (in other words, a nomothetic orientation) and the task of the human sciences as understanding particular phenomena in their sociohistorical contexts (an idiographic orientation) (for discussion of these positions, see, e.g., Frisby, 1976; Hammersley, 1989; von Wright, 1971).

There has been a tendency for ethnographers and others looking back on this history to see it as the story of a conflict between two sides: the positivist paradigm on the one hand against the interpretive or hermeneutic paradigm on the other, with ethnography assumed to belong to the latter (Filstead, 1970; J. K. Smith, 1989; Smith & Heshusius, 1986). This is a misleading picture, however. What we find when we look more closely is a diversity of ideas about the character of human social life and how it is to be understood, as well as about the nature of method in natural science and its relevance to the study of human behavior. To illustrate this point we shall look briefly at two of the key phases in the development of ethnography in the twentieth century: the work of the founders of modern anthropology and that of the Chicago school of sociology.

It makes little difference for our purposes here whom one takes as the key figure in the founding of modern anthropology. All three of the main candidates—Boas, Malinowski, and Radcliffe-Brown—were committed to anthropology as a science, albeit perhaps as a special sort of science. And ethnography was central to their idea of what was scientific about anthropological work: It involved the collection of information firsthand by the anthropologist and the description of the social and cultural characteristics of existing "primitive" societies—as against attempts to infer their history or to judge them in terms of evolutionary level. In other words, the prime motivation on the part of all three founders was the rejection of speculation in favor of empirical investigation, a theme that has always been a central characteristic of empiricism, though not exclusive to it. Furthermore, they all took the natural sciences as an important model for anthropology,

114

though not one to be followed slavishly. Radcliffe-Brown's (1948) aim of creating a "natural science of society" was not discrepant, in broad terms, with the orientations of Malinowski or Boas (see also Harris, 1969; Leach, 1957). At the same time, all three believed that social and cultural phenomena were different in character from physical phenomena and had to be understood in terms of their distinctive nature, an idea that led some of their followers (notably those of Boas) subsequently to deny the appropriateness of the scientific model (for example, see Radin, 1931/1965; see also the discussion in Harris, 1969). But that model, in some form, was never completely abandoned by the bulk of anthropologists, though it probably is under more pressure today than ever before. The tension within ethnography, between science and the humanities, was present from the start; and, as we shall see, it has never been resolved (Redfield, 1962).

Although Chicago sociology of the 1920s and 1930s does not seem to have been strongly influenced by anthropology, its orientation was similar in many respects. Most striking of all, to us today, there was little questioning of the relevance of natural science as a methodological model for social research. Even the debate between advocates of case study and statistical method that raged in the 1920s and 1930s was framed in terms of conflicting interpretations of science rather than acceptance and rejection of it (Bulmer, 1984; Hammersley, 1989; Harvey, 1987). The most influential figure at Chicago was of course Robert Park, who wedded a newspaper reporter's concern with the concrete and unique to a neo-Kantian philosophical justification for such a focus in terms of the idiographic character of the cultural sciences. And yet he, like William I. Thomas before him, blended this with a nomothetic interest in the discovery of sociocultural laws (Park & Burgess, 1921, 1969). An important influence on this attempt by many in the Chicago school to fuse scientific and hermeneutic influences was pragmatist philosophy, especially the writings of William James, John Dewey, and George Herbert Mead. All these philosophers sought to combine a scientific orientation to the study of human behavior with the heritage of German idealism and historicism. Indeed, they seem to have regarded a scientific reading of Hegel as providing a means of overcoming divisions such as that between the sciences and the humanities. Once again, however, this attempted synthesis must be judged to have been by no means entirely successful.[3]

The subsequent history of ethnography, both in anthropology and sociology, reflects the continuing tension between attraction to and rejection of the model of the natural sciences; yet with few abandoning one pole wholeheartedly for the other. Furthermore, in recent years ethnography has witnessed great diversification, with somewhat different approaches being adopted in different areas, guided by different concerns (from traditional sociocultural description, through applied work designed to inform policy makers, to a commitment to advocacy and furthering political emancipation). And these different goals are variously associated with different forms of ethnographic practice: traditional, long-term, in-depth investigation sometimes being abandoned for condensed field-work or primary reliance on unstructured interviews, or for consultancy work or participation in political struggles.

In the next section we shall look in more detail at the major debates to which the ambivalent history and diverse character of modern ethnography have led: the question of whether ethnography is or can be scientific; questions about the proper relationship between ethnographic research and social and political practice; and, finally, arguments surrounding the textual strategies used by ethnographers to represent the lives of others, and the methodological, aesthetic, ethical, and political issues raised by these. These various themes are, of course, frequently closely interrelated.

◆ Ethnography: Science or Not?

As we noted in the previous section, the question of whether there can be a science of social life has preoccupied social scientists for more than a century, and it has been an especially important element in much methodo-logical thinking about ethnography. However, this question is not one that can usefully be answered simply in the affirmative or negative. There is a wider range of possible answers. There are three dimensions structuring this range of possibilities:

- ◆ There can be differences in views about which of the natural sciences is to be taken as paradigmatic for scientific method.
- ◆ There can be various interpretations even of any method held to be charac-teristic of particular sciences at particular times.
- ◆ There can be disagreements about what aspects of natural scientific method should and should not be applied to social research.

Much thinking about ethnographic methodology in recent years has been based on a rejection of "positivism," broadly conceived as the view that social research should adopt scientific method, that this method is exemplified in the work of modern physicists, and that it consists of the rigorous testing of hypotheses by means of data that take the form of quantitative measurements. Quantitative sociological research is often seen as exemplifying this positivist viewpoint, and it has been criticized by ethnographers for failing to capture the true nature of human social behavior. This arises because it relies on the study of artificial settings (in the case of experiments) and/or on what people say rather than what they do (in the case of survey research); because it seeks to reduce meanings to what is "observable"; and because it treats social phenomena as more clearly defined and static than they are, and as mechanical products of social and psychological factors. This is not to say that quantitative methods are rejected in toto by ethnographers; indeed, structured forms of data collection and quantitative data analysis are frequently employed to some degree or other in ethnographic work. What is rejected is the idea that these methods are the only legitimate, or even the most important, ones. This implies a rejection not so much of quantitative method or even of natural science as a model, but rather of positivism.[4]

However, in recent years a more radical attitude has appeared that *does* seem often to involve rejection of both quantitative method and the scientific model. Whereas at one time ethnographers questioned the frequently assumed relationship between science and quantification, this is now less common; often, the two are rejected together (see, e.g., Lincoln & Guba, 1985; J. K. Smith, 1989). In part, this reflects a general cultural disillusionment with natural science. It is now widely seen as the source of highly destructive weaponry and of substantial planetary pollution, for example. Indeed, some regard it as an oppressive force that dominates the modern world. Elements of this view are to be found in the writings of critical theorists (see Held, 1981; Wellmer, 1969/1974) and the work of feminists, where science is sometimes associated with male aggression and patriarchy (see, for instance, Harding, 1986). Both of these approaches have become influential among ethnographers and have led many to move away from the model of science toward exploring alternatives that reopen links with the humanities (see, e.g., Eisner, 1985, 1988, 1991).

In part, what is involved here is a questioning of the objectivity of social research, ethnographic research included. For instance, it is argued by feminists that the findings of much social research, including ethnographic work, reflect the masculinist assumptions of researchers. It is not just that they have tended to neglect and occasionally to disparage the activities and experiences of women, but that the whole perspective on the world that they provide is limited by their male point of view. This is not dissimilar in character to earlier Marxist criticisms of the ideological character of bourgeois social science, and analogous criticisms have long been found among advocates of black sociology (for a discussion that draws these parallels, see Hammersley, 1992a).

Increasingly, however, this challenge to the objectivity of ethnographic (and other) research has been developed into a more fundamental questioning of the very possibility of social scientific knowledge. It is pointed out that the accounts produced by researchers are constructions, and as such they reflect the presuppositions and sociohistorical circumstances of their production. This is held to contradict the aspiration of social science (including much ethnography) to produce knowledge that is universally valid, in other words, that captures the *nature* of the social world. In the past, ethnographers very often relied precisely on arguments about the greater capacity of their approach to represent the nature of social reality accurately (see, e.g., Blumer, 1969). Such arguments are rarer these days, under the influence of various forms of antirealism, whether constructivism (Guba, 1990), philosophical hermeneutics (J. K. Smith, 1989), or post-structuralism (Clough, 1992; Denzin, 1990; Lather, 1991).

An interesting illustration of the last of these influences is to be found in commentaries by Denzin and Richardson on a recent dispute about the accuracy of Whyte's (1955) classic ethnographic study of Boston's North End. Whyte's pioneering study was concerned with documenting various aspects of the lives of people in this community, especially the "Corner Boys." The accuracy of Whyte's account is questioned by Boelen (1992) on the basis of some recent interviews, though the original account is defended by a surviving member of the Corner Boys (Orlandella, 1992). Moving off at a tangent, Denzin (1992) and Richardson (1992) effectively dismiss this dispute on the grounds that all accounts are constructions and that the whole issue of which account more accurately represents reality is meaningless.

Also associated with this radical critique has been a tendency to direct some of the criticisms that have long been applied to quantitative research at traditional ethnography itself. It too is now seen by some as reifying social phenomena, as claiming illegitimate expertise over the people studied, as being based on relationships of hierarchy, control, and so on. Indeed, it has been argued that it represents a subtler form of control than quantitative research because it is able to get closer to the people studied, to discover the details of their behavior and the innards of their experience (Finch, 1986; Stacey, 1988).

The epistemological challenge to the credentials of ethnography that is at the root of these criticisms is undoubtedly fruitful in many respects. Some of the arguments used to promote ethnography against quantitative method and to justify its features are open to serious question. To take just one example, the whole notion of what counts as a theory in ethnography is ill defined, and the concept of "theoretical description" that has guided much ethnographic research in sociology is of doubtful value (Hammersley, 1992b, chap. 1). At the same time, there is a tendency for this questioning to lead to skepticism and relativism. It is not always clear how thoroughgoing this relativism and skepticism is. Often it seems to be applied selectively, but without much indication of what principles might underlie the selectivity (Woolgar & Pawluch, 1985, refer to this in another context as "ontological gerrymandering"). Where the attempt is made to embrace skepticism and relativism wholeheartedly, on the other hand, the end point seems likely to be a debilitating nihilism. What is required, it seems to us, is a careful reassessment of the methodological and philosophical arguments surrounding the concept of science and of the relationship of ethnography to this. Above all, we must not be misled into assuming that we are faced merely with a choice between dogmatism and relativism, between a single oppressive conception of science and some uniquely liberating alternative.

◆ Theory and Practice

Another area of disagreement and debate that has become of great salience in recent years is the question of the relationship between ethnographic research and social and political practice. In the past, and probably still today, most ethnography has been directed toward contributing to disciplinary knowledge rather than toward solving practical problems. Although such work may ultimately contribute knowledge of wide public relevance, this contribution has not usually been very immediate or specific. Furthermore, the knowledge produced has often been presented as valuable for its own sake as much as for any instrumental value it has.

Although ethnographers have usually wished to address those beyond the boundaries of their disciplinary communities, very often this has not involved any marked deviation from the sort of research, or even the sort of written presentation, appropriate to academic work. The relationship between research and practice assumed here is what has been called the enlightenment model (Bulmer, 1982; Janowitz, 1971; for a more elaborate conception of the various possible roles of the researcher, see Silverman, 1985, 1989). However, not all ethnographic research has operated on this model. For a long time, the applied anthropology movement in the United States has exemplified a different stance, being specifically concerned with carrying out research that is designed to address and contribute directly to the solution of practical problems. This is a tradition that has flourished and transformed itself in recent years, coming to be applied within mainstream U.S. society, not just outside it (Eddy & Partridge, 1978; van Willigen, 1986). In addition, its practical and political orientation has spread more widely, with the disciplinary model coming under increasing criticism.

Even those anthropologists and sociologists primarily concerned with contributing to disciplinary knowledge have sometimes felt it necessary to engage in advocacy on the part of the people they have studied. Furthermore, there have been calls for this to be developed further—indeed, to be integrated into the research process (Paine, 1985). It is suggested that by its very nature anthropology (and the point can be extended without distortion to ethnographic work in general) involves a "representation" of others even when it does not explicitly claim to speak for or on behalf of them. And it is argued that there are ethical and political responsibilities arising from this fact.

However, neither this argument nor the sort of practice recommended on the basis of it is straightforward. Drawing on their own experience, Hastrup and Elsass (1990) point out that the context in which any advocacy is to take place is a complex one: It is not composed simply of an oppressed and an oppressor group but of a diversity of individuals and groups motivated by various ideals and interests, and pursuing various political strategies. Furthermore, the group to be "represented" is not always internally homogeneous and is rarely democratically organized. Also, there is often genuine uncertainty about what is and is not in the interests of the group and of members of it. In particular, there is the danger of adopting ethnographic myths, such as that Indian groups represent "islands of culture" that must be defended against the apparently cultureless settlers, or that informants speak "cultural truths."

In recent years there has also been a growing application of ethnographic methods, by sociologists, anthropologists, and others, in applied fields such as education, health, and social policy. This reflects, in part, a decline of confidence in quantitative research on the part of funders and a willingness on the part of some of them to finance qualitative research. In Britain, ironically, this trend has been more obvious in the field of commercial market research than in government-funded work, though there are signs of change (Walker, 1985). This change is also evident in the United States, where, for example, federally funded evaluations in education have increasingly involved ethnographic components (see Fetterman, 1988; Fetterman & Pitman, 1986; Rist, 1981). At the same time, there has been some debate about whether, and in what senses, this applied research is ethnographic. Some anthropologists, in particular, see it as abandoning key elements of what they regard as ethnography (Wolcott, 1980). And it is true that in several respects this trend has resulted in significant modification of ethnographic practice. An interesting example is the condensed fieldwork advocated and practiced by some researchers in the field of educational evaluation (see, e.g., Walker, 1978; for an assessment, see Atkinson & Delamont, 1985).

Sometimes associated with the moves toward more applied forms of ethnographic work have been calls for collaborative research. In part, these have arisen out of concern about the lack of impact that ethnographic (and other) research has had on social and political practice. Some believe that its impact would be greater if practitioners were themselves involved in the research process, both because that involvement would be likely to change the research and make it more practically relevant and because they would be more motivated to draw on it as a result of being involved. There have been other important influences pushing in the direction of collaborative research, however, notably Marxist critical theory and feminism. These demand that research contribute to the political struggles of oppressed groups, not merely the working class, but also women, ethnic minorities, the disabled, and so on. And the commitment to collaboration stems from a reconceptualization of the central political goal of the Left as the extension of democracy, and the belief that those committed to that goal must exemplify their commitment to it in the practice of research. From this point of view, traditional ethnographic work has been criticized for embodying a hierarchical and therefore undemocratic relationship between researcher and researched, because it is the former who makes the decisions about what to study and how to study it, and whose voice is represented in the written ethnography (see, for example, Gitlin, Siegel, & Boru, 1989).

There is little doubt of the need for ethnographers to rethink the relationship between their work and social and political practice. However, it would be a mistake in our view to seek to restructure ethnography on the basis of a single conception of that relationship. Above all, it is of considerable importance that we do not lose sight of what has hitherto been the goal of ethnographic research, namely, the production of knowledge. We should not replace this with the pursuit of practical goals that, although sometimes valuable in themselves, are no *more* worthy in general terms of our time and effort than the pursuit of knowledge. This is especially so when these goals are of a kind that we may be much less able to achieve. It is true that conventional research never changes the world at a stroke, and that often it may not have much effect even over the long term. But that does not mean that it is of no value. It is also worth remembering that changing the world can be for the worse as well as for the better. Utopian attempts to do politics by means of research are of no service to anyone.

◆ Rhetoric and Representation

In recent years the literature on ethnography and participant observation has been enriched by a growing corpus of reflections on the rhetoric of ethnographic accounts. Attention has been given, for example, to the aesthetics and ethics of ethnographic texts, including the relationship between authority and authorship, and indeed to the connections among rhetoric, representation, and logic generally. This "rhetorical turn" among ethnographers is part of a much broader movement of scholarship toward an interest in the rhetoric of inquiry that has been manifested in many of the human and social disciplines. It has engaged with various important (if often diffuse) theoretical and methodological tendencies—not least feminism, poststructuralism, and postmodernism. The most significant contributions, and the earliest, from social scientists came from cultural and social anthropologists. More recently, attention has been paid to this issue by sociologists. Although the respective disciplines have slightly different emphases, the broad themes have been similar: the conventionality of ethnographic texts, the representation of "Self" and "Other" in such texts, the character of ethnographies as a textual genre, the nature of ethnographic argumentation and the rhetoric of evidence.

122

The starting point for this "rediscovery of rhetoric" has been the acknowledgment that there is no perfectly transparent or neutral way to represent the natural or social world. For example, however "impersonal" and formulaic the work of the natural scientist, it stands in no "natural" relationship to the phenomena and events it describes. On the contrary, the textual products of natural science are highly conventional. Their apparent guarantee of authenticity and credibility is dependent on readers' adopting shared strategies of reading and interpretation.

In just the same way, the human sciences draw on common sets of conventional devices to construct and convey their characteristic portrayals of social scenes, actors, and cultural meanings. Thus White's (1973) extensive writing on the writing of historical texts has exerted an influence far beyond historiography. Likewise, McCloskey's (1985) wry and erudite commentaries on the rhetoric of economics have provided important benchmarks and exemplars. Among social and cultural anthropologists, the standard ethnography or monograph was—to a considerable extent—a taken-for-granted format. As Boon (1983) points out, however, the typical framework of anthropological monographs imposed a common pattern on, rather than revealing one in, the vast array of human societies they described. He argues that the "classic" form of the anthropological monograph was a direct, if implicit, embodiment of the domain assumptions of functionalist anthropology.

The watershed of critical awareness of ethnographic textuality was the highly influential collection of papers edited by Clifford and Marcus (1986), *Writing Culture.* The works brought together in that collection all emphasize, in various ways, the nature of the textual imposition that anthropology exerts over its subject matter. They emphasize the complex interplay of literary and rhetorical, historical, and ideological influences on the production and reception of anthropological ethnographies.

Clifford and Marcus's volume is partly, but not perfectly, parallel to that of Geertz (1973), who began to assert that anthropological writings could be regarded as "fiction," in the sense that they are made: They are crafted by their authors and shaped by "literary" conventions and devices. Geertz (1988) went on later to document the distinctive literary styles used by a number of founding figures, British and American. In the same way, several contributors to the Clifford and Marcus volume sought to illuminate the "literary" antecedents and parallels for ethnographic writing. Pratt (1986, 1991), for instance, developed there—and elsewhere—the parallels and self-conscious contrasts between anthropological ethnography and travel writing.

In a similar vein, an early contribution from Atkinson (1982) explored some of the literary origins and parallels for sociological ethnography associated with the Chicago school. In common with many of the anthropological commentaries appearing at that time, Atkinson's work was influenced by aspects of contemporary literary criticism. Structuralist and poststructuralist theory emphasized that the "realism" of realist fictional writing drew on particular conventions of reading and writing. In the same way, it was possible to explore how the authenticity of "factual" accounts, such as ethnographies, was generated through equally (and very similar) conventional means.

Some aspects of the "literary" antecedents and convergences have been sketched in the literature. For anthropology, commentators have drawn attention to literary as well as biographical affinities between the work of Malinowski and Conrad (Clifford, 1988), between surrealism and French ethnography (Clifford, 1988), and in the poetic writing of Benedict and Sapir (Brady, 1991; Prattis, 1985). To a rather lesser extent, sociological traditions have been explored from a similarly literary perspective. Atkinson (1982) makes a preliminary identification of Chicago school urban ethnographies with the naturalistic and realistic novels of American literature. But if the respective intellectual communities wish to pursue these schemes, there is much yet to do. We still have rather few detailed examinations of the general cultural and—in the widest sense—"literary" contexts within which particular ethnographic traditions have been formed. In Britain, for example, the sociological foundations laid by urban investigators such as Booth and Rowntree have major affinities with several literary models. The investigative journalism of more popular writers, and the fictional products of authors such as Dickens, provide rich mixtures of realism, melodrama, and the grotesque that find their parallels in the tone, style, and sensibilities of the sociological tradition. Likewise, the long and rich tradition of "community" studies on both sides of the Atlantic needs careful reading against the kind of literary analyses of the contrast between the urban and the rural furnished by, say, Raymond Williams (1973).

The point of such "literary" analysis is not merely to create "interesting" parallels and contrasts, nor yet to attempt to trace the literary antecedents of particular anthropological or sociological texts. It is, rather, to remove the false distinction between "science" and "rhetoric." The essential dialectic between the aesthetic and humanist, on the one hand, and the logical and scientific, on the other, is thus reaffirmed. A recognition of the conventional quality and literary antecedents of the ethnographic text in turn raises questions about the distinctive characteristics of ethnography as a genre of textual product. It is not enough, in the eyes of many contemporary commentators, simply to note that our texts are (in Geertz's sense) fiction. It is important to map the conventions that are deployed in constructing particular anthropological and sociological styles. It is thus possible to explore relationships among schools of thought, traditions, and individual authorship with repertoires of textual device through which scholarly accounts are constructed.

This identification of style and genre has taken various turns. A group of British anthropologists (Fardon, 1990) has explored how different textual styles have accorded with different regional biases and preoccupations. (They in turn criticize several of the "textual" critics for treating anthropological ethnography as a more or less undifferentiated textual type.) Likewise, Van Maanen's (1988) highly influential contribution explores the characteristics of various modes of ethnographic writing. Most notably, perhaps, he contrasts the styles of "realist" and "confessional" accounts by sociologists and anthropologists, the former style typically being central, the latter traditionally being more marginal, perhaps relegated to a methodological appendix. This contrast, which is built into a great deal of ethnographic output, is itself a textually based convention whereby the tension between the "personal" and the "impersonal" has been managed by successive authors and schools of ethnography.

In the "classic" ethnographies of urban sociology and anthropology, the conventions of textual production were not always apparent. The reason is simple: Their authors and readers drew on textual paradigms and devices that were entirely familiar and "natural." Thus the highly "readable" ethnographies, such as Whyte's *Street Corner Society* (1955), conveyed vivid accounts of social settings by virtue of their "literary" qualities. As Gusfield (1990), among others, has pointed out in an analysis of Liebow's *Tally's Corner* (1967), such a realist ethnography achieves its effects through its narrative structures and its rhetorical and stylistic devices. Similarly, drawing explicitly on models from literary criticism, as well as on the work of previous commentators (e.g., Brown, 1977; Edmondson, 1984), Atkinson (1990) identifies the recurrent textual methods and motifs by which ethnographic texts have been constructed. He looks at several standard elements of literary analysis, and thus examines the use of various major devices and tropes. For example, narrative forms are used to convey accounts of social action and causation. Likewise, the "characters" or actors in the account are assembled out of narrative and descriptive fragments. Hence ethnographers use their "literary" competence to reconstruct social action and social actors. In common with many other critics and commentators, Atkinson traces the use of various figures of speech—tropes—such as metaphor, irony, and synecdoche. The demonstration that the "ethnography" is based on conventional literary resources does not, of course, invalidate their use. It commends a disciplined use of them: The use of ethnographic realism can never be innocent in the future. But there is no reason on that score alone to search out alternative literary forms, although some critics and commentators have advocated and practiced ethnographic writing that departs from the conventional realist text in various ways (for examples, see Crapanzano, 1980; Dwyer, 1982; Krieger, 1983; Shostak, 1981; Woolgar, 1988).

In the hands of many, the textual or rhetorical turn serves not just aesthetic or methodological interests, but has inescapably ethical and political implications. A good deal of anthropological reflection has focused on the textual representation of the Author and of the Other in the ethnography. Here, of course, anthropologists find common interest with more general cultural critics, such as Said's (1978) account of Orientalism, or Spivak (1989) (see Pratt, 1992, for an exemplar that brings the interests together). It is argued that a paradox lies at the heart of the ethnographic endeavor and of "the ethnography" as a textual product. On the one hand is the ethnographer's epistemological, personal, and moral commitment to his or her hosts. The image—often, the reality—of prolonged immersion in "the field" and the emphasis on participant observation commit the ethnographer to a shared social world. He or she has become a "stranger" or "marginal native" in order to embark upon a process of cultural learning that is predicated on a degree of "surrender" to "the Other" (see Wolff, 1964). The epistemology of participant observation rests on the principle of interaction and the "reciprocity of perspectives" between social actors. The rhetoric is thus egalitarian: observer and observed as inhabitants of a shared social and cultural field, their respective cultures different but equal, and capable of mutual recognition by virtue of a shared humanity. The classic texts of ethnography, on the other hand, have (it is claimed) all too often inscribed a radical distinction between the Author and the Other. The "realist" techniques of standard ethnographic reportage may implicitly endow the ethnographer—as the implied Narrator—with a privileged gaze that reproduces the authorial omniscience characteristic of many examples

126

of narrative fiction. The text brings actors and culture together under the auspices of a single, all-encompassing point of view. By contrast, the Other is rendered solely as the object of the ethnographer's gaze. The voice of the ethnographer is privileged, that of the Other is muted. As a consequence, there have been various moves to produce ethnographic texts that replace the "monologic" mode with more "dialogic" forms, in which the text allows for a multiplicity of "voices." This perspective brings together a textual, methodological, and moral commitment. Dwyer's (1982) self-conscious adoption of a dialogic textual format is a benchmark contribution to this style of presentation, although it falls short of a full-fledged dialogic approach.

The moral concerns of commentators on ethnographic rhetoric have been echoed by advocates of feminist points of view (see Stanley & Wise, 1983). The textual practices of a privileged "Western" observer may be compared to the inscription of a privileged masculine discourse. There have, therefore, been attempts to produce feminist texts that subvert the taken-for-granted formats. Krieger's (1983) "stream-of-consciousness" style is offered as an exemplar (see DeVault, 1990). The feminist appraisal of ethnographic writing is in turn part of a more general appraisal of social scientific writing and an interest in various genres—most notably biography and autobiography (see Stanley, 1990, 1992; see also D. Smith, 1987, pp. 105ff.). Stanley and Wise, Smith, and others provide an interesting link between a feminist standpoint and a readiness to treat textual forms as problematic. The concern is epistemological and ethical, personal and professional. From the feminist standpoint, of course, they are all implicative of one another.

The rhetorical turn is also intimately related to a "postmodern" tendency in the construction of ethnography. The postmodern ethnography explores the discontinuities, paradoxes, and inconsistencies of culture and action. In contrast with the supposed "modern" ethnography, it does so not in order to resolve or to reconcile those differences. The classic modern ethnography (the postmodernist holds) brought the various fragmentary representations of social life under the auspices of a dominant narrative and a single, privileged point of view. The postmodern author seeks to dissolve that disjuncture between the observer and the observed. The trope of "participant observation," which captures the ambivalence of distance and familiarity, is replaced by one of "dialogue," showing "the cooperative and collaborative nature of the ethnographic situation" (Tyler, 1986, p. 126).

Moreover, the postmodern ethnography is held to adopt a radically alternative attitude toward its textual character. Tyler (1986), for instance, rejects any claim that the ethnography can be said to "represent" the social world. He prefers the terminology and imagery of "evoking" (though he omits consideration of just what is being evoked). A sophisticated discussion of evocation and ethnographic "complexity" is also provided by Strathern (1991). The subject matter of postmodernity and postmodern ethnographic texts are dialectically related. This is aptly illustrated in Dorst's (1989) account of an American town, *Chadd's Ford*. There Dorst describes how this Pennsylvania suburb creates itself through various forms of representation and acts of identification (not least identification with and through the paintings of Andrew Wyeth). Dorst collates various local devices whereby surface appearances of the locality itself are contrived.

Rose (1989) has written an even more extreme version of such a postmodern text. Again, it depends on the collation and juxtaposition of strikingly different collections of materials. It incorporates not just radical shifts of subject matter and perspective but also strikingly different styles of writing. (As has been pointed out, Bateson's ethnography *Naven,* 1936, was an early example of a textually variegated ethnographic account; see Clifford, 1988, p. 146.) Although the "realist" ethnography clearly remains alive and well, it is also clear that—for better or worse—the postmodern turn will encourage some sociologists and anthropologists to experiment with textual styles and formats. In doing so, they will help to focus attention on the conventional character of all ethnographic reportage. It will become part of the craft knowledge of ethnographic authors that textual forms and styles will be self-consciously recognized and explored (see Atkinson, 1990). In this way, a variety of textual styles may become characteristic of the genres of ethnography.

In recent years there has been such a consistent emphasis on the rhetoric or "poetics" of ethnography that there has been some danger of undue attention to these literary and aesthetic issues. Problems of logic and inference have been obscured. Recognition that scholarly texts have conventional and literary aspects seems to have led some practitioners to undue extremes. As we have noted, textual experimentation—sometimes to the point of obscurantism—has now been undertaken, particularly in the name of "postmodernism." This emphasis on textuality is, however, in danger of privileging the rhetorical over the "scientific" or rational. Hammersley (1991, 1993) suggests that we need to pay attention to strategies of reading and writing ethnography, but primarily in order to evaluate the quality of arguments and the use of evidence. Like most of the "textual" commentators, he acknowledges that much of the sociological or anthropological argument proceeds implicitly. It is conveyed in the textual arrangement of narrative, descriptions, and tropes. But he advocates explicit critical attention to those textual elements in order to evaluate the quality of the arguments—however conveyed. He thus reaffirms the more "scientific" aspect of the overall evaluation of the ethnographic enterprise.

◆ Toward a Conclusion: Contemporary Crises and Renewals

Ethnographic approaches to social research have been adopted in numerous disciplines and applied fields: social and cultural anthropology, sociology, human geography, organization studies, educational research, cultural studies. It is noteworthy that in none of these disciplinary areas is there a single philosophical or theoretical orientation that can lay unique claim to a rationale for ethnography and participant observation. Across the spectrum of the social sciences, the use and justification of ethnography is marked by diversity rather than consensus. On that basis, it is arguable that it is futile to try to identify different types of "qualitative research." Rather, one has to recognize different theoretical or epistemological positions, each of which may endorse a version of ethnographic work. It is certainly a mistake to try to elevate "ethnography" (or some equivalent category) to the status of a quasi-paradigm in its own right. There are some common threads, of course, but it is noticeable that many recent or contemporary advocates define their activities in terms of what they are not—in opposition to less preferred perspectives—rather than in a positive way.

Historically, for instance, there has been little in common between the methodological appeals of sociology and anthropology. And those appeals in turn are not very accurately grounded in the actual histories of the respective fields. Many sociologists have claimed an elective affinity (at least) between participant observation and symbolic interactionism (Williams, 1976). One can indeed find many points of contact between the interactionists' view of the social actor, social action, and social order and the practical accomplishment of fieldwork. Both stress the extent to which meanings and understandings emerge through processes and transactions of interaction. In that context, Chicago school sociology is often invoked as the originating inspiration. It is, therefore, ironic that Chicago sociology itself was not especially dominated by ethnographic fieldwork; that early Chicago school urban ethnography was not necessarily very similar to more recent approaches; that earlier Chicago urban sociology was not exclusively predicated on "symbolic interactionism"—which was largely a subsequent codification of presuppositions.

Likewise, others identify an ethnomethodologically informed ethnography. Here the stress is on the investigation of everyday methods for the practical accomplishment of social life. It often involves something of a relaxation of a "pure" version of ethnomethodology. The latter is drawn on, often eclectically and in combination with other perspectives, to illuminate topics and problems of interest to a more conventional, mainstream sociology. Whether or not ethnomethodology can be shown to live up to the claims of some of its practitioners that it is a uniquely fundamental or "foundational" discipline, there is no doubt that it has furnished significant subject matter, and new research questions, for ethnographic orientations. It has, however, introduced some specific limitations. With their emphasis on the detailed analysis of spoken interaction, some versions of ethnomethodology have tended to encourage a rather restricted view of what constitutes "the field." If too great reliance is placed on the analysis of spoken interaction, then the field of investigation may become reduced to those settings and situations for which audio or video recordings can be made. By the same token, the special contribution of participant observation is negated, or reduced to a very minor role in the acquisition of background knowledge of the social context (Atkinson, 1992). The same point may be made about the contribution of discourse analysis (see, for example, Potter & Wetherell, 1987). Close attention to the forms of language and social interaction are undoubtedly important adjuncts to more general, holistic ethnographic approaches. But they cannot fully substitute for ethnographic inquiry.[5]

In other quarters, an emphasis on semiotics or hermeneutics has informed ethnographic data collection and analysis. Here an attention to culture as a system of signs and texts provides the major impetus. In ethnography the textual metaphor of culture has found its major proponent in Geertz, whose formulation of "thick description" stresses the interpretation of cultural meaning. This interpretive perspective in cultural anthropology contrasts clearly with more formal and—according to the interpretivists—reductionist views such as structuralism or ethnoscience. The interpretive approach implies a relativism that eschews a nomothetic approach, while warranting the capacity of the ethnographer to interpret cultures and their local manifestations. Interpretivism in this mode conceives of "culture" in terms of its own poetics—its metaphors, tropes, and other forms of representation. This sense of the "textuality" of social life has in turn been linked to a heightened awareness of the textual character of "the ethnography" itself, as we mentioned earlier.

There are common threads and recurrent motifs running through the entire ethnographic tradition. Yet there is no simple one-to-one relationship between ethnography and any given theoretical perspective. It is not the case that all ethnography has been undertaken under the auspices of one epistemological orthodoxy. Rather, the distinctive characteristics of ethnographic work have been differentially appealed to by different disciplines and tendencies. As we have tried to show, this has produced a highly complex and contentious discursive field.

◆ Notes

1. There are researchers who have intentionally "gone native" for the purposes of research, for example, Jules-Rosette (1978).

2. We should not forget the nineteenth-century precursors of this work, the writings of Engels (1845/1968), Booth (1889-1902), and Webb and Webb (1932), though they were more concerned with documenting living conditions than culture.

3. Its instability is exemplified in the disputes about how their work should be interpreted and what lessons should be drawn from it for sociology. See, for example, Bales (1966), McPhail and Rexroat (1979), Lewis and Smith (1980), Stewart (1981), Blumer (1983), and Fine and Kleinman (1986).

4. Blumer's methodological writings exemplify this (see Blumer, 1969; for discussions, see Baugh, 1990; Hammersley, 1989).

5. Their appeal for some researchers undoubtedly rests on the appearance of greater precision and rigor, analysis being restricted to what can be validated on the basis of the availability of permanent recordings. And, indeed, some ethnomethodological writing has a strongly empiricist streak, see Atkinson (1988).

◆ References

Arensberg, C., & Kimball, S. (1940). *Family and community in Ireland.* Cambridge, MA: Harvard University Press.

Asad, T. (Ed.). (1973). *Anthropology and the colonial encounter.* New York: Humanities Press.

Atkinson, P. A. (1982). Writing ethnography. In H. J. Helle (Ed.), *Kultur und Institution* (pp. 77-105). Berlin: Dunker & Humblot.

131

Atkinson, P. A. (1988). Ethnomethodology: A critical review. *Annual Review of Sociology,* *14,* 441-465.

Atkinson, P. A. (1990). *The ethnographic imagination: Textual constructions of reality.* London: Routledge.

Atkinson, P. A. (1992). *Understanding ethnographic texts.* Newbury Park, CA: Sage.

Atkinson, P. A., & Delamont, S. (1985). Bread and dreams or bread and circuses? In M. Shipman (Ed.), *Educational research: Principles, policies and practices* (pp. 26-45). London: Falmer.

Bales, R. (1966). Comment on Herbert Blumer's paper. *American Journal of Sociology, 71,* 547-548.

Bateson, G. (1936). *Naven.* Cambridge: Cambridge University Press.

Baugh, K. (1990). *The methodology of Herbert Blumer.* Cambridge: Cambridge University Press.

Blumer, H. (1969). On the methodological status of symbolic interactionism. In H. Blumer, *Symbolic interactionism* (pp. 1-60). Englewood Cliffs, NJ: Prentice Hall.

Blumer, H. (1983). Going astray with a logical scheme. *Symbolic Interaction, 6,* 127-137.

Boelen, W. A. M. (1992). *Street corner society:* Cornerville revisited. In *Street corner society* revisited [Special issue]. *Journal of Contemporary Ethnography, 21,* 11-51.

Boon, J. A. (1983). Functionalists write too: Frazer, Malinowski and the semiotics of the monograph. *Semiotica, 46,* 131-149.

Booth, C. (1889-1902). *Life and labour of the people of London* (17 vols.). London: Macmillan.

Brady, I. (Ed.). (1991). *Anthropological poetics.* Lanham, MD: Rowman & Littlefield.

Brown, R. H. (1977). *A poetic for sociology.* Cambridge, MA: Harvard University Press.

Bulmer, M. (1982). *The uses of social research.* London: Allen & Unwin.

Bulmer, M. (1984). *The Chicago school of sociology.* Chicago: University of Chicago Press.

Burgess, R. G. (Ed.). (1982). *Field research: A source book and field manual.* London: Allen & Unwin.

Clifford, J. (1988). *The predicament of culture: Twentieth-century ethnography, literature, and art.* Cambridge, MA: Harvard University Press.

Clifford, J., & Marcus, G. E. (Eds.). (1986). *Writing culture: The poetics and politics of ethnography.* Berkeley: University of California Press.

Clough, P. T. (1992). *The end(s) of ethnography: From realism to social criticism.* Newbury Park, CA: Sage.

Cole, J. W. (1977). Anthropology comes part way home: Community studies in Europe. *Annual Review of Anthropology, 6,* 349-378.

Crapanzano, V. (1980). *Tuhami: Portrait of a Moroccan.* Chicago: University of Chicago Press.

Denzin, N. K. (1990). The spaces of postmodernism: Reading Plummer on Blumer. *Symbolic Interaction, 13,* 145-154.

Denzin, N. K. (1992). Whose Cornerville is it, anyway? In *Street corner society* revisited [Special issue]. *Journal of Contemporary Ethnography, 21,* 120-132.

DeVault, M. L. (1990). Women write sociology: Rhetorical strategies. In A. Hunter (Ed.), *The rhetoric of social research: Understood and believed* (pp. 97-110). New Brunswick, NJ: Rutgers University Press.

Dorst, J. D. (1989). *The written suburb: An ethnographic dilemma.* Philadelphia: University of Pennsylvania Press.

Dwyer, K. (1982). *Moroccan dialogues: Anthropology in question.* Baltimore: Johns Hopkins University Press.

Eddy, E. M., & Partridge, W. L. (Eds.). (1978). *Applied anthropology in America.* New York: Columbia University Press.

Edmondson, R. (1984). *Rhetoric in sociology.* London: Macmillan.

Eisner, E. (1985). On the differences between artistic and scientific approaches to qualitative research. In E. Eisner, *The art of educational evaluation: A personal view.* London: Falmer.

Eisner, E. (1988). The primacy of experience and the politics of method. *Educational Researcher, 17*(5), 15-20.

Eisner, E. (1991). *The enlightened eye: Qualitative inquiry and the enhancement of educational practices.* New York: Macmillan.

Engels, F. (1968). *The condition of the working class in England in 1844.* London: Allen & Unwin. (Original work published 1845)

Fardon, R. (Ed.). (1990). *Localizing strategies: Regional traditions of ethnographic writing.* Edinburgh: Scottish Academic Press.

Fetterman, D. M., & Pitman, M. A. (Eds.). (1986). *Educational evaluation: Ethnography in theory, practice, and politics.* Beverly Hills, CA: Sage.

Fetterman, D. M. (Ed.). (1988). *Qualitative approaches to evaluation in education: The silent scientific revolution.* New York: Praeger.

Filstead, W. J. (1970). Introduction. In W. J. Filstead (Ed.), *Qualitative methodology.* Chicago: Markham.

Finch, J. (1986). *Research and policy: The uses of qualitative research in social and educational research.* London: Falmer.

Fine, G., & Kleinman, S. (1986). Interpreting the sociological classics: Can there be a "true" meaning of Mead? *Symbolic Interaction, 9,* 129-146.

Freilich, M. (Ed.). (1970). *Marginal natives: Anthropologists at work.* New York: Harper & Row.

Frisby, D. (1976). Introduction to the English translation. In T. Adorno, H. Albert, R. Dahrendorf, J. Habermas, H. Pilot, & K. Popper, *The positivist dispute in German sociology* (pp. ix-xliv). London: Heinemann.

Geertz, C. (1973). *The interpretation of cultures: Selected essays.* New York: Basic Books.

Geertz, C. (1988). *Works and lives: The anthropologist as author.* Stanford, CA: Stanford University Press.

Gitlin, A., Siegel, M., & Boru, K. (1989). The politics of method: From leftist ethnography to educative research. *Qualitative Studies in Education, 2,* 237-253.

Gold, R. (1958). Roles in sociological field observations. *Social Forces, 36,* 217-223.

Guba, E. (Ed.). (1990). *The paradigm dialog.* Newbury Park, CA: Sage.

Gusfield, J. (1990). Two genres of sociology. In A. Hunter (Ed.), *The rhetoric of social research: Understood and believed* (pp. 62-96). New Brunswick, NJ: Rutgers University Press.

Hammersley, M. (1989). *The dilemma of qualitative method: Herbert Blumer and the Chicago tradition.* London: Routledge.

Hammersley, M. (1991). *Reading ethnographic research: A critical guide.* London: Longman.

Hammersley, M. (1992a). On feminist methodology. *Sociology, 26,* 187-206.

Hammersley, M. (1992b). *What's wrong with ethnography? Methodological explorations.* London: Routledge.

Hammersley, M. (1993). The rhetorical turn in ethnography. *Social Science Information, 32*(1), 23-37.

Hammersley, M., & Atkinson, P. (1983). *Ethnography: Principles in practice.* London: Tavistock.

Hannerz, U. (1969). *Soulside.* New York: Columbia University Press.

Harding, S. (1986). *The science question in feminism.* Milton Keynes, UK: Open University Press.

Harris, M. (1969). *The rise of anthropological theory.* London: Routledge & Kegan Paul.

Harvey, L. (1987). *Myths of the Chicago school of sociology.* Aldershot, UK: Gower.

Held, D. (1981). *An introduction to critical theory.* London: Hutchinson.

Hastrup, K., & Elsass, P. (1990). Anthropological advocacy: A contradiction in terms? *Current Anthropology, 31,* 301-311.

Janowitz, M. (1971). *Sociological methods and social policy.* New York: General Learning.

Jules-Rosette, B. (1978). The veil of objectivity: Prophecy, divination and social inquiry. *American Anthropologist, 80,* 549-570.

Junker, B. (1960). *Field work.* Chicago: University of Chicago Press.

Kaberry, P. (1957). Malinowski's contribution to field-work methods and the writing of ethnography. In R. Firth (Ed.), *Man and culture: An evaluation of the work of Bronislaw Malinowski* (pp. 71-91). New York: Harper & Row.

Krieger, S. (1983). *The mirror dance: Identity in a women's community,* Philadelphia: Temple University Press.

Lather, P. (1991). *Getting smart: Feminist research and pedagogy with/in the postmodern.* New York: Routledge.

Leach, E. (1957). The epistemological background to Malinowski's empiricism. In R. Firth (Ed.), *Man and culture: An evaluation of the work of Bronislaw Malinowski* (pp. 119-139). New York: Harper & Row.

Lewis, J. D., & Smith, R. L. (1980). *American sociology and pragmatism.* Chicago: University of Chicago Press.

Lincoln, Y. S., & Guba, E. G. (1985). *Naturalistic inquiry.* Beverly Hills, CA: Sage.

Malinowski, B. (1922). *Argonauts of the western Pacific.* London: Routledge & Kegan Paul.

Marcus, G., & Fischer, M. (1986). *Anthropology as cultural critique: An experimental moment in the human sciences.* Chicago: University of Chicago Press.

McCloskey, D. N. (1985). *The rhetoric of economics.* Madison: University of Wisconsin Press.

McPhail, C., & Rexroat, C. (1979). Mead vs. Blumer. *American Sociological Review, 44,* 449-467.

Orlandella, A. R. (1992). Boelen may know Holland, Boelen may know Barzini, but Boelen "doesn't know diddle about the North End!" In *Street corner society* revisited [Special issue]. *Journal of Contemporary Ethnography, 21,* 69-79.

Paine, R. (Ed.). (1985). *Advocacy and anthropology: First encounters.* St. Johns: Memorial University of Newfoundland, Institute of Social and Economic Research.

Park, R., & Burgess, E. (Eds.). (1921). *Introduction to the science of sociology.* Chicago: University of Chicago Press.

Park, R., & Burgess, E. (Eds.). (1969). *Introduction to the science of sociology* (3rd ed.). Chicago: University of Chicago Press.

Potter, J., & Wetherell, M. (1987). *Discourse and social psychology*. London: Sage.

Pratt, M. L. (1986). Fieldwork in common places. In J. Clifford & G. E. Marcus (Eds.), *Writing culture: The poetics and politics of ethnography* (pp. 27-50). Berkeley: University of California Press.

Pratt, M. L. (1992). *Imperial eyes: Travel writing and transculturation*. London: Routledge.

Prattis, J. I. (Ed.). (1985). *Reflections: The anthropological muse*. Washington, DC: American Anthropological Association.

Radcliffe-Brown, A. R. (1948). *A natural science of society*. New York: Free Press.

Radin, P. (1965). *Method and theory of ethnology*. New York: Basic Books. (Original work published 1931)

Redfield, R. (1962). Relation of anthropology to the social sciences and the humanities. In R. Redfield, *Human nature and the study of society* (pp. 107-121). Chicago: University of Chicago Press.

Richards, A. (1939). The development of field work methods in social anthropology. In F. C. Bartlett (Ed.), *The study of society* (pp. 272-316). London: Routledge and Kegan Paul.

Richardson, L. (1992). Trash on the corner: Ethics and technography. In *Street corner society* revisited [Special issue]. *Journal of Contemporary Ethnography, 21,* 103-119.

Rist, R. (1981). On the application of qualitative research to the policy process: An emergent linkage. In L. Barton & S. Walker (Eds.), *Social crisis and educational research* (pp. 153-170). London: Croom Helm.

Rose, D. (1989). *Patterns of American culture: Ethnography and estrangement*. Philadelphia: University of Pennsylvania Press.

Rowe, J. H. (1965). The Renaissance foundation of anthropology. *American Anthropologist, 67,* 1-20.

Said, E. (1978). *Orientalism*. New York: Pantheon.

Shostak, M. (1981). *Nisa:.The life and words of a !Kung woman*. Cambridge, MA: Harvard University Press.

Silverman, D. (1985). *Qualitative methodology and sociology*. Aldershot, UK: Gower.

Silverman, D. (1989). The impossible dreams of reformism and romanticism. In J. F. Gubrium & D. Silverman (Eds.), *The politics of field research: Beyond enlightenment* (pp. 30-48). Newbury Park, CA: Sage.

Smith, D. (1987). *The everyday world as problematic*. Boston: Northeastern University Press.

Smith, J. K. (1989). *The nature of social and educational inquiry*. Norwood, NJ: Ablex.

Smith, J. K., & Heshusius, L. (1986). Closing down the conversation: The end of the quantitative-qualitative debate among educational inquirers. *Educational Researcher, 15*(1), 4-12.

Spivak, G. C. (1989). *In other worlds*. London: Methuen.

Stacey, J. (1988). Can there be a feminist ethnography? *Women's Studies International Forum, 11,* 21-27.

Stanley, L. (1990). *Feminist praxis*. London: Routledge.

Stanley, L. (1992). *The auto/biographical I: The theory and practice of feminist auto/biography*. Manchester, UK: Manchester University Press.

Stanley, L., & Wise, S. (1983). *Breaking out: Feminist consciousness and feminist research.* London: Routledge & Kegan Paul.

Stewart, R.L. (1981). What George Mead should have said. *Symbolic Interaction, 4,* 157-166.

Strathern, M. (1991). *Partial connections.* Lanham, MD: Rowan & Littlefield.

Suttles, G. (1968). *The social order of the slum: Ethnicity and territory in the inner city.* Chicago: University of Chicago Press.

Tyler, S. A. (1986). Post-modern ethnography: From document of the occult to occult document. In J. Clifford & G. E. Marcus (Eds.), *Writing culture: The poetics and politics of ethnography* (pp. 122-140). Berkeley: University of California Press.

Van Maanen, J. (1988). *Tales of the field: On writing ethnography.* Chicago: University of Chicago Press.

van Willigen, J. (1986). *Applied anthropology: An introduction.* South Hadley, MA: Bergin & Garvey.

von Wright, G. (1971). *Explanation and understanding.* London: Routledge & Kegan Paul.

Walker, R. (1978). The conduct of educational case studies. In B. Dockerill & D. Hamilton (Eds.), *Rethinking educational research* (pp. 30-63). London: Hodder & Stoughton.

Walker, R. (Ed.). (1985). *Applied qualitative research.* Aldershot, UK: Gower.

Wax, R. H. (1971). *Doing fieldwork: Warnings and advice.* Chicago: University of Chicago Press.

Webb, S., & Webb, B. (1932). *Methods of social study.* London: Longmans Green.

Wellmer, A. (1974). *Critical theory of society.* New York: Seabury. (Original work published 1969)

White, H. (1973). *Metahistory: The historical imagination in nineteenth century Europe.* Baltimore: Johns Hopkins University Press.

Whyte, W. F. (1955). *Street corner society: The social structure of an Italian slum* (2nd ed.). Chicago: University of Chicago Press.

Whyte, W. F. (1981). *Street corner society: The social structure of an Italian slum* (3rd ed.). Chicago: University of Chicago Press.

Williams, R. (1973). *The country and the city.* London: Chatto & Windus.

Williams, R. (1976). Symbolic interactionism: Fusion of theory and research. In D. C. Thorns (Ed.), *New directions in sociology* (pp. 115-138). Newton Abbott: David & Charles.

Wolcott, H. F. (1980). How to look like an anthropologist without really being one. *Practicing Anthropology, 3*(2), 56-59.

Wolff, K. H. (1964). Surrender and community study: The study of Loma. In A. J. Vidich, J. Bensman, & M. R. Stein (Eds.), *Reflections on community studies* (pp. 233-263). New York: Harper & Row.

Woolgar, S. (Ed.). (1988). *Knowledge and reflexivity.* London: Sage.

Woolgar, S., & Pawluch, D. (1985). Ontological gerrymandering: The anatomy of social problems explanations. *Social Problems, 32,* 214-227.

Young, M. W. (1979). Introduction. In M. W. Young (Ed.), *The ethnography of Malinowski: The Trobriand Islands 1915-18* (pp. 1-20). London: Routledge & Kegan Paul.

6

Phenomenology, Ethnomethodology, and Interpretive Practice

James A. Holstein & Jaber F. Gubrium

◆ From the 1960s through the 1970s, a family of qualitative research
approaches concerned with reality-constituting interpretive practice
hovered at the periphery of sociology, generating almost as much puzzle-
ment—and even hostility—as it did empirical findings (see Atkinson, 1988;
Coser, 1975; J. Douglas, 1970; Gouldner, 1970; Mehan & Wood, 1976).
Harold Garfinkel's (1967) disruptions of the social order and his description of a transsexual's management of femininity, methodological critiques
of conventional sociology (Cicourel, 1964; Garfinkel, 1967; Kitsuse &
Cicourel, 1963), and even Peter Berger and Thomas Luckmann's (1966)
claim that reality is socially constructed piqued the discipline, spawning
both vitriol from the old guard and a rich body of theory and research on
a new front. The approaches still seem radical to some, challenging many
of the presuppositions of more familiar brands of sociology. Yet recent
developments of phenomenologically and ethnomethodologically informed
empirical programs have led to an almost grudging acceptance if not
appreciation of the approaches as neighbors residing in the "suburbs" of
sociology (Pollner, 1991).

This chapter discusses phenomenology, ethnomethodology, and related
sociological programs of inquiry concerned with interpretive practice.

Although the approaches bear a resemblance, their differences are not mere variations on a single enterprise. Clearly they are all indebted to the phenomenological tradition, but the analytic paths taken from the basic tenets diverge into a rich variety of constructionist, ethnomethodological, conversation-analytic, and interpretive strains. Researchers are now making new attempts to begin to consider interpretive practice for the ways that the objectivity of the world is locally accomplished and managed with reference to broad organizational, social, and cultural resources, thus tying what Garfinkel (1967) called "artfulness" to established interpretive structures. The link between interpretive practice and interpretive structures provides a way of understanding the deprivatization of experience as contemporary life is increasingly conducted in public organizational spheres. We begin our discussion by outlining the phenomenological tenets of the approaches.

◆ Phenomenological Tenets

Approaches to the study of interpretive practice share a set of subjectivist assumptions about the nature of lived experience and social order, derived most directly from Alfred Schutz's attempt to develop a social phenomenology bridging sociology with Edmund Husserl's (1970) more philosophical phenomenology. Concerned with the experiential underpinnings of knowledge, Husserl insisted that the relation between perception and its objects was not passive. He argued that human consciousness actively constitutes the objects of experience. This has become foundational for the qualitative study of reality-constituting practices, but it has been turned in a variety of directions.

Schutz (1962, 1964, 1967, 1970) took up Husserl's interest in the ways in which ordinary members of society constitute and reconstitute the world of everyday life, introducing a set of tenets that provide the basis for subsequent phenomenological, ethnomethodological, and constructionist theorizing and empirical work. Stressing the constitutive nature of consciousness and interaction, Schutz (1964) argued that the social sciences should focus on the ways that the life world—that is, the experiential world every person *takes for granted*—is produced and experienced *by members*: "The safeguarding of the subjective point of view is the only but sufficient guarantee that the world of social reality will not be replaced by a fictional non-existing world constructed by the scientific observer" (p. 8). In this view, subjectivity is paramount as the scientific observer deals with how social objects are made meaningful. The emphasis is on how those concerned with objects of experience apprehend and act upon the objects as "things" set apart from observers.

This is a radical departure from the experiential assumptions of the *natural attitude* (Schutz, 1970)—the everyday interpretive stance that takes the world to be principally "out there," separate and distinct from any act of perception or interpretation. In the natural attitude, persons assume that the life world exists before they are present and will be there after they depart. Schutz's recommendation was to study social action that takes place within the natural attitude by *bracketing* the life world, that is, setting aside one's taken-for-granted orientation to it. All ontological judgments about the nature and essence of things and events are suspended. The observer can then focus on the ways in which members of the life world themselves interpretively produce the recognizable, intelligible forms they treat as real.

The orientation to the subjectivity of the life world led Schutz to examine the commonsense knowledge and practical reasoning members use to "objectify" its social forms. Schutz noted that an individual approaches the life world with a *stock of knowledge* composed of common-sense constructs and categories that are social in origin. These images, theories, ideas, values, and attitudes are applied to aspects of experience, making them meaningful. Stocks of knowledge are resources with which persons interpret experience, grasp the intentions and motivations of others, achieve intersubjective understandings, and coordinate actions.

Stocks of knowledge produce a familiar world, one with which members already seem to be acquainted. In part this is because of the typified manner by which knowledge is articulated. The myriad phenomena of everyday life are subsumed under a more limited number of ostensibly shared constructs and categories, general and flexible guidelines for understanding and interpreting experience. *Typifications* make it possible to account for experience, rendering things and occurrences recognizable as being of a particular type or realm. At the same time, typifications are indeterminate, adaptable, and modifiable. Stocks of knowledge are always essentially incomplete, open-ended. Meaning requires the interpretive application of a category to the concrete particulars of a situation.

If human consciousness necessarily typifies, Schutz (1970) argued, language is the central medium for transmitting typifications and thereby meaning. This provides a methodological orientation for a phenomenology of social life concerned with the relation between language use and the

139

objects of experience. Within the contrasting natural attitude, the meaning of a word is taken to be what it references, corresponds with, or stands for in the real world—following a correspondence theory of meaning. In this framework, the essential task of language is to convey information, to describe reality. Viewed as a system of typifications, however, words can be seen as the constitutive building blocks of everyday reality. Accordingly, social phenomenology rests on the tenet that social interaction constructs as much as conveys meaning.

Finally, Schutz noted that our taken-for-granted use of language and typifications creates a sense that the life world is substantial; it is always there apart from our apprehension of it. The majority of one's experiences confirm and reinforce the notion that individuals who interact with one another do so in a world that is experienced in fundamentally the same fashion by all parties, even though mistakes may be made in its apprehension. In other words, we assume that others experience the world basically in the way we do, and that we can therefore understand one another in our dealings in and with the world. We take our subjectivity for granted, overlooking its constitutive character, presuming that we *intersubjectively* share the same reality. Schutz points out that this intersubjectivity is an ongoing accomplishment, a set of understandings sustained from moment to moment by participants in interaction.

Schutz's social phenomenology aimed for a social science that would "interpret and explain human action and thought" through descriptions of the foundational structures of "the reality which seems self-evident to men remaining within the natural attitude" (Schutz & Luckmann, 1974, p. 3). This was an uncompromising interpretive enterprise focused on everyday subjective meaning and experience, the goal of which was to explicate how objects and experience are meaningfully constituted and communicated in the world of everyday life. The program was to treat subjectivity as a topic for investigation in its own right, not as a methodological taboo.

◆ Ethnomethodological Contours

Although ethnomethodology is indebted to Schutz's social phenomenology, it is not a mere extension of his program. Ethnomethodology addresses the problem of order by combining a "phenomenological sensibility" (Maynard & Clayman, 1991) with a paramount concern for constitutive social practice (Garfinkel, 1967). From an ethnomethodological standpoint, the world of "social facts" is accomplished through members' interpretive work—activity through which actors produce and organize the very circumstances of everyday life.

In part, Garfinkel's (1952, 1967) foundational program for ethnomethodology was a response to his teacher Talcott Parsons's (1968) theory of action (Heritage, 1984). For Parsons, social order was made possible through institutionalized systems of norms, rules, and values. Garfinkel sought an alternative to this approach in which social actors, as Garfinkel wrote, were portrayed as "judgmental dopes" responding to external social forces and motivated by internalized directives and imperatives. Garfinkel's response was a model of social order built through the contingent, embodied, ongoing interpretive work of ordinary members of society. He viewed persons as possessing practical linguistic and interactional competencies through which the observable, accountable, orderly features of everyday reality were produced—"members" whose activity constitutes social order. Ethnomethodology's topic became members' practical everyday procedures— that is, "ethnomethods"—for creating, sustaining, and managing a sense of objective reality.

Empirical investigation of "members' methods" has its point of departure in phenomenological bracketing. Adopting a policy of "ethnomethodological indifference" (Garfinkel & Sacks, 1970), the analyst suspends all commitments to an a priori or privileged version of social structure, focusing instead on how members accomplish, manage, and reproduce a *sense* of social structure. Analysis centers on the properties of practical reasoning and the constitutive work that produces the unchallenged appearance of a stable reality, while resisting judgmental characterizations of the "correctness" of members' activities. Contrary to conventional sociology's tendency to ironicize and criticize members' commonsense formulations in comparison with sociologists' views, ethnomethodologists focus on folk methods and commonsense reasoning, abiding by the maxim "Don't argue with the members" (Pollner, personal communication, 1993).

Ethnomethodologists have examined a variety of aspects of social order. One objective, for example, is the description of how order—say, recognizable structures of observable behavior, systems of motivation, or causal ties between motivations and patterns of behavior—is made visible through members' descriptive and accounting practices (Zimmerman & Wieder, 1970). Whereas conventional sociology focuses on rules, norms, and shared meanings as explanations for patterned behavior, ethnomethodology also makes rules topical, but in a distinctly different way. It sets aside the notion that behavior is rule governed or motivated by shared values and expectations in order to observe how conduct is described and explained with reference to rules, values, motives, and the like. The appearance of behavior as being the consequence of a rule is treated as just that—the appearance of an event as an instance of compliance or noncompliance with a rule. By invoking rules and elaborating their sense for specific cases, members describe their activities as rational, coherent, precedented, and orderly (Zimmerman, 1970).

A juror in the midst of deliberation, for instance, may account for her verdict by saying that the judge's instructions on how to consider the case at hand compelled her to decide in her fashion. A rule—the judge's instruction—is used to make sense of the juror's decision making, giving it the appearance of rationality, legality, and correctness because it was done "according to the rule" (Holstein, 1983). Another juror might account for his verdict by saying it was serving the interest of "justice," in this case citing a moral value or principle to explain the decision (Maynard & Manzo, 1993). From an ethnomethodological standpoint, the legal correctness of these decisions is not at issue; instead, the focus is on the use of rules, values, principles, and the like as sense-making devices. The aim is not to provide causal explanations of patterned behavior, but to describe how members recognize, describe, explain, and account for the order of their everyday lives (Zimmerman & Wieder, 1970).

Ethnomethodology's emphasis on the practical production of a sense of reality forms its specific analytic contours. Rather than assuming that members share meanings and definitions of situations, ethnomethodologists note how members continuously rely upon the interpretive capacities of coparticipants in interaction to assemble and reveal a locally visible sense of order. Social structures are locally produced, sustained, and experienced as normal environments—that is, routine, taken-for-granted states of affairs. Indeed, the notion of a singular, objective reality itself is sustained by everyday practices of mundane reason (Pollner, 1987).

If realities are produced "from within," by way of members' interpretive procedures, members' social circumstances are *self-generating*. This implicates two essential properties of meaning revealed by ethnomethodological analysis. First, meanings are essentially *indexical,* that is, they depend on context. Objects and events have equivocal or indeterminate meanings without a visible context. It is only through their situated use in talk and interaction that objects and events become concretely meaningful. Second, the circumstances that provide the context for meaning are themselves self-generating. Interpretive activities are simultaneously *in* and *about* the settings to which they orient, and that they describe. Socially accomplished realities are thus *reflexive*; descriptive accounts of settings give shape to those settings while simultaneously being shaped by the settings they constitute. Opposite sides of the same coin, indexicality and reflexivity are unavoidable features of social reality; their manifestations and consequences are central ethnomethodological research topics (for example, see Pollner, 1991; Wieder, 1988). Studies of situated interpretive practice necessarily require close attention to the fine details of talk and interaction. Ethnomethodological analysis focuses on the interactionally unfolding features of social settings, treating talk and interaction as topics for analysis rather than as mere communications about more sociologically important underlying phenomena.

Whereas much ethnomethodological research has been ethnographic (e.g., Emerson, 1969; see Maynard & Clayman, 1991, for a review of other studies), it pays especially close attention to the interactional, particularly discursive aspects of the settings studied. Traditional ethnographies generally assume that language is a neutral conduit for description; words represent or tell about culturally circumscribed realities (Atkinson, 1990; Clifford & Marcus, 1986; Clough, 1992; Geertz, 1988; Gubrium & Silverman, 1989). In contrast, an ethnomethodological approach treats objective reality as an interactional and discursive accomplishment; descriptions, accounts, or reports are not merely about some social world as much as they are constitutive of that world. The approach does not attempt to generate information about interaction or discourse through interviews or questionnaires, but relies upon naturally occurring talk to reveal the ways ordinary interaction produces social order in the settings where the talk occurs. When subjects or informants talk, their utterances are not taken as more or less accurate or authentic reports about circumstances, conduct, states of mind, or other reportables. Instead, the talk is considered as the very action through which local realities are accomplished.

From a procedural standpoint, ethnomethodological research must be keenly attuned to naturally occurring discourse and interaction as constitutive elements of the settings studied (see Atkinson & Drew, 1979; Maynard, 1984, 1989; Mehan & Wood, 1975; Sacks, 1972). The point of departure, however, may vary. Although always concerned with the domain of talk and interaction, more ethnographically oriented studies emphasize discourse-in-context, looking more to the situated content of talk as constitutive of local meaning. At the other end of the continuum, the

143

analyst may be more inclined to emphasize the sequential structuring of talk as a means of building context and meaning. Although particular aspects of the domain may be highlighted, structure, context, and content all remain central ethnomethodological concerns.

The emphasis on talk-in-interaction (rather than talk and interaction) has been developed into what some claim is a distinct variant of ethnomethodology—conversation analysis (see Heritage, 1984; Sacks, Schegloff, & Jefferson, 1974; Zimmerman, 1988). Although some contend that its connection to ethnomethodology is tenuous (Atkinson, 1988; Lynch & Bogen, 1994; for counterarguments, see Maynard & Clayman, 1991; ten Have, 1990), conversation analysis may be linked to ethnomethodology by their common interest in the local, embodied, methodical construction of intelligible and analyzable social action (Maynard & Clayman, 1991).

Focusing on the competencies that underlie ordinary social activities, conversation analysis attempts to describe and explicate the collaborative practices speakers use and rely upon when they engage in intelligible interaction. Both the production of conduct and its interpretation are seen as the accountable products of a common set of methods or procedures (Heritage, 1984). It is through these procedures that the intelligibility of the social world is made evident. As Emanuel Schegloff and Harvey Sacks (1973) argue regarding the patterned conversations they observed: "Insofar as the [conversational] materials we worked with exhibited orderliness, they did so not only to us . . . but for the co-participants who produced them. If the materials were . . . orderly, they were so because they had been methodically produced by the members of society for one another" (p. 290).

John Heritage (1984) summarizes the fundamentals of conversation analysis in three premises. First, interaction is structurally organized, and this may be observed in the regularities of ordinary conversation. All aspects of interaction can be found to exhibit organized patterns of stable, identifiable structural features. They stand independent of the psychological or other characteristics of particular speakers, representing ubiquitous features of talk-in-interaction itself to which participants orient. Second, all interaction is contextually oriented in that talk is both productive of and reflects the circumstances of its production. Third, these two properties characterize all interaction so that no order of detail can be dismissed as disorderly, accidental, or irrelevant to the ongoing interaction.

This focus on the real-time, sequential details of ordinary conversation requires naturalistic methods of study. Naturally occurring talk is tape-recorded (increasingly, videotaping is encouraged) and transcribed to reproduce the fine-grained detail of speech exchanges (see Atkinson & Heritage, 1984). Analysis then centers on the collaborative, constantly emerging structure of conversation itself, identifying principles that underpin the sequential organization of talk, the local management of turn taking, and practices relating to opening, sustaining, and closing orderly sequences. In brief, talk is systematically examined for the methodical, structured ways that the orderliness of interaction is recurrently accomplished.

Another strain of contemporary ethnomethodology has proceeded in a significantly different direction, concentrating more on detailed descriptions of the features of practical actions through which order is accomplished. In contrast to what some have labeled the "enriched positivism" of conversation analysis (Lynch & Bogen, 1994) as it has been promoted by Sacks and his circle, Garfinkel (1988) and others have begun to elaborate a "post-analytic" (Lynch & Bogen, 1994) ethnomethodology that is less inclined to universalistic generalizations regarding the enduring structures or machineries of ordinary interaction. This work concentrates on the highly localized competencies that constitute various domains of "work"— most notably the work of the sciences, for example, astronomy (Garfinkel, Lynch, & Livingston, 1981), biology and neurology (Lynch, 1985), and mathematics (Livingston, 1986). The goal is to specify the "quiddity" or "just whatness" of social practices within tightly circumscribed, specialized domains of knowledge and action (Heritage, 1987). These studies focus on the embodied conceptualizations and practices that practitioners within a particular domain of work recognize as belonging to that domain (Heritage, 1987). The emphasis is antitheoretical (Fish, 1989) in that it discourages the formulation of comprehensive frameworks for investigating the myriad practices that constitute social order. Instead, the program advocates studies of specific interactional practices through which order is manifested and rendered accountable in highly specific social, historical, and practical circumstances (Bogen & Lynch, 1993).

◆ Expanding the Scope

The ethnomethodological emphasis on practice is shared by several newly developing variations of the approach. The following subsections describe some adaptations, elaborations, and reformulations of ethnomethodological themes that are expanding the theoretical and empirical scope of Garfinkel's original program.

Local Interpretive Resources

The agent at the center of one variation remains that of the practitioner of everyday life who works at discerning and designating the recognizable and orderly parameters of everyday life in order to get on with the business at hand. Although the work is seen as practical and "artful" in the ethnomethodological sense of the term, the practitioner is not viewed as building reality "from scratch"—from the ground up, as it were—on each and every interpretive occasion. Rather, interpretive work is conditioned by arrays of local interpretive resources—recognizable categories, familiar vocabularies, organizational missions, professional orientations, group cultures, and other existing frameworks for assigning meaning to matters under consideration. At the same time, these contexts of interpretation are themselves ongoing accomplishments, reflexively supplying meaning to actions and objects as those meanings maintain, elaborate, or alter the circumstances in which they occur (Garfinkel, 1967; Heritage, 1984).

The use of local interpretive resources is typically astute; resources are crafted to the demands of the occasion. Meaning is never completely predetermined; it must always be convincingly and accountably articulated with concrete particulars. At the same time, interpretive practice engages institutional frameworks, formal and informal categories, and long-standing cultural patterns—socially established structures of meaning (Geertz, 1973, 1983). Description and interpretation often seem quite familiar; they must make sense. Not only must adequate descriptions be recognizable (Sacks, 1974), but they are accountable in that they must convince socially defined competent agents that the circumstances in question warrant the attributions that are attached. Thus, although social reality is situationally and artfully constructed, this is accomplished in relation to concrete interpretive parameters. Social order is assembled from "cultural particulars" (Silverman, 1985) that may be widely available yet contingently asserted.

The combined concern for interpretive resources and artful practice offers a perspective that has been applied to a wide variety of topics, including family (Gubrium & Holstein, 1990, 1993a, 1993b; Holstein & Gubrium, 1993), the life course (Gubrium, Holstein, & Buckholdt, 1994), human service work (G. Miller, 1991a, 1991b), domestic violence and battered women's shelters (Loseke, 1992), mental illness and involuntary commitment (Holstein, 1993), family therapy (Gubrium, 1992), social

146

problems (Holstein & Miller, 1993; Miller & Holstein, 1989; L. J. Miller, 1993), and trouble and deviance (Emerson & Messinger, 1977).

The linkage between interpretive practice and resource is facilitated by reference to some well-known disciplinary concerns, in particular, aspects of Durkheim's (1961) reflections on collective representation and various formulations of the role of culture, institutional context, and discourse structures.

Collective Representations

Contemporary positivist sociology traces some of its roots to Emile Durkheim's (1964) call for the scientific study of social facts. Read interpretively, aspects of Durkheim's work also provide a basis for studying how meaning is attached to objects of everyday life (Pfohl, 1992; Silverman, 1985). Durkheim (1961) referred to widely available categories of meaning and understanding—social forms such as religion, community, family, and home—as collective representations. By this he meant that social objects and categories can be viewed as abstractly representing the organization of persons' lives. As Mary Douglas (1986) notes, Durkheim considered collective representations to be "publicly standardized ideas [that] constitute social order" (p. 96). Durkheim paid little attention to the interactive processes through which social order is achieved, but this reading of his framework is useful for orienting to meaning as socially, not individually, accomplished.

Interpretive practice can be understood to involve the articulation of publicly recognized structures, categories, or images with aspects of experience in ways that accountably produce broadly recognizable instances of the objects or events so categorized (Gubrium, 1988; Holstein, 1993). David Silverman (1985) sees this practical linkage of interpretive structure and "artfulness" as a way of establishing a middle ground between such polar sociological extremes as so-called macro and micro forms of analysis.

Collective representations enter into the interpretive process in a manner similar to Schutz's (1970) "schemes of interpretation," as widely available, experientially acquired frameworks for organizing and making sense of everyday life. The schemes collectively represent the social forms or structures of our lives, such as the popular stage models of human development that are taken to reflect personal experience in relation to time (Gubrium, Holstein, & Buckholdt, 1994). The schemes mediate

147

individual biography and interpersonal relations, reflecting and perpetuating culturally promoted understandings of, and orientations to, everyday experience. Interpretation is shaped by the resources that are locally available, recognized, and accepted, making meaningful experience—its perception, representation, and authenticity—a socially rather than privately constructed phenomenon (Silverman, 1987).

Rhetorics of Everyday Life

One way of analyzing interpretive structures is to explicate the rhetorics of collective representation. Cultural studies of various types provide insight into the array of interpretive resources and categories available for use in constituting everyday realities. Studies of social movements and their role in the formation of public issues and promulgation of interpretive categories for personal troubles also have this aim.

The constructionist approach to social problems is a prominent instance of this line of research in sociology. Spector and Kitsuse (1987), for example, outline a program for studying social problems as "the activities of individuals or groups making assertions of grievances and claims with respect to some putative condition" (p. 75). The study of social problems from this perspective requires descriptions of the emergence, nature, and maintenance of claims-making and responding activity that constitutes "condition categories" (Ibarra & Kitsuse, 1993) used to identify social problems. Center stage is the large-scale and mass-media rhetoric or "publicity" (Gubrium, 1993) that promotes "images of issues" (Best, 1989) that may be applied to categorize experience.

Accenting the artful, other studies in this vein focus on the activities through which collective representations are locally applied to personal troubles (see Mills, 1959). Jaber Gubrium (1986) shows how the Alzheimer's disease movement provides a medical rhetoric for interpreting the cognitive ravages of aging. Such personal troubles as the stress of caregiving and the fear of institutionalization collectively represent a disease experience. Similarly, Gale Miller (1991a) documents how the rhetoric of labor market conditions and job applicant attitudes collectively constitute social relations in a work incentive program. Donileen Loseke (1992) deconstructs the claims forming the collective representations of wife abuse and battered women, then explicates the organizational practices through which shelter workers attach the images to actual persons and events. Concrete instances of battered women and wife abuse, Loseke explains, are the interpretive result of a newly recognized public category for viewing individual cases.

Local Culture, Discourse Structures, and Organizational Embeddedness

Meaning structures are public, but they are also locally circumscribed. In a sense, Clifford Geertz (1983) recognized this when he argued that knowledge is "always ineluctably local" (p. 4). As the corpus of local knowledge coalesces into a local culture—that is, a set of more or less regularized ways of assigning meaning and responding to things (Gubrium, 1989)—interpretive practice reflects local circumstances and resources.

Local culture comes in various guises. Small groups, formal organizations, and other domains of everyday life condition what we encounter and how we make sense of it. Mary Douglas (1986) goes so far as to suggest that human reason is organized and expressed through processes of "institutional thinking." Applying the phrase metaphorically, she argues that socially organized circumstances provide models of social order through which experience is assimilated and organized. She states, for example, that "an answer is only seen to be the right one if it sustains the institutional thinking that is already in the minds of individuals as they try to decide" (p. 4).

According to Douglas, institutions are organized social conventions involving typical and routine ways of representing social reality. As she formulates them, these representational conventions are similar to what Michel Foucault (1972) calls "discursive formations." Contextually grounded discourses, vocabularies, and categories form local interpretive resources or cultures for defining and classifying aspects of everyday life. Parenthetically, as Sacks (1974) notes, "a culture . . . does not, so to speak, merely fill brains in roughly the same way, it fills them so that they are alike in fine detail" as well, providing an ethnomethodological contour (p. 218).

Interpretive practice also is *organizationally embedded* (Gubrium, 1988; Gubrium & Holstein, 1990). This is a shorthand way of saying that interpretation reflects publicly recognized contexts, that social objects are constituted within discernibly organized circumstances. We use the term *organizational* in its most general sense—any socially organized circumstance— while recognizing that interpretation is increasingly conditioned by the more strictly defined parameters of formal organizations (see Gubrium & Holstein, 1990). As everyday life is more and more conducted within formally organized settings, the formulation of meaning becomes decidedly public—deprivatized—as it is conditioned by organizationally promoted ways of making sense of experience. Indeed, the organizational embeddedness of experience has so diversified the meanings of self and our social relations as to transform modern institutional life into a postmodern form (Gubrium, 1992; Gubrium, Holstein, & Buckholdt, 1994).

Although organized settings provide accountable modes of representation, the settings do not determine interpretive practice. Concertedly local, interpretation relies upon delimited cultural categories that are diversely and artfully articulated with, and attached to, experience. Whether the local culture under consideration is characteristic of a particular organization, profession, ethnic or gender group, or another collectivity or setting, the culture supplies *resources* for interpretation, not injunctions or absolute directives. Experience constituted in a particular organization or setting may take on the general qualities that the organization or setting promotes, but interpretation also is practical, artfully maneuvering what is locally available and circumstantial. Practitioners of everyday life are not "organizational dopes," mere extensions of organizational thinking. They exercise interpretive discretion, mediated by complex layerings of interpretive influence. They also carry with them the biographical basis for resistance, personal and interpersonal histories that compete with organizational categories as means for interpreting experience (Gubrium & Holstein, 1993a).

Prevailing interpretations thus emerge as provisional adaptations of diverse local resources and conditions, serving the practical needs at hand, until further notice. Culture orients and equips the process, but interpretive inventiveness and serendipity intervene. The process repeatedly and reflexively turns back on itself, as substance, structure, and practice are enmeshed in the ongoing production, reproduction, and redesignation of meaning and order.

◆ Emerging Classic Themes

Some recent developments in ethnomethodology and related approaches have turned to classic sociological themes. This represents a further broadening of the enterprise, one that also bridges what have been conceived as incompatible micro- and macro-level concerns. Richard Hilbert (1992), for example, argues that many of ethnomethodology's central considerations also reside in the theoretical writings of Max Weber and Durkheim. Hilbert suggests that modern interpreters—most notably Talcott Parsons—have obscured or suppressed many of the radical themes of the classics. Ethnomethodology, he claims, has rediscovered and reinvigorated theoretical arguments that Durkheim and Weber initiated, and thus addresses problems at the very core of the discipline.

Although ethnomethodology has generally been considered a microsociological orientation, Dorothy Smith combines ethnomethodological, Marxist, and feminist insights to develop a different set of classic themes. Taking her point of departure from women's experience, Smith argues that what she calls "textually mediated" activity and "relations of ruling" combine in practice to articulate the meanings of being female—especially the meaning of motherhood. Her studies of women's work as mothers (Griffith & Smith, 1990; Smith, 1989; Smith & Griffith, 1990) show how the working discourse of mothers' institutional linkages with home, work, and school articulates an everyday world for mothers that reproduces their subordination to a system of patriarchy.

Smith extends her critique to the "relations of ruling" operating in social science research practices that virtually "rule" women because typical research designs are insensitive to women's lived experience. For example, Smith takes exception to William J. Wilson's (1987) taken-for-granted distinction between "intact" families and those that are not intact (Smith, 1993). She argues that Wilson's view of family life is "SNAF-mediated," meaning that the view is a kind of text based on an idealized image of the "standard North American family." Wilson's reliance on this view leads his research to "overrule" women's diverse and legitimate familial experiences.

Closer to more traditional ethnomethodological concerns, David Silverman's (1987) research on communication and medical practice focuses on the role of context in interpretation, but with a decided social policy orientation. His studies of doctor-patient interactions in various medical settings show that although talk and interaction constitute the meaning of patienthood, the family, and the illness experience, the working medical vocabularies of particular settings mediate understandings of illnesses, intervention, progress, and recovery. Silverman's work not only examines the organizational embeddedness of discourse, but also provides directives for refashioning social relations, especially when he asks such questions as, "What can social science contribute?" (Silverman, 1985, chap. 9).

A new set of conversation-analytic studies has also turned to "institutional talk" (Drew & Heritage, 1993). Although the point of departure remains the transsituational regularities of conversational structure, more emphasis is being given to the ways that institutional or organizational context conditions interactional practice. Drew and Heritage (1993), for example, note that institutional talk is normally informed by the goal orientations of relatively restricted, organizationally conventional forms. Institutional location also tends to constrain the ways that members participate in interaction, and presents inferential frameworks and procedures to which they may orient. Although they rely less upon the analytic apparatus of conversation analysis, studies such as Robert Dingwall and Phil Strong's (1985) examination of the role of language and practical reasoning in the production of organizational realities elaborate the theme of talk and organizational context.

Gubrium's (1992) comparative ethnography of clinical discourse in two family therapy programs also underscores institutional groundings, linking broader issues of rationalization with more ethnomethodological concerns. Gubrium shows how organizational communication constructs domestic disorder, making it visible in locally understandable terms. Contrasting images of home life in the two therapeutic settings—one viewing domestic order as a system of authority, the other seeing it as a configuration of emotional bonds—serve to articulate different senses of family troubles, of being "out of control." The idea that the reality of home life and domestic troubles are embedded in organizational activities and mediated by institutional images provides a basis for arguing that domestic life is both socially constructed and manifoldly rationalized—that is, constituted under the auspices of the many organizations that suffuse contemporary life. Gubrium argues that as everyday reality is increasingly grounded in diverse public settings, its rationalization is more artful and local—less total—than in Weber's (1947) conceptualization.

◆ Conclusion

All told, the range of qualitative research approaches manifesting "phenomenological sensibilities" has grown considerably. Indeed, although Maynard and Clayman (1991) celebrate the "diversity of ethnomethodology," proclaiming the "enormous range of ethnomethodological research" over the past three decades, their assessment seems too modest, perhaps even parochial. More broadly, studies of interpretive practice evincing an "ethnomethodological sensibility" but moving beyond the traditional purview are flourishing. New analytic resources are being mobilized, as, for example, Durkheimian and Foucauldian insights into overarching collective representations and discourse structures are linked to local interpretive procedures. New issues are being raised regarding linkages between classic and contemporary questions of social order, between ostensibly micro- and macro-level concerns. New analytic resources are developing to explicate more fully the roles of discourse, conversational structure, and the content and context of interactional exchanges.

With the new connections, interpretation is being thrust into the context of the postmodern and beyond. It might be argued that ethnomethodology represents something of a deconstructionist (Derrida, 1977) turn in sociology, with its concern for the reflexivity of social interaction and context paralleling in some ways Derrida's attention to the continuous "play of difference"—the constant swirl of reality-constituting activity—that produces perennially new realities in literary texts. Highlighting both interpretive resources and interpretive practice, however, provides a means of linking the play of difference to the *in situ* activities that produce, manage, and contain social order. The focus on broader interpretive contexts at least partially binds the play of difference to the relatively circumscribed resources of organizational and institutional settings as contexts.

This moves the analytic enterprise in a post-Derridian direction (Gubrium, 1992; Gubrium & Holstein, 1990; Holstein, 1993). The interpretation of lived experience (compared with, say, literary text) is shaped by contexts that may be relatively fixed, that mediate reality production accordingly. The accomplishment of order and meaning is highly localized, artful yet contextually conditioned. The focus on interpretive resources reappropriates classic sociological themes—rationalization and collective representation, for example—to the enactment of meaningful reality, blurring the distinction between macro and micro. Practice remains the common thread as some of the recent occupants of sociological "suburbs" are rediscovering the analytic verve of older cities.

◆ References

Atkinson, J. M., & Drew, P. (1979). *Order in court*. Atlantic Highlands, NJ: Humanities Press.

Atkinson, J. M., & Heritage, J. (Eds.). (1984). *Structures of social action*. Cambridge: Cambridge University Press.

Atkinson, P. A. (1988). Ethnomethodology: A critical review. *Annual Review of Sociology, 14,* 441-465.

Atkinson, P. A. (1990). *The ethnographic imagination: Textual constructions of reality.* London: Routledge.

Berger, P. L., & Luckmann, T. (1966). *The social construction of reality.* Garden City, NY: Doubleday.

Best, J. (1989). *Images of issues.* Hawthorne, NY: Aldine de Gruyter.

Bogen, D., & Lynch, M. (1993). Do we need a general theory of social problems? In J. A. Holstein & G. Miller (Eds.), *Reconsidering social constructionism: Debates in social problems theory* (pp. 213-237). Hawthorne, NY: Aldine de Gruyter.

Cicourel, A. V. (1964). *Method and measurement in sociology.* New York: Free Press.

Clifford, J., & Marcus, G. E. (Eds.). (1986). *Writing culture: The poetics and politics of ethnography.* Berkeley: University of California Press.

Clough, P. T. (1992). *The end(s) of ethnography: From realism to social criticism.* Newbury Park, CA: Sage.

Coser, L. (1975). Two methods in search of a substance. *American Sociological Review, 40,* 691-700.

Derrida, J. (1977). *Of grammatology.* Baltimore: Johns Hopkins University Press.

Dingwall, R., & Strong, P. M. (1985). The interactional study of organizations. *Urban Life, 14,* 205-232.

Drew, P., & Heritage, J. (Eds.). (1993). *Talk at work.* Cambridge: Cambridge University Press.

Douglas, J. (Ed.). (1970). *Understanding everyday life.* Chicago: Aldine.

Douglas, M. (1986). *How institutions think.* Syracuse, NY: Syracuse University Press.

Durkheim, E. (1961). *The elementary forms of the religious life.* New York: Collier-Macmillan.

Durkheim, E. (1964). *The rules of sociological method.* New York: Free Press.

Emerson, R. M. (1969). *Judging delinquents.* Chicago: Aldine.

Emerson, R. M., & Messinger, S. (1977). The micro-politics of trouble. *Social Problems, 25,* 121-134.

Fish, S. (1989). *Doing what comes naturally: Change, rhetoric, and the practice of theory in literary and legal studies.* Durham, NC: Duke University Press.

Foucault, M. (1972). *The archaeology of knowledge.* New York: Pantheon.

Garfinkel, H. (1952). *The perception of the other: A study in social order.* Unpublished doctoral dissertation, Harvard University.

Garfinkel, H. (1967). *Studies in ethnomethodology.* Englewood Cliffs, NJ: Prentice Hall.

Garfinkel, H. (1988). Evidence for locally produced, naturally accountable phenomena of order, logic, reason, meaning, method, etc. in and as of the essential quiddity of immortal ordinary society (I of IV): An announcement of studies. *Sociological Theory, 6,* 103-109.

Garfinkel, H., Lynch, M., & Livingston, E. (1981). The work of a discovering science construed with materials from the optically discovered pulsar. *Philosophy of the Social Sciences, 11,* 131-158.

Garfinkel, H., & Sacks, H. (1970). On the formal structures of practical actions. In J. C. McKinney & E. A. Tiryakian (Eds.), *Theoretical sociology* (pp. 338-366). New York: Appleton-Century-Crofts.

Geertz, C. (1973). *The interpretation of cultures: Selected essays.* New York: Basic Books.

Geertz, C. (1983). *Local knowledge: Further essays in interpretive anthropology.* New York: Basic Book.

Geertz, C. (1988). *Works and lives: The anthropologist as author.* Stanford, CA: Stanford University Press.

Gouldner, A. W. (1970). *The coming crisis of Western sociology.* New York: Avon.

Griffith, A. I., & Smith, D. E. (1990). "What did you do in school today?": Mothering, schooling, and social class. In G. Miller & J. A. Holstein (Eds.), *Perspectives on social problems* (Vol. 2, pp. 3-24). Greenwich, CT: JAI.

Gubrium, J. F. (1986). *Oldtimers and Alzheimer's: The descriptive organization of senility.* Greenwich, CT: JAI.

Gubrium, J. F. (1988). *Analyzing field reality.* Newbury Park, CA: Sage.

Gubrium, J. F. (1989). Local cultures and service policy. In J. F. Gubrium & D. Silverman (Eds.), *The politics of field research: Beyond enlightenment* (pp. 94-112). Newbury Park, CA: Sage.

Gubrium, J. F. (1992). *Out of control: Family therapy and domestic disorder.* Newbury Park, CA: Sage.

Gubrium, J. F. (1993). For a cautious naturalism. In J. A. Holstein & G. Miller (Eds.), *Reconsidering social constructionism: Debates in social problems theory* (pp. 89-101). Hawthorne, NY: Aldine de Gruyter.

Gubrium, J. F., & Holstein, J. A. (1990). *What is family?* Mountain View, CA: Mayfield.

Gubrium, J. F., & Holstein, J. A. (1993a). Family discourse, organizational embeddedness, and local enactment. *Journal of Family Issues, 14,* 66-81.

Gubrium, J. F., & Holstein, J. A. (1993b). Phenomenology, ethnomethodology, and family discourse. In P. Boss, W. Doherty, R. LaRossa, W. Schum, & S. Steinmetz (Eds.), *Sourcebook of family theory and methods* (pp. 649-670). New York: Plenum.

Gubrium, J. F., Holstein, J. A., & Buckholdt, D. R. (1994). *Constructing the life course.* Dix Hills, NY: General Hall.

Gubrium, J. F., & Silverman, D. (Eds.). (1989). *The politics of field research: Beyond enlightenment.* Newbury Park, CA: Sage.

Heritage, J. (1984). *Garfinkel and ethnomethodology.* Cambridge: Polity.

Heritage, J. (1987). Ethnomethodology. In A. Giddens & J. Turner (Eds.), *Sociological theory today* (pp. 224-271). Stanford, CA: Stanford University Press.

Hilbert, R. A. (1992). *The classical roots of ethnomethodology.* Chapel Hill: University of North Carolina Press.

Holstein, J. A. (1983). Jurors' use of judges' instructions. *Sociological Methods and Research, 11,* 501-518.

Holstein, J. A. (1993). *Court-ordered insanity: Interpretive practice and involuntary commitment.* Hawthorne, NY: Aldine de Gruyter.

Holstein, J. A., & Gubrium, J. F. (1993). Constructing family: Descriptive practice and domestic order. In T. R. Sarbin & J. I. Kitsuse (Eds.), *Constructing the social* (pp. 232-250). London: Sage.

Holstein, J. A., & Miller, G. (1993). Social constructionism and social problems work. In J. A. Holstein & G. Miller (Eds.), *Reconsidering social constructionism: Debates in social problems theory.* Hawthorne, NY: Aldine de Gruyter.

Husserl, E. (1970). *Logical investigation.* New York: Humanities Press.

Ibarra, P. R., & Kitsuse, J. I. (1993). Vernacular constituents of moral discourse: An interactionist proposal for the study of social problems. In J. A. Holstein & G. Miller (Eds.), *Reconsidering social constructionism: Debates in social problems theory* (pp. 25-58). Hawthorne, NY: Aldine de Gruyter.

Kitsuse, J. I., & Cicourel, A. V. (1963). A note on the uses of official statistics. *Social Problems, 11,* 131-139.

Livingston, E. (1986). *The ethnomethodological foundations of mathematics.* London: Routledge & Kegan Paul.

Loseke, D. R. (1992). *The battered woman and shelters: The social construction of wife abuse.* Albany: State University of New York Press.

Lynch, M. (1985). *Art and artifact in laboratory science.* London: Routledge & Kegan Paul.

Lynch, M., & Bogen, D. (1994). Harvey Sacks' primitive natural science. *Theory, Culture & Society, 11*(4), 65-104.

Maynard, D. W. (1984). *Inside plea bargaining: The language of negotiation.* New York: Plenum.

Maynard, D. W. (1989). On the ethnography and analysis of discourse in institutional settings. In J. A. Holstein & G. Miller (Eds.), *Perspectives on social problems* (Vol. 1, pp. 127-146). Greenwich, CT: JAI.

Maynard, D. W., & Clayman, S. E. (1991). The diversity of ethnomethodology. *Annual Review of Sociology, 17,* 385-418.

Maynard, D. W., & Manzo, J. (1993). On the sociology of justice. *Sociological Theory, 11,* 171-193.

Mehan, H., & Wood, H. (1975). *The reality of ethnomethodology.* New York: John Wiley.

Mehan, H., & Wood, H. (1976). De-secting ethnomethodology. *American Sociologist, 11,* 13-31.

Miller, G. (1991a). *Enforcing the work ethic: Rhetoric and everyday life in a work incentive program.* Albany: State University of New York Press.

Miller, G. (1991b). Family as excuse and extenuating circumstance: Social organization and use of family rhetoric in a work incentive program. *Journal of Marriage and the Family, 53,* 609-621.

Miller, G., & Holstein, J. A. (1989). On the sociology of social problems. In J. A. Holstein & G. Miller (Eds.), *Perspectives on social problems* (Vol. 1, pp. 1-18). Greenwich, CT: JAI.

Miller, L. J. (1993). Claims-making from the underside: Marginalization and social problems analysis. In J. A. Holstein & G. Miller (Eds.), *Reconsidering social constructionism: Debates in social problems theory* (pp. 349-376). Hawthorne, NY: Aldine de Gruyter.

Mills, C. W. (1959). *The sociological imagination.* New York: Oxford University Press.

Parsons, T. (1968). *The structure of social action.* New York: Free Press.

Pfohl, S. (1992). *Death at the Parasite Cafe.* New York: St. Martin's.

Pollner, M. (1987). *Mundane reason: Reality in everyday and sociological discourse.* Cambridge: Cambridge University Press.

Pollner, M. (1991). Left of ethnomethodology: The rise and decline of radical reflexivity. *American Sociological Review, 56,* 370-380.

Sacks, H. (1972). An initial investigation of the usability of conversational data for doing sociology. In D. Sudnow (Ed.), *Studies in social interaction* (pp. 31-74). New York: Free Press.

Sacks, H. (1974). On the analyzability of stories by children. In R. Turner (Ed.), *Ethnomethodology* (pp. 216-232). Harmondsworth: Penguin.

Sacks, H., Schegloff, E., & Jefferson, G. (1974). A simplest systematics for the organization of turn-taking for conversation. *Language, 50, 696-735*.

Schegloff, E. A., & Sacks, H. (1973). Opening up closings. *Semiotica, 7, 289-327*.

Schutz, A. (1962). *The problem of social reality*. The Hague: Martinus Nijhoff.

Schutz, A. (1964). *Studies in social theory*. The Hague: Martinus Nijhoff.

Schutz, A. (1967). *The phenomenology of the social world*. Evanston, IL: Northwestern University Press.

Schutz, A. (1970). *On phenomenology and social relations*. Chicago: University of Chicago Press.

Schutz, A., & Luckmann, T. (1974). *The structures of the life world*. London: Heinemann.

Silverman, D. (1985). *Qualitative methodology and sociology*. Aldershot: Gower.

Silverman, D. (1987). *Communication and medical practice*. London: Sage.

Smith, D. E. (1993). The standard North American family: SNAF as an ideological model. *Journal of Family Issues, 14, 50-65*.

Smith, D. E. (1989). Women's work as mothers: A new look at the relation of class, family, and school achievement. In J. A. Holstein & G. Miller (Eds.), *Perspectives on social problems* (Vol. 1, pp. 109-127). Greenwich, CT: JAI.

Smith, D. E., & Griffith, A. I. (1990). Coordinating the uncoordinated: Mothering, schooling, and the family wage. In G. Miller & J. A. Holstein (Eds.), *Perspectives on social problems* (Vol. 2, pp. 25-44). Greenwich, CT: JAI.

Spector, M., & Kitsuse, J. I. (1987). *Constructing social problems*. Hawthorne, NY: Aldine de Gruyter.

ten Have, P. (1990). Methodological issues in conversation analysis. *Bulletin de Methodologie Sociologique, 27, 23-51*.

Weber, M. (1947). *Theory of social and economic organization*. New York: Free Press.

Wieder, D. L. (1988). *Language and social reality*. Washington, DC: University Press of America.

Wilson, W. J. (1987). *The truly disadvantaged: The inner city, the underclass, and public policy*. Chicago: University of Chicago Press.

Zimmerman, D. H. (1970). The practicalities of rule use. In J. Douglas (Ed.), *Understanding everyday life* (pp. 221-238). Chicago: Aldine.

Zimmerman, D. H. (1988). On conversation: The conversation-analytic perspective. In J. A. Anderson (Ed.), *Communication yearbook 11* (pp. 406-432). Newbury Park, CA: Sage.

Zimmerman, D. H., & Wieder, D. L. (1970). Ethnomethodology and the problem of order. In J. Douglas (Ed.), *Understanding everyday life* (pp. 285-295). Chicago: Aldine.

7

Grounded Theory Methodology

An Overview

Anselm Strauss & Juliet Corbin

◆ The purpose of this chapter is to give an overview of the origins, purposes, uses, and contributions of grounded theory methodology. We will not address the methodology's suggested procedures or much of the logic lying behind them, as these have been discussed extensively elsewhere (see, e.g., Corbin & Strauss, 1990; Glaser, 1978; Glaser & Strauss, 1967; Strauss, 1987; Strauss & Corbin, 1990; see also Charmaz, 1983, 1990). We will assume here that readers either are acquainted with some of those writings or, if sufficiently interested in this chapter, will turn to those sources.

Grounded theory is a *general methodology* for developing theory that is grounded in data systematically gathered and analyzed. Theory evolves during actual research, and it does this through continuous interplay between analysis and data collection. A central feature of this analytic

AUTHORS' NOTE: This summary statement represents the authors' views as participants in, contributors to, and observers of grounded theory's evolution. Others who have been part of this intellectual movement will differ in their views of some points made here and the relative importance we give to them. We thank Leonard Schatzman for his careful reading of the manuscript and some very useful comments.

approach is "a general method of [constant] comparative analysis" (Glaser & Strauss, 1967, p. vii); hence the approach is often referred to as the *constant comparative method* (for the original formulation, see Glaser, 1965/1967). Since its introduction 25 years ago, a number of guidelines and procedures have evolved through the research experience of its users; these are designed to enhance the effectiveness of this methodology *in* research. The suggested guidelines and procedures allow much latitude for ingenuity and are an aid to creativity (see below for further discussion).

In this methodology, theory may be *generated* initially from the data, or, if existing (grounded) theories seem appropriate to the area of investigation, then these may be *elaborated* and modified as incoming data are meticulously played against them. (For this second point, see Strauss, 1987; see also a similar approach by a sociologist influenced by Glaser & Strauss's *The Discovery of Grounded Theory,* 1967—Diane Vaughan, 1992; she terms it "theoretical elaboration.") Researchers can also usefully carry into current studies any theory based on their *previous research,* providing it seems relevant to these— but again the matching of theory against data must be rigorously carried out.

Grounded theory methodology explicitly involves "generating theory and doing social research [as] two parts of the same process" (Glaser, 1978, p. 2). In proposing this approach to the development of theories, Glaser and Strauss were fully cognizant that alternative approaches to creating and elaborating theory—without explicit linkage to actual research—were popular, or assumed, or vigorously argued for (at the time, these included those of Parsons, Merton, and Blau); they still are (see Laumann, Habermas, or Alexander). In that sense, but also in its inclusion of both general guidelines and, over the years, more specific procedures for producing grounded theories, this approach is still unique. Impressed by this radical *research* approach to theory development, Baszanger (1992, pp. 52-53), a French sociologist, has recently commented on the concerted and detailed "hard work" entailed in generating the resultant concepts and tracing their relationships.

◆ Some Similarities and Differences With Other Modes

Similarities

Grounded theory studies share some similarities with other modes of carrying out qualitative research. Sources of data are the same: interviews and field observations, as well as documents of all kinds (including diaries, letters, autobiographies, biographies, historical accounts, and newspaper and other media materials). Videotapes may also be used. Like other qualitative researchers, grounded theorists can utilize quantitative data or combine qualitative and quantitative techniques of analysis (see the discussion below, but also see Glaser & Strauss, 1967, pp. 185-220). Advocates of this methodology assume, as do many other researchers, that some form of social science is possible and desirable. Also, as have others, grounded theorists have redefined the usual scientific canons for the purposes of studying human behavior (see explicit discussions in Glaser & Strauss, 1967, pp. viii, 224; Strauss & Corbin, 1990). As Glaser and Strauss (1967) assert:

> In this book we have raised doubts about the applicability of these [the usual] canons of rigor as proper criteria for judging the credibility of theory based on the use of this methodology. We have suggested that criteria of judgment be based instead on the detailed elements of the actual strategies used for collecting, coding, analyzing, and presenting data when generating theory, and on the way in which people read the theory. (p. 224)

Involved in this commonly shared redefining is an insistence that ours is interpretive work and, as described below, that interpretations *must* include the perspectives and voices of the people whom we study. Interpretations are sought for understanding the actions of individual or collective actors being studied. Yet, those who use grounded theory procedures share with many other qualitative researchers a distinctive position. They accept responsibility for their interpretive roles. They do not believe it sufficient merely to report or give voice to the viewpoints of the people, groups, or organizations studied. Researchers assume the further responsibility of interpreting what is observed, heard, or read (we comment further on this later in the chapter).

Differences

The major difference between this methodology and other approaches to qualitative research is its emphasis upon theory development. Researchers can aim at various levels of theory when using grounded theory procedures. However, most grounded theory studies have been directed at developing substantive theory. This is because of the overwhelming sub-

160

stantive interests of grounded theory researchers rather than the nature of their methodology. As will be discussed later, higher-level "general" theory is also possible, but when grounded this differs from more deductive types of general theory because of its generation and development through interplay with data collected in actual research (for an example, see Glaser & Strauss, 1970). Regardless of level of theory, there is built into this style of extensive interrelated data collection and theoretical analysis an explicit mandate to strive toward *verification* of its resulting hypotheses (statements of relationships between concepts). This is done *throughout the course* of a research project, rather than assuming that verification is possible only through follow-up quantitative research. Enhanced also by its procedures is the possibility of developing theory of great conceptual density and with considerable meaningful variation. *Conceptual density* refers to richness of concept development and relationships—which rest on great familiarity with associated data and are checked out systematically with these data. (This is different from Geertz's "thick descriptions," where the emphasis is on description rather than conceptualization.)

Other Distinguishing Characteristics: Procedures

Certain other general procedures have made this methodology effective and influential. Besides the constant making of comparisons, these include the systematic asking of generative and concept-relating questions, theoretical sampling, systematic coding procedures, suggested guidelines for attaining conceptual (not merely descriptive) "density," variation, and conceptual integration. More recently, the conceptualization and diagramming of a "conditional matrix" (Corbin & Strauss, 1988; Strauss & Corbin, 1990) helps toward specifying conditions and consequences, at every level of scale from the most "macro" to the "micro," and integrating them into the resulting theory.

As we shall refer to the conditional matrix below, a few words about this analytic tool should be useful. This matrix can be visualized "as a set of circles, one inside the other, each [level] corresponding to different aspects of the world. . . . In the outer rings stand those conditional features *most distant* to action/interaction; while the inner rings pertain to those conditional features bearing *most closely* upon an action/interaction sequence" (Strauss & Corbin, 1990, p. 161). Levels include conditions running from international through national, community, organizational and institutional, suborganizational and subinstitutional, group, individual, and collective to action pertaining to a phenomenon. In any given study, the conditions at all levels have relevance, but just how needs to be traced. "The researcher needs to fill in the specific conditional features for each level that pertain to the chosen area of investigation," regardless of which particular level *it* is (Strauss & Corbin, 1990, p. 161).[1]

◆ Evolution in the Use of the Methodology

Early History

Grounded theory was presented initially by Glaser and Strauss in *The Discovery of Grounded Theory* (1967). This book had three avowed purposes. The first was to offer the rationale for theory that was *grounded*—generated and developed through interplay with data collected during research projects. This type of theory, Glaser and Strauss argued, would contribute toward "closing the embarrassing gap between theory and empirical research" (p. vii). Grounded theories and their possibilities were posed against dominant functionalist and structuralist theories (represented by those of such theorists as Parsons, Merton, and Blau), which Glaser and Strauss regarded as inordinately speculative and deductive in nature. The second purpose was to suggest the logic for and specifics of grounded theories. The third aim was to legitimate careful qualitative research, as by the 1960s this had sunk to a low status among an increasing number of sociologists because it was not believed capable of adequate verification.

Ironically, *Discovery* soon achieved its third aim, becoming an early instance of today's strong rationale that underpins qualitative modes of research. It took about two decades, however, before American sociologists, especially those doing qualitative research, showed much appreciation for the more explicit and systematic conceptualization that constitutes theory. It was then that this aspect of the methodology began to become more widely appreciated, probably in conjunction with increasing numbers of books and papers using this methodology and its suggested procedures. The publication of additional methodological writings—as cited above—by grounded theorists also made it more visible and available.

The simultaneous publication of *Discovery* in the United States and England made "grounded theory" well-known, at least among qualitatively inclined researchers and their graduate students in those countries. In the years after its publication, first Glaser and then Strauss taught a continuing seminar in qualitative analysis, grounded theory-style, to graduate students in the Department of Social and Behavioral Sciences at the University of California in San Francisco. Many graduates have published monographs and papers using grounded theory methodology about a variety of phenomena. These writings have undoubtedly contributed to making qualitative researchers increasingly aware of this mode of analysis. This has been true especially for medical sociologists, because the first two grounded theory monographs were about dying in hospitals (Glaser & Strauss, 1964, 1968).

Because grounded theory is a general methodology, a *way of thinking about and conceptualizing data,* it was easily adapted by its originators and their students to studies of diverse phenomena. To name only a few, these included professional socialization (Broadhead, 1983), policy arenas (Wiener, 1981), remarriage after divorce (Cauhape, 1983), interaction between builders and a would-be homeowner (Glaser, 1972), homecoming (Hall, 1992), the management of a hazardous pregnancy (Corbin, 1992), ovarian egg donation between sisters (Lessor, 1993), spousal abuse (Lempert, 1992), experiences with chronic illness (Charmaz, 1980), and the work of scientists (Clarke, 1990a, 1990b; Fujimura, 1987; Star, 1989a, 1989b), as well as the development of general theory about status passages (Glaser & Strauss, 1970), negotiation (Strauss, 1978), and the control of information ("awareness contexts") (Strauss, 1987, 1991; for more studies, see the appendix to this chapter). Meanwhile, additional books explicating this style of analysis were also published, contributing to a wider international awareness of the methodology and its procedures (Glaser, 1978; Strauss, 1987; Strauss & Corbin, 1990; see also Charmaz, 1983, 1990).

Developments in Use of Grounded Theory

Although much of the original research using grounded theory procedures was done by sociologists, probably the use of these procedures has never been entirely restricted to this group. Researchers in psychology and anthropology are increasingly using grounded theory procedures. Researchers in practitioner fields such as education, social work, and nursing have increasingly used grounded theory procedures alone or in conjunction with other methodologies. These include phenomenology, in its various social science versions (see Benner, 1989), particular techniques (scales and other instruments), and in combination also with quantitative methods. That practitioners would find grounded theory methodology of use in their studies was signaled as an anticipated possibility in *Discovery,* where Glaser and Strauss (1967) asserted, in a chapter titled "Applying Grounded Theory," that an important feature of a grounded theory is its "fitness":

> A grounded theory that is faithful to the everyday realities of a substantive area is one that has been carefully *induced* from diverse data. . . . Only in this way will the theory be closely related to the daily realities (what is actually going on) of substantive areas, and so be highly applicable to dealing with them. (pp. 238-239)

As with any general methodology, grounded theory's actual use in practice has varied with the specifics of the area under study, the purpose and focus of the research, the contingencies faced during the project, and perhaps also the temperament and particular gifts or weaknesses of the researcher. For instance, Adele Clarke (1990a, 1990b) and S. Leigh Star (1989a) each utilized historical data in conjunction with fieldwork and interview data because their research purposes included gaining an understanding of historical origins and historical continuities in the scientific disciplines they studied. Carolyn Wiener (1981), in her study of the national alcohol arena and its many participants and issues, largely relied on published contemporary documents supplemented by intensive interviews and observations at conferences. Individual researchers invent different specific procedures. Almost always too, in handling the difficult problem of conceptual integration, they learn that advice given in the methodological writings and/or the grounded theory seminar requires adaptation to the circumstances of their own thought processes. Personal histories of dealing with particular bodies of data also affect adaptation of the general methodology.

Researchers utilizing grounded theory have undoubtedly been much influenced by contemporary intellectual trends and movements, including ethnomethodology, feminism, political economy, and varieties of postmodernism. Thus the specific uses and views of grounded theory have been either directly influenced or indirectly affected, in terms of thinking through the different assumptions and emphases of alternative modes of analysis (for an instance, see the thoughtful paper by Joan Fujimura, 1991). Our interpretation of this development in the use and conceptualization of grounded theory is not that its central elements—especially constant comparison—are altering, but that additional ideas and concepts suggested by contemporary social and intellectual movements are entering analytically as *conditions* into the studies of grounded theory researchers.

This methodology's stance on such matters is one of openness, including, as we now interpret that openness, in conditional matrix terms. One of the methodology's central features is that its practitioners can respond to and change with the times—in other words, as conditions that affect behavior change, they can be handled analytically, whether the conditions are in the form of ideas, ideologies, technologies, or new uses of space. The general procedure is to ask, What is the influence of gender (for instance), or power, or social class on the phenomena under study?—then to trace this influence as precisely as possible, as well as its influence flowing in reverse direction. Grounded theory procedures force us to ask, for example: What is power in this situation and under specified conditions? How is it manifested, by whom, when, where, how, with what consequences (and for whom or what)? Not to remain open to such a range of questions is to obstruct the discovery of important features of power *in situ* and to preclude developing its further conceptualization. Knowledge is, after all, linked closely with time and place. When we carefully and specifically build conditions into our theories, we eschew claims to idealistic versions of knowledge, leaving the way open for further development of our theories.

Diffusion of the Methodology

In reflecting about the increasing numbers and kinds of research in which grounded theory has been utilized, we have been struck by certain features of its diffusion. Ordinarily, an intellectual trend spreads out from an inventive group or institution largely through face-to-face teaching. In the instance of this methodology, the diffusion appears largely to have taken place—and is today occurring—through its literature, including foreign-language translations and computer software (e.g., NUD•IST—see Richards, Richards, McGalliard, & Sharrock, 1992; and ATLAS/ti—see Mühr, 1992; see also Tesch, 1990) that claims relationships to grounded theory methods.

The diffusion of this methodology seems recently to be increasing exponentially in numbers of studies, types of phenomena studied, geographical spread, and disciplines (education, nursing, psychology, and sociology, for example). The diffusion of grounded theory procedures has now also reached subspecialties of disciplines in which we would not have anticipated their use—and does not always appear in ways that other grounded theorists would recognize as "grounded theory." For instance, there are studies of business management, communication studies concerning such areas as the use of computers by the physically disabled, and "grounded theory" applied to the building of a theoretical model of the epistemology of knowledge production. (We say more about the extension of the methodology later in this chapter.)

Risks Attending Diffusion

This methodology now runs the risk of becoming fashionable. Part of the risk is that users do not understand important aspects of the methodology (as indicated earlier), yet claim to be using it in their research. For instance, they discover a basic process but fail to develop it conceptually, because they overlook or do not understand that variation gives a grounded theory analysis its conceptual richness. People who think they are doing grounded theory studies often seem to concentrate on coding as this methodology's chief and almost exclusive feature, but do not do *theoretical* coding. ("Theoretical codes conceptualize how the substantive codes may relate to each other as hypotheses to be integrated into a theory"; Glaser, 1978, p. 72.) Also, even theoretical coding, unless done in conjunction with the making of constant comparisons, is unlikely to produce conceptually rich theory. Another part of the risk attending grounded theory's rapid diffusion is that some researchers deliberately do not aim at developing theories. Therefore, they ignore this central feature of the methodology, often using its procedures inappropriately or overlooking alternative methodologies that could serve their purposes better.

Also, researchers are still claiming to use "grounded theory methods" because their studies are "inductive." Certainly, thoughtful reaction against restrictive prior theories and theoretical models can be salutary, but too rigid a conception of induction can lead to sterile or boring studies. Alas, grounded theory has been used as a justification for such studies. This has occurred as a result of the initial presentation of grounded theory in *Discovery* that has led to a persistent and unfortunate misunderstanding about what was being advocated. Because of the partly rhetorical purpose of that book and the authors' emphasis on the need for *grounded* theories, Glaser and Strauss overplayed the inductive aspects. Correspondingly, they greatly underplayed both the potential role of extant (grounded) theories and the unquestionable fact (and advantage) that trained researchers are theoretically sensitized. Researchers carry into their research the sensitizing possibilities of their training, reading, and research experience, as well as explicit theories that might be useful if played against systematically gathered data, in conjunction with theories emerging from analysis of these data (Corbin & Strauss, 1990; Glaser, 1978; Strauss, 1987). Many people still get their conceptions of grounded theory from the original book, and have missed the later more realistic and balanced modifications of that book's purposeful rhetoric.

Quantitative Methods and Grounded Theory

Here is an observation about the historic relationship—or, better, lack of relationship—between quantitative researchers and grounded theory, and what may currently be happening to this relationship. As mentioned earlier, *Discovery* made clear that grounded theory was a general methodology, applicable to quantitative as well as qualitative studies. ("We believe that *each form of data is useful for both verification and generation of theory*, whatever the primacy of emphasis. Primacy depends only on the circumstances of research, on the interests and training of the researcher, and on the kinds of material [needed for] theory. . . . *In many instances, both forms of data are necessary*"; Glaser & Strauss, 1967, pp. 17-18.) However, the emphasis and the subtitle of *Discovery* (*Strategies for Qualitative Research*), perhaps combined with the dominance of quantitative methods in sociology and elsewhere for the two decades following its publication, seemingly ensured that only qualitative researchers would pay attention to its messages. Glaser's later publication, *Theoretical Sensitivity* (1978), has had its impact almost wholly on qualitative researchers. We ourselves wrote specifically for qualitative researchers, as the titles of our books signaled (see, e.g., Strauss & Corbin, 1990; but also Strauss, 1987). Increasingly, quantitative researchers seem dissatisfied with purely quantified results and are turning toward supplementary qualitative analyses, while qualitative researchers have become less defensive about their modes of analysis and more open to working with quantitative researchers on research projects. Sometimes they combine quantitative methods with their qualitative ones. Grounded theory research will undoubtedly be affected by these trends.

◆ Theory and Interpretation

This methodology is designed to further the development of effective theory. Why theory? After all, the entire conception of a social "science" is under attack today, especially by some postmodernist and feminist scholars. This is not the appropriate place to counter that attack (and anyhow, a number of defenders of the scientific faith have reexplained and defended the rationale for science). One certainly does not have to adopt a positivistic position or the procedures and specific methods of the physical and biological sciences to argue for the desirability of a social science.

On the other hand, neither does one have to insist that all social inquiry, or even qualitative research, must lead to the development or utilization of theory. Qualitative modes of interpretation run the gamut from "Let the informant speak and don't get in the way," on through theme analysis, and to the elucidation of patterns (biographical, societal, and so on), theoretical frameworks or models (sometimes only loosely developed), and theory formulated at various levels of abstraction (Tesch, 1990). All of these modes certainly are useful for some purposes and not so useful for others. So we do *not* argue that creating theory is more important than any other mode of interpretation, or that it produces more useful or significant results; we argue only that theory should be grounded in the sense described earlier—in interplay with data and developed through the course of actual research.

That said, we turn next to some very brief remarks directed toward the following questions insofar as they pertain to grounded theories. What does theory *consist* of? What does it look like when presented? What is its relation to *"reality"* and *"truth"*? How does it relate to actors' perspectives? Of what use is it, and what responsibilities do researchers/theorists have for producing it?

What Does Theory Consist Of?

Theory consists of *plausible* relationships proposed among *concepts* and *sets of concepts*.[2] (Though only plausible, its plausibility is to be strengthened through continued research.) Without concepts, there can be no propositions, and thus no cumulative scientific (systematically theoretical) knowledge based on these plausible but testable propositions. (On this point, we recommend Herbert Blumer's ironically titled paper "Science

Without Concepts," 1934/1969, in which he clearly outlines the necessity of concepts and conceptual relationships for scientific understanding.)

Grounded theory methodology is designed to guide researchers in producing theory that is "conceptually dense"—that is, with many conceptual relationships. These relationships, stated as propositions, are, as in virtually all other qualitative research, presented in discursive form: They are embedded in a thick context of descriptive and conceptual writing (Glaser & Strauss, 1967, pp. 31-32; Strauss, 1987, pp. 263-264). Discursive presentation captures the conceptual density and conveys descriptively also the substantive content of a study far better than does the natural science form of propositional presentation (typically couched as "if-then").

Theoretical conceptualization means that grounded theory researchers are interested in *patterns* of action and interaction between and among various types of social units (i.e., "actors"). So they are not especially interested in creating theory about individual actors as such (unless perhaps they are psychologists or psychiatrists). They are also much concerned with discovering *process*—not necessarily in the sense of stages or phases, but of reciprocal changes in patterns of action/interaction and in relationship with changes of conditions either internal or external to the process itself.[3] When stages or phases are distinguished for analytic purposes by the researcher, this signifies a conceptualization of what occurs under certain conditions: with movement forward, downward, up and down, going one way then another—all depending on analytically specified conditions. Insofar as theory that is developed through this methodology is able to specify consequences and their related conditions, the theorist can claim predictability for it, in the limited sense that *if* elsewhere approximately similar conditions obtain, *then* approximately similar consequences should occur.

Perhaps a few words should be added to counter possible reactions that this version of theory is overly austere and formal in nature, even if not so in presentation. Earlier we alluded to the relevance ("fit") of substantive grounded theories in terms of what the researcher has actually seen and/or heard, and later more will be said about the relevance of theory in its application. Here we would only note two additional features of grounded theories, regardless of what their levels of abstraction may be. First, theories are always traceable to the data that gave rise to them—within the interactive context of data collecting and data analyzing, in which the analyst is also a crucially significant interactant. Second, grounded theories are very "fluid" (this is the adjective used to characterize them by Joan Fujimura in a personal communication). Because they embrace the inter-action of multiple actors, and because they emphasize temporality and process, they indeed have a striking fluidity. They call for exploration of each new situation to see *if* they fit, *how* they might fit, and how they *might not* fit. They demand an openness of the researcher, based on the "forever" provisional character of every theory. For all that, grounded theories are not just another set of phrases; rather, they are systematic statements of plausible relationships.

What Grounded Theory Writing Looks Like

One reviewer of an earlier version of this chapter suggested that readers might profit from one or two extended quotations illustrating what a grounded theory looks like. In turn, we suggest they might sample from the list of substantive writings by us, our working colleagues, and our ex-students contained in the references as well as the appendix to this chapter. Short of that, we quote from a chapter about "closed awareness context" that is probably quite well-known:

> There are at least five important structural conditions which contribute to the existence and maintenance of the closed awareness context. [These are then discussed in detail for two and a half pages. Then types of interaction that occur under closed awareness conditions are presented both descrip-tively (with quotations) and with analytic sensitivity. Then, since process is important, the authors write:] Inherently, this closed awareness context tends toward instability, as the patient moves either to suspicion or full awareness of . . . terminality. The principal reasons for the instability . . . re-quire only brief notation, as they have already been adumbrated. First, any breakdown in the structural conditions that make for the closed awareness context may lead to its disappearance. Those conditions include [examples are given]. . . . Some unanticipated disclosures or tip-offs, stemming from organizational conditions, can also occur. [More examples are given, in-cluding variations by ward.] New symptoms understandably are likely to perplex and alarm the patient; and the longer his retrogressive course, the more difficult it becomes to give him plausible explanations, though a very complicated misrepresentational drama can be played for his benefit. Even so, it becomes somewhat more difficult to retain . . . trust over a long time. [More comparisons and variations are given.] . . . Another threat to closed awareness . . . is that some treatments make little sense to a patient who

does not recognize that he is dying. . . . At times, moreover, a patient may be unable to cope with his immensely deteriorating physical condition, unless nurses interpret that condition and its symptoms to him. To do this, nurses may feel forced to talk of his dying. Not to disclose . . . can torture and isolate the patient, which runs counter to a central value of nursing care, namely to make the patient as comfortable as possible. . . . The danger that staff members will give the show away . . . also increases as the patient nears death, especially when the dying takes place slowly. . . . This last set of conditions brings us to the question of whether, and how, personnel actually may engineer a change of the closed awareness context. [Examples are given of observations of how this is done.] Indeed, when the family actually knows the truth, the hazards to maintaining closed awareness probably are much increased, if only because kin are more strongly tempted to signal the truth. [There follows then a systematic detailing of consequences: for patients, nurses, physicians, kin, ward, and hospital.] (Glaser & Strauss, 1964, pp. 29-46)

Relationship of Theory to Reality and Truth?

Nowadays there is much debate about these two questions. We follow closely here the American pragmatist position (Dewey, 1937; Mead, 1917): A theory is not the formulation of some discovered aspect of a preexisting reality "out there." [4] To think otherwise is to take a positivistic position that, as we have said above, we reject, as do most other qualitative researchers. Our position is that truth is enacted (Addelson, 1990): Theories are interpretations made from given perspectives as adopted or researched by researchers. To say that a given theory is an interpretation—and therefore fallible—is not at all to deny that judgments can be made about the soundness or probable usefulness of it.

All interpretations, whether or not they have the features or status of theory, are temporally limited—in a dual sense. First, they are always provisional, they are never established forever; their very nature allows for endless elaboration and partial negation (qualification). Second, like many other kinds of knowledge, theories are limited in time: Researchers and theorists are not gods, but men and women living in certain eras, immersed in certain societies, subject to current ideas and ideologies, and so forth. Hence as conditions change at any level of the conditional matrix, this affects the validity of theories—that is, their relation to contemporary social reality. Theories are constantly becoming outdated or in need of qualification because, as one of us once wrote:

We are confronting a universe marked by tremendous fluidity; it won't and can't stand still. It is a universe where fragmentation, splintering, and disappearance are the mirror images of appearance, emergence, and coalescence. This is a universe where nothing is strictly determined. Its phenomena should be partly determinable via naturalistic analysis, including the phenomenon of men [and women] participating in the construction of the structures which shape their lives. (Strauss, 1978, p. 123)

In short, theories are embedded "in history"—historical epochs, eras, and moments are to be taken into account in the creation, judgment, revision, and reformulation of theories.

The interpretive nature of grounded theories means that such conceptualizing is an intellectual process that extends throughout the entire course of a given research project. This is a very complex process, and the next pages will in some sense elaborate its complexity.

Multiple Actors' Perspectives and Analytic Interpretations

Grounded theory methodology incorporates the assumption, shared with other, but not all, social science positions concerning the *human* status of actors whom we study. They have perspectives on and interpretations of their own and other actors' actions. As researchers, we are required to learn what we can of their interpretations and perspectives. Beyond that, grounded theory requires, because it mandates the development of theory, that those interpretations and perspectives become incorporated into our own interpretations (conceptualizations).

Grounded theory procedures enhance this possibility, directing attention, for instance, to *in vivo* concepts that reflect actors' own deep concerns; or its procedures force researchers to question and skeptically review their own interpretations at every step of the inquiry itself. A major argument of this methodology is that *multiple perspectives* must be systematically sought during the research inquiry. This tenet contributes to building theory inclusive of lay conceptions and helps to prevent getting captured by those. Perhaps not every actor's perspectives can be discovered, or need be, but those of actors who sooner or later are judged to be significantly relevant must be incorporated into the emerging theory. (In the language of our contemporaries, multiple "voices" are attended to, but note that these are *also* interpreted conceptually by the researcher who

172

follows our methodology.) Coding procedures—including the important procedures of constant comparison, theoretical questioning, theoretical sampling, concept development, and their relationships—help to protect the researcher from accepting any of those voices on their own terms, and to some extent forces the researcher's own voice to be questioning, questioned, and provisional.

In grounded theory, concepts are formulated and analytically developed, conceptual relationships are posited—but we are emphasizing here that they are inclusive of the multiple perspectives of the actors. Thus grounded theories, which are abstractions quite like any other theories, are nevertheless grounded directly and indirectly on perspectives of the diverse actors toward the phenomena studied by us. Grounded theories connect this multiplicity of perspective with patterns and processes of action/interaction that in turn are linked with carefully specified conditions and consequences.

Effective theoretical coding is also greatly enhanced by theoretical sensitivity (Glaser, 1978; Strauss & Corbin, 1990). This consists of disciplinary or professional knowledge, as well as both research and personal experiences, that the researcher brings to his or her inquiry. This point links with previous discussion of the conditional matrix, because the more theoretically sensitive researchers are to issues of class, gender, race, power, and the like, the more attentive they will be to these matters. The procedures of theoretical sampling and constant comparison are allied with theoretical sensitivity.

Apropos of theoretical sensitivity, we should add that in all modes of qualitative research the interplay between researcher and the actors studied—if the research is intensive—is likely to result in some degree of reciprocal shaping. This is because researcher and data (words and phrases, actions, videotapes) speak to each other. In grounded theory studies, the conversation is centered on theoretical analysis, so the shaping is also related to the process of becoming increasingly theoretically sensitive. During or at the end of the study, the researcher may give information back to the actors, in the form of a final theoretical analysis or framework or, more frequently, through observations informed by an evolving theory. In turn, the theorist, over the course of the research project, may be much affected by the experience of analysis itself (contributed to in some sense by the respondents). Also, the theorist is affected by experiences *with* the respondents, who may not incidentally be contributing ideas, concepts (including *in vivo* concepts), and enduring perspectives to the analysis. In short, the researcher-theorist is becoming increasingly theoretically sensitized, including, as noted earlier, scrutinizing the literature for received theories that might possibly be relevant to the emerging theory developed largely through the continuing conversation with "the data." [5]

Theorists' Responsibilities and Uses of Theory

Emphasizing as it does the theoretical aspects of social research, grounded theory pushes its practitioners toward theoretical interpretations. Thereby they have obligations to contribute to the knowledge of their respective disciplines or professions. However, we who aim at grounded theories also believe (as do many other researchers) that we have obligations to the actors we have studied: obligations to "tell their stories" to them and to others—to give them voice—albeit in the context of their own inevitable interpretations. We owe it to our "subjects" to tell them verbally or in print what we have learned, and to give clear indications of why we have interpreted them as we have. Furthermore, as noted in *Discovery*, a grounded theory "must correspond closely to the data if it is to be applied in daily situations" (Glaser & Strauss, 1967, p. 238). And this faithfulness to the substantive data, this "fit" to a substantive area, is a powerful condition for usefulness in the practical life of the theory. Its usefulness can be a matter of "understanding" as well as of direct application.

Certainly, this does not mean every grounded theory must have immediate or direct application, yet we do have an obligation also toward "society," at least to those social worlds toward which we have commitments. These commitments carry responsibilities to develop or use theory that will have at least some practical applications, that can be of service to wider audiences than are strictly constituted by our disciplinary or professional colleagues or even the *specific* groups, organizations, or social worlds that we have studied. Translation of even well-grounded substantive theory is not necessarily immediate, and ultimately the responsibility may rest on educators or actual practitioners "in the field." One example of a successful application through combined efforts of two researchers/theorists (a sociologist and a researcher/nurse educator) and clinical nurses/educators is the extension of the concept of "trajectory" into a model fairly directly applicable to the giving of nursing care and to research on nursing care (Woog, 1992).

174

Grounded theories can also be relevant and possibly influential either to the "understanding" of policy makers or to their direct action. As an instance of the former, we point to a policy book on health care (Strauss & Corbin, 1990) that offers a critique of the present health care system and a blueprint for a rather different one that has typically been rejected by practical-minded policy readers but has opened horizons of understanding to those not so committed to current arrangements.

Our stand on this third obligation, to the wider society, seems at variance with others taken by those who would confine actions, or reform activities, only to improving the lot of the people actually studied. Because all theory carries implications for action, we would not so confine its applicability. Careful grounded theory is likely to be used, and used in ways other than any dreamed of by us researchers/theorists—far beyond our commitments and desires. Hence we bear the special responsibility of attempting to reach at least the audiences that we ourselves wish to reach.

◆ Higher-Order Grounded Theories

In *Discovery*, a chapter titled "From Substantive to Formal Theory" (1967) begins with a very important set of ideas; indeed, they seem even more important now. Their significance lies both in the continued predominance of substantive theory (or substantive studies *sans* theorizing) and the paucity of higher-level social theories that are *grounded in specific research inquiries*. Here is the quotation:

> Since substantive theory is grounded in research on one particular substantive area (work, juvenile delinquency, medical education, mental health) it might be taken to apply only to that specific area. A theory at such a conceptual level, however, may have important general implications and relevance, and become almost automatically a springboard or stepping stone to the development of a grounded formal [or as is more usually said, "general"] theory. . . . Substantive theory is a strategic link in the formulation and generation of grounded formal theory. We believe that although formal theory can be generated directly from data, it is more desirable, and usually necessary, to start the formal theory from a substantive one. The latter not only provides a stimulus to a "good idea" but it also gives an initial direction in developing relevant categories and properties and in choosing

175

possible modes of integration. Indeed it is difficult to find a grounded formal theory that was not in some way stimulated by a substantive theory. Often the substantive and formal theories are formulated by different authors. Sometimes in formal theory the substantive theory is implicit, having been developed previously by the author or another writer. (Glaser & Strauss, 1967, p. 79)

In the pages that followed this statement, Glaser and Strauss noted the drawbacks of formulating formal theory on the basis of data from only one rather than several substantive areas. In a book published three years later (1970), those authors presented a formal theory about status passages that was both a development of previous conceptualizations and based on data amassed from a multitude of substantive areas. A later book offered a theory of negotiation (Strauss, 1978), taking off from a theoretical formulation known as "negotiated order" (Strauss, Bucher, Ehrlich, Sabshin, & Schatzman, 1963, 1964), and from an examination of data drawn both from various substantive areas and several monographs or social and political theorists' writings. Earlier, Strauss (in a 1970 work reprinted in 1987, pp. 306-311) published a paper titled "Discovering New Theory From Previous Theory" that suggested in detail how a grounded substantive theory could be greatly extended, leading either to a more elaborated substantive theory or to formal theories developed in conjunction with multiarea data. (For similar discussions of substantive and formal theories, see Glaser, 1978, pp. 143-157; Strauss, 1987, pp. 241-248.)

As mentioned earlier, Diane Vaughan (1992), a thoughtful theorist and excellent researcher, has written about an alternative but related approach to producing general theory. She advocates "theory elaboration," which consists of taking off from extant theories and developing them further in conjunction with "qualitative case analysis." By *theory,* she means "theoretical tools in general," including (formulated) theory, models, and concepts. By *elaboration,* she means "the process of refining the theory, model or concept in order to specify more carefully the circumstances in which it does or does not offer potential for explanation" (p. 175). (Her examples, however, are mostly of her own grounded theories and research, but she also utilizes some existing substantive grounded ones.) From reading her, we have gained an appreciation of further techniques for attaining theories that are more general, that embrace but transcend the substantive while at the same time linking those with previous theories (see also Gerson, 1991). It is apparent that we will face complexities in developing theories at different levels or degrees of abstraction. These complexities have not yet been clarified in the literature. (The terms *general* and *formal* are too crude to catch those degrees or levels of theory.)

So here is a challenge that should be faced by anyone who believes theory should be grounded! We should not settle only for substantive theories, no matter how stimulating or useful they are—for furthering theory development, for understanding phenomena, for *Verstehen* of people and actions, or for their practical use in guiding behavior or policy. General theory also has its place as a powerful tool for all those same purposes. The danger of such theorizing is not that it is abstract—for that can be a great advantage—but that it can be speculatively remote from the phenomena it purports to explain. Grounded theory methodology insists that no matter how general—how broad in scope or abstract—the theory, it should be developed in that back-and-forth interplay with data that is so central to this methodology.

Yet whether general or substantive theory is sought, there is a potential danger in using this methodology if a researcher is overly familiar with and attached to the concepts and conceptual frameworks presented in previous grounded theory studies. The danger is that these may be used without genuine grounding in the current study. They too must be grounded in the interplay with data, just as are those taken from other sources.

◆ Social and Intellectual Trends and Grounded Theory

To round off this chapter, the editors of this volume have requested that we make a guess at what the future might hold for grounded theory. Crystal gazing is not our forte, but we can at least anticipate the following. First, consider certain strong social and intellectual trends that are likely to affect greatly the awareness, rejection, and varied uses of this methodology:

1. the continued fragmentation of traditional social and behavioral science disciplines into subdisciplines, each with its currently distinctive issues, types of data, and often specific research procedures

2. an increasing interest in and the presumed necessity for social research within various professions and their subunits, and directed toward an increasing or at least changing set of issues

3. a continued reliance on qualitative methods alone or in conjunction with quantitative ones, by increasing numbers of professional and disciplinary researchers

4. an increasing interest in theoretical interpretations of data, along with divergent definitions of theory believed to fit the nature of one's materials

5. a continuation of the current trend of antagonism toward anything that goes by the name of science and especially toward its canons

6. the spread of postmodernism, but a variegated spread, given that there are many and sometimes divergent directions within this general intellectual movement

7. a continued trend toward the use of computer programs to order and interpret data, perhaps with visual and oral accompaniments

8. in the world at large, probably a continued and even greater emphasis on individual and collective identity (nationalism, for instance), requiring improved methods for understanding the meanings and symbolization of actors

All of these trends should profoundly affect the use and evaluation of grounded theory. Think, if you will, of this general methodology as in early stages of the comparable development of survey research circa 1940. What researchers did with survey methodology, once aware of it, was to reject it for one reason or another, or over the years to use it in its original formulation, elaborate it, or adapt it in various ways, including combining it with other methodologies. The fate of grounded theory methodology should not be appreciably different.

So at least it can be safely predicted, keeping the previously noted social-intellectual conditions in mind, that the following *processes* will occur:

1. Researchers in additional substantive and professional areas and countries will experiment with and use or adapt the methodology.

2. Adaption will include combining it with other methodologies (hermeneutical, phenomenological, for instance). It will also be combined with quantitative methods on predominantly quantitative or predominantly qualitative projects, or on projects of equal emphasis.

3. Particular fields will combine the methodology with other methodologies rather than consider them to be competing. (For instance, researchers in nursing use various combinations of ethnography, phenomenology, and grounded theory; presumably psychologists will combine or are combining the latter with more traditional or emerging research methods.)

4. An increasing number of computer programs will include the possibility of utilizing the methodology, and these programs will become more sophisticated and will be used increasingly for this purpose.

5. The procedures suggested or used in the current grounded theory literature will become elaborated *and* specific adaptations will be made by
researchers for a greater range of phenomena. This elaboration and adaption will include also multisite studies in a variety of settings, including
cross-cultural work.

6. Varieties of theory (or "interpretation") will be developed by different
researchers and in different areas, all of whom will use one or another
adapted/elaborated version of the methodology.

Recently, an astute sociologist asked us to say something about the outer
limits of research that *we* would or could continue to call "grounded theory."
The features of this methodology that we consider so central that their
abandonment would signify a great departure are the grounding of theory
upon data through data-theory interplay, the making of constant comparisons, the asking of theoretically oriented questions, theoretical coding, and
the development of theory. Yet no inventor has permanent possession of
the invention—certainly not even of its name—and furthermore we would
not wish to do so. No doubt we will always prefer the later versions of
grounded theory that are closest to or elaborate our own, but a child once
launched is very much subject to a combination of its origins and the
evolving contingencies of life. Can it be otherwise with a methodology?

APPENDIX:
A SAMPLING OF SUBSTANTIVE
WRITINGS BY UCSF RESEARCHERS

Biernacki, P. (1986). *Pathways from heroin addiction.* Philadelphia: Temple University
Press.

Charmaz, K. (1987). Struggling for a self: Identity levels of the chronically ill. In P.
Conrad & J. Roth (Eds.), *The experience of chronic illness.* Greenwich, CT: JAI.

Corbin, J., & Strauss, A. (1991). Comeback: Overcoming disability. In G. Albrecht & J.
Levy (Eds.), *Advances in medical sociology* (Vol. 2). Greenwich, CT: JAI.

Fagerhaugh, S., & Strauss, A. (1977). *The politics of pain management.* Menlo Park, CA:
Addison-Wesley.

Fagerhaugh, S., Strauss, A., Suczek, B., & Wiener, C. (1987). *Hazards in hospital care.* San
Francisco: Jossey-Bass.

Rosenbaum, M. (1981). *Women on heroin.* New Brunswick, NJ: Rutgers University Press.

Strauss, A., Fagerhaugh, S., Suczek, B., & Wiener, C. (1985). *The organization of medical
work.* Chicago: University of Chicago Press.

Strauss, A., & Glaser, B. (1970). *Anguish: A case history of a dying trajectory.* San Francisco:
Sociology Press.

Wiener, C., Strauss, A., Fagerhaugh, F., & Suczek, B. (1979). Trajectories, biographies, and the evolving medical scene: Labor and delivery and the intensive care nursery. *Sociology of Health and Illness, 1,* 261-283.

◆ Notes

1. Here is a nice illustration of tracing effects of conditions, or in the authors' (ex-students of Strauss's) words, "things, attributes, elements are *in the situation itself.* . . . For example, Fujimura (1987) noted that stockholders in biotechnology companies are very present elements in the laboratory (though rarely in person), and not merely contextual. Stockholders routinely constrained decision making in the construction of doable problems and what the next step in a project might be. The claims and other products that emerge from the situation embody all the elements within it, human and nonhuman alike. Therefore specifying the elements is a highly significant task" (Clarke & Fujimura, 1992, pp. 17-18).

2. "A coherent group of general propositions used [provisionally] as principles of explanation for a class of phenomena" (Stein & Urdang, 1981, p. 1471).

3. *"To capture process analytically,* one must show the evolving nature of events by noting why and how action/interaction—in the form of events, doings or happenings—will change, stay the same . . . ; why there is progression of events or what enables continuity of a line of action/interaction, in the face of changing conditions, and with what consequences" (Strauss & Corbin (1990, p. 144; but see discussion, pp. 143-157).

4. The pragmatists emphasized consequences and the antecedent conditions that precipitated them, and urged abandonment of the impossible quest for Truth. Grounded theory advocates follow this general position. Reading an earlier version of this chapter, one reviewer asked about our position on the relationships of ideology and power to truth. In brief: Power certainly affects the ability to convince audiences, including probably oneself, if one takes one's power seriously. Ideologies we all have—we all have political and other positions—but unquestioning allegiance to those, with little or no attempt to challenge or "test" them, leads sociologists like Irving Horowitz, quite correctly, we believe, into battle with sociological ideologues. Grounded theory has procedures that help one to challenge one's own ideologies and implicit positions. The feminist critique of the objective biases of traditional science seems to us correct insofar as some scientists may assume they are just human instruments reporting on nature (it used to be God's nature) "out there." Contemporary physical and biological scientists seem to understand quite well the naïveté of such a position, although they also, sometimes, individually display awesome hubris.

A related point, raised by another reviewer, is that "researchers often *write* as though order were implicit . . . and inhered in the data, when what they really meant was that order emerged from interaction between the researcher, his/her data, and some theoretical sensitivity suggested by the original research question." That is exactly the point!

5. A reviewer of an earlier version of this chapter suggested that our statement about theoretical sensitivity is an overstatement because naive researchers "may be even more likely to see things that don't make sense, and therefore asks questions why? or may be more

likely to ask why don't you think about it (do it) this way?" He has a point, given that new perspectives can precipitate significant and even radical issues. Personal experiences are also immensely vital to theoretical sensitivity (Corbin & Strauss, 1990; Glaser, 1978).

◆ References

Addelson, K. (1990). Why philosophers should become sociologists (and vice versa). In H. Becker & M. McCall (Eds.), *Symbolic interaction and cultural studies* (pp. 119-147). Chicago: University of Chicago Press.

Baszanger, I. (1992). Introduction. In *La Trame de la Negociation: Sociologie Qualitative et Interactionnisme* (pp. 11-63). Paris: L'Harmattan.

Benner, P. (1989). *The primacy of caring: Stress and coping in health and illness*. Menlo Park, CA: Addison-Wesley.

Blumer, H. (1969). Science without concepts. In H. Blumer, *Symbolic interactionism: Perspective and method* (pp. 153-170). Englewood Cliffs, NJ: Prentice Hall. (Reprinted from *American Journal of Sociology, 1934, 36*, 515-533)

Broadhead, R. (1983). *Private lives and professional identity of medical students*. New Brunswick, NJ: Transaction.

Cauhape, E. (1983). *Fresh starts: Men and women after divorce*. New York: Basic Books.

Charmaz, K. (1980). The construction of self-pity in the chronically ill. *Studies in Symbolic Interaction, 3*, 123-145.

Charmaz, K. (1983). The grounded theory method: An explication and interpretation. In R. Emerson (Ed.), *Contemporary field research* (pp. 109-126). Boston: Little, Brown.

Charmaz, K. (1990). "Discovering" chronic illness: Using grounded theory. *Sociology of Health and Illness, 30*, 1161-1172.

Clarke, A. (1990a). Controversy and the development of reproductive sciences. *Social Problems, 27*, 18-37.

Clarke, A. (1990b). A social worlds research adventure: The case of reproductive sciences. In S. Cozzens & T. Gieryn (Eds.), *Theories of science in society* (pp. 23-50). Bloomington: Indiana University Press.

Clarke, A., & Fujimura, J. (Eds.). (1992). *The right tools for the job: At work in twentieth-century life sciences*. Princeton, NJ: Princeton University Press.

Corbin, J. (1992). Caregiving. *Revue Internationale d'Action Communautaire, 28*, 39-49.

Corbin, J., & Strauss, A. (1988). *Unending work and care: Managing chronic illness at home*. San Francisco: Jossey-Bass.

Corbin, J., & Strauss, A. (1990). Grounded theory method: Procedures, canons, and evaluative criteria. *Qualitative Sociology, 13*, 3-21.

Dewey, J. (1937). *Logic: The theory of inquiry*. New York: Holt.

Fujimura, J. (1987). Constructing doable problems in cancer research: Articulating alignment. *Social Studies of Science, 17*, 257-293.

Fujimura, J. (1991). On methods, ontologies, and representation in the sociology of science: Where do we stand? In D. Maines (Ed.), *Social organization and social process* (pp. 207-248). New York: Aldine de Gruyter.

Gerson, E. (1991). Supplementing grounded theory. In D. Maines (Ed.), *Social organization and social process* (pp. 285-301). New York: Aldine de Gruyter.

Glaser, B. (1967). The constant comparative method of qualitative analysis. In B. Glaser & A. Strauss, *The discovery of grounded theory: Strategies for qualitative research* (pp. 101-116). Chicago: Aldine. (Reprinted from *Social Problems*, 1965, 12, 436-445)

Glaser, B. (1972). *Experts versus laymen: A study of the patsy and the subcontractor.* New Brunswick, NJ: Transaction.

Glaser, B. (1978). *Theoretical sensitivity.* Mill Valley, CA: Sociological Press.

Glaser, B., & Strauss, A. (1964). *Awareness of dying.* Chicago: Aldine.

Glaser, B., & Strauss, A. L. (1967). *The discovery of grounded theory: Strategies for qualitative research.* Chicago: Aldine.

Glaser, B., & Strauss, A. (1968). *Time for dying.* Chicago: Aldine.

Glaser, B., & Strauss, A. (1970). *Status passages.* Chicago: Aldine.

Hall, C. (1992). *Homecoming: The self at home.* Unpublished doctoral thesis, University of California, San Francisco, Department of Social and Behavioral Sciences.

Lempert, L. (1992). *The crucible: Violence, help seeking, and abused women's transformations of self.* Unpublished doctoral thesis, University of California, San Francisco, Department of Social and Behavioral Sciences.

Lessor, R. (1993). All in the family: Social processes in ovarian egg donation between sisters. *Sociology of Health and Illness, 15,* 393-413.

Mead, G. (1917). Scientific method and the individual thinker. In J. Dewey (Ed.), *Creative intelligence* (pp. 167-227). New York: Holt.

Mühr, T. (1992). *ATLAS/ti user manual: Beta version 0.94c.* Berlin: Berlin Technical University.

Richards, T., Richards, L., McGalliard, J., & Sharrock, B. (1992). *NUD•IST 2.3:* Users manual. La Trobe, Australia: Replee Pty/La Trobe University.

Star, S. L. (1989a). *Regions of the mind: Brain research and the quest for scientific certainty.* Stanford, CA: Stanford University Press.

Star, S. L. (1989b). The structure of ill-structured solutions: Boundary objects and heterogeneous distributed problem solving. In M. Huhns & L. Gasser (Eds.), *Distributed artificial intelligence* (Vol. 3, pp. 37-54). Menlo Park, CA: Morgan Kauffmann.

Stein, J., & Urdang, L. (1981). *The Random House dictionary of the English language.* New York: Random House.

Strauss, A. (1978). *Negotiations: Varieties, contexts, processes and social order.* San Francisco: Jossey-Bass.

Strauss, A. (1987). *Qualitative analysis for social scientists.* New York: Cambridge University Press.

Strauss, A. (1991). *Creating sociological awareness.* New Brunswick, NJ: Transaction.

Strauss, A., Bucher, R., Ehrlich, D., Sabshin, M., & Schatzman, L. (1963). The hospital and its negotiated order. In E. Freidson (Ed.), *The hospital in modern society* (pp. 147-169). New York: Free Press.

Strauss, A., Bucher, R., Ehrlich, D., Sabshin, M., & Schatzman, L. (1964). *Psychiatric ideologies and institutions.* New York: Free Press.

Strauss, A., & Corbin, J. (1990). *Basics of qualitative research: Grounded theory procedures and techniques.* Newbury Park, CA: Sage.

Tesch, R, (1990). *Qualitative research: Analysis types and software tools.* New York: Falmer.

Vaughan, D. (1992). Theory elaboration: The heuristics of case analysis. In H. Becker & C. Ragin (Eds.), *What is a case?* (pp. 173-202). New York: Cambridge University Press.

Wiener, C. (1981). *The politics of alcoholism.* New Brunswick, NJ: Transaction.

Woog, P. (Ed.). (1992). *The chronic illness trajectory framework: The Corbin and Strauss nursing model.* New York: Springer.

8

Biographical Method

Louis M. Smith

Biographers write lives.
—Leon Edel, *Writing Lives,* 1984

◆ A Perspective on Biography: Domain, Variety, and Complexity

This statement, "Biographers write lives," is not so simple as it sounds. It is the first line in Leon Edel's (1984) "manifesto" on doing biography. "Writing lives" carries connotations that seem more than a bit broader than biography per se. Handbooks and handbook chapters, such as this, are codifications, statements of rules of practice useful to practitioners—in this instance, practitioners of qualitative research methods. When one writes lives, so I would argue, one finds that every rule, even when so simply stated as a "rule of thumb," always plays through some individual person and becomes his or her interpretation as the rule is thought about or put into practice. And when one writes a handbook chapter, giving form to an idea, such as "biographical method," the individual author expresses a personal point of view. In an unusual sense, I would argue, every text that is created is a self-statement, a bit of autobiography, a statement that carries an individual signature. Such reasoning suggests that all writing should be

AUTHOR'S NOTE: As usual, I want to thank my colleagues and students in the Department of Education at Washington University. In particular, the members of my recent seminars have been most helpful.

184

in the first person, reflecting that individual voice, even when one writes a chapter in a handbook. At an extreme, paraphrasing Saroyan, I almost want to make the case that it's autobiography, all down the line.

In this essay I will speak in the first person, in spite of some conventional wisdom that suggests "handbooks" are more detached summaries of general knowledge. My audience is students and scholars of qualitative methods who are interested in adding biographical method and life writing to their inquiry repertory. My outline is fairly simple. First is a brief overview of domain or "turf." Second, I present a process account of "doing biography," the problems one encounters, the alternatives available, the trade-offs, and the decisions one tries to live with. The third section is a too-brief excursion into the place of biography in the several intellectual disciplines that make use of life writing. Finally, I offer a few tentative generalizations to integrate the overall perspective.

The Domain of Biography: General and Personal

Formally, biography is "the written history of a person's life"—so says *Webster's Dictionary*. The *Oxford English Dictionary* nearly agrees, but not quite. "A written record of the life of an individual" is that volume's second usage. The word *life* appears in both definitions. *Person* and *individual* seem close synonyms, although some might argue that a person, a human being, is only one kind of individual within the larger category of individuals. And some might argue that *record* is different from *history*, perhaps less interpretive. Finally, *written* defines oral traditions as outside the genre. A too-limiting constraint for contemporary students and scholars? Obviously, yes! But the major point of this personal perspective and more formal definitional introduction lies in the domain or turf to be encompassed in any discussion of biography. The *OED*, in its first definition, confounds further the domain of biography as it states, "the history of the lives of individual men, as a branch of literature." Women are excluded. The social sciences of anthropology, psychology, and sociology are excluded. From this point on, the concept of biography, and the activity it signifies, becomes contentious—some would argue "political." And that is an important generalization.

Finally, part of what I want to say in this chapter draws upon several vivid personal professional experiences I have had in qualitative research. Three decades ago, I spent a long semester in an elementary classroom taught by a man named William Geoffrey. We wrote a book about that experience, *The Complexities of an Urban Classroom* (Smith & Geoffrey, 1968). It was cast as a "microethnography" of the classroom, a study of a small social system. In another sense the book was a piece of a biography, the story of one semester of Geoffrey and his teaching. In a further sense, it became part of my autobiography, the most important professional learning experience of my life, an "epiphany" or "turning point," in Denzin's (1989) interpretive theory of biography. The text carried, in a subdued way, both of those personal stories. At the time, neither of us thought about the experience or the book as his or my biography or autobiography. But, I would say now, it can be reconstrued in this alternative way.

The second personal experience that is very pertinent was a follow-up study, the "life histories" of the teachers and administrators of the Kensington Elementary School and the Milford School District. We called that *Educational Innovators: Then and Now* (Smith, Kleine, Prunty, & Dwyer, 1986). Life histories, at least as we developed them in this instance from long, two- to seven-hour, interviews, are briefer, more focused biographies, mostly told from the teachers' own perspectives. One of the major personal outcomes of that work was the realization that at some point I wanted to do what I came to call "a real biography." I am now in the middle, actually toward the end, of that experience, a biography that carries the title *Nora Barlow and the Darwin Legacy* (Smith, in press). That effort, as process and product, will flow in and out of this essay. Each of these experiences has led to considerable reflection on "how we did what we did," what we have called "miniature theories of methodology," often written as "methodological appendices." For me, writing this chapter on "biographical method" is not a simple, detached, impersonal exercise. And that may be good or bad, as we shall see.

Variants of Biography

Life writing comes with many labels—portrayals, portraits, profiles, memoirs, life stories, life histories, case studies, autobiographies, journals, diaries, and on and on—each suggesting a slightly different perspective under consideration. Most of these can be tracked through dictionary definitions, illustrations in this text, and various sources listed in the references. Noting variety in biography is perhaps too simple a point. But the world seems full of true believers, individuals who want to restrict options to one or just a few alternatives in creating or criticizing biography.

Further, one of the points I want to make is that life writing is in serious contention among readers, critics, and practitioners of biography. For instance, one of the most investigated individuals in the Western world is Charles Darwin.[1] A brief glance at him, his interpreters, and the written records involving him suggests the range of possibilities in doing life writing and the difficulties of interpretation for anyone contemplating biography.

Darwin's first major publication—life writing, if you will—was his journal (1839) of the five-year voyage of HMS *Beagle* as it circumnavigated the world between 1831 and 1836. Also in 1839, FitzRoy, captain of the *Beagle,* published his journal, a companion volume about the voyage. In 1845, Darwin revised, with significant additions and abridgments, his journal. New, but only slightly different, editions appeared in 1860 and 1870. Some hundred years after the voyage, in 1933, Nora Barlow published *Charles Darwin's Diary of the Voyage of the H.M.S. Beagle.* Approximately one-fourth of the material in that publication was new, previously unpublished. Barlow included a number of footnotes, a list of *dramatis personae* with brief identifying biographical information, maps, six pages of "bibliography," of Darwin publications from the *Beagle* period, and other related material.

In his late 60s, Darwin wrote an autobiography for the "amusement" of his family. Darwin's son Francis published the autobiography in 1888 as part of the three-volume *Life and Letters of Charles Darwin.* But the autobiography had been expurgated. In 1958, Nora Barlow published a "de-edited" version of the autobiography, restoring some 6,000 words. In recent years, additions to a long list of major biographies continue to appear. Bowlby (1990) and Desmond and Moore (1991) have contributed at great length (500 and 800 pages) major new views. The list continues,[2] but the major point here is that biography, "life writing," comes in multiple forms, lengths, focuses, and perspectives. A related point is the importance of insight and creativity on the part of the biographer in the studying, constructing, and writing of lives or parts of lives.

The Special Instance of Autobiography

Autobiography is a special case of life writing. Writing autobiographies and critiques of autobiography is one of the most rapidly developing and, recently, one of the most controversial forms (Lejeune, 1989; Olney, 1980; Stanley, 1992). Autobiography suggests the power of agency in social and literary affairs. It gives voice to people long denied access. By example, it usually, but not always, eulogizes the subjective, the "important part of human existence" over the objective, "less significant parts of life." It blurs the borders of fiction and nonfiction. And, by example, it is a sharp critique of positivistic social science. In short, from my perspective, autobiography in its changing forms is at the core of late twentieth-century paradigmatic shifts in the structures of thought. And that is quite an agenda. Even as I state these tentative generalizations, I have to pull back, at least to a degree, for the eminent and consummate behavioristic psychologist B. F. Skinner (1977, 1979, 1983) has written a three-volume autobiography that denies every one of the points. The simple lesson is, Don't generalize or evaluate too quickly about life writing!

With tantalizing good humor, Pritchett (1977), in his presidential address to the English Association, pushed some of the limits of "autobiography." In his opening paragraph he posed one controversial version of the difficulties this variant of life writing creates for the scholar as reader: "It is common among knowing reviewers to lump autobiography and the novel together as examples of two different ways of telling agreeable lies." For anyone with "scientific" leanings, doing "fiction" is anathema. *Caveat emptor* is an immediate response. The paragraph continues:

> But, of course, you have only to start writing your autobiography to know how crucial the distinction is. The novelist distributes himself in disguise among the characters in his work. It is easy for him to pretend he's a man, woman, or child and, if he likes, in the first person. The autobiographer on the other hand comes forward as the hero or the anti-hero of his story and draws other people into himself.

But Pritchett can't quite let the audience off so easily as he concludes the paragraph with the bon mot:

> In a sense he is sort of stripper: the suspense of his story lies in guessing how far he will undress. Or, of course—if he is writing about his career—we see him putting more and more important clothes on. (p. 3)

In a penetrating essay, Gusdorf (1980) makes a similar point more pithily, that autobiography is "a sort of posthumous propaganda for posterity" (p. 36).

For the reader, determining what one learns from an autobiography becomes an exercise in critical judgment. Few would argue that they have not learned something of importance from reading an autobiography. But here as well, readers must do their own constructing, reconstructing, and evaluating. Reading Eakin (1989) reinforces such a conclusion.

The larger theory of knowledge issues and dilemmas—What do we know? How confident can we be in our knowledge?—becomes clearly visible in assaying this kind of scholarly inquiry. Olney (1980), in his historical and critical overview, does a kind of analysis on the label per se:

auto	bios	graphy
self	life	writing

As his argument proceeds, Olney sees the self in a never-ending transition, ending only in death. And that self will see the life from a different point of view at different points in the life. Finally, and this point is made even more strongly in Gusdorf's (1980) essay from the same volume, the very act of writing forces a self-examination that changes both the self and quite possibly the life as well. In a sense, three open-ended systems are in constant flux, flow, and interchange. From my point of view, positive knowledge about anything in the human condition is a misconstrual. At the same time, one knows more than "nothing." Knowledge has a quality of a balancing act. The problems are both more subtle and more complex than Pritchett's metaphor of robing and disrobing and Eakin's analysis of Lejeune's definitional problems, although these are important parts of the dilemma.

In related disciplines, the historian Hexter (1971) speaks of the first and second records in historical inquiry. The first is the something "out there" that has happened over time in the past. The "second record" is what each historian brings to the first record—the questions, the values, the beliefs, and the idiosyncratic life experiences, some professional and some personal. If his distinction is credible, history has a quality of being "autohistory." The anthropologist Malinowski (1922) makes a similar point, that the anthropologist should bring along the best of contemporary theory when he or she goes into the field setting. In this personal intellectual baggage, Malinowski makes an oft-quoted distinction between "foreshadowed problems" and "preconceived solutions," a distinction often hard to define in the particular situation. And those foreshadowed problems do not remain static but take on a life of their own in the field and in the writing of ethnographic reports, monographs, and books. The autobiographical, if not autobiography in the formal sense—that is, the personal—enters into any creative intellectual construction. Other students, especially the feminists and minority members of our culture, see larger political and ethical issues within the genre. Liberation, oppression, and multicultural themes get writ large in much autobiography, a point I shall raise later in this essay. Conceptual labels such as "auto/biographical" (Stanley, 1992) attempt to reflect and redirect inquiry in life writing.[3]

◆ What Life Writers Do: The Craft of Biography

Writing lives is the devil.
—Virginia Woolf (quoted in Edel, 1984, p. 17)

Several years ago, Donald Schön (1983, 1987) introduced the concept of the "reflective practitioner" into the professional literature. In one sense, his argument is simple. Professional practitioners, be they physicians, architects, or teachers—or, one might add, craftspersons or artists—face "situations of practice" characterized by complexity, uncertainty, instability, uniqueness, and value conflict. In my view, that is a formidable set of dimensions. In Schön's view, the problems professionals face cannot be solved by the formulas of "technical rationality." I would extend his view to social scientists in general and those doing qualitative case studies in particular. The problems and dilemmas confronting life writers as they practice some aspect or form of the craft of biography have the same quality. The decisions biographers make are constituted by ambiguity, and that is part of the excitement and the agony of doing biography (Smith, 1990, 1992).

Among a number of life writers illustrating the particulars of the processes involved in the craft of biography, none surpasses the insights of Catherine Drinker Bowen (1959, 1968), James Clifford (1970), and Leon Edel (1984). Each of their books is an autobiographical statement of its author's perspective on biography: Edel—"all my writings on biography which I wish to preserve" (p. 248); Bowen—"the biographer's way of life, which to my mind is a pleasant way" (p. ix); and Clifford—"the operative concerns of a writer who decides to recreate the career of another person" (p. vii). It is to them, and a few others, I turn for an outline of understandings and generalizations in the practice of the biographical craft.

Selecting a Subject and First Inquiries

The obvious first task of biography is the decision concerning a person to write about. One must select a hero or heroine, be he or she recognized as such or not by the population at large. The autobiographer solves this first problem simply, although questions arise immediately as to why an individual would think his or her life worth telling—for example, has a kind of self-deception already begun? In contrast, the biographer needs to think carefully and analytically, to perceive intuitively an anomaly, or to be serendipitous, that is, just plain lucky. The literature is full of examples of each variant of what social scientists call "problem finding," a major element in creativity. And if one wants to complicate these simple interpretations, and perhaps make oneself a bit uneasy, follow Leon Edel (1984) as he reflects: "In a world full of subjects—centuries crowded with notables and dunces—we may indeed ask why a modern biographer fixes his attention on certain faces and turns his back on others" (p. 60). The biographer's personality—motives, fears, unconscious conflicts, and yearnings— reaches out to responsive, if not similar, territory in the person to be subject. The dance of Boswell and Johnson, of Strachey and his eminent Victorians, and of more recent American biographers and their choices is analyzed vividly by Edel. In a compelling short preface to *Young Man Luther,* Erik Erikson (1962) poses the issues this way:

> I have attempted in this preface to give a brief rationale for writing this book; I doubt, though, that the impetus for writing anything but a textbook can ever be rationalized. My choice of subject forces me to deal with problems of faith and problems of Germany, two enigmas which I could have avoided by writing about some other young great man. *But it seems that I did not wish to avoid them.* (p. 9; emphasis added)

What meets the eye is never quite what it seems—so Edel and others show and tell us.

Often the problem finding is mixed with discovering an important new pool of data. Derek Hudson (1972) commented in the introduction to his biography of A. J. Munby, the "hero" of the Hannah Cullwick story:

> I first became aware of A. J. Munby in the autumn of 1968. I was looking through *The Oxford Companion to English Literature* and came to the heading: MUNBY, ARTHUR JOSEPH (1828-1910). After mentioning

various books of his verse, the brief entry concluded: "Munby was secretly and happily married to his servant, who refused to quit her station. The fact explains some of the allusions in his poems." (p. 1)

Then began his chase to find the manuscripts. That exciting adventure of biographer Derek Hudson is told briefly in the introduction and epilogue to the biography *Munby: Man of Two Worlds*. Later, others picked up on Hudson's efforts (Hiley, 1979; Stanley, 1984) and Hannah Cullwick, maid-of-all-work, became a nineteenth-century heroine. Photographic records would illuminate her life, Munby's life, and the nether side of women's work, women's lives, and social class in the Victorian era in England. One finds one improbable biographical story after another.

And, if you want to laugh and cry, and sometimes get angry, read Catherine Drinker Bowen's *Adventures of a Biographer* (1959). Her stories of being denied the role of authorized biographer of Chief Justice Holmes, of being made to feel an outsider at the American Historical Association, and of being snubbed at a display of John Adams's artifacts will make at least some of you want to become biographers. Some of the hellishness of life writing becomes clearer here, as well.

These exploratory activities and experiences, finding the pieces of the jigsaw puzzle, Clifford labels "outside research."[4] Clifford contrasts these with "inside research," the utilizing of library resources. He is content to tell a half dozen of these fascinating and improbable stories of his own adventures and those of others. He does not reach for patterns or conceptualizations of the activities. In contrast, in telling some of my own stories (Smith, 1990, 1992), I initially labeled the outside activity "anthropological biography"; later, I called it "ethnographic biography." The broader and compelling insight, for me, was the similarity between aspects of doing biography and ethnography, the latter having its own well-developed modes of inquiry. What a windfall it would seem if the ethnographic ideas of Bronislaw Malinowski, William Foote Whyte, and Clifford Geertz, among others, could be brought to bear on the craft of biography! The possibilities of intellectual integration and synthesis become readily apparent. One hopes that such possibilities will spill over into practice.

But my central point is the vagaries involved in selecting an individual to be the subject of one's biography and in beginning the inquiries into the life. A further corollary is caution in criticizing or judging too quickly anyone's motivation and selection of a subject for his or her life writing. Major personal issues may be involved.

Creating and/or Using an Archive

Life writing as an empirical exercise feeds on data: letters, documents, interviews. In these days of high intellectual specialization, many biographers miss the joys and the frustrations of creating an archive. But in the doing of archival creation, one runs into a number of interesting difficulties.

In general, part of my personal problem-solving strategy is to have several "tentative models" in my head whenever I approach new problems. As I began on the Nora Barlow task, I had heard that the Margaret Mead archive was housed in the Library of Congress. I already knew that Barlow and Mead were friends. I telephoned the Library of Congress to find out if any of the Barlow letters were in the Mead collection. I was told, "Yes, we have a number of her letters." During an American Educational Research Association meeting in Washington I stole away for a couple of half days and photocopied some 80 letters. Substantively, I learned that in her letters Barlow rarely discussed her Darwin work with either Mead or Gregory Bateson. Even as she was working on the HMS *Beagle* materials, Darwin's time "in the field," Mead and Bateson were getting married and were researching in Bali and elsewhere—that is, doing their own creative ethnographic work. And somehow no connections were ever drawn. I was amazed at that. That experience led to one of the most significant driving questions in the biography: Who did Nora Barlow talk to about her intellectual work? From a symbolic interactionist perspective, one's immediate social intellectual world is important in what one does. The thematic question is both relevant and important. I have spent several years answering that question; it is a large part of the structure of the biography per se. And it arose as I was building an archive of Nora Barlow's letters.

My wife and I spent parts of three summers creating the Nora Barlow archives—more than 1,000 A-4 envelopes in 38 R-Kive 725 Bankers Boxes and a small catalogue as well. In very practical terms, we have separate boxes for letters: immediate family, extended family, and friends and colleagues. They are arranged alphabetically and chronologically. Similarly, we have boxes of published and unpublished manuscripts, also ordered chronologically. There are also photos and books and more photos and books. All are now stored in the large temperature- and humidity-controlled wing adjacent to the Manuscripts Room of the Cambridge University Library. It makes one feel almost a "real" archivist. As Edel (1984) says, in his usual pithy style, "Biography, like history, is the organization of human memory. Assembled and hoarded papers are bits and pieces of that memory" (p. 93).

In addition, a major outcome of the archival activity is an overview of the life—original materials over nine or ten decades of her life span of 103 years. The archival work begins the construction of the life. "Becoming an archivist" (Smith, 1992) carries its own stories and theoretical implications. Other biographers "just" confront someone else's archival efforts. But what would one, you or I, do with Margaret Mead and 600 feet of data? But then, I have never been in a presidential library—Truman, Kennedy, Johnson, Nixon. What does one do with that kind of archival wealth? McCullough (1992) hints at all that in the acknowledgments at the end of his recent *Truman*.

Finally, no one library or home study, even one as full as Nora Barlow's, contains all of the papers that are important for the life story. "Pools of data" exist in all sorts of likely and unlikely places. Finding those is another story in doing biography, as my discussion has already indicated. The intellectual and social process turns back upon itself, in spite of attempts at analytic clarity. The general point is clear: One either finds or builds a data file, an archive, as one step in the process of doing biography. Resourcefulness and imagination can and should occur here as elsewhere in the process.

Finding and Developing One's Theme

One of the most difficult decisions facing the biographer as he or she practices the craft of biography resides in the slant, perspective, or theme that is needed to guide the development of the life to be written. Sometimes the theme comes early, based on an insight from preliminary knowledge and an overview of the subject's life. In two previous essays I have recounted in some detail knowing early that "the Darwin legacy" was the theme to integrate the life of Nora Barlow (Smith, 1987, 1990). The perception was grounded in the knowledge of her four books, written late in life, the first as she turned 50, and then one each in her 60s, 70s, and 80s. But sometimes also, reconstruals vie with the original decision as new data enter, new facets of the life begin to form, new views of the significance of the story arise, and new audiences appear or become salient. The biographer's agony is caught with what might be called "the restless theme" (Smith, 1992). In the biography of Nora Barlow, the "intellectual aristocracy" became a major competing theme. I agonized over that during much of my spring 1990 sabbatical in Cambridge. Which theme is superordinate and which is subordinate? Which will carry better the burden of the evidence of the life? And for which audience? The biographer's internal argument over which theme is the more powerful eventually is entangled in the question of "audience" and publisher. To whom does one want to speak, and who wants to produce the book?

The decisions regarding theme are both part of, and followed closely by, what Bowen (1968) calls "plotting the biography." "Conflict," "suspense," "humor," and "humanity" are some of the terms she uses to highlight issues and decisions regarding plot. Chronology is always important, but a simple chronology of birth, education, marriage, career, and death won't do—for her. What is the book to say about the hero or heroine? Is it a happy or tragic life? And what of the times the central figure lived through? And what scenes and incidents give the life a fullness and a richness? And who are the friends and acquaintances who breathe vitality into the existence? And how do they come and go over the years? In Bowen's view the life writer must have all this finding, settling on, and developing the theme in mind as he or she starts to put words linearly onto sheets of paper. And then, at least in some instances, the writing takes over and transforms things—such as a theme—once again.

"The Figure Under the Carpet"

In the flow of interrelated problems and decisions—picking a subject, developing a theme, becoming aware of the multilayered contexts of lives—none is more difficult than insight into "the figure under the carpet," as Leon Edel (1979) phrases the problem of coming to know the essence of one's subject. The metaphor is mixed but vivid. From one perspective, the view can make one pause, if not forget that "essences" are in high debate these days, and the best one can do is construct a pattern that fits well the data one has of the life of the person being studied and written about. The figure under the carpet is not so much found as constructed. The "mask of life"—the appearance, the facade, the overt behavior one sees (or finds in letters, diaries, and other documents)—and the underlying "life myth"—the major inferences into the character and personality of the person being written about—are like a tapestry, which shows images on its front side and displays the underlying construction on the back. In three pages, Edel dissects Ernest Hemingway—the macho, warring, champion of all he undertook tapestry and "the troubled, uncertain, insecure figure, who works terribly hard to give himself eternal assurance," the figure under the carpet (p. 27). Great biographers look for that figure, construct it carefully, and paint it convincingly; lessor ones never do. Edel, thinking and acting like a composite of Sherlock Holmes and Sigmund Freud, hunts among slips of the tongue, anomalies in everyday behavior, the significant gestures, and the moving and poignant statement in a letter, essay, or novel for clues to that elusive figure.

Bowen, denied the letters of Justice Holmes, which were reserved for the official, the definitive, the authorized biography, talked to, so it seems, nearly everyone who had known Holmes. Eleven of his twelve law secretaries agreed to be interviewed by her. And often she sought out the places where Holmes had lived and worked. Through small detail she pursued the figure under the carpet. Even here, however, subtleties occur. As Bowen (1959) notes, "But the subject of a biography cannot remain at one age—at fifty, at twenty-five, at forty. He must grow old and the reader must see and feel the process" (p. 65). And what, we might ask, of the life myth? How does it evolve, change, grow, and decline—if it does?

Each biographer carries his or her own conception of personality, or character, as it is called by literary biographers. To Virginia Woolf (1927 /1960), biography was about the truthful transmission of personality. The truth is like "granite," and personality, at least in the selection of which truths to present, is like a "rainbow." In Woolf's view, truth and personality make one of the biographer's perennial dilemmas. Present-day scholars often see truth as less than granite. As I will argue shortly, sometimes the implicit personality theories can be helpful as sensitizing concepts, and at other times they can be blinders. Once again, Edel (1984) suggests imaginative—and perhaps impractical—ways of coming to terms with such problems—reading psychoanalytic literature, being psychoanalyzed, or even entering into collaborative relationships with an analyst in doing biography. From my perspective, and in a not so simple manner, the biographer brings all of his or her own personality, understandings, and experience to the task of creating a view of the individual under study. If that be true, it poses severe problems for traditional social science, for the sources and implementation of creativity can only be bolstered by technocratic procedures, not carried by them. That raises a long and tortuous argument for those of us working in that tradition.

Form and Shape

Even as one comprehends databases, themes, and underlying patterns or figures in the biography, other dilemmas and choices remain. One of the biographer's major decisions lies in the form or type of biography to be attempted. Clifford (1970) presents a taxonomy of types and a discussion of the factors to be considered in the decision. The underlying dimension of the classification is the degree of objectivity to subjectivity, perhaps better labeled the degree of intrusion of the author into the manuscript. He suggests five points on the continuum.

The "objective biography" is impossible in an absolute sense, but some biographies tend toward a factual collation, usually held together by chronology, with minimal biographer interpretation. In terms of an earlier perspective, if not cliché, "the facts speak for themselves." This type of biography shades into the "scholarly-historical," a form retaining heavy factual emphasis and a strong chronological organization, but with increasing historical background and attempts to develop the underlying character of the subject as defining features. The intruding author is beginning to construct a form with context. This is perhaps the most prevalent type among academic biographers.

The "artistic-scholarly" form involves some of the same exhaustive research, but the biographer takes the role "of an imaginative creative artist, presenting the details in the liveliest and most interesting manner possible" (p. 85). The rainbow is coming to dominate the granite. According to Clifford, most of Catherine Drinker Bowen's biographies fall here. And these efforts are damned by some as "popular." In this regard, I find Bowen's (1959) comment as she attended a frustrating-to-her meeting of the American Historical Association particularly instructive: "There are ways to come at history, I thought, pursuing my way down the hotel corridor. Let us say the professors come at it from the northeast and I from the southwest. Either way will serve, provided the wind blows clean and the fog lifts" (p. 102). Domains of intolerance and true belief infuriated her, and sometimes the wind does not blow clean and the fog does not lift.

"Narrative biography" involves a fictionalizing of scenes and conversations, based on letters and documents, that make the writing both factual and highly imaginative at the same time. The end of the continuum is the fifth form, the "fictional biography," almost a historical novel, with minimal attention to original research and primary resources. The difficulty in putting biographies into these categories appears when one names Irving Stone as an instance of an author whose work falls into the fifth category. For example, correspondence in the Nora Barlow archives contains questions from him to her about items such as the nature of the china used in the Darwin household, asked as Stone wrote his biography of Darwin, *The Origin.*

The continuum is helpful for biographers as they think about the kind of book they want to write or feel they are able to write. And that, the special talents and skills the biographer brings to the task, is an undertreated issue in my view.[5]

Context and Writing

Heroes and heroines do not exist in isolation. Contexts exist in lives and context exists in writing lives. In a vivid illustration, Bowen suggests the problems in beginning and ending the written biography per se. In *Yankee From Olympus,* Oliver Wendell Holmes, Jr., does not appear in the first 80 pages (seven chapters) of the biography, for to understand Holmes, Bowen argues, one must understand New England, Yankee traditions, and Holmes's father, the senior Oliver, who was poet, physician, professor, and storytelling author of "Autocrat of the Breakfast Table." Other biographies begin alternatively. If the subject is well-known, the "opening scene" can be of his or her birth; if the subject is unknown, it might be better to present "some scene to catch the reader's attention, show that the hero and his doings are important and exciting and perhaps have a bearing upon history" (Bowen, 1968, p. 21). So Bowen contributes to a reflective conversation with her fellow biographers on a particular dilemma of the craft.

Bowen (1968) also addresses the issue of how the biographer thinks through the "end scene." Most striking perhaps is her account of her book *John Adams and the American Revolution.* Adams's last words were "Thomas Jefferson survives"; he was unaware that Jefferson had died the same day. As Bowen notes, "This double departure of the heroes was epic, tremendous, and needed only to be set down in its bare facts. How could a biographer miss, I asked myself, and looked forward with relish from the day Adams was chosen as subject" (p. 38). But she lost her plot, the proportions of the life, and the original shape of the book, and she had a manuscript already book length with some 50 years to go before 1826. She ended the story in 1776, not a bad eventful moment, but still not the grander ending scene she really wanted. Along the way in her essay, Bowen raises important ideas, such as the "burden of the whole," the keeping of the totality in mind as one writes, the fact that "sometimes luck favors the biographer," the joy in finding a key note lost for years; she notes that "history came at least to a partial rescue" in her case, in the form of what would become Independence Day, July 4. And that provided a significant way of ending the biography, even if less than the possibilities of 1823.

Following upon Bowen, a neophyte biographer can be sensitized and begin thinking through his or her specific subject and situation. Critical judgment, reflective practice, is never right or wrong in some absolute or technical rule-application sense. Nonetheless, some decisions work out better than others, and helping with all this is what a theory of biographical method should be about.

A Brief Conclusion on Craft

Virginia Woolf was half right: Writing lives *is* the devil. But a strand of intellectual excitement, approaching ecstasy, also exists. If one is fortunate to find a heroine or hero from another time, place, and culture, the biographical activity takes on a strong cast of ethnography. Earlier craft skills come into play, even though always with a bit different flavor. The intellectual problems seem to demand more of creativity than of technical or rule-governed problem solving. And that is a challenge to the practice of traditional social science. Some of my students and colleagues suggest that the integration might occur in "metacognition," self-directed thinking about thinking. My own tentative choice of guiding labels is "reflective practice," caught vividly by Donald Schön (1987): "Clearly, it is one thing to be able to reflect-in-action and quite another to be able to reflect on our reflection in action so as to produce a good verbal description of it; and it is still another thing to be able to reflect on the resulting description" (p. 31). The problems of the craft of biography are "messy," not "well-formed." The problems contain elements of ambiguity, complexity, uncertainty, value conflict, and uniqueness.

In too-brief fashion I have presented some of the dilemmas and some of the several taxonomies of resolutions used by such master biographical practitioners as Catherine Drinker Bowen, James Clifford, and Leon Edel. Thinking along with them creates images and metaphors for handling one's own devils. Doing biography is a great way to live.

◆ Disciplinary Strands: Alternative Interpretations

> There is no theory that is not a fragment, carefully prepared,
> of some autobiography.
> —Paul Valéry (quoted in Olney, 1980, preface)

Biographical method can be viewed in alternative, and perhaps more abstract, ways than as a craft or process. For better and worse—that is, the benefits of focused vision and the limits of sometimes narrowed vision—much intellectual activity is organized as academic disciplines. Several of the disciplines have claims on biography and biographical method. Even though they can be clustered into literature, history, social science, education, and feminist and minority perspectives, each of these can be differentiated further. Even a cursory scanning of references and illustrations indicates that these disciplinary points of view often run relatively independent of each other.[6] That independence seems limiting, if not tragic, for students and scholars who want diverse images and models of how life writing might be conceived and carried out, to enhance their own intellectual creativity. And lurking behind, almost hauntingly so, is the idea of autobiography, undermining many of the claims of detachment and specialization from the disciplines. Are our theories, as Valéry suggests, "simple" extensions of our autobiographies? If so, what then becomes of social science?

Literary Biography

Reading literary biographies and accompanying statements of biographical method is exciting, especially if one is partial to competition, conflict, and sharp jousting. The contentiousness is neither superficial nor limited to domains and turf, but spills over into style and substance of the biography. Note the strongly stated positions of two eminent English intellectuals and biographers. In his preface to *Eminent Victorians,* Strachey (1918) reoriented English biography with his critique of traditional biographies: "Those two fat volumes with which it is our custom to commemorate the dead—who does not know them, with their ill-digested masses of material, their slipshod style, their tone of tedious panegyric, their lamentable lack of selection, of detachment, of design?" (p. viii). In his view, "it is perhaps as difficult to write a good life as it is to live one."

In 1932, G. M. Trevelyan, in a new preface to an older biography (1876) seemed to write almost in rebuttal and in elaboration to Strachey. He comments regarding the "life and letters" biography:

> My father [G. O. Trevelyan] certainly chose the form of biography most suitable to his uncle [Lord Macaulay]. He had not Boswell's rare gift of reproducing the essence of conversation, nor did Macaulay's real strength lie, like Dr. Johnson's in his tongue, but rather in his pen. His letters would reveal him and amuse the reader. It would have been equally beside the mark to treat Macaulay in a subjective, psychological character sketch, such as "the new biography" prefers, with the documents and letters omitted. Macaulay was not subtle enough for such subtleties, and his letters are much too good to miss. His description of his interview with the clergyman who thought Napoleon was the Beast in Revelations (p. 342) both amuses us more and tells us more about Macaulay than a page of psychological analysis. In this book the man lives and speaks for himself. (pp. v-vi)

In this short paragraph, Trevelyan raises a much more complex set of events facing the biographer: the special talents of the biographer, the special strengths of the subject, the importance of an interpretive character sketch versus letting the individual speak for him- or herself, and the need for or desirability of a psychological analysis.

The debate continues to the present. Other perspectives are possible as well. More recently, Horner (1987), in her brief introduction to the Radcliffe Biography Series, has noted that "fine biographies give us both a glimpse of ourselves and a reflection of the human spirit. Biography illuminates history, inspires by example, and fires the imagination to life's possibilities. Good biography can create lifelong models for us" (p. ix). That position opens further doors insofar as it is reminiscent of Kluckhohn's (1949) powerful statement of anthropology being a "mirror of man." Concepts and metaphors of biography run in many directions.

Earlier transformations occurred as well. Boswell's *Life of Johnson* dominated the English scene after its publication in 1791. Rogers, in an introduction to the 1980 Oxford University Press edition, comments on the book with phrases such as "lonely eminence," "towered over lesser works," and "dominated the skyline" of biography. In my view, Boswell's own eight-page introduction is a marvelous and strikingly modern essay in its own right. He presents a view of his relationship to Johnson—in my words, that of "humble servant." He was a friend of some 20 years; had the biography in mind from the start; cleared his "rights of human subjects," in that Johnson knew what he was about; kept voluminous records of activities, conversations, and events; cautioned against "panegyrick"; urged the importance of chronology; argued the method of conversation as the method to "best display his character"; cited Plutarch on the importance of an action of small note, a short saying, or a jest as the door to an individual's "real" character; quoted Johnson about how to study and understand Johnson; and staked his territory vis-à-vis other biographers who knew Johnson less well. Boswell read widely and knew about biography; he reflected well upon the process, and he wrote a memorable biography.

Illuminating Boswell's eight pages is Edel's (1984) brilliant essay on Boswell. Here we find Boswell arranging meetings, setting scenes, and determining the course of conversations—shades of Monet arranging and planting his gardens at Giverny to enhance his paintings of the bridge and lily ponds! Who and what is to be believed about anything in biography? It seems that one pits one's own intelligence against the world and others' views of the world, if they be two phenomena, gathers data and evidence from whatever simple and esoteric sources one can find, and does the best one can. And that can be exciting, frustrating, and terrifying—if one has high need of certainty.

So change and contentiousness exist, and have existed for centuries, in and around literary biography. Further implications for the life writer seem to follow on this generalization. In situations of intellectual conflict considerable room exists for multiple alternatives, choices, reflection, and creativity, that is, individual agency. Artistry as well as factual representation and reality, in varying proportions, vie with each other. Granite and rainbows again! That seems another important generalization for individuals who want to write lives.

History

History lies somewhere between the humanities and the social sciences. However, construed in a disciplinary sense, history has claims on biography, as our introductory definitions indicate. In a series of three major essays, Lawrence Stone (1981) has addressed the relationship of history to the social sciences, the nature and place of prosopography in historical thinking, and the changing emphasis on narration in history. But it is the "prosopography" essay that is most germane here. In resurrecting the classical label for "group biography," Stone argues for its contemporary importance.

The collective study of lives, Stone asserts, leads to insight into two of the most basic problems in history. The roots of political actions lie in the motives, personalities, and characters of key individual actors in any set of important historical events. Private events and papers relate a different facet of politics than do public events and speeches. And it is not only the great men and women who are important, but also the other people who surround them in complex social events. Stone argues that not only is biography important, but group biography, that is, prosopography, adds a further dimension. The social and symbolic interactionists from other social sciences would strongly agree.[7] Second, the study of group biography gives insight into the larger problems of social structure and social mobility. Networks, overlapping boards, connections, and family relationships are built on individual people interacting together for their own interests. Mapping those careers and linkages is an important means of understanding.

In a small way, we found this kind of approach, what we called life histories of a group of educational administrators and teachers who had created the innovative Kensington Elementary School, to be a powerful way of understanding the rise and fall of the school and the complexities of educational innovation and reform (Smith et al., 1986; Smith, Dwyer, Prunty, & Kleine, 1988; Smith, Prunty, Dwyer, & Kleine, 1987). Overall we blended history, ethnography, and life history as inquiry methods. Part of our rationale concerned the idea of a case study, a bounded system, in our view. The individual life history pieces or brief biographies were interlinked because of the time the staff taught and administered together in the Kensington Elementary School and the Milford School District. That linkage presented possibilities of understanding beyond any one individual biography. Powerful group patterns emerged in their lives.

One of Stone's conclusions is that group biography can link together "constitutional and institutional history" and "personal biography," two of the oldest and best developed parts of the historian's craft, but ones that have run too independent of each other. Biography becomes not an end in itself, but a helpful element in the pursuit of other ends.[8] In addition, the rise of oral history, investigative journalism in the political domain, and the making of archives into presidential libraries offers an array of possibilities to the historian as life writer. Old ideas and methods take on a fresh look and open up imaginative possibilities in new contexts.

Social Science Perspectives

Although variation exists among social scientists, most argue that biography should move beyond narration and storytelling of the particular into more abstract conceptualizations, interpretations, and explanations. Writing lives can serve multiple purposes. In general, "scientists" seek patterns in the forms of concepts, hypotheses, theories, and metaphors. These patterns are both the fruits of scientific inquiry and practice and the stimulus for further inquiry and improved practice. For convenience, I divide the social scientists by discipline—anthropologists, psychologists, and sociologists. Some might argue that a trichotomy of conservative, liberal, and radical is a more powerful split. And others see the paradigmatic assumptions—positivism, neopositivism, interpretivism, and critical theory as more powerful organizing conceptions. Finding the joints at which to cut "nature" seems more and more difficult. Some would argue that Plato was wrong—at least for social science and the humanities.

Anthropologists. Anthropologists have had a long relationship with biography, mostly under the rubrics of "life histories" and "culture and personality." Langness (1965: Langness & Frank, 1981) presents an overview of this history and the multiple approaches being used. To pick only one strand, Oscar Lewis and Robert Redfield illustrate some of the excitement in the field. Both did ethnographies of Tepoztlan, attempts at a total view, Redfield's (1930) in the 1920s and Lewis's (1951) "restudy" two decades later. But the views were different: the positive side, bright view of Redfield contrasted with the dark side, nether view of Lewis. And that posed a severe intellectual problem for holistic anthropologists. Redfield (1955) responded with *The Little Community,* one of the most provocative and, I would maintain, underappreciated methodological books in social science. Essentially, he argued for a half dozen approaches for studying the small community. Three chapters are particularly important for the interpretations here—"A Typical Biography," "A Kind of Person," and "An Outlook on Life." The sequence of events as an individual passes through a culture during the course of a life is one view of that culture. And the resulting kind of person and his or her outlook on life are related additional ways of viewing a culture. These views play off against ecological, social structural, and historical perspectives. Cultures can be written through lives. And that is part of some of the best of Lewis's later work, life stories of individuals and families who moved from rural Tepoztlan to urban Mexico

City. In *Five Families* (1959) and *The Children of Sanchez* (1961), Lewis tape-recorded individual life stories and, with only minor editing, presented them as documents of lives, "multiple autobiographies," to use his label. Out of this work came the controversial conception of the "culture of poverty." Valentine (1968) raised a "critique and counterproposals" of Lewis's use of the long autobiographical life story data for the kind of theoretical interpretations lying within the conception of the "culture of poverty."

After writing one of the most autobiographically laden accounts of fieldwork ever presented in his "Deep Play: Notes on the Balinese Cockfight" (in Geertz, 1973), Geertz, in a more recent book, *Works and Lives: The Anthropologist as Author* (1988), faces directly the issue of the dual role of the anthropological investigator between the horns of the "other," the individual or the culture being studied, and the "text," the narrative written about the world "out there." With his usual persuasive style, he makes the point that the reader's acceptance of the text occurs not because of its factual weight or the theoretical places being created, but rather because of its narrative strength, based on rhetorical devices, convincing the reader that he, the anthropologist, was really there. "Vas you dere Sharlie?" is his paraphrase of an earlier literary statement. And what better, in his earlier "Deep Play," than the scramble by Geertz and his wife to escape the police breaking up the cockfight and the charade of having tea with a local dignitary when all the postfight commotion was occurring. Geertz's "host" had not only been at the cockfight but had helped organize it. Geertz's more recent analysis, without reference to the early piece, is a vivid exposition of that earlier writing strategy. For Geertz the incident was a major breakthrough in community acceptance of his fieldwork. For the reader, it authenticated everything substantive he had to say about Bali. I was left with the feeling, "After that episode, how could he have gotten anything wrong?" But Geertz in 1988 writes not only of the relationship between the investigator and the community or individual being studied, but mainly of the relationship between the investigator and the kind of text he or she has written. Although not intended as biography, the narrative of his argument is carried by the intellectual and professional lives of four major anthropologists—Lévi-Strauss, Evans-Pritchard, Malinowski, and Benedict. The writing of lives can and does serve many purposes.

Recently, Rabinow (1977) and Crapanzano (1980), both writing Moroccan culture and biography, suggest difficulties and creative possibilities in understanding and blending life writing and cultural analysis. The identities of literature and science are lost and recreated brilliantly.

Psychologists. Psychologists have trouble with biography. On the one hand, psychoanalytic literature has influenced countless life writers; Leon Edel is one of the more noteworthy. With a psychoanalytic perspective, almost as a wand, he probes problems, issues, and interpretations with ease and facility as he writes biographies, critiques biographies, and surveys the tremendous volume of literature on biography. But academic psychologists have never lived easily with psychoanalysis. On the other hand, too, psychologists have a passion for truth, and a particular kind of truth at that, exemplified in experimentation, quantification, and tested propositions. Some see psychology as physics writ large. Garraty (1954, 1957), citing varied attempts at quantification of life documents, such as graphology, content analysis, and discomfort-relief quotients, turns his hand to issues of personality in biography. Though raised in that tradition, I now find it chilling to the creativity involved in the writing of lives.

A kind of middle ground is found in the work of Gordon Allport and Henry Murray. Allport, an out-of-step third-force psychologist, produced a fascinating set of books relevant to biography. His well-received *Personality* (1937) was followed by his classic *The Use of Personal Documents in Psychological Science* (1942), and the brilliant *Letters from Jenny* (1965). In the last, he presented and then explored a large collection of letters written by a woman named Jenny, mostly to her son and daughter-in-law. They are vivid, troubling, introspective accounts of both her life as a working woman and mother and her accompanying mental states. The exploration involved Allport in a consideration of several competing theories for understanding and explaining the letters. Existential psychology and Freudian psychoanalysis vied with his own structural-dynamic approach. He concluded with an estimate of Jenny's mental health. The life story, told mostly in the letters, with minimal commentary, was in the service of general theory. Allport also took up the challenge of Stefan Zweig in his infamous quote regarding writers such as Proust and Flaubert: "Writers like these are giants in observation and literature, whereas in psychology the field of personality is worked by lesser men, mere flies, who have the safe anchorage of a frame of science in which to place their petty platitudes and minor heresies" (quoted in Allport, 1960, p. 6). Allport (1960) makes the case for both literature and psychology in his "Personality: A Problem for Science or a Problem for Art?"

Henry Murray's contribution to biography also lies in his explorations in personality, and in a book by the same title (Murray et al., 1938); in his invention of the TAT, the thematic apperception test; and in his collaboration with a remarkable group of colleagues and students who have pursued problems in the nature of lives. With the anthropologist Clyde Kluckhohn he edited the well-recognized *Personality in Nature, Society, and Culture* (Kluckhohn & Murray, 1953). Concepts such as needs, presses, proceedings, serials, plans, schedules, ego strength, and proactive systems guided the work of several generations of American psychologists interested in lives and life writing. *Lives in Progress* (White, 1952) is a major illustration of the post-Murray approach. The eclectic emphasis on biology, family, social circumstances, and the individuals themselves appears and reappears. Erikson, another former Murray colleague, in his *Childhood and Society* (1963) and his *Young Man Luther* (1962) brought the "eight ages of man," "identity crises," and other conceptualizations to life writing. The ideas of Murray and others in the psychobiography and psychohistory traditions are extended in McAdams and Ochberg (1989) and Runyan (1982, 1988).

In the more recent *Seasons of a Man's Life,* Levinson (1978) accents the stages in adult life and the difficult transitions—most noteworthy, the midlife crisis—as a framework for the consideration of a life. The dilemma of the general and the particular appears once again. Academic psychologists tend to pursue the former with greater zeal. Although major disagreements exist here, Coles, in a series of books that includes *Women of Crisis II* (Coles & Coles, 1980), attacks vigorously the social scientists and the theorists, even while developing and presenting, mostly implicitly, his own more subtle theoretical point of view (Smith et al., 1986, pp. 21-23). It is an exciting world; the granite and rainbow dichotomy does not rest easily within psychology.

As much as any disciplinary group, psychologists have used biography in the service of other ends. One illustration must suffice. In his very stimulating *Contrary Imaginations,* Liam Hudson (1966) collected short, open-ended autobiographical statements of clever English schoolboys. "Just describe those aspects of your life which seem to you interesting or important" provoked responses useful in clarifying major hypotheses in his study. More far-reaching was his turning the autobiographical perspective on himself and his career shifts from experimental psychology to a more humanistic kind of psychology in his *The Cult of the Fact* (1972). He sets his authorial position with a powerful initial sentence: "The story begins in Cambridge, in the spring of 1968; my eleventh year in Cambridge, and my third in the superlative if stagey ambiance of King's College" (p. 15). For anyone who has spent any time in Cambridge, the invitation is irresistible. Insights and personal help come in strange ways! I have now a major lead toward revising and extending my *Doing Ethnographic Biography: A Reflective Practitioner at Work During a Spring in Cambridge* (1992). Serendipity once again! Psychologists really should have less trouble with biography.

Sociologists. Like psychologists and anthropologists, sociologists have been ambivalent toward biography. But writing lives, in the form of life histories, became part of the world of the Chicago school with the publication of Clifford Shaw's *The Jack-Roller* in 1930. And life history was only one of the broader category of qualitative inquiries, labeled better as "case studies." From the Gold Coast to the Ghetto, they were to have a permanent impact on sociological thought and method. And out of such work, and the seminal thought of George Herbert Mead, was to come the very influential symbolic interactionism as a social science point of view. In two short introductions, one to a republication of Shaw's book and the other to his own collected essays, Howard Becker (1966, 1970) makes the case for both this kind of "close-up" sociology and the place of biographical and autobiographical life histories in sociology.

I can remember reading several of the Chicago case study books in a general sociology course when I was an undergraduate, being absorbed in them and the four wishes of Thomas as discussed in Waller (1932), but not being able to integrate all that into the kind of "scientific" psychology I was to learn in graduate school. Now, several decades later, as a latter-day practitioner of case studies of schools, curricula, and school districts, and life histories of teachers, and now of more formal biography, I find the power of the Chicago perspective awesome.

Becker makes the argument for life histories as part of a "mosaic" of community and institutional investigations, as important "touchstones" for considering any abstract theory of person and community, and the testing of implicit assumptions about human beings in the larger sociological studies. Biography has an overriding dimension, the chronology between birth and death. In a social science that often makes pleas for "process" interpretations, the clash between the synchronic and the diachronic usually ends in the victory of the more structural synchronic. Biography, and history as well, opens the theorist to data organized on a diachronic timeline. In addition, biography with a concern for the way a specific individual perceives and construes the world also moves the sociological interpreter toward the subject's perspective rather than the observer's point of view, a major issue labeled by the anthropologist Clifford Geertz as "experience near" versus "experience distant" conceptualizations.

Following in these same traditions, Denzin (1989) raises his sociological perspective as "interpretive biography," the creating of literary and narrative accounts and stories of lived experience. He pursues in great analytic detail the development of taxonomies and concepts; the multiple ways lives can be studied, construed, and written; and the implications of taking one perspective or another. "Turning points," the never-ending construction and reconstruction of lives, and obituaries as documents (that is, brief life statements), the cultural categories we use in describing lives, and the ethical responsibilities in studying lives, suggest the creative range of ideas his brand of sociology brings to the biographical task. In much the same tradition, with some stronger overtones of radicalism as well, Bertaux (1981) edited an international collection of essays, *Biography and Society: The Life History Approach in the Social Sciences.* Sociology is reclaiming one of its important roots. C. Wright Mills (1959) would be pleased as history, biography, and social structure have moved a step closer to productive syntheses.

Taking the sociological position just a shade more toward journalism are life writers such as Studs Terkel (1970, 1972), who describes his study *Hard Times* as an "oral history." In a page or two to a half dozen pages he presents brief vignettes of the lives of individuals who lived through the Depression years of the 1930s in the United States. One might see it as a collection of "episodes" in autobiographical life stories, with some biographical editing by Terkel from his tape-recorded interviews. In his introduction, labeled "A Personal Memoir," he classifies the effort this way:

> This is a memory book, rather than one of hard fact and precise statistic. In recalling an epoch, some thirty, forty, years ago, my colleagues experienced pain, in some instances; exhilaration, in others. Often it was a fusing of both. A hesitancy, at first, was followed by a flow of memories: long-ago hurts and small triumphs. Honors and humiliations. There was laughter, too. (Terkel, 1970, p. 17)

Inner perspectives, experience near phrasings and conceptualizations, and tidal waves of feeling and emotion present individuals and their lives. These coalesce into larger images and patterns. Whether journalism, or oral history, or a kind of sociology, the labels seem less relevant than the power

Terkel brings to the reporting and evoking of images. Most social scientists would envy his ability to capture his focus in *Working*:

> It is about search, too, for daily meaning as well as daily bread, for recognition as well as cash, for astonishment rather than torpor; in short, for a sort of life rather than a Monday through Friday sort of dying. Perhaps immortality, too, is part of the quest. To be remembered was the wish, spoken and unspoken, of the heroes and heroines of this book. (Terkel, 1972, p. xiii)

Creativity and insight come in varied forms. Honoring them is high on my list of life-writing priorities.

Feminist and Minority Perspectives

Anyone who has ever felt left out, ignored, or powerless has the beginnings of an understanding of the feminist and minority perspectives that have arisen in recent decades with great vigor and anger in the field of biography and autobiography. From the *Oxford English Dictionary*'s early limiting definitions of who is included and excluded to the more personal reports of experience, the argument grows. In a small but poignant and potent personal experience, while walking through the corridors of the Cambridge University Library, actually from the Manuscripts Room on the third floor to the Tea Room in the basement, while working on the biography of Nora Barlow, I noted an exhibition of books from the seventeenth century focusing on the "Worthies of England" (Smith, 1992). Though "worthies" was a label new to me, it seems to say it all. In that era it was clear who was important and who decided on the criteria of importance. That human experience is gendered is the fundamental truth underlying the feminist perspective. Race and class as categories of individuals echo, follow quickly upon, similar assumptions.

Examining issues in equity, power, social structure, agency, self-definition, and their interrelations, so it is argued by feminists, will be enhanced by the writing of all kinds of personal narratives of all kinds of lives of all kinds of women. Images, models, and insights for change exist in the life-writing narratives and critical reflections upon those stories. A gripping particularistic account of these issues appears in the "Origins" chapter of the Personal Narratives Group (1989) book, *Interpreting Women's Lives*. Variations in lifestyles, with their attendant satisfactions and deep dissatisfactions, appear along with an array of conceptual attempts to broaden the meaning of the experiences recounted. This broadening occurs with counternarratives as illustrations and arguments for women who are not thinking or feeling or behaving as they are "supposed to," constructing and negotiating new alternatives, and the troubling constraints posed by one's disciplinary training in the humanities versus the social sciences.

Ultimately, the Personal Narratives Group structured its book around four major sensitizing concepts: context, narrative form, narrator-interpreter relations, and truths. Each of these "lenses" or "pieces of madras cloth" illuminates the meanings of women's life stories. *Context* refers to the particular conditions that prevail in any society at any moment in time. *Narrative forms,* the fluid shapes into which one's creative constructions of lives flow, are rich with alternatives. The *narrator-interpreter* relations conception addresses the multiple people involved in living, narrating, writing, critiquing, and meaning making in biography, and also the complex interrelationships of the individuals themselves. *Truths* refers to "the multiplicity of ways in which a woman's life story reveals and reflects important features of her conscious experience and social landscape, creating from both her essential reality" (p. 14).

If those abstractions, retold here for brevity, lose their concrete meaning, the reader has only to go to any of the individual essays for the particulars. For instance, Swindells's essay reinterprets Stanley (1984) on the Hannah Cullwick diaries. The diaries were written by a Victorian maidservant, a "maid-of-all-work," at the urging of A. J. Munby, "man of two worlds," her male exploiter and later husband (if these be different). Recently they were published by a feminist press and interpreted by the editor (Stanley, 1984). More recently, the diaries have been reinterpreted by Swindells, and given additional interpretation by the Personal Narratives Group editors. Now each reader, with the help of Derek Hudson's (1972) biography of Munby and Hiley's (1979) book of photographs (mostly Munby's) *Victorian Working Women: Portraits From Life,* can make his or her own interpretation. It is an incredible story—or set of interrelated stories. The exciting complexities of "auto/biographical" methods, to use Stanley's phrasing, in the late twentieth century are readily apparent.

Alternative, more conventional if not more tempered, accounts appear in such highly discussed books as Mary Catherine Bateson's (1990) *Composing a Life* and Carolyn Heilbrun's (1988) *Writing a Woman's Life.* Bateson's five biographical stories of lives raise conceptualizations such as "unfolding stories," "improvisation" versus "a vision already defined," "patchwork quilt" as a metaphor for a life, and "a rethinking of the concept of achievement." I was reminded of an earlier and personally influential book by Gruenberg and Krech (1952), *The Many Lives of Modern Woman,* which provided a metaphor and guided the decisions of some of us a generation or two ago.

Heilbrun's opening sentence gives pause to anyone contemplating any aspect of the topic "biography and women." She begins:

> There are four ways to write a woman's life: the woman herself may tell it, in what she chooses to call an autobiography; she may tell it in what she chooses to call fiction; a biographer, woman or man, may write the woman's life in what is called a biography; or the woman may write her own life in advance of living it, unconsciously, and without recognizing or naming the process. (p. 11)

"Nostalgia," "anger," and "taking control of their own lives" are concepts that appear early and throughout her analysis. Early autobiographies by women, and many of the more recent as well, read "flat" to Heilbrun, especially as she contrasts the autobiographies with the more emotional books of letters. Perhaps it is my contentiousness, but I find some of her interpretations open to further exploration. She cites the differences between two of May Sarton's autobiographical books: *Plant Dreaming Deep* (1968) tends toward a positive, upbeat flavor, whereas *Journal of a Solitude* (1973) tends to probe the nether side of life, but, in my view, tragedy as well as anger. And for reasons not clear to me as reader, Heilbrun does not mention the earlier *I Knew a Phoenix: Sketches for an Autobiography* (1959), in which Sarton draws portraits of her parents: George Sarton, the historian of science, and Mabel Elwes Sarton, painter, interior decorator, and artisan, and the joys and despair of Europe in the World War I era. Her own youth is caught in a series of sketches, "The Education of a Poet." May Sarton, as person, writer, and text, seems much more complex than Heilbrun's brief comments and interpretations indicate.

And Heilbrun is very complex as well. I encountered her first as writer of the introductory essays to two of Vera Brittain's *Testament* books, a kind of "documentary" history through autobiography (see, e.g., Heilbrun, 1981). Much of *Writing a Woman's Life* appears there. Vera Brittain and Winifred Holtby seem, to me as a bit more than casual observer, to have influenced Heilbrun mightily. More recently I have started reading the Amanda Cross mystery novels. Picture this: Heilbrun writes under the pseudonym of Amanda Cross (mystery writers don't get tenure in literature at Columbia, she says); the heroine of the novels is Kate Fansler, a detective and university literary critic, and in one of the more recent novels, *The Players Come Again* (1990), heroine Fansler is writing a biography of a woman who is allegedly the author of her husband's world-famous stream-of-consciousness novel. Perhaps all this life writing will be clearer when I have read the rest of Heilbrun's long series of books and essays. For the moment—what a provocative set of ambiguous interpretive possibilities!

Further, what Heilbrun calls "the claim of achievement, the admission of ambition, the recognition that accomplishment" was earned appeared in the letters of some writers but not in their formal autobiographies. In her view, scripts, other than reflecting men's stories, for telling life stories seldom existed in the lives of eminent women. In my view, Healey's (1986) *Wives of Fame* gives the beginning of a kind of redressing of the comment "I didn't know he had a wife" regarding Jenny—and Marx; and Mary—and Livingstone; and Emma—and Darwin. Heilbrun's own anecdotes and stories continue excitedly, culminating in statements about aging, courage, freedom, and endings. She argues that being 50 years old is an important transition time. To a social scientist, many of these interpretations are empirically testable propositions. Another agenda?

The life-writing literature by minority and ethnic groups is immense and growing as well. From the early autobiographies of Booker T. Washington and Frederick Douglass to the more recent ones by Malcolm X and Maya Angelou, the multiple definitions of the black experience have continued to cumulate. Butterfield's *Black Autobiography in America* (1974) presents a vivid historical picture of major transitions from the early slave narrative period, to one of search, and now to the period of rebirth, to use his phrases. The first sentence of the introduction presages the overall perspective of the book:

> George Orwell's image of the future in *1984* was of a boot stamping on the human face forever. He could have used the same image to represent the Negro past in America, fitting the boot easily to the foot of a slavetrader, overseer, master, policeman, soldier, vigilante, capitalist, and politician. (p. 1)

Overall, his interpretation of autobiography is a mix of history and literature and an attempt to integrate "objective fact and subjective awareness." In his later, more interpretive chapters, Butterfield analyzes issues of constructing black identity in terms of politics, separatism, and revolution among many young black writers. In his essay "The Language of Black Satire" he cites powerful short excerpts from Cleaver, Seale, and others, most of whom spent time in prison. Butterfield's "history as subjective experience" is an exercise in a set of propositions linking personal experience to individuality, an awakening of a "truer and better self," and the birth of a new world. Example follows example.

As I read Haley's epilogue at the end of *The Autobiography of Malcolm X*, multiple "biographical method" questions arose. In what sense is the book Malcolm X's autobiography and in what sense is it Haley's biography of him? Is Stanley's phrasing "auto/biography" the more viable alternative? And what should we make of the point in time in which the book was narrated and written? While the book was in process, Malcolm X parted company with Elijah Muhammad. The climax of the book was now different. Should the early materials be rewritten? Malcolm said no. What problems were created for Haley, the writer of the auto/biography? The questions run on insistently.

As I reread Anne Moody's *Coming of Age in Mississippi* (1968), a larger essay loomed in my mind. Life stories can be a powerful influence on creativity, and that is no mean accomplishment. I believe it was her four-part table of contents—"Childhood," "High School," "College," and "The Movement"—and the vivid vignettes and brief stories from the text per se that seemed so simply similar to many of my interests and perspectives. I saw the possibilities of comparisons and contrasts between her book and the very different but equally powerful *Period Piece: A Cambridge Childhood*, Gwen Raverat's (1952) auto/biography of the Darwin family at the turn of the century. In addition, our multiple ethnographic case studies of pupils, teachers, and schools in and around the metropolitan area of St. Louis and the central Midwest in the United States, all of which have biographical and autobiographical strands, would provide a large further comparison and contrast. Bridging some of these differences is Wilma Wells, my colleague and coauthor of *"Difficult to Reach, Maintain, and Help" Urban Families in PAT: Issues, Dilemmas, Strategies, and Resolutions in Parent Education* (Smith & Wells, 1990). This was very heavily an auto/biographical account of struggles to educate poor urban mothers in child-rearing practices. As I think about such work, family, schooling, class, and caste cut across gender, generations, and continents. Now, the larger essay and this paragraph seem like a promissory note for a new, autobiographical book that will bring together numerous loose ends, nagging unsolved problems, from a professional lifetime. At this point I feel I am co-opting someone else's narrative. But Anne Moody is alive, and not so well, in St. Louis's urban ghetto in 1993.

The influential life-writing literature from the feminist and minority perspectives reflects back on some of the intellectual cynicism regarding autobiography. Some believe that autobiography is impossible, as noted earlier in this essay. Criticism has its own complexities and power.

Professional Education

Much of recent life writing in professional education carries the same intellectual flavor of the feminist and minority perspective, finding voice among the disenfranchised, the powerless, or those with alternative visions. Marilyn Cohn and Robert Kottkamp (1992) gave their book *Teachers* the subtitle *The Missing Voice in Education.*

Several strands seem especially important. Representative of a first strand are collections of essays such as Ball and Goodson's (1985) *Teachers' Lives and Careers* and Goodson's (1992) *Studying Teachers' Lives.* Conceptually the major thrust lies in the accenting of "agency," of teachers in the daily give and take of teaching in classrooms and schools. This is particularly important in a domain that experiences fads of curriculum reform and school innovation under the control of central office administrators, university educationists, and subject matter specialists. Perhaps the most telling illustration was the development of "teacher-proof" curricula in the 1960s by disciplinary specialists. The new materials were supposed to be so powerful and well done that even incompetent teachers, like you and me, could not spoil them in the transmission from text to students. Similarly, the field of school innovation and change, exemplified by the "RD&D" (research, development, and diffusion) model, placed the classroom teacher as one technocratic spot in the conveyor belt of school change. Images of Charlie Chaplin on the assembly line in *Modern Times* suggest the frenetic, but not so hilarious, life of the teacher. Teacher life stories attempt to change both the teachers themselves and the educational system of which they are a part. Another minority group is seeking a voice.

A second strand with both distant roots and recent flowering is made up of those teachers with alternative visions. A. S. Neill is best known for his *Summerhill* (1960), but even more impressive is his *A Dominie's Log* and the other two dominie books (see Neill, 1975). The *Log* contains all the significant material that he was not permitted to include in the official records he had to keep for the inspectorate. Sylvia Ashton-Warner's *Teacher* (1963) brings a personal view of New Zealand, multiculturalism, and a more organic way of teaching. And the "romantics" of the 1960s and 1970s, such as Hentoff (1966), Hernden (1966, 1971), and Holt (1964), present powerful life-writing statements. Nonmainstream voices entered into the dialogue about schooling.

A third strand that seldom is described as life writing is the growing interest in "action research." As described by Elliott (1991) and others, action research involves teachers studying their own teaching. In a cycle that involves proposing, planning, implementing, observing, recording (through diaries and journals), reflecting, and writing, teachers have begun to talk about their teaching, their hopes and desires, the immediate context of a particular group of pupils, a particular set of curriculum materials, and a particular school with its particular principal and staff of colleagues. Although the focus is usually on an innovative teaching strategy or piece of curriculum, I would argue that a more powerful way of thinking about action research is to construe the activity as "really" a piece of teacher autobiography. And if this be true, then action researchers should be including more personal context, larger chunks of autobiography, in their research statements. For educationists, the epigraph from Valéry with which I began this section needs to be extended beyond "theory" to "practice" as well.

◆ Conclusions

No foundation. All the way down the line.
—William Saroyan, *The Time of Your Life*, 1939

Several conclusions, not quite foundations, in the form of patterns, tentative generalizations, or lessons seem to follow reasonably closely upon the arguments presented in this chapter. In wrestling with the theme and audience of this chapter I found I wanted to say something of the multiple and conflicting definitions and perspectives of life writing; I wanted to address the process or craft aspects of doing biography; and finally I wanted to acquaint any one disciplinarian with images of life writing from other disciplines. Eventually, integration or talking across boundaries was on my agenda. My focal audiences, as frequently is the case, are my graduate students interested in doing one form or another of qualitative inquiry. They seem not too far from a larger population of students and scholars.

Underlying this essay is an image of an ideal. For reasons I understand only partially, I am drawn to those scholars who write interesting and important biographies, who seem to know huge amounts of the relevant literature on life writing, and who reflect insightfully upon the craft, the process of doing biography—an awesome and nearly unattainable ideal! In attempting to actualize such an ideal, I have raised a few of the older, more classical biographers and their perspectives as well as the more contemporary. In addition, and as part of a perspective on the importance of the individual as agent, I have written in the first person and about some of my own efforts, even though the chapter is part of a "handbook," which usually assumes a more detached perspective.

For the educational and social science researcher interested in qualitative methods, biography—and its variants, autobiography, life history, and life story—seems a rich and only partially exploited form of inquiry for reaching multiple intellectual goals and purposes. In her recent book, Stanley (1992) makes a strong case for the label "auto/biographical." In an important summary, Lancey (1993) suggests "personal accounts." *Life writing* might be the more apt generic label.

Although this discussion has not been organized explicitly on a historical or chronological basis, it is clear that the nature, purpose, form, and function of life writing have evolved over recent years and decades, as well as centuries. For scholars with even a bit of an innovative or experimentalist set of values, current biographical forms and formats should be seen as only tentative guidelines toward their own creative inquiry endeavors. Any constraining formalistic definitions and rules about the nature and function of biography seem out of keeping with the vigor of intellectual activity under way.

Almost as a corollary of the prior generalizations, biographical inquiry is in high contention among scholars within and among different disciplines—literature, history, sociology, psychology, and anthropology. Each of these traditions has evolved its own standards and perspectives on life writing. Conflict seems everywhere. Each discipline, and subgroups within disciplines, vents its anger and displeasure upon other groups and traditions. Ecumenical approaches often are not seen as desirable. Large personal, professional, and disciplinary issues and interests are at stake. The best counsel seems to be, Realize that this is happening, come to know as much of the variety as time permits, and integrate the differences in ways that contribute to one's own creativity in life writing.

The kind of data drawn upon by different researchers—letters, interviews, documents, self-statements, and so on—as they construct their biographies will vary in amount, quality, relevance, and perceived significance. Autobiographies—sometimes as statements in their own right and sometimes as data for other statements—seem to draw disdain from several quarters and high support from others. Critics and evaluators will need to use their own judgment, just as the biographer per se must do, to assess the meaning and the quality of the effort. In my view, building a rationale for any particular form of life writing as legitimate inquiry seems possible in the diversity of orientations presented here. The important test case for an academic might well be: What variants are permissible as Ph.D. dissertations? Clearly, formal biographies of eminent white males qualify. But what of a Moody or a latter-day Cullwick? Would their autobiographies or diaries count? I would argue yes, but others might disagree. And the debate would continue: Purposes? Limits? Criteria?

In my view, doing biography is an active constructionist activity, from the picking of a hero or heroine to the seeking of data pools, to the selection of issues and themes, and to the final image or portrait that is drawn. The importance of serendipity in selecting a subject for a biography, in determining a particular theme and perspective, and in working one's way through the doing of the biography needs to be noted as a significant possibility in both purpose and strategy. While searching for one solution, life writers seem to find other things. Serendipity needs to be contrasted with more formal intellectual approaches, which are often, in my view, an illustration of reconstructed logic rather than logic in use. Theories of biography remain partial and limited in scope.

One of my major aspirations in this essay has been the presentation of ideas and people who espouse the ideas, that is, the perspectives that will "move along" the inquiries of the readers. At a minimum, if I have intrigued any of you who have never done life histories or biographies, or those of you who have never read Bowen, Clifford, or Edel, among others, to begin those journeys, this essay will have been a success.

Finally, many social scientists who worry about the relationships among inquiry, theory, and practice speak of the importance of "sensitizing concepts," "models," and "metaphors" as aids to thinking about and doing practical activity. Engaging in life-writing inquiry is, in part, a craft, an instance of practice. In my interpretation of these views, I believe an essentially pragmatic perspective arises. I believe that the stories and ideas that one creates should be useful for solving further problems in one's professional life. Autobiography is writ large, at least implicitly. Reflective practice is another of the broader and more significant conceptions. This essay on "biographical method" is intended to fall within these traditions.

◆ Notes

1. A similar extended illustration could be drawn using the multiple life writings by and about a figure such as Virginia Woolf (1929, 1938, 1940). Bell's (1972) two-volume biography of Woolf contrasts sharply with the more recent biography by DeSalvo (1989), who accents a sexual abuse theme.

2. The Darwin illustration can be pursued further with such variants as Kohn (1985), Barrett (1977), Gruber (1981), Healey (1986), Marks (1991), Darwin and Seward (1903), F. Darwin (1909), and Barlow (1946, 1967).

3. My current views presented here are in transformation once again as I participate in a Washington University faculty seminar on "autobiography." The stimulating discussion ranges across the humanities—comparative literature, performing arts, romance languages— and occasionally the social sciences.

4. Clifford (1970) tells a similar set of fascinating stories under the heading "the vague footnote," which sent him off to Wales in the 1930s.

5. Bowen (1968, p. 11) suggests an alternative typology: narrative, topical, or essay for forming and shaping the biography. See, for example, Sarton's (1959) *I Knew a Phoenix*, which carries the subtitle *Sketches for an Autobiography*.

6. Even as this essay is being revised, my Washington University colleagues in the faculty seminar have inundated me with literally dozens (hundreds?) of references, especially from comparative literature, that I have never seen. It is a humbling experience.

7. A number of sources exist in the symbolic interactionist tradition; classically, Blumer's (1969) "Chicago school" of sociology's extension of George Herbert Mead is critical. Recently, Hargreaves (1986) has presented, especially for the educationist, a potent summary perspective with the title "Whatever Happened to Symbolic Interactionism?" Dexter's (1970) methodological book *Elite and Specialized Interviewing* is grounded in a similar view (see, e.g., p. 5).

8. The relationship of shorter biographical studies in the service of other inquiry approaches is a major intellectual and practical issue in itself. I have touched on it only briefly and in passing.

◆ References

Allport, G. W. (1937). *Personality*. New York: Holt.
Allport, G. W. (1942). *The use of personal documents in psychological science*. New York: Social Science Research Council.
Allport, G. W. (1960). Personality: A problem for science or a problem for art? In G. W. Allport, *Personality and social encounter* (pp. 3-15). Boston: Beacon.

Allport, G. W. (1965). *Letters from Jenny*. New York: Harcourt, Brace & World.

Ashton-Warner, S. (1963). *Teacher*. New York: Simon & Schuster.

Ball, S., & Goodson, I. (Eds.). (1985). *Teachers' lives and careers*. London: Falmer.

Barlow, N. (Ed.). (1933). *Charles Darwin's diary of the voyage of the H.M.S. Beagle*. Cambridge: Cambridge University Press.

Barlow, N. (Ed.). (1946). *Charles Darwin and the voyage of the Beagle*. New York: Philosophical Library.

Barlow, N. (Ed.). (1958). *The autobiography of Charles Darwin 1809-1882*. London: Collins.

Barlow, N. (Ed.). (1967). *Darwin and Henslow: The growth of an idea. Letters 1831-1860*. Berkeley: University of California Press.

Barrett, P. (Ed.). (1977). *The collected papers of Charles Darwin* (Vols. 1-2). Chicago: University of Chicago Press.

Bateson, M. C. (1990). *Composing a life*. New York: Plume/Penguin.

Becker, H. S. (1966). Introduction. In C. Shaw (Ed.), *The jack-roller: A delinquent boy's own story* (pp. v-xviii). Chicago: University of Chicago Press.

Becker, H. S. (1970). *Sociological work*. Chicago: Aldine.

Bell, Q. (1972). *Virginia Woolf: A biography* (Vols. 1-2). New York: Harcourt Brace Jovanovich.

Bertaux, D. (Ed.). (1981). *Biography and society: The life history approach in the social sciences*. Beverly Hills, CA: Sage.

Blumer, H. (1969). *Symbolic interactionism*. Englewood Cliffs, NJ: Prentice Hall.

Bowen, C. D. (1959). *Adventures of a biographer*. Boston: Little, Brown.

Bowen, C. D. (1968). *Biography: The craft and the calling*. Boston: Little, Brown.

Bowlby, J. (1990). *Charles Darwin: A new life*. New York: W. W. Norton.

Butterfield, S. (1974). *Black autobiography in America*. Amherst: University of Massachusetts Press.

Clifford, J. L. (1970). *From puzzles to portraits: Problems of a literary biographer*. Chapel Hill: University of North Carolina Press.

Cohn, M., & Kottkamp, R. (1992). *Teachers: The missing voice in education*. Albany: State University of New York Press.

Coles, R., & Coles, J. H. (1980). *Women of crisis II: Lives of work and dreams*. New York: Delacorte.

Crapanzano, V. (1980). *Tuhami: Portrait of a Moroccan*. Chicago: University of Chicago Press.

Cross, A. (1990). *The players come again*. New York: Random House.

Darwin, C. (1839). *Journal of researches into the geology and natural history of the various countries visited by H.M.S. Beagle, under the command of Captain Fitzroy, R.N., from 1832-1836*. London: Henry Colburn.

Darwin, F. (Ed.). (1888). *Life and letters of Charles Darwin* (Vols. 1-3). London: Murray.

Darwin, F. (Ed.). (1909). *The foundations of the* Origin of Species: *Two essays written in 1842 and 1844 by Charles Darwin*. Cambridge: Cambridge University Press.

Darwin, F., & Seward, A. (Eds.). (1903). *More letters of Charles Darwin* (Vols. 1-2). London: J. Murray.

Denzin, N. (1989). *Interpretive biography*. Newbury Park, CA: Sage.

DeSalvo, L. (1989). *Virginia Woolf: The impact of childhood sexual abuse on her life and work.* New York: Ballantine.

Desmond, A., & Moore, J. (1991). *Darwin.* London: Michael Joseph.

Dexter, L. A. (1970). *Elite and specialized interviewing.* Evanston: Northwestern University Press.

Eakin, P. J. (1989). Foreword. In P. Lejeune, *On autobiography* (pp. vii-xxviii). Minneapolis: University of Minnesota Press.

Edel, L. (1979). The figure under the carpet. In M. Pachter (Ed.), *Telling lives: The biographer's art* (pp. 16-34). Washington, DC: New Republic Books.

Edel, L. (1984). *Writing lives: Principia biographica.* New York: W. W. Norton.

Elliott, J. (1991). *Action research for educational change.* Milton Keynes, UK: Open University Press.

Erikson, E. H. (1963). *Childhood and society* (2nd ed.). New York: W. W. Norton.

Erikson, E. H. (1962). *Young man Luther: A study in psychoanalysis and history.* New York: W. W. Norton.

FitzRoy, R. (1839). *Proceedings of the second expedition, 1831-1836.* London: Henry Colburn.

Garraty, J. (1954). The interrelations of psychology and biography. *Psychological Bulletin, 51,* 569-582.

Garraty, J. (1957). *The nature of biography.* New York: Alfred A. Knopf.

Geertz, C. (1973). *The interpretation of cultures: Selected essays.* New York: Basic Books.

Geertz, C. (1988). *Works and lives: The anthropologist as author.* Stanford, CA: Stanford University Press.

Goodson, I. (Ed.). (1992). *Studying teachers' lives.* London: Routledge.

Gruber, H. E. (1981). *Darwin on man: A psychological study of scientific creativity* (2nd ed.). Chicago: University of Chicago Press.

Gruenberg, S., & Krech, H. (1952). *The many lives of modern woman.* Garden City, NY: Doubleday.

Gusdorf, G. (1980). Conditions and limits of autobiography. In J. Olney (Ed.), *Autobiography: Essays theoretical and critical* (pp. 28-48). Princeton, NJ: Princeton University Press.

Hargreaves, D. (1986). Whatever happened to symbolic interactionism? In M. Hammersley (Ed.), *Controversies in classroom research.* Milton Keynes, UK: Open University Press.

Healey, E. (1986). *Wives of fame: Mary Livingstone, Jenny Marx, Emma Darwin.* London: New English Library, Hodder & Stoughton.

Heilbrun, C. (1981). Introduction. In V. Brittain, *Testament of a friendship* (pp. xv-xxxii). New York: Wideview.

Heilbrun, C. (1988). *Writing a woman's life.* New York: W. W. Norton.

Hentoff, N. (1966). *Our children are dying.* New York: Viking.

Hernden, J. (1966). *The way its spozed to be.* New York: Bantam.

Hernden, J. (1971). *How to survive in your native land.* New York: Bantam.

Hexter, J. (1971). *The history primer.* New York: Basic Books.

Hiley, M. (1979). *Victorian working women: Portraits from life.* London: Gordon Fraser.

Holt, J. (1964). *How children fail.* New York: Pitman.

Horner, M. S. (1987). The Radcliffe Biography Series. In R. Coles (Ed.), *Simone Weil: A modern pilgrimage* (pp. ix-x). Reading, MA: Addison-Wesley.

Hudson, D. (1972). *Munby: Man of two worlds.* London: Murray.

Hudson, L. (1966). *Contrary imaginations: A psychological study of the English schoolboy.* Harmondsworth: Penguin.

Hudson, L. (1972). *The cult of the fact.* London: Jonathan Cape.

Kluckhohn, C. (1949). *Mirror for man: The relation of anthropology to modern life.* New York: McGraw-Hill.

Kluckhohn, C., & Murray, H. A. (1953). *Personality in nature, society, and culture.* New York: Alfred A. Knopf.

Kohn, D. (Ed.). (1985). *The Darwin heritage.* Princeton, NJ: Princeton University Press.

Lancey, D. (1993). *Qualitative research in education.* New York: Longman.

Langness, L. L. (1965). *The life history in anthropological science.* New York: Holt, Rinehart & Winston.

Langness, L. L., & Frank, G. (1981). *Lives: An anthropological approach to biography.* Novato, CA: Chandler & Sharp.

Lejeune, P. (1989). *On autobiography.* Minneapolis: University of Minnesota Press.

Levinson, D., with Darrow, C. N., Klein, E. B., Levinson, M. H., & McKee, B. (1978). *The seasons of a man's life.* New York: Alfred A. Knopf.

Lewis, O. (1951). *Life in a Mexican village: Tepoztlan restudied.* Urbana: University of Illinois Press.

Lewis, O. (1959). *Five families.* New York: Basic Books.

Lewis, O. (1961). *The children of Sanchez.* New York: Random House.

Malinowski, B. (1922). *Argonauts of the western Pacific.* London: Routledge & Kegan Paul.

Marks, R. (1991). *Three men of the Beagle.* New York: Alfred A. Knopf.

McAdams, D., & Ochberg, R. (Eds.). (1980). *Psychobiography and life narratives.* Durham, NC: Duke University Press.

McCullough, D. (1992). *Truman.* New York: Simon & Schuster.

Mills, C. W. (1959). *The sociological imagination.* London: Oxford University Press.

Moody, A. (1968). *Coming of age in Mississippi.* New York: Dell.

Murray, H. A., et al. (1938). *Explorations in personality: A clinical and experimental study of fifty men of college age.* New York: Oxford University Press.

Neill, A. S. (1960). *Summerhill: A radical approach to child rearing.* New York: Hart.

Neill, A. S. (1975). *The dominie books of A. S. Neill: A dominie's log; A dominie in doubt; A dominie dismissed.* New York: Hart.

Olney, J. (Ed.). (1980). *Autobiography: Essays theoretical and critical.* Princeton, NJ: Princeton University Press.

Personal Narratives Group. (1989). *Interpreting women's lives: Feminist theory and personal narratives.* Bloomington: Indiana University Press.

Pritchett, V. S. (1977). *On autobiography.* London: English Association.

Rabinow, P. (1977). *Reflections on fieldwork in Morocco.* Berkeley: University of California Press.

Raverat, G. (1952). *Period piece: A Cambridge childhood.* London: Faber & Faber.

Redfield, R. (1930). *Tepoztlan: A Mexican village.* Chicago: University of Chicago Press.

Redfield, R. (1955). *The little community.* Chicago: University of Chicago Press.

Rogers, P. (1980). Introduction. In J. Boswell, *Life of Johnson* (pp. v-xxxvi). Oxford: Oxford University Press.

Runyan, W. (1982). *Life histories and psychobiography.* New York: Oxford University Press.

Runyan, W. (Ed.). (1988). *Psychology and historical interpretation.* New York: Oxford University Press.

Sarton, M. (1959). *I knew a phoenix: Sketches for an autobiography.* New York: W. W. Norton.

Sarton, M. (1968). *Plant dreaming deep.* New York: W. W. Norton.

Sarton, M. (1973). *Journal of a solitude.* New York: W. W. Norton.

Schön, D. (1983). *The reflective practitioner: How professionals think in action.* New York: Basic Books.

Schön, D. (1987). *Educating the reflective practitioner: Toward a new design for teaching and learning in the professions.* San Francisco: Jossey-Bass.

Shaw, C. (1930). *The jack-roller: A delinquent boy's own story.* Chicago: University of Chicago Press.

Skinner, B. F. (1977). *Particulars of my life.* New York: Alfred A. Knopf.

Skinner, B. F. (1979). *The shaping of a behaviorist: Part two of an autobiography.* New York: Alfred A. Knopf.

Skinner, B. F. (1983). *A matter of consequences: Part three of an autobiography.* New York: Alfred A. Knopf.

Smith, L. M. (1987). The voyage of the *Beagle*: Fieldwork lessons from Charles Darwin. *Educational Administration Quarterly, 23,* 5-30.

Smith, L. M. (1990). One road to historical inquiry: Extending one's repertory of qualitative methods. In W. Eaton (Ed.), *History, politics, and methodology in American education: Collected essays* (pp. 79-109). New York: Teachers College Press.

Smith, L. M. (1992). *Doing ethnographic biography: A reflective practitioner at work during a spring in Cambridge.* Manuscript submitted for publication.

Smith, L. M. (in press). *Nora Barlow and the Darwin legacy.* Ames: Iowa State University Press.

Smith, L. M., Dwyer, D. C., Prunty, J. J., & Kleine, P. F. (1988). *Innovation and change in schooling: History, politics, and agency.* London: Falmer.

Smith, L. M., & Geoffrey, W. (1968). *The complexities of an urban classroom.* New York: Holt, Rinehart & Winston.

Smith, L. M., Kleine, P. F., Prunty, J. J., & Dwyer, D. C. (1986). *Educational innovators: Then and now.* London: Falmer.

Smith, L. M., Prunty, J. J., Dwyer, D. C., & Kleine, P. F. (1987). *The fate of an innovative school: The history and present status of the Kensington School.* London: Falmer.

Smith, L. M., & Wells, W. (1990). *"Difficult to reach, maintain, and help" urban families in PAT: Issues, dilemmas, strategies, and resolutions in parent education* (Final report to the Smith-Richardson Foundation). St. Louis, MO: Washington University.

Stanley, L. (Ed.). (1984). *The diaries of Hannah Cullwick, Victorian maidservant.* New Brunswick, NJ: Rutgers University Press.

Stanley, L. (Ed.). (1992). *The autobiographical I: The theory and practice of feminist auto/biography.* Manchester, UK: Manchester University Press.

Stone, L. (1981). *The past and the present.* Boston: Routledge & Kegan Paul.

Strachey, L. (1918). *Eminent Victorians.* New York: Harcourt, Brace.

Terkel, S. (1970). *Hard times: An oral history of the Great Depression.* New York: Avon.

Terkel, S. (1972). *Working.* New York: Avon.

Trevelyan, G. M. (1932). Preface. In G. O. Trevelyan, *The life and letters of Lord Macaulay* (pp. v-vii). London: Oxford University Press.

Valentine, C. (1968). *Culture and poverty: Critique and counterproposals.* Chicago: University of Chicago Press.

Waller, W. (1932). *The sociology of teaching.* New York: John Wiley.

White, R. W. (1952). *Lives in progress.* New York: Dryden.

Woolf, V. (1929). *A room of one's own.* New York: Harcourt, Brace.

Woolf, V. (1938). *Three guineas.* New York: Harcourt, Brace.

Woolf, V. (1940). *Roger Fry: A biography.* New York: Harcourt, Brace.

Woolf, V. (1960). *Granite and rainbow.* London: Hogarth. (Original work published 1927)

9

Historical Social Science

Methodologies, Methods, and Meanings

Gaye Tuchman

◆ One question logically precedes any advice about the use of historical methods in social science research: What do social scientists mean by *historical research*? Articles distinguishing between historical sociology and sociological history tend to develop ideal-typical portraits of each endeavor.[1] Rather than presenting ideal types, this essay will unfold as much qualitative research does—by inference. Nonetheless, this essay has an implicit theme: Whether done by social scientists or by historians, historical work requires a point of view. A point of view necessarily includes an interpretive framework that implicitly contains some notion of the "meaning of history."

The theoretical use of historical data also implies a methodology. I do not use the term *methodology* in its current sense of "application of a specific method," such as analysis of documents or participant observation. Rather, I use *methodology* in its classic sense: the study of the epistemo-

AUTHOR'S NOTE: I am grateful to librarian Scott Kennedy for showing me how to locate research tools in a computerized library. I profited from readings of a very early draft by Douglas Heckathorn and Myra Marx Ferree, and Norman Denzin and Yvonna Lincoln provided marvelous suggestions for improving subsequent drafts.

logical assumptions implicit in specific methods. I thus assume that a methodology includes a way of looking at phenomena that specifies how a method "captures" the "object" of study.

I have placed the terms *captures* and *object* in quotation marks in the preceding statement because they are problematic. Not all methodologies imply that the researcher should "capture" the "object" of study. Feminist methodologies oppose these terms, because they imply that a researcher is trying to dominate the phenomenon under consideration (see Keller, 1985). Other chapters in this volume review some of the implications of current methodologies. This essay necessarily adopts a methodology; to wit, adequate social science includes a theoretical use of historical information. Any social phenomenon must be understood in its historical context. To grasp historical information, one must have a point of view, including an interpretive framework that includes some notion of the "meaning" of history.

However, just as the nature of social science is widely debated, so too what history "means" is problematic. Indeed, that "meaning" is precisely what historians debate. Sometimes they debate the relevance of theories shared with the social sciences: Does a Marxist or a Weberian interpretation of a specific phenomenon best capture its "essence"? How, if at all, is geography central to grasping the development of specific regions, such as the development of the Mediterranean area (Braudel, 1972)? Which social group should historians study and why: elites, the poor, intellectuals? What are the consequences of studying which group? What picture of the past does the historian create by her or his choice?[2] Sometimes historians debate periodization, or how the division of history into periods influences generalizations (Kelly, 1977). Sometimes they debate the nature of historical narratives: Is there a "grand narrative" that can tell the story of, say, European development? Can the history of other continents (or minority peoples) be incorporated in a grand narrative? Or even, Is the historian's task the development of a grand narrative (Coontz, 1992; Himmelfarb, 1987)?

There are no simple answers to questions about the "meaning of history," just as there are no ready answers to the "meaning" of social science or—to draw an admittedly foolish comparison—to the meaning of life. Given that I do not believe there are a series of correct answers, I will ask such questions as the following: How have empirically minded sociologists grappled with distinctions between the historical and sociological enterprises? How has historical information figured in social science classics? Within the past few decades, how have historians seemingly modified the nature of the historical enterprise? How are those modifications relevant to social scientific research?

◆ Defining Social Science as Different From History

To establish their legitimacy, early American sociologists tried to identify how their field differed from more traditional fields of study. In 1921, Robert Park and Ernest Burgess reflected on the nature of history and sociology. Both, they wrote, "are concerned with man as a person, as a 'political animal,' participating with his fellows in a common fund of social traditions and cultural ideals" (p. 10). According to these early qualitative American sociologists:

> History . . . seeks to reproduce and interpret concrete events as they actually occurred in time and space. Sociology . . . seeks to arrive at natural laws and generalizations in regard to human nature and society, irrespective of time and place. . . . History seeks to find out what actually happened and how it all came about. Sociology . . . seeks to explain, on the basis of a study of other instances, the nature of the process involved. (p. 11)

However, today many European and North American historians and sociologists reject Park and Burgess's formulation. Since the publication of Park and Burgess's classic *Introduction to the Science of Sociology* (1921), historians have increasingly "compared instances" and have frequently adopted quantitative methods to do so. Sociologists have come to recognize that the great nineteenth-century European sociologists, now canonized as classic theorists, were not writing theory that "reject[s] the application of theoretical statement to the empirical world, declaring empirical evidence to be irrelevant for . . . theorizing" (Scheuch, 1992, p. 769). Rather, they were writing "theory of . . . "—theory relevant to empirical issues. Their questions were as broad as, What is the meaning of capitalism for contemporary societies? To glean answers, they had to "do history." To address the historical processes relevant to their questions, they examined cross-national data. Some of these data were quantitative.

◆ Classical Theory and Historical Data

I will discuss the canonized work of Karl Marx and Max Weber as prototypical examples because their work has been so central to social science. Because books by these men are often assigned in undergraduate and graduate courses, my discussion assumes that the reader has passing familiarity with these classic texts. In each of the texts considered, historical knowledge is essential to interpretation of the argument. To read the works of Marx and Weber, one must also understand how nineteenth-century historians interpreted the past.

Marx

To understand Marx and Engels's "political pamphlet" *The Communist Manifesto,* one must understand the social relationships and processes associated with feudalism, including both the interdependence of the church and state and the economic interdependence of families. Otherwise it seems incomprehensible that more serfs did not flee the land. Similarly, unless one knows of the existence of dress codes in medieval cities (not discussed in Marx), one cannot comprehend the failure of many urban servants to flee their masters.

I chose these two examples because of an incident in one of my classes: A Kenyan graduate student had not realized the full impact of feudalism as a system of peonage that forced serfs to give a large share of their agricultural produce to the feudal aristocracy, supported extensive land-holdings of the church, which also bound serfs to their land, and encouraged familial ties between the aristocracy and the church hierarchy. When this student grasped how severe the oppression of serfs had been, he could not understand why they did not flee. Having little appreciation of the flora available in, say, France, he supposed fleeing serfs could find food and shelter in forests in winter and could freely kill animals without fear of laws against poaching. The Kenyan student accepted the assurance of a French student that one could not easily survive in many European forests. But then the Kenyan faced another problem: He supposed that serfs in one region would gladly take in a fleeing refugee. He did not appreciate the degree of interdependence among serfs—how in traditional European societies an individual could not hope to survive outside of the local collectivity because these traditional societies did not embrace strangers. (This "mechanical solidarity," to use Durkheim's phrase, is captured by the

TABLE 9.1 The Association Between Education and Religion

	Protestant (%)	Catholic (%)	Jews (%)
Gymnasium	43	46	9.5
Realgymnasium	69	31	9
Oberrealschulen	52	41	7
Realschulen	49	40	11
Höhere Bürgerschulen	51	37	12
Average	48	42	10
Percentage in population	37	61.3	1.5

SOURCE: Weber (1904-1905/1976, pp. 188-189); last line added from the text of Weber's footnote 8.
NOTE: All rows do not add to 100%.

very term *outlaw,* a person sentenced to be "out"side of the protective "law" for a year, a fate that endangered survival.) Lacking this historical background, the student could not comprehend why Marx discussed the dire exploitation afflicting the early nineteenth-century proletariat as "progress" over medieval oppression. In sum, without the appropriate historical background, the Kenyan found the argument of the *Communist Manifesto* difficult to grasp.

Weber

Some appreciation of past realities is also necessary to grasp the thrust of Max Weber's classic *The Protestant Ethic and the Spirit of Capitalism* (1904-1905/1976): Early modern European capitalism was different in kind than earlier forms of capitalism, and its character was influenced by ideas associated with Protestantism, as well as by other factors. I start with a minor example, Weber's footnote 8. It concerns the association between religion and education and is part of Weber's attempt to argue against objections to his historical interpretation. The footnote includes the table reproduced here as Table 9.1. It also includes a translator's note, for translator Talcott Parsons felt he had to provide definitions of terms in the table for the data to be meaningful.

The passage in the text reads: "It may be, as has been claimed, that the greater participation of Protestants in the positions of ownership and management in modern economic life may to-day be understood, in part at least, simply as a result of the greater material wealth they have inherited. But there are other phenomena which cannot be explained in the same way" (p. 37). Next comes Weber's example: the association between religion and the percentage of students and graduates of higher-education institutions relative to the proportion of individuals of specified religions in the population of Baden. The paragraph ends:

> But among the Catholic graduates themselves the percentage of those graduating from the institutions preparing, in particular, for technical studies and industrial and commercial occupations, but in general from those preparing for middle-class business-life, lags still farther behind the percentage of Protestants. On the other hand, Catholics prefer the sort of training which the humanistic Gymnasium affords. That is a circumstance to which the above explanation does not apply, but which, on the contrary is one reason why so few Catholics are engaged in capitalistic enterprise. (p. 38)

Footnote 8 (pp. 188-189) presents the percentage of Protestants, Catholics, and Jews in Baden in 1895 and what percentage of each of five types of schools was composed of Protestants, Catholics, and Jews. Parsons's translator's note then explains, "In the *Gymnasium* the main emphasis is on the classics. In the *Realgymnasium* Greek is dropped and Latin is reduced in favour of modern languages, mathematics and science. The *Realschule* and *Oberrealschule* are similar to the latter except that Latin is dropped entirely in favour of modern languages." I have added a line to the table; it gives the percentage of each religious group in the population of Baden in 1895.

Parsons has not told the reader what was taught in the *Höhere Bürgerschulen,* higher city schools, nor why Jews are so overrepresented in these schools. But, for now, merely note that Parsons recognized that the meaning of the table—its relevance to the text—is incomprehensible if one does not know what each school taught. (Later I will use this table to discuss the relevance of chasing down byways to interpret the frame of an argument.)[3]

Although the data in the previous example concern education and religion at roughly the time Weber was writing *The Protestant Ethic and the Spirit of Capitalism* (1904-1905/1976) today commentators agree that Weber used historical data to rebut Herbert Spenser and Karl Marx, even as he offered his own "theory of" the development of capitalism. Though Weber does not provide direct citation to Spenser and Marx, his language is redolent of theirs. For instance:

Thus the capitalism of to-day, which has come to dominate economic life, educates and selects the economic subjects which it needs through a process of economic survival of the fittest. But here one can easily see the limits of the concept of selection as a means of historical explanation. In order that a manner of life so well adapted to the peculiarities of capitalism could be selected at all, i.e. should come to dominate others, it had to originate somewhere, and not in isolated individuals alone, but as a way of life common to whole groups of men. This origin is what needs explanation. (p. 55)

Weber continues, "Concerning the doctrine of the more naive historical materialism, that such ideas originate as a reflection or superstructure of economic situations, we shall speak of more in detail below. At this point it will suffice for our purposes to call attention to the fact that without doubt . . . the spirit of capitalism . . . was present before the capitalistic order" (p. 55).[4]

To go beyond the argument over antecedents (and so causality), one must have some historical sophistication. Pertinent questions include the following: How did capitalism change from its mercantile beginnings? Was the process of change "uniform" across various countries? Without being able to assess how and why Weber disagreed with Spenser and Marx, one may suspect that Weber is merely offering a refutation to earlier theories. But, although in *Protestant Ethic* Weber seems to feel that historical materialism is naive, his conclusion—that "the cloak of [Protestant] ascetic rationalism" had developed into an "iron cage"—is as bitter a condemnation of the social organization of advanced capitalism as anything Marx wrote. And Weber is certainly more pessimistic about attempts to ameliorate capitalism than is Marx. Historical knowledge—some grasp of the differences between English capitalism in the 1840s and German capitalism at the turn of the century—helps one to interpret Weber's attitude, although aspects of his biography are germane as well. By the beginning of the twentieth century, the advent of bureaucratic organization, emerging management techniques, and the ability of capitalism to withstand revolutionary attack in Western societies made it clear that capitalism was not about to dissolve.

Historical knowledge is also necessary if one is to interpret what Weber identifies as the nub of his argument. Toward the end of a four-page footnote, Weber writes:

The essential point of the difference is . . . that an ethic based on religion places certain psychological sanctions (not of an economic character) on the maintenance of the attitude prescribed by it, sanctions which, so long as the religious belief remains alive, are highly effective, and which mere worldly wisdom . . . does not have at its disposal. Only in so far as these sanctions work, and above all, in the direction in which they work, which is *often different from the doctrine of the theologians,* does such an ethic gain an independent influence on the *conduct of life* and thus on the economic order. This is, to speak frankly, the point of this whole essay, which I had not expected to find so completely overlooked. (p. 197; emphasis added)

Although Weber seems determined to make his intent clear, this footnote still permits conflicting interrogations. Each scrutiny is truly a "cross"-examination, for each implies a different interpretation of past practices (and so a different interpretation of the text) and simultaneously a different interpretation of the text (and so a different interpretation of past practices). Does Weber offer a social psychological interpretation of capitalism, as the functionalists taught? Is the essence of this argument that the spirit of capitalism arose from the psychological loneliness experienced by Protestants who yearned for assurance that they belonged to God's Elect? Does it arise from the social organization of Protestant life, exemplified by the New England Puritans? Is Weber engaging in a cultural analysis based in a humanistic sociology of knowledge[5] that stresses daily practice? Is Weber most interested in how a phenomenon—the spirit of capitalism—became transformed over time?

I do not wish to offer my own interpretation of Weber's classic, or to delve into historians' refutations of Weber. (Those refutations concern the validity of Weber's evidence.) Rather, I note that the theoretical use of historical data implies methodological issues. The term *methodological* affirms the late nineteenth-century German insight that any empirical study, including any historical study, requires an interpretive approach—a philosophy of method, an epistemology—that guides the identification of appropriate data. Given that it is clear that Weber's use of specific historical data was intentional, one must ask of Weber much the same questions one would ask of any essay or monograph: Why these data? Why does the argument of *The Protestant Ethic and the Spirit of Capitalism* turn on Benjamin Franklin's maxims, Puritan daily practices, and, less heavily, theology?

In sum, Marx and Weber wrote as though one must come to grips with historical realities to explore the *meaning* of contemporary practices and processes. To interpret their theoretical work, one must appreciate what they took for granted as characteristic of *their* time *and* their interpretations of the past. For instance, Weber's refutation of Marx draws on the late nineteenth- and early twentieth-century assumption that Marx's writings were crude, unidimensional materialism. But both these classic theorists realized that contemporary practices are historically embedded. To use today's theoretical concepts: Social meanings are recursive (Giddens, 1984). The past continues to speak to the present. All that we take for granted as "natural" is a product of both historical and contemporary processes. Our task as social scientists is to interpret those multifaceted meanings, including their interactions with one another.[6] How to choose a point of view that serves as an interpretive frame is quite another matter.

◆ Contemporary Cliometrics and Point of View

As do other academic specialists, historians argue about the point of view appropriate to their research. For the past 20 years, they have argued about whether what we call history—the story of people and societies across time—concerns the perceptions and activities of elites or of "ordinary" folk (social history). To some extent, the research practices of different types of historians have involved different sorts of data. For instance, in the 1970s social historians saw themselves as young Turks battling against more traditional historians, whom they accused of an atheoretical acceptance of the version of events promulgated by members of the elites whose activities the more traditional historians studied. The social historians wanted to demonstrate that those past elites (and so present historians) had misinterpreted "concrete events as they actually occurred in time and space" (Park & Burgess, 1921, p. 11). And so many social historians turned to statistics (named *cliometrics* to honor Clio, the ancient Greek muse of history).

Cliometrics can be used to study any phenomenon for which there are reliable and valid data.[7] Such data may concern the wages of factory workers, patterns of literacy, or the education of elites. I offer two examples of cliometrics. The first juxtaposes two views of the participation of women in the English labor force during the Industrial Revolution. One is a statement made in 1838 by a member of the British Parliament; the other, a summary of tables about the distribution of women and men in the paid labor force in Great Britain (in 1851) and France (in 1866). The second case involves the literary activities of the middle and upper classes.

Example 1: The Participation of Women in the Nineteenth-Century Workforce

The member of Parliament expressed "one of the enduring images of industrialization, created by contemporaries and transmitted by historians"— "the female factory worker" as "prototype of the wage-earning woman . . . a young 'mill girl' or a married 'operative,' turned from her family by the need to earn wages" (Tilly & Scott, 1978, p. 63). His words:

> Amongst other things I saw a cotton mill—a sight that froze my blood. The place was full of women, young, all of them, some large with child, and obliged to stand twelve hours each day. . . . The heat was excessive in some of the rooms, the stink pestiferous, and in all an atmosphere of cotton flue. I nearly fainted. The young women were all pale, sallow, thin, yet generally fairly grown, all with bare feet—a strange sight to English eyes. (quoted in Tilly & Scott, 1978, p. 64)

Interpreting quantitative data, Tilly and Scott (1978) announce that this depiction is misleading:

> Industrialization did mean that many more women had to help their families earn wages. Instead of contributing their labor to household production, they had to sell their labor power and bring in cash. Textile factories did create jobs for women. But these factories were neither the only nor the predominant form of female wage-earning activity during the nineteenth century in England. . . . *The impact of industrialization on women's employment was more varied and far less dramatic than the standard image of the mill girl implies.* (p. 64; emphasis added)

Their reasoning continues, although England and France had quite different economies in the nineteenth century, "in both countries, women tended to be concentrated in unmechanized, 'traditional' sectors of the economy, except for the textile industry. The mechanized textile industry's growth in these countries marked the entry of women into wage labor in factory settings. Nevertheless it was only part of the picture."

Tilly and Scott then use the language of statistics: "In the economy outside of textiles, the smaller the scale of organization, the larger the size of the female work force" (p. 68). Even in the more industrialized England, most women workers were not in manufacturing: "Overall, textile workers represented 22 percent of the female labor force. In contrast, domestic service claimed 40 percent" (p. 68). Thus *domestic service was the typical form of female employment outside of agriculture before industrialization. In England, it apparently expanded as an occupation as the country industrialized*" (p. 68). Tilly and Scott's cliometrics rebut past understandings of the role of women in industrialization as surely as Weber intended his analysis of a cultural phenomenon—the spirit of Protestantism—to rebut what he understood to be "crude historical materialism."

But Tilly and Scott's cliometrics cannot refute aspects of standard historical interpretations: The elite clearly identified female employment with the textile industry, and elites behaved as though their interpretation were accurate. Their interpretation had consequences; to paraphrase W. I. Thomas's classic insight: If people believe that a phenomenon is real, it is real in its consequences. By debating women's employment *as though* work in the textile industry were ideal-typical, the early nineteenth-century British elite constructed and acted on a version of reality that did not correspond to the conditions of working-class women.

Thus Tilly and Scott's cliometrics raise two different issues. One may be phrased as a research question: How did elites' "fictive" definition of the situation affect their actions and so influence the life conditions experienced by nineteenth-century British working-class women? The other related issue is more philosophical: How does the deconstruction of the past influence one's story of the past? Tilly and Scott proclaim that historians have misinterpreted the situation of working women. They present what they believe to be the "true" story. Can this "true" story be accepted at face value, or do the conflicting stories present a more complex task? Again, I phrase the relevant issues as questions: How are we to adjudicate between the two stories as constructions of historians? Can we hope to achieve some adjudication without coming to grips with the sociohistorical meanings of power? In my use, the phrase *sociohistorical meanings of power* has several referents: (a) nineteenth-century interpretations and contestation of power between the elite and the working class and, within social classes, between women and men; and (b) differential distributions of professional power among twentieth-century historians, who contest the quality of one another's scholarship and so credibility and who also contest the "proper" subjects of historical scholarship.

The contrast between social history and what I have termed *traditional history* raises other issues as well, namely, the *reliability* of informants and the discernment of *patterns*. Presumably, the member of Parliament quoted above commented on characteristics of female factory workers after he had toured many factories. He could claim to be what a participant observer might call a "reliable informant" about women operatives and about factory conditions, but *not* about the pattern of women's employment. To be a reliable informant about the general pattern (in this case, the distribution of women workers), he would have had to have noticed a phenomenon he appears to have taken for granted: the pervasiveness of women domestics in upper-middle-class homes, including presumably his own. We can assume that the M.P. took this form of employment for granted because it was so fundamental to Victorian life—so beyond notice. I infer from such novels as Mrs. Gaskell's *Cranford* and George Eliot's *Middlemarch* that one can classify a family's economic status by the number and kind of servants it employed.[8] Thus I conclude that the M.P.'s observations are reliable about some things, but not others: A highly placed government official was in a position to report about phenomena in which he participated. We might trust his reflections, including his description of patterns, if we felt he was an astute observer whose impartiality or biases we could independently assess. But simultaneously we must also realize that *often people cannot see patterns, precisely because those patterns are so central to their lives that they take the patterns for granted.*

Cliometrics can provide information about historical patterns that may not have been obvious (or even discernible) to people living when those patterns existed. If one accepts the positivist assumption that information can be accurately transformed into quantitative data, and if one accepts the reliability of the sources from which Tilly and Scott gleaned these data, then one can accept as "accurate" the patterns they present. But patterns are just that: *merely patterns.* Attributing *meaning* to patterns is quite another matter. Sometimes one can discern meanings—or make historical generalizations—only with the help of a knowledgeable informant, a historical figure who has been in a position to gather reliable information. Let me be more concrete.

Example 2: The Literary Activity
of Victorian Women

When starting the research that became *Edging Women Out: Victorian Novelists, Publishers, and Social Change* (Tuchman with Fortin, 1989), I had a simple hypothesis: When the British novel was a relatively unimportant genre, women wrote it; as, for a variety of reasons, the novel became more important, men redefined it as "high culture" and as an enterprise best undertaken by males. The methods appropriate to test this hypothesis included development of quantified data that could be analyzed statistically.[9] After reading literary histories to determine periodization, Nina Fortin and I found the hypothesized patterns concerning the acceptance or rejection of fiction and nonfiction manuscripts submitted to Macmillan and Company (London) from November 1866 through December 1917. But we needed reliable informants to attribute *meaning*. Our "informants" were nineteenth-century writers whom we needed to interview retrospectively.

We needed to learn whether "informants"—the "referees" who had served as editorial consultants and analyzed the merits of submissions—were reliable.[10] We had to know not merely what they had said about which manuscript (available through archives), but what they had published, how their own work had been received, and how their contemporaries had assessed their literary and editorial competence. We had to learn whether the reports written by Macmillan's editorial consultants used the same criteria and were penned in the same style as reports submitted to other publishing houses. We also had to know the historical context, including information about the production and distribution of Victorian books over time, economic factors influencing sales, shifts in the business cycle, and shifts in literary tastes among both the elite and what literary critics have called "the common reader." Such information enabled us to flesh out our description of three periods.

The following fleshed-out interpretation is still rather bare: Until roughly 1840, most British novelists were women. Then, as women novelists in England and on the Continent achieved both glory and, in some instances, considerable income, some men realized that writing novels might bring them fame and fortune. Nonetheless, through roughly 1880, women were more likely than men to submit fiction manuscripts to Macmillan. Women were also more likely than men to have their novels accepted—although Macmillan's editorial consultants often denigrated rejected women's fiction, whereas they identified the rejected novels of men as the work of youth.

From roughly 1880 through 1900, both male critics and their female compatriots who had accepted male standards as universal standards worked to define the realistic novel as the high-culture novel. At Macmillan and Company, fiction submissions grew significantly relative to submissions of nonfiction. Submissions by men account for this increase. They were at least as likely to be accepted as those of women. And Macmillan's editorial consultants identified rejected novels by women as "old-fashioned romances," noted that the talented women novelists of the 1840s had virtually disappeared, and continued to find masculine virtues in the rejected novels of men.

At the beginning of the twentieth century, the situation shifted once again. In part because of changes in the system used to distribute the novel, mainly the collapse of the hegemony previously enjoyed by Charles Mudie's Select (Circulating) Library, in part because of the new vogue for theater, in part because of the strictures the Great War placed on both women and men, fiction submissions to Macmillan decreased—both in raw numbers and relative to nonfiction. Nonetheless, men's hegemony over the esteemed novel had been institutionalized: although through 1917 women submitted more fiction than did men, novels by men were more likely to be accepted than were those proffered by women. At Macmillan, an elite Victorian publishing house—still celebrated as one of the seven major fiction houses of the Victorian era—men had edged women out.

But even though Macmillan's editorial consultants were lauded "English *Men* of Letters," questions remained. Were the rejected manuscripts any good? Were their authors serious writers or ninnies? We would have liked to use qualitative data: to read accepted and rejected manuscripts. Often it is more difficult to discern patterns in qualitative than in quantitative data, but qualitative data are richer: They are more likely to be meaningful(l)—more likely to let a researcher see *how* a social world seemed and felt to a variety of its members. They are more likely to reveal process. Some scientists believe that the key scientific question is *how,* not *why.* For instance, evolutionary biologists believe that *why* tends to devolve into a search for origins, whereas *how* enables comments about process. Unfortunately, we could not locate qualitative data and had to make do with such quantitative data as the reconstructed publishing careers of rejected male and female authors. These data enabled us to infer that men did not edge

238

women out of the occupation of novelist. They edged women out of being high-culture novelists.

Such statements provide only a preliminary grounding of observed patterns in historical reality. They cannot tell what it meant to be a male or female novelist in Victorian England: what it felt like, how women novelists were treated, how their works were read. I cannot provide here the historical context we used to place these issues in the context of a changing literature system. But one idea does bear repetition: Without a historical context, even quantitative patterns are meaningless.

Another idea is implicit in this summary of the process of doing this research. It bears formal introduction: *In historical research, as in all other kinds of research, the data to be used depend upon the question the researcher wishes to answer and the information the researcher can find to answer the question.* Let me return to the classics. Weber made it clear that he examined Benjamin Franklin's aphorisms because (a) he wanted to look at the *"ethos"* of capitalism as it appeared in daily life; (b) others had identified those aphorisms as "the supposed confession of faith of the Yankee," a creature who seemed to be the apotheosis of bourgeois capitalism; and (c) Western capitalism differs from the "greed of the Chinese Mandarin, the old Roman aristocrat, or the modern peasant" (p. 56)—all of whom cared about money. Weber's question about the origin of capitalism, including his desire to develop a multicausal argument, required him to establish the historical antecedents of conceptual artifacts—"ideal types"— across societies with different economies and cultures. He wished, among other things, to establish differences in kind. So, too, Marx and Engels had to demonstrate differences in kind—the feudal modes of production versus the capitalist mode of production; the feudal class system versus the capitalism class system; oppression versus exploitation—to posit "laws" or patterns of historical development.[11]

The problem, of course, is that to understand one's question one needs some background in the relevant historical period. Unfortunately, most American-educated researchers do *not* have historical knowledge at hand. American academic training has taken place in a national culture firmly dominated by "anti-intellectualism, pragmatism, materialism, [and] populism" (Lamont & Wuthnow, 1990, p. 302), so that the American social sciences tend to be "ahistorical, pragmatic, and scientistic" (see Wolff, 1981, on American studies of culture), as is also true of most American sociology. Furthermore, the American intellectual tradition tends to define power more narrowly than does its European counterparts (Lamont & Wuthnow, 1990, p. 298), who view power in a historical scope. For instance, British considerations of power relations (in media, including advertising) "can be read as refining Marx and Engels' dominant ideology thesis which centers on the role of ideology in cementing relations of domination by camouflaging exploitation and differences in class interest" (Lamont & Wuthnow, 1990, p. 298).

◆ History as the Story of Lived Experience

But how are Americans to gain the required historical sophistication? One answer is that social scientists need to grasp (a) that history is more than the passage of events whose sequence may be memorized and (b) that the past has continuing relevance for the present.[12] Most simply, we all live history, and not merely in the grand sense of wars, recessions, and political transformation. Rather, we live out the assumptions of our *époque* in the most mundane aspects of our daily lives. Sometimes we are conscious of how our activities articulate with our times: When the member of Parliament reported his horror of the experiences of mill girls, he was doing so for a reason—presumably to eradicate this evil. Why else could he have spoken as he did in this public forum? Sometimes, we are not conscious of how history pervades our activities. What Raymond Williams (1977) has called the "structure of feeling" of an era guides the minutiae of everyday life. But we often take for granted that structure of feeling.

Gravestones provide a good example of how history is a living story that speaks both the tension between past and present and an era's structure of feelings. When a family member tells a stone carver what to inscribe on the tombstone of a relative, the words chosen are meaningful.[13] They express groups norms about the information and sentiments appropriate for a tombstone, such as how to sum up a life and the attitude to be taken toward death.[14] A late eighteenth-century tombstone inside a church in lower Manhattan bears the following description of a man who died in his mid-20s: "He lived a useful life." Similar sentiments do not grace Victorian gravestones. These "remember" the deceased with "love." The contrast between the gravestones of the two periods bespeaks the very different attitudes toward life and death of people living a mere 100 years apart.[15]

A gravestone may also consciously deviate from norms; it may hide some "facts" about a person's life to highlight others. Sometimes one may infer group norms from just such deviations. An example from my own family reveals how past (European) family norms influenced a mid-twentieth-century (American) gravestone. This example illustrates another principle as well: the need for corroborative data in oral history as in all historical research.

In the 1920s, one of my European-born great-uncles married his European-born niece. Their marriage followed Eastern European, but not American, custom. It seemed shameful to their American-born children and nieces and nephews. At least, so I infer. Several pieces of evidence support my inference. Gravestones in my family's plot report individuals' English names and Hebrew names. Hebrew names take the form "first and middle name, daughter (or son) of first and middle name of father." Rather than declaring her "real Hebrew name" (Tova, daughter of Maier), this woman's gravestone declares in Yiddish "Tova, daughter of a good man." [16] When in 1986 I asked relatives then in their 70s the name of Tova's father, no one would say. I inferred the truth when my mother's first cousin became befuddled during a conversation and explained that my great-grandparents had given two of their daughters the identical name. I knew her explanation went against traditional naming practices and inferred Tova's parentage. When confronted, my mother confirmed my surmise and swore me to secrecy lest I hurt the feelings of other members of our family. Tova's own niece (then in her 60s) had never been told that Tova was her mother's sister. The intricacies of my own family are of little consequence, but the example illustrates how one may reason with information to learn how deviations from the norm highlight potential conflicts between past and present practices.

Not only do "documentary" history and oral history require corroborative data from several reliable informants (or sources), they also require both inductive and deductive methods. One of the first people I had asked about Tova's parentage was indeed the woman whose feelings my mother wanted to protect: Tova's sister's 60-year-old daughter. A good informant on our mutual relatives in their 50s and 60s, she was not reliable about older relatives.[17] Had I spoken only with her, I would not have solved the riddle of the gravestone, nor could I have solved the riddle without some knowledge of the naming practices of European Jews who immigrated to the United States at the turn of nineteenth century. This knowledge, part of the "stock of knowledge at hand" with which I grew up, helped to provide a point of view.

◆ Learning History

But how can a novice acquire a historical point of view, especially if she or he is dealing with unfamiliar materials? Let us suppose for the moment that a young researcher has a question that has a historical dimension, appreciates that history is more than a laundry list of names, events, and dates, but is not schooled in the relevant periods. That lack of formal knowledge may impede serious research precisely because historians bring their own points of view to their arguments about the past. Without some familiarity with the issues about which historians argue, one has difficulty reading their texts in a meaningful way. One needs knowledge of the main lines of dispute to grasp why they chose to present some data, but not others. Accordingly, the researcher's first task is to acquire the necessary background—not only to learn the dates, names, and key events, but also to master controversies among historians about whether, how, and why those dates, names, and events matter.

There are several ways to learn about a specific period or topic. The easiest is to take a good history course that covers the material (and arguments) one needs to know. As academic schedules often make additional course work impossible, there are other alternatives. One may ask friends, colleagues, and historians for help in locating an expert who can compile a reading list. Lacking access to an expert (or a required reading list), one can go to the reference section of a research library and construct a reading list from specialized bibliographies, handbooks, and dictionaries. A reference librarian can help to locate the relevant books; so can the favorite tool of many reference librarians—*The Guide to Reference Books* (Sheehy, 1986) and its supplements. One can check the utility of the reading list one has compiled by consulting the *Social Science Citation Index* to learn whether many researchers have used the items on a "homemade" reading list in their own work. The second alternative borders on self-instruction; the third alternative requires self-instruction.

Autodidacticism, even quasi-autodidacticism, takes longer: It may take a researcher six months to a year to figure out what questions the historians are asking, especially because historians' texts do not use the conventions associated with publication in the social sciences. Historians tend to write narrative, not theory. Generally, they do not begin their work with an introductory theoretical section (or chapter) and end it with a concluding section (or chapter). Judged by the authorial conventions of the social sciences, most books by historians "just end." As historians tend to weave their ideas into their stories, one must read carefully enough to know what the stories are about. Sometimes one must read very carefully indeed even to know with whom historians are taking issue and why. Without some guidance, one may simply miss the point.[18]

Another warning is in order. Supposedly, the social scientist has come to a historical question because of the nature of his or her own research problem. That question was probably inspired by questions in his or her own field, not by the issues historians debate. Possible exceptions include problems currently stimulating interdisciplinary research, such as issues in women's studies. But even when a question has been inspired by interdisciplinary reading, chances are that a historian would frame the question differently than would a member of another discipline. It is tempting, but dangerous, to confuse historians' disputes with one's own theoretical aim. Their disputes best serve as sensitizing devices: ways of interpreting their data, of approaching what went on in the past and of understanding how, in the past, different people in different life situations saw their world.

Let me return to a previous example, footnote 8 of Weber's *The Protestant Ethic and the Spirit of Capitalism*. Recall that it concerned the association between religion and education. Weber reproduced this table from a contemporary source, but the presentation is nonetheless incorrect. One row adds to 109%. Weber "percentaged" in the wrong direction: The table uses school as an independent variable to predict religion, not religion as an independent variable to predict type of schooling.

Weber made a common error. Such errors are good for a chuckle, but may be irrelevant to a theory. Weber's mistake does *not* invalidate his argument. The data in footnote 8 concern religion and schools in 1895. Weber's argument concerns the advent of modern capitalism during the Reformation. To be sure, Weber also presents arguments about the character of late nineteenth-century capitalism. But Weber never claimed that the Protestant ethic caused "ascetic rationalism" to become an "iron cage." Rather, he believed that "religious asceticism" had "escaped from the cage" of contemporary capitalism and that early twentieth-century capitalism "needs its support no longer" (pp. 181-183).

Just as squabbles about the correct presentation of quantitative data may be irrelevant to the nub of a theory, so too historians' disputes may be irrelevant to a social scientist. Again, an example: Suppose one wishes to learn about the meaning of television commercials in contemporary life. The problem clearly has a historical dimension: Advertisements predate television. Because cultural practices are recursive, we may wish to learn more about the first ads, but historians disagree about when the first ads appeared. Some trace advertising to the early Greeks. Others point to eighteenth-century English practices. One could travel the byways to decide which historian gives the "right" date, but the "right" date is irrelevant to the meaning of television ads in contemporary life. As Williams (1980) explains, it would be more fruitful to explore a historical issue germane to communication theory, namely, the changing articulation among ads, production and distribution systems, and consumption patterns. As always, the researcher must decide which aspects of these relationships are relevant to the problem.

◆ Historiography

One must also learn how to find data. Ideally, one would take a course in historiography (historical methods). Such courses come in at least two variations: philosophy of method (or narrative) and the hands-on approach (nuts and bolts). The appendix to this chapter presents information on the second approach; it stresses that even "nuts and bolts" raise interpretive issues.

Interpretive issues are at the core of today's debates about philosophy of method and narrative. Many contemporary historians extend the interpretive issues implicit in data collection to the construction of a historical narrative. But just as one cannot speak about sociological theory as though it were a unified endeavor, so too one cannot write of historians' views of their enterprise as though they share a common view. The most pertinent example is debate about the construction of narrative.

History as Text

Just as the debate about the utility of cliometrics tended to be associated with social history, so too many of the current debates in historiography arose with the advent of cultural history, a relatively new field practiced by the (momentarily) "newest young Turks." There are several ways to

244

interpret the term *cultural history*. It can refer to (a) the history of culture, narrated according to standard practice (i.e., the division of culture into periods or the influence of such changing technologies as the electronic media on cultural phenomena); (b) an exploration of the meanings of cultural practices (e.g., how the first books were rendered part of "oral cultures" and used by some Catholics in supposedly "Protestant ways"; Davis, 1975); (c) a historical explication of cultural texts to learn about social relationships (e.g., how a story about an incident in a printer's Paris shop reveals tensions between guild members and apprentices that, in turn, contravene assumptions about guilds as corporate actors; Darnton, 1984); or (d) an analysis of cultural myths and practices as "representations." [19]

The term *representation* invokes specific theories. It means much more than depiction, illustration, image, or portrayal. Rather, it serves as a referent to postmodernist theories, which see both written documents and mundane activities as "texts." Initially based in the ideas of linguist Ferdinand de Saussure, these theories argue that the assumptions of an era (an *époque*) are both inscribed and embedded in (documentary or lived) texts. Texts are to be analyzed as parts of webs or systems of signification that may be viewed as "a set of language systems." Because language systems are characteristic of an era (place, class, or situation), one can analyze any particular text in relationship to other texts; that is, as part of a *structure* of meaning. Indeed, the analyst's (researcher's) task is to elucidate that structure. Hence these theories are called "structuralist."

Poststructuralist notions of representation follow this idea to its logical conclusions. Mukerji and Schudson (1991) explain: "If no one is the author, perhaps everyone is the author. Probably the central tenet of post-structuralist analyses is that texts are multivocal. Texts are seen as having a variety of potential meanings, none of which is the real meaning to be derived by some superior reader" (p. 46). They continue:

> Poststructuralists have generally been more interested in the variability of readings than in the perfectibility of the reading process. They claim not only that different interpretations are a necessary part of reading because different readers approach texts with different assumptions about writing and reading, but also that texts themselves are . . . riddled with contradictions. All texts . . . , subtly or openly, intentionally or unconsciously, allude to or incorporate other texts, so they make themselves inevitably open to multiple readings. (pp. 46, 47)

This poststructuralist tenet about texts has several implications. One is that there is no "true," "objective" reading of history as text. The potential multiplicity of meanings do not mean that any one interpretation is incorrect; rather, any one reading of a historical datum may coexist with other readings that are also "true."

Historian's Account as Text

These theories also imply that the historian's account is an assembled text. It, too, is multivocal and bespeaks the context of its production. It, too, is an assemblage that bespeaks the historian's *époque* rather than the voice of the historian-author. How, then, should we read the accounts of historians? Again the answers vary.

Some historians are wed to the idea of the "grand narrative," the all-encompassing story that relates the march of humanity through civilization(s) or some corner of time and place. Indeed, through much of the twentieth century, historians have interpreted their task as the production of grand narratives, which include either implicit or de facto explanations of the relationships among phenomena across time and place. These historians view poststructuralisms and postmodernisms as anathema, for these new theories obviously subvert the very notion of *the* grand narrative (see Himmelfarb, 1987).

Historians who pledge allegiance to positivism also find postmodernisms antithetical to their basic methodological tenets. They use the word *speak* quite differently than do those influenced by linguistic structuralism. If the facts speak for themselves, the facts cannot be "multivocal." "Speaking facts" do not require the historian as interpreter: If and when facts seem to contradict one another, one should gather more facts to deduce "the truth." In this view, "facts" guide explanation (or what I have described as the interpretive enterprise). For these historians, basic historiographic rules about the reliability and validity of facts and sources (see the appendix to this chapter) themselves guide the acceptance of a phenomenon as a fact. Their text is not an assemblage.

Still other historians speak for eclecticism and refuse to adopt any one philosophy of history. Instead, they recognize the potential utility of many approaches and note, as does Joan Scott (1988, 1989), that a plurality of approaches can be useful, especially within specialty areas. This pluralistic view embraces "historical texts as montage." So-called women's history provides an apt series of examples. For instance, some historical work easily classified as women's history uses cliometrics. Other historians of women detest cliometrics and view it as a positivistic endeavor. (As used here, the word *positivism* is not a compliment.) Yet others would say that they are "merely" trying to make sense of a specific historical phenomenon from the point of view of women—to be "gynocentric." [20] Still other historians of women identify themselves as practitioners of "cultural studies," an interdisciplinary approach that draws on European Marxisms, postmodernisms, and a concern with how cultural phenomena influence social arrangements. Although no one of these approaches may document "the truth," together they present a revealing montage.

I have borrowed the word *montage* from art. It is also used in cinema. However, *montage* is not part of a historian's professional vocabulary. The word is useful precisely because it suggests that artistry is necessarily implicated in the historian's endeavor. But even the most accomplished art historian might blanch if asked to explain how he or she distinguishes a "good" montage from a "poor" one.

The problem of distinction affects the social sciences as well. For instance, social scientists, whose work involves the generation of "meaningful" accounts from qualitative data, find it difficult to agree upon how one should construct an ethnography. Is one's task to reproduce or to interpret?[21] Is the task of the ethnographer (or historian) to assemble data so skillfully that a sophisticated reader would learn "how to be" the resident of a small village in Taiwan or of an eighteenth-century New England hamlet? The monographs of some ethnographers and historians read *as though* their authors were trying to "reproduce"—to explain "how to." For others, "how to" does not suffice. Rorty explains:

> The anthropologist is not doing his job if he merely offers to teach us how to bicker with his favorite tribe, how to be initiated into their rituals, etc. What we want to be told is whether that tribe has anything interesting to tell us—interesting to *our* light, answering to *our* concerns, informative about what *we* know to exist. Any anthropologist who rejects this assignment on the grounds that filtering and paraphrase would distort and betray the integrity of the tribe's culture would no longer be an anthropologist, but a sort of cultist. He is, after all, working for *us*, not *them*.

The passage continues, "Similarly, the historian of X, where X is something we feel to be real and important, is working for those of us who share that knowledge, not for our unfortunate ancestors, who did not" (Rorty, quoted in Harlan, 1989a, p. 608; emphasis in Harlan; but see Hollinger, 1989; Rorty, Schneewind, & Skinner, 1984). But some historians would demur. They find a topic interesting precisely because it was important to our "unfortunate" ancestors, even though it may not seem germane to us.

Harlan's distinction is unfortunate. Whether an ethnographer or historian is working for *us* or *them,* that person still faces the task of assembling a credible story, of creating a montage that *speaks.* It may speak what the author wants to tell, or the author may identify his or her text as multivocal—a text that speaks itself. As previously indicated, how or what the historian's text speaks is yet another issue of historiographic debate. Harlan (1989a, 1989b) argues that historians should decry the new postmodernisms introduced to American scholarship by literary theorists. He talks of the implications of postmodernisms for history as the "return of literature" to historical discourse after a century's absence. He feels many historians "are afraid that if they once let themselves be distracted by theory they will spend their days wandering in a cognitive labyrinth from which they will find no way to depart. Literary criticism is clearly the worst of these labyrinths, especially its postmodern version" (Harlan, 1989a, p. 583). For others, those labyrinths may be important sensitizing devices, insisting— as they do—that both the historian and the qualitative social scientist are engaged in interpretive endeavors.

Ultimately, of course, these arguments about how to do historical research and how to write history are debates about the nature of history. Joan Scott (1989) has explained that the contemporary debate about historiography is an argument about both power *among* historians and power *in* history. She deserves the last substantive word:

> By "history," I mean not what happened, not what "truth" is "out there" to be discovered and transmitted, but what we *know* about the past, what the rules and conventions are that govern the production and acceptance of the knowledge we designate as history. My first premise is that history is not purely referential but is rather constructed by historians. Written history both reflects and creates relations of power. Its standards of inclusion and exclusion, measure of importance, and rules of evaluation are not objective criteria but politically produced conventions. What we know as history is, then, the result of past politics; today's contests are about how history will be constituted for the present.

Scott continues:

History is inherently political. There is no single standard by which we can identify "true" historical knowledge. . . . Rather, there are contests, more and less conflictual, more and less explicit, about the substance, uses, and meanings of the knowledge that we call history. . . . This process is about the establishment [and challenge] and protection [and contestation] of hegemonic definitions of history.

◆ Conclusion

At the start of this essay, I stated that early twentieth-century sociologists distinguished between history and sociology. The utility of Park and Burgess's 1921 contrast has virtually disappeared. What remains in both fields is recognition that research is an interpretive enterprise. The debates about interpretation abound. I have not attempted to find a theoretical pattern underlying how historians argue these issues. Rather, their disagreements are meaningful precisely because they raise the very epistemological issues that qualitative social scientists are confronting. They are familiar, if contested, terrain. The historical debates matter to social scientists because, reading "new" histories and experimenting with historical methods, we must be able to call on our training in theoretical literatures to interpret our encounters with the historians. To use some of the jargon that besets historians (as it besets social scientists), the crisis in historiography speaks the general crisis of meaning and knowing that afflicts our own episteme.

APPENDIX:
NUTS AND BOLTS

The hands-on approach to historiography asks, How does one find information and how does one assess it? The classic text is Barzun and Graff's *The Modern Researcher* (1957). This book is still useful as a guide to the sort of reasoning one would use to find data and to judge reliability, but many of its suggestions are simply out of date. Most research libraries have introduced electronic tools since the publication of *The Modern Researcher*. Some work once done by an assiduous search of reference books may now be done through "hard copy" (books), CD-ROM, or electronic rental of a database, such as *Historical Abstracts, American History and Life,* or *Sociological Abstracts.* Many research libraries have these databases on line.

Perhaps the distinction most pertinent to a novice is that between secondary and primary sources. Like all attempts to draw a line, the demarcation is more easily stated than accomplished. To wit, secondary sources are books and articles written by historians and social scientists about a topic. Primary sources are most often the historical data (documents or practices) of the period one is trying to explain. But the distinction is fuzzy. For instance, should one consider an acclaimed nineteenth-century article about eighteenth-century literature a primary or a secondary document? Does it make sense to say that an individual doing research about nineteenth-century culture should view the article as a primary source, but one doing research about the eighteenth century should view it as a secondary source? The discussion below assumes that secondary sources are books and articles written by historians, social scientists, or critics within the past 50 years.

Secondary Sources

Once one has read enough history to have some familiarity with a period, one may change the kind of material one is reading. What one reads next depends on one's research question. For instance, if one's question pertains to nineteenth-century women's magazines, four bodies of literature are relevant: those by (a) communications specialists, (b) literary critics, (c) historians, and (d) scholars in women's studies. If one already knows of a particularly good monograph relevant to the topic, one may check its references. For instance, on this topic one might check what such historians as Barbara Welter (1976) have written about the "cult of true womanhood," for part of her argument is based on nineteenth-century women's magazines. To learn more, one might check her sources or use the *Social Science Citation Index* and the *Arts and Humanities Citation Index* to see who has cited them and how.

There are also alternative procedures for locating examples of the relevant literatures. One might turn to "Homer," the most common computerized index to a library. Experimentation would reveal whether a library has holdings relevant to women's magazines. Here is the logic of such a computerized search. At the University of Connecticut's Homer Babidge Library (currently classifying its collection), 5,000 titles are now classified under "literature." The subclassification "literature-periodicals" includes item 1437, *The Literary Index to American Magazines, 1815-1865* (Wells, 1980). An additional search of the 793 items classified under "feminism" locates the subcategory "feminist periodicals, 1855-1984."

Following the computer's categories, one might then check for relevant material under "women's studies" (95 entries) or "women's periodicals" (22 entries). Indeed, these subcategories lead to *American Women's Magazines: An Annotated Historical Guide* (Humphreys, 1989).

Other searches might follow a slightly variant logic. If one wants to know about the regulation of the newspaper industry at the turn of the nineteenth century, one might start a search either by using Homer or by checking in such a useful source as *The International Encyclopedia of Communications* (Barnouw, 1989). If one's question pertains to the regulation of television or radio, books and articles by communications scholars, economists, and historians are probably relevant and can be located through Homer, the *International Encyclopedia of Communications,* or *Mass Media Bibliography: An Annotated Guide to Books and Journals for Research and Reference* (Blum & Wilhoit, 1990), and even the OCLC (On-line Computer Library Center), which has replaced the hard-copy *Union Catalogue* and lists which library owns which books.

Unfortunately, locating secondary sources does not end one's task. One must discover whether the scholarship meets acceptable standards. One way to check on sources is to see whether they are frequently cited. Reference books facilitate this task. For instance, one may look up an article or book in either the *Social Science Citation Index* or the *Arts and Humanities Citation Index.* In theory, the more an article or book is cited, the greater its contribution to the literature and so the greater its utility in your attempt to learn what you want to know. However, two caveats are in order. First, some books and articles may be cited because other authors believe they are wrong. One might find a frequently cited article only to discover subsequently (through further reading) that it is used as the classic example of, say, a common misinterpretation. Second, some articles or books that have made major contributions may not be cited very much, because they are in a very specialized area. Even the best work in an arcane area may receive few citations.

Whatever the route one chooses to locate relevant secondary sources and to check their utility, one must ask of these texts the same questions one asks of other texts: Why is this author making this argument? Do other scholars dispute this argument? Why these particular materials, but not others? Do the author's questions suggest other issues relevant to the project at hand?

Lacking a good answer, one can check book reviews in the scholarly journals of the time to see how the material under consideration was received. Let me take an immodest example, my own book *Making News* (Tuchman, 1978). To learn about its reception, one might use the *Social Science Citation Index* to locate reviews. Discovering that Todd Gitlin reviewed *Making News* in *Contemporary Sociology*, one would read the review and use a citation index to learn about Gitlin. A reference to Gitlin's *The Whole World Is Watching* (1980) might suggest checking his book to learn his perspective and to discover other useful references. Indeed, because one is trying to locate materials and assessments of materials, one must pay assiduous attention to footnotes. If necessary, one may use OCLC to locate a library that owns the material one needs and then borrow it through interlibrary loan.

Primary Sources

Finding and assessing primary historical data is an exercise in detective work. It involves logic, intuition, persistence, and common sense—the same logic, intuition, persistence, and common sense that one would use to locate contemporary data or information pertinent to one's daily life. For instance, if one needed a part for a refrigerator whose manufacturer had gone out of business, one would contact a specialist—an appliance service—to learn whether that firm has the part. If it does not, one might contact a series of appliance services. One will either find the part or learn that it is no longer available. Specialists know things that nonspecialists do not know.

Academic are specialists, too. For instance, virtually any researcher who studies news knows of the existence of the Vanderbilt University Television News Archives. (It has tapes of television nightly news broadcasts from August 1968 through the present and publishes an index and abstracts available through many university libraries.)[22] Similarly, the existence of such compendia as *Facts on File* and the *Index to the New York Times* is common knowledge. Most researchers also realize the utility of legal records, often available through the Freedom of Information Act. Because legal disputes and government hearings are arguments, they revolve around what different parties believe to be the implications of regulations and taken-for-granted norms.

Frequently, however, common knowledge does not cross academic specialties. During their graduate school education, twentieth-century historians learn how to use the Freedom of Information Act to obtain American documents.[23] Historians also accumulate information about the location of specific archives in much the same way sociologists accumulate information about the variables included in some standard quantitative data sets.[24] One may discover whether there is an archive to mine by asking an accomplished historian. Another way is to consult annotated lists of archives available in the libraries of research universities or other major libraries. One useful source is the *National Inventory of Documentary Sources in the United States* (NIDS) (Agee, Bertelsen, Holland, & Wivel, 1985). It includes information about federal documents and libraries. Another is the *Directory of Archives and Manuscript Repositories in the United States* (National Historical Publications and Records Commission, 1988). One can also use OCLC to locate other commercial bibliographies that might provide the names of useful collections. But again, simply locating an archive is not the end of one's task. Archives are often less convenient to use than are data sets. One may order a data set in a computer-mountable tape or even in CD-ROM and so use it through a PC. Frequently, one must go to an archive. There are exceptions; some archives are being issued in microfiche or on film, as one can discover through assiduous use of such appropriate reference books as NIDS, but many are not.

If one cannot afford to travel to the appropriate archive (or get a grant to do so), one can try to imagine what data appropriate to one's question would look like. If one is working in, say, the early twentieth century, one may check sociological journals to learn whether anyone has written articles related to the problem under study. If the author is still alive, he or she may have saved the data. If the person is dead, he or she, or his or her descendants, may have deposited the relevant data in the library of an institution where the author taught. For instance, the University of Chicago has a collection of Robert Park's work; the Pennsylvania State University houses the papers of L. L. Bernard.

Quantitative historical data contain all of the problems associated with contemporary quantitative data—and then some. Quantitative data are collected and coded with particular questions in mind. Additionally, ideologies of the era in which the data were collected are frequently embedded in the coding categories.

Official censuses serve as a useful example of how ideologies are captured in coding categories. Bose (1987) explains, "The international debate among census statisticians at the end of the 19th century . . . confirms that the methods of reporting female and child labor were subject to political ideology and social influences" (p. 101). Britain wanted to portray itself as a "community of workers and a strong nation." It classified unpaid domestic workers and the female relatives of farmers and small businessmen in their own separate category. Two Australian colonies demurred from this approach; each tried another method. One classified these women under their fathers' and husbands' occupations; the others did not assume that the women participated in the family enterprises. In 1890, the Australian colonies called a conference to resolve their conflict. Its participants agreed to classify the whole population into "breadwinners" and "dependents," for the Australians wanted to create an image of a country where women did not need to work.[25]

Qualitative data present problems too. Let us assume that women's letters and diaries are pertinent to one's research question and that one can locate pertinent examples. One cannot simply read them. As in the previous examples about gravestones, one must read enough examples to infer the norms for what could be written and how it could be expressed. For instance, in the early nineteenth century, some (primarily female) school-teachers instructed girls in journal writing and read their journals to do so. How would such instruction have influenced the journals kept by these girls as adults? Delving into the diary writer's psychology will not necessarily answer this question. Rather, it is useful to view the nineteenth-century journal writer as an informant. Just as one tries to understand how a contemporary informant speaks from a specific social location, so too one would want to establish the social location of a historical figure. One might ask of these and other diaries: What is characteristic of middle-class female diary writers? What is characteristic of this informant? How should one view what this informant writes? These same questions are germane to correspondence.

Archival data present other problems as well. Who saved them and why? Who sorted them and how? These inferential tasks have a contemporary analogy. Let me create its scenario: An academic department has a head clerk who has devised an idiosyncratic filing system. You have to find a form in order to receive your pay and the clerk is not available. If the form is not under "forms," maybe it's under "pay." Maybe it's under "salaries." Maybe it's under "incoming students." Maybe it's under "personnel." What categories might an idiosyncratic person have used to construct those files? Unless the files are random (unlikely, because then the clerk would not be able to find anything either), there are limited possibilities. One must discover them and check the possibilities in order of likelihood. The option selected depends on which alternatives looks as though it will yield the result most quickly. As in any other kind of research, one must decide how much time or money one is willing to expend to get what one needs.

If one cannot locate the data one needs, there are alternative ways to proceed. One can ask the archivist the most likely location. One can sample the archive by requesting documents in different categories to discover what each category means. By understanding the system used to identify main categories, one may narrow the search among subcategories. Again, locating documents is not the end of the process. A social scientist wants to infer patterns. That process resembles how one makes inferences from any qualitative data. Detecting a pattern requires being open to the material (just as one must be open to hearing what one's informants say in an interview) and having some imagination. Now, however, one must have both a social science and a historical imagination. By *historical imagination,* I mean some grasp of how a document would have been interpreted in its time.

Any researcher has at hand material that might help in the process of reconstructing meaning. Because the researcher started this project by reading the work of historians, he or she may have some sense of the period and some "feel" for the materials under investigation—a grasp of "structures of feeling" (Williams, 1977). But other materials help too. Let us consider again a very common historical document, a letter. One needs to understand it—not just what it says explicitly, but what it means. To understand meaning, one must understand the literary form.[26] Some eighteenth- and nineteenth-century letters have been included in memoirs (see Roberts, 1834); others have been collected in books (Johnson, 1925). Suppose the improbable: One cannot find examples of eighteenth-century letters. As usual, there is an alternative. If one is working in the eighteenth century, one can read an epistolary novel (such as Fanny Burney's *Evelina*) to infer letter-writing conventions. But one would want to realize the implications of using any alternative. Because Burney was writing a novel, she used her fictive letters to draw character. Does another late eighteenth-century novel use the same epistolary conventions?

Using different types of data, such as newspapers, one would ask slightly different questions, but they too would involve trying to grasp contemporary conventions.[27] The communication literature is replete with information about how news was gathered and processed. But if the research produced since 1940 does not help one to understand how newspapers work, one may check legal records, especially libel suits against the news media. Particularly in the past 15 years, libel suits have included information about the routines of news coverage. Indeed, it is possible that the court records and supporting documents of a significant libel suit, such as

Westmoreland v. CBS, may make television news coverage of the Vietnam War more open to some kinds of theoretical interpretation than a content analysis would.

If one could summarize these "nuts and bolts," the moral of this appendix would be: Ask questions of all data, primary and secondary sources. Do not assume that anything about data is "natural," inevitable, or even true. To be sure, a datum has a physical presence: One may touch the page, picture, tombstone, or microfiche one has located. But that physical truth may be radically different from the interpretive truth needed to assess the application or test a theory.

◆ Notes

1. These articles ask, How does *sociological history* differ from *historical sociology*? (These are but two of the terms invoked in the debate.) Some authors stress that sociologists use historical data to test sociological concepts and theories, whereas historians use sociological ideas to understand historical data (Bonnell, 1980). Others object that "the divergent practices of sociologically oriented historians and historically oriented sociologists have helped to reinforce the sense that the aims of historians are divergent from those of theory constructors" (Megill, 1989, p. 635). Meanwhile, theorists inspired by what I shall be discussing as "postmodernisms" seek to identify the different narrative practices used by historians and sociologists to clarify the ideal-typical distinctions of their endeavors (Hall, 1992). I believe such discussions are more useful to people who wish to draw boundaries between sociology and history than they are to people who have questions they wish to answer.

2. For a debate on these issues, see the June 1989 issue of the *American Historical Review.*

3. Later I will discuss a quantitative error in this table that the translator did not mention.

4. Some commentators also suggest that Weber adopted the interpretation of Marx dominant at the beginning of the twentieth century. That interpretation defined Marx as an economic determinist. Some late twentieth-century commentators reject this view of Marx. Others criticize Parsons's translation of *The Protestant Ethic and the Spirit of Capitalism.* They say that Parsons rendered some meanings so as to make Weber's ideas more compatible with Parsons's own theories.

5. The German term used to classify Weber's enterprise—*Geisteswissenschaft*—may be translated as either "the sociology of knowledge" or "the study of the humanities."

6. This sentence obviously implies that one can know "what actually happened." Some contemporary historiographers do not accept this assumption, but see historical texts as constructed accounts. Assessments of the reliability and validity of those accounts may themselves be determined by the systems of meanings fostered and accepted by our own historical era.

7. I am assuming that when one discusses quantitative patterns, one applies standard definitions of validity and reliability.

8. One obvious implication is that one may read novels as historical documents about social practices, as done by a group of literary critics and historians called the "New Historicists" (see, e.g., Greenblatt, 1988; Hunt, 1992).

9. I write as though this were a simple task. It took roughly seven people-years to gather, code, and transform the relevant data into computerized data sets.

10. Our consultants were reliable observers. One was a major Victorian critic whose works are still in print. We learned about them through literary histories, contemporary literary criticism, biographies, and obituaries.

11. The term *laws* implies a positivist orientation.

12. Historically constructed meanings become the raw materials for new cultural creation. However, long-standing cultural meanings also set limits on what groups can use to construct new collective activities and forms of identity (see Tuchman & Levine, 1993).

13. Note the cultural supposition that a family member selects the gravestone and decides what is to be written on it.

14. Indeed, Western groups assume that gravestones provide the opportunity for a commentary on life and death.

15. Ann Douglas uses gravestones to trace the development of Victorian attitudes toward the deaths of children.

16. None of the other gravestones uses Yiddish, although I suppose that language might have been used for such inscriptions when the family lived in Europe.

17. I first called Tova's niece because of another research priority, conservation of funds. I could reach her with a local phone call.

18. Narrative is also the virtue of historical writing. Historians sometimes tell deceptively simple stories. Much prose in the social sciences would be improved if the authors could construct narratives as elegant as those required of historians.

19. See, for example, the journal *Representations*.

20. Joan Kelly's (1977) article "Did Women Have a Renaissance?" is an apt example. She argues that what for men was a "rebirth" was for women a loss of the power to define the sort of knowledge they needed and to teach it one another.

21. I assume that all description involves interpretation.

22. A telephone call to the archives placed November 5, 1992, produced the unhappy information that this nonprofit source may close for lack of funds.

23. A telephone call to the general recording at the Library of Congress produced the telephone number for the National Reference Service. Its information expert kindly produced the names of two possible sources: *How to Use the Freedom of Information Act* (Sherick, 1978) and *The Citizen's Guide on How to Use the Freedom of Information Act and the Privacy Act in Requesting Government Documents* (U.S. House of Representatives, 1977). The latter is a periodical. The information expert also noted that almost all federal agencies maintain Freedom of Information Act offices and that one should check with an agency to see exactly what it requires before submitting a written request for information.

24. Historians also record their data differently than do social scientists. When using archives, they record bin, drawer, and call numbers, as well as date and publisher. There are good reasons to follow the historians' example. Suppose you need to double-check a datum, but you are in Texas and the datum is in New York. If you have recorded everything needed

to find the information, a friend of a friend can copy it for you. Also, if you eventually wish to publish your work with a house that favors the style of historical references, you will need to know bin and drawer numbers.

25. Bose (1987) also explains how ideology may be embedded in instruction to coders who must classify a woman as belonging to one or another paid occupation.

26. Letters to friends were a "female literary form" in the eighteenth and nineteenth centuries.

27. Even such sources as the *Congressional Record* have built-in biases (see Leonard, 1986). Representatives and senators may enter materials, including speeches, that they never introduced on the floor of the House or Senate.

◆ References

Agee, V., Bertelsen, J., Holland, R. J., & Wivel, C. (Comps.). (1985). *National inventory of documentary sources in the United States* (compiled for the National Historical Publications and Records Commission). Teaneck, NJ: Chadwyck-Healey.

Barnouw, E. (Ed.). (1989). *The international encyclopedia of communications.* New York: Oxford University Press.

Barzun, J., & Graff, H. (1957). *The modern researcher.* New York: Harcourt, Brace.

Blum, E., & Wilhoit, F. G. (1990). *Mass media bibliography: An annotated guide to books and journal for research and reference* (3rd ed.). Urbana: University of Illinois Press.

Bonnell, V. (1980). The use of theory, concepts and comparison in historical sociology. *Comparative Studies in Society and History, 22,* 156-173.

Bose, C. (1987). Devaluing women's work: The undercount of women's employment in 1900 and 1980. In C. Bose, R. Feldberg, & N. Sokoloff (Eds.), *Hidden aspects of women's work* (pp. 95-115). New York: Praeger.

Braudel, F. (1972). *The Mediterranean and the Mediterranean world in the age of Philip II.* New York: Harper & Row.

Coontz, S. (1992). *The way we never were: Families and the nostalgia trap.* New York: Basic Books.

Darnton, R. (1984). *The great cat massacre and other episodes in French cultural history.* New York: Basic Books.

Davis, N. Z. (1975). *Society and culture in early modern France.* Stanford, CA: Stanford University Press.

Giddens, A. (1984). *The constitution of society.* Berkeley: University of California Press.

Gitlin, T. (1980). *The whole world is watching: The role of the media in the making and unmaking of the New Left.* Berkeley: University of California Press.

Greenblatt, S. J. (1988). *Shakespearean negotiations: The circulation of social energy in Renaissance England.* Berkeley: University of California Press.

Hall, J. R. (1992). Where history and sociology meet: Forms of discourse and socio-historical inquiry. *Sociological Theory, 10,* 164-193.

Harlan, D. (1989a). Intellectual history and the return of literature. *American Historical Review, 94,* 581-609.

Harlan, D. (1989b). Reply to David Hollinger. *American Historical Review, 94,* 622-626.

Himmelfarb, G. (1987). *The new history and the old*. Cambridge, MA: Harvard University Press.

Hollinger, D. A. (1989). The return of the prodigal: The persistence of historical knowing. *American Historical Review, 94,* 610-621.

Humphreys, N. K. (1989). *American women's magazines: An annotated historical guide.* New York: Garland.

Hunt, L. (1992). *The family romance of the French Revolution*. Berkeley: University of California Press.

Johnson, R. B. (1925). *Letters of Hannah More*. London: John Lane.

Keller, E. F. (1985). *Reflections on gender and science*. New Haven, CT: Yale University Press.

Kelly, J. (1977). Did women have a Renaissance? In R. Bridenthal & C. Koontz (Eds.), *Becoming visible: Women in European history*. Boston: Houghton Mifflin.

Lamont, M., & Wuthnow, R. (1990). Betwixt and between: Recent cultural sociology in Europe and the United States. In G. Ritzer (Ed.), *Frontiers of social theory* (pp. 287-315). New York: Columbia University Press.

Leonard, T. C. (1986). *The power of the press: The birth of American political reporting.* New York: Oxford University Press.

Megill, A. (1989). Recounting the past: Description, explanation, and narrative in historiography. *American Historical Review, 94,* 627-653.

Mukerji, C., & Schudson, M. (1991). Introduction. In C. Mukerji & M. Schudson (Eds.), *Rethinking popular culture: Contemporary perspectives in cultural studies*. Berkeley: University of California Press.

National Historical Publications and Records Commission. (1988). *Directory of archives and manuscript repositories in the United States*. Phoenix: Oryx.

Park, R., & Burgess, E. (Eds.). (1921). *Introduction to the science of sociology*. Chicago: University of Chicago Press.

Roberts, W. (1834). *Memoirs of the life and correspondence of Mrs. Hannah More*. London: R. B. Seeley & W. Burnside.

Rorty, R., Schneewind, J. B., & Skinner, Q. (Eds.). (1984). *Philosophy in history*. New York: Cambridge University Press.

Scheuch, E. K. (1992). German sociology. In E. F. Borgatta & M. L. Borgatta (Eds.), *Encyclopedia of sociology* (Vol. 2, pp. 762-772). New York: Macmillan.

Scott, J. W. (1988). *Gender and the politics of history*. New York: Columbia University Press.

Scott, J. W. (1989). History in crisis? The others' side of the story. *American Historical Review, 94,* 680-692.

Sheehy, E. P., with the assistance of Keckeissen, R. G. (1986). *The guide to reference books* (10th ed.). Chicago: American Library Association.

Sherick, L. G. (1978). *How to use the Freedom of Information Act*. New York: Arco.

Tilly, L., & Scott, J. W. (1978). *Women, work and family*. New York: Holt, Rinehart & Winston.

Tuchman, G. (1978). *Making news: A study in the construction of reality*. New York: Free Press.

Tuchman, G., with Fortin, N. E. (1989). *Edging women out: Victorian novelists, publishers, and social change*. New Haven, CT: Yale University Press.

Tuchman, G., & Levine, H. G. (1993). New York Jews and Chinese food: The social construction of an ethnic pattern. *Journal of Contemporary Ethnography, 22*(3).

U.S. House of Representatives, Committee on Government Operations. (1977). *The citizen's guide on how to use the Freedom of Information Act and the Privacy Act in requesting government documents.* Washington, DC: House Committee Periodicals.

Weber, M. (1976). *The Protestant ethic and the spirit of capitalism* (T. Parsons, Trans.). New York: Charles Scribner. (Original work published 1904-1905)

Wells, D. A. (1980). *The literary index to American magazines, 1815-1865.* Metuchen, NJ: Scarecrow.

Welter, B. (1976). *Dimity convictions: The American woman in the nineteenth century.* Athens: Ohio University Press.

Williams, R. (1977). *Marxism and literature.* New York: Oxford University Press.

Williams, R. (1980). Advertising: The magic system. In R. Williams, *Problems in materialism and culture* (pp. 170-195). London: Verso.

Wolff, J. (1981). *The social production of art.* New York: St. Martin's.

10

Three Approaches
to Participative Inquiry

Peter Reason

◆ From one perspective, the orthodox scientific worldview is the product of the Enlightenment and represents a liberating step for human society in releasing itself from the bonds of superstition and Scholasticism. From another perspective, it is a movement to narrow our view of our world and to monopolize knowing in the hands of an elite few, and is fueled by patriarchy, alienation, and materialism; it is the product of a society committed to the domination of nature and of other peoples, of a society committed to a transcendental theology that sees man (*sic*) in the image of God and thus outside His creation (Baring & Cashford, 1991). So whereas on the one hand the scientific perspective has taught us the value of critical public testing of what is taken as knowledge, another consequence has been to place the researcher firmly outside and separate

AUTHOR'S NOTE: My colleague Judi Marshall has been a constant source of comment, encouragement, and challenge throughout the writing of this chapter. Our graduate research students' stimulating questions invited us to address the similarities and differences of different participative approaches. Dave Brown, John Clark, John Gaventa, Davydd Greenwood, Budd Hall, Marja Liisa Swantz, Rajesh Tandon, and Gary Woodhill all made helpful suggestions along the way. John Heron, Iain Mangham, David Sims, and Bill Torbert critically read early drafts. The official reviewers, Professors Giroux, Kuzel, and Whyte, provided helpful feedback on earlier drafts. Finally, Yvonna Lincoln and Norman Denzin were both supportive and challenging in their role as editors of the volume.

from the subject of his or her research, reaching for an objective knowledge and for one separate truth (Bateson, 1972b).

I believe and hope that there is an emerging worldview, more holistic, pluralist, and egalitarian, that is essentially participative. It is fueled by holistic and systemic thinking (Bateson, 1972b; Maturana & Varela, 1986; Skolimowski, 1992), feminism (Lichtenstein, 1988; Plant, 1989; Reinharz, 1992), liberationist education (Freire, 1970; Rogers, 1969), an extended epistemology (Habermas, 1972), new visions of spirituality and theology (Fox, 1991), deep ecology (Naess, 1989), and the metaphors of "new" physics, mathematics, and biology (Schwartz & Ogilvy, 1980). This worldview sees human beings as cocreating their reality through participation: through their experience, their imagination and intuition, their thinking and their action (Heron, 1992). As Skolimowski (1992) puts it, "We always partake of what we describe" (p. 20), so our "reality" is a product of the dance between our individual and collective mind and "what is there," the amorphous primordial givenness of the universe. This participative worldview is at the heart of inquiry methodologies that emphasize participation as a core strategy.

Let me be clear that my personal and professional commitment is to contribute to the emergence of this more participative worldview; that I write this chapter as an advocate of the methods presented rather than as an outside reviewer. I have devoted the past 15 years of my professional life to the development and application of co-operative inquiry in which the emphasis is on working with groups as co-researchers. As I look at the practice of action inquiry I am excited and awed by the challenge of developing the kind of self-reflexive critical awareness-in-action it demands. As I read about the work of practitioners of participatory action research, whose emphasis is on establishing liberating dialogue with impoverished and oppressed peoples, I understand the link between power and knowledge and realize the privileged position that I am in as a white male European academic. It seems to me to be urgent for the planet and for all its creatures that we discover ways of living in more collaborative relation with each other and with the wider ecology. I see these participative approaches to inquiry and the worldview they foster as part of this quest.

I have chosen three approaches to research as participation as the focus of my discussion: co-operative inquiry, participatory action research, and action inquiry. These three seem to me to be well articulated in both theory and practice and to stand together in quite radical contrast to orthodox

262

scientific method; at the same time, all start from quite different premises and emphasize different aspects of the participative inquiry process. I acknowledge that in making my choices I have left out other approaches: appreciative inquiry (Cooperrider & Srivastva 1987), "emerging varieties" of action research (Elden & Chisholm, 1993), applied anthropology (Stull & Schensul, 1987), critical ethnography (Quantz, 1992), research partnerships (Whitaker, Archer, & Greve, 1990), and others.

In this chapter I take each approach separately and set out what I see as its underlying assumptions and practice. I attempt to give a flavor of the language and perspective of each, to do justice to the three as separate traditions. Then, in later sections of the chapter, I explore some of the similarities and differences among the three approaches and make critical comparisons. I attempt to show how the three approaches complement each other, so that together they stand as the beginnings of a robust "paradigm" of research with people.

Before proceeding further, let me acknowledge the paradox of writing "about" research with people, for I cannot really do it alone. In its complete version, participation belongs to the people who participate, and thus to all those who have joined in this kind of research, who include disadvantaged people in Asia, Africa, and South America; factory workers in the United States and Scandinavia; medical and nursing practitioners in England; and aboriginal people in Australia. In some ways to write (and to read) "about" these people's experience in coming to understand their own worlds is to repossess it as an academic subject that can be studied from outside. These approaches to inquiry through participation need to be seen as living processes of coming to know rather than as formal academic method. And, as we shall see, one of the key questions about research is the political one: Who owns the knowledge, and thus who can define the reality?

One final word of caution: Although I attempt to provide the flavor of each of three approaches, I am not able to provide an exhaustive review of each, nor can I explore some of the subtleties of theory and practice. I have the feeling that those who are closely identified with any of these methods may find my presentation biased and inadequate, whereas some of those coming from more traditional research strategies may be put off by the language, which is often passionate and committed, and will want a more formal definition of each approach. So I have the strange feeling that I am not merely entering a lion's den, but that I am entering several lions' dens simultaneously. So be it.

◆ Co-Operative Inquiry

Co-operative inquiry has its roots in humanistic psychology, in the idea that persons can with help choose how they live their lives, free from the distress of early conditioning and restrictive social custom (e.g., Heron, 1977; Maslow, 1968; Rogers, 1961; Rowan, 1976), and that working together in a group with norms of open authentic communication will facilitate this (see, e.g., Randall & Southgate, 1980; Srivastva, Obert, & Neilson, 1977).

The proposal for co-operative experiential inquiry was first made by John Heron (1971; see also Heron, 1981a, 1981b, 1992; Reason, 1988, 1994; Reason & Heron, 1986). At the heart of his critique of orthodox inquiry is the idea that its methods are neither adequate nor appropriate for the study of *persons,* for persons are to some significant degree self-determining. Orthodox social science inquiry methods, as part of their rationale, exclude the human subjects from all the thinking and decision making that generates, designs, manages, and draws conclusions from the research. Such exclusion treats the subjects as less than self-determining persons, alienates them from the inquiry process and from the knowledge that is its outcome, and thus invalidates any claim the methods have to be a science of persons.

To say that persons are self-determining is to say that they are the authors of their own actions—to some degree actually, and to a greater degree potentially. In other words, their intentions and purposes, their intelligent choices, are causes of their behavior. One can do research on persons in the full and proper sense of the term only if one addresses them as self-determining, which means that what they do and what they experience as part of the research must be to some significant degree determined by them. So in co-operative inquiry all those involved in the research are both co-researchers, whose thinking and decision making contribute to generating ideas, designing and managing the project, and drawing conclusions from the experience, and *also* co-subjects, participating in the activity being researched.

Ideally, there is full reciprocity, so that each person's agency is fundamentally honored in both the exchange of ideas and the action. This does not necessarily mean that all those involved in the inquiry enterprise contribute in identical ways. An inquiry group, like any human group, has to struggle with the problems of inclusion, influence, and intimacy; people will take different roles, and there will be differences in both the quality and quantity of members' contributions. In particular, one or more members may have initiated the inquiry as part of their organizational role or more informally; these members or others may act as facilitators of the inquiry process. How the group manages these potential differences in power will affect the quality of its work. Thus, although ideally full consensus will be reached on all decisions, this is rarely practical; at a minimum, everyone involved needs to be initiated into the inquiry process and needs to give free and informed assent to all decisions about process and outcome. (For discussion of these pragmatic issues in establishing an inquiry group, see Reason, 1988, 1994.)

Heron (1981b) also suggests an extended epistemology that includes at least three kinds of knowledge: (a) *Experiential knowledge* is gained through direct encounter face-to-face with persons, places, or things; (b) *practical knowledge* concerns "how to" do something—it is knowledge demonstrated in a skill or competence; and (c) *propositional knowledge* is knowledge "about" something, and is expressed in statements and theories. In research on persons, the propositional knowledge stated in the research conclusions needs to be rooted in and derived from the experiential and practical knowledge of the subjects in the inquiry. If the propositions are generated exclusively by a researcher who is not involved in the experience being researched, and are imposed without consultation on the practical and experiential knowledge of the subjects, we have findings that directly reflect neither the experience of the researcher nor that of the subjects.

Recently, Heron (1992) has clarified the additional notion of *presentational knowledge* as the process by which we first order our tacit experiential knowledge into patterns, and that is expressed in images, dream, story, creative imagination. The development of presentational knowledge is an important (and often neglected) bridge between experiential knowledge and propositional knowledge.

Methodology

Co-operative inquiry can be described as taking place in four phases of action and reflection.

Phase 1. Co-researchers agree on an area for inquiry and identify some initial research propositions. They may choose to explore some aspect of their experience, agree to try out in practice some particular skills, or seek to change some aspect of their world. They also agree to some set of procedures by which they will observe and record their own and each other's experience. This phase involves primarily *propositional* knowing.

For example, health visitors in southwest England were invited by one of their colleagues to form an inquiry group to explore the sources of stress in their work. After much resistance to the idea that they could be "researchers," the members of the group decided to explore the stress that comes from the "hidden agendas" in their work—the suspicions they had about problems such as depression, child abuse, and drug taking in the families they visit that are unexpressed and unexplored (Traylen, 1989, 1994).

Phase 2. The group then applies these ideas and procedures in their everyday life and work: They initiate the agreed actions and observe and record the outcomes of their own and each other's behavior. At this stage they need to be particularly alert for the subtleties and nuances of experience, and to ways in which their original ideas do and do not accord with experience. This phase involves primarily *practical* knowing.

Thus the health visitors first explored among themselves their feelings about these "hidden agendas" and decided to experiment with confronting them. They practiced the skills they thought they would need through role play, and then agreed to try raising their concerns directly with their client families.

Phase 3. The co-researchers will in all probability become fully immersed in this activity and experience. They may be excited or bored, engaged or alienated; they may sometimes forget they are involved in an inquiry project; they may forget or otherwise fail to carry out and record the agreed-upon procedures; or they may stumble on unexpected and unpredicted experiences and develop creative new insights. This stage of full immersion is fundamental to the whole process: It is here that the co-researchers, fully engaged with their experience, may develop an openness to what is going on for them and their environment that allows them to bracket off their prior beliefs and preconceptions and so see their experience in a new way. This phase involves mainly *experiential* knowing.

The health visitors' experience of trying out these new behavior strategies was both terrifying and liberating in ways none of them had expected. On the one hand, they felt they were really doing their job; on the other hand, they were concerned about the depth of the problems they would

266

uncover and whether they had adequate skills to cope with them. The initiator in particular was anxious and had disturbing dreams.

Phase 4. After an appropriate period engaged in Phases 2 and 3, the co-researchers return to consider their original research propositions and hypotheses in the light of experience, modifying, reformulating, and rejecting them, adopting new hypotheses, and so on. They may also amend and develop their research procedures more fully to record their experience. Thus this phase involves a critical return to *propositional* knowing.

The health visitors met periodically to review and make sense of their experiences. One outcome of their work was changes they made in their own professional practice; another was the report they wrote in their own language about their experiences that was made available to their colleagues and managers; a third was the master's dissertation written by the initiator (Traylen, 1989).

Validity in Co-Operative Inquiry

Co-operative inquiry claims to be a valid approach to research with persons because it "rests on a collaborative encounter with experience" (Reason & Rowan, 1981). This is the touchstone of the approach in that any practical skills or theoretical propositions that arise from the inquiry can be said to derive from and be congruent with this experience. The validity of this encounter with experience in turn rests on the high-quality, critical, self-aware, discriminating, and informed judgments of the co-researchers, which may be called "critical subjectivity" (Reason & Rowan, 1981, chap. 10).

Critical subjectivity is a state of consciousness different from either the naive subjectivity of "primary process" awareness and the attempted objectivity of egoic "secondary process" awareness. Critical subjectivity means that we do not suppress our primary subjective experience, that we accept that our knowing is from a perspective; it also means that we are *aware of* that perspective and of its bias, and we *articulate* it in our communications. Critical subjectivity involves a self-reflexive attention to the ground on which one is standing and thus is very close to what Bateson (1972a) describes as Learning III. (The notion of critical subjectivity also appears close to Keller's [1985] notion of "dynamic objectivity.")

267

This notion of critical subjectivity means that there will be many versions of "reality" to which people may hold with a self-reflexive passion. It also means that the method is open to all the ways in which human beings fool themselves and each other in their perceptions of the world, through faulty epistemology, cultural bias, character defense, political partisanship, spiritual impoverishment, and so on. In particular, co-operative inquiry is threatened by unaware projection and consensus collusion.

Unaware projection means that we deceive ourselves. We do this because inquiring carefully and critically into those things we care about is an anxiety-provoking business that stirs up our psychological defenses. We then project our anxieties onto the world we are supposed to be studying (Devereaux, 1967), giving rise to a whole variety of self-deceptions in the course of the inquiry. *Consensus collusion* means that the co-researchers may band together as a group in defense of their anxieties, so that areas of their experience that challenge their worldview are ignored or not properly explored.

It is important to find ways to explore and counteract these defensive tendencies, as the health visitors challenged themselves to look at aspects of their work that caused profound anxiety. A comprehensive set of procedures has been developed that serve to engage with and explore (but not eliminate) these threats to validity. These include cycling and recycling between action and reflection so that issues are examined several times in different ways, exploring the authenticity of participation within the group, using self-development methods to look at the impact of unacknowledged anxiety, and establishing norms whereby group members can challenge unwarranted assumptions (Heron, 1988; Reason & Rowan, 1981; De Venney-Tiernan, Goldband, Rackham, & Reilly, 1994).

These validity procedures are useful for systematically reviewing the quality of inquiry work. Their application does not mean that the experiential, practical, or propositional knowing that comes out of the research is valid in any absolute sense of the term, but rather that it is possible to see more clearly and communicate to others the perspective from which that knowing is derived, and to illuminate the distortions that may have occurred.

◆ Participatory Action Research

Participatory action research (PAR) is probably the most widely practiced participative research approach; it is important because it emphasizes the political aspects of knowledge production. There are several different communities of PAR practitioners who represent their work in different ways; what follows is necessarily a generalized account in which I have drawn strongly on Fals-Borda and Rahman's recent book *Action and Knowledge* (1991), and to a lesser extent on other discussions of PAR: Fernandes and Tandon (1981); Hall, Gillette, and Tandon (1982); Tandon (1989); Cancian and Armstead (1992); Hall (1993). For a comprehensive bibliography, see Cancian and Armstead (1993).

Fals-Borda and Rahman (1991) place PAR firmly within the long tradition of liberationist movements: "Those who adopted PAR have tried to practice with a radical commitment that has gone beyond usual institutional boundaries, reminiscent of the challenging tradition of Chartists, utopians, and other social movements of the nineteenth century" (p. vii). Similarly, the brochure for PRIA (n.d.), the Society for Participatory Research in Asia, states, "Participatory Research implies an effort on the part of the people to understand the role of knowledge as a significant instrument of power and control."

Thus the primary task of PAR is the "enlightenment and awakening of common peoples" (Fals-Borda & Rahman, 1991, p. vi). Given this orientation, the PAR tradition starts with concerns for power and powerlessness, and aims to confront the way in which the established and power-holding elements of societies worldwide are favored because they hold a monopoly on the definition and employment of knowledge. Concerns for epistemology and methodology appear secondary to this primary concern.

A second important starting point is the lived experience of people, and the idea that through the actual experience of something we may "intuitively apprehend its essence; we feel, enjoy, and understand it as reality" (Fals-Borda & Rahman, 1991, p. 4). Thus in PAR the knowledge and experience of people—often oppressed groups—is directly honored and valued.

So the PAR strategy has a double objective. One aim is to produce knowledge and action directly useful to a group of people—through research, adult education, and sociopolitical action. The second aim is to empower people at a second and deeper level through the process of constructing and using their own knowledge: They "see through" the ways in which the establishment monopolizes the production and use of knowledge for the benefit of its members. This is the meaning of consciousness-raising or *conscientization,* a term popularized by Paulo Freire (1970) for a "process of self-awareness through collective self-inquiry and reflection" (Fals-Borda & Rahman, 1991, p. 16).

A third important starting point for PAR is authentic commitment. PAR values the processes of genuine collaboration, which it sees as "rooted in cultural traditions of the common people . . . which are resplendent with feelings and attitudes of an altruistic, cooperative and communal nature and which are genuinely democratic" (Fals-Borda & Rahman, 1991, p. 5). Those agents of change who initiate PAR processes among oppressed peoples must embrace a genuine commitment to work with these democratic values and to honor the wisdom of the people. A key notion here is dialogue, because it is through dialogue that the subject-object relationship of traditional science gives way to a subject-subject one, in which the academic knowledge of formally educated people works in a dialectical tension with the popular knowledge of the people to produce a more profound understanding of the situation.

Some practitioners (e.g., Hall, 1992) claim that the term *participatory action research* was originally used to describe this form of liberationist inquiry in the underprivileged parts of both the "Third World" and the developed West (Gaventa, 1991). Other practitioners have applied the term to their work in Western organizations (Cohen, Greenwood, & Harkavay, 1992; Greenwood, Whyte, & Harkavay, 1993; Whyte, 1991), borrowing, it is argued, the terminology of the "original" version. Many PAR practitioners object to this: It is offensive, first, because it is seen as a way in which the rich establishment is once again co-opting and colonizing the world of the underprivileged; second, because this approach is based on a liberal rather than a radical ideology and holds quite different assumptions about the relationship between popular knowledge and "scientific knowledge"; and third, because to use the same term for significantly different processes confuses the necessary debate between the variety of collaborative inquiry approaches (Brown, 1993; but see also Whyte, 1992).

Critique of Orthodox Research

Practitioners of PAR work mainly in communities that are vulnerable to colonization by the dominant culture. The primary critique of nonparticipatory research is that it serves this dominant culture through monopolizing the development and use of knowledge to the disadvantage of the communities in which the research takes place, and is thus exploitive.

Tandon (1982) offers four points in his critique of monopolistic research. The *absolutist* critique argues that pure knowledge generation cannot be the aim of social research because the assumption that there can be one pure truth in social research is erroneous. The *purist* critique attacks the social science crusade for objectivity: When strict separation is maintained between researcher and subject in the guise of maintaining rigor, all control of the research is retained in the hands of the researcher. The *rationalist* critique points out that the classical research paradigm has, in the interests of maintaining objectivity, overemphasized thinking as the means of knowing, neglecting feeling and acting. And the *elitist* critique points out that as the dominant research paradigm is available only to a body of professionals who enjoy elite status, the research they conduct is most likely to enhance the economic and ideological advantage of their class.

Tandon (1989) has developed this critique to argue that, in contrast, PAR values the people's knowledge, sharpens their capacity to conduct their own research in their own interests, helps them appropriate knowledge produced by the dominant knowledge industry for their own interests and purposes, allows problems to be explored from their perspective, and, maybe most important, liberates their minds for critical reflection, questioning, and the continuous pursuit of inquiry, thus contributing to the liberation of their minds and the development of freedom and democracy.

Methods in Participatory Action Research

In reading the literature on PAR it is easier to discover the ideology of the approach than a detailed description of what actually takes place. As Tandon (1989) points out, PAR is a *methodology* for an alternate system of knowledge production based on the people's role in setting the agendas, participating in the data gathering and analysis, and controlling the use of the outcomes. The PAR methodology may use diverse *methods,* both quantitative and qualitative, to further these ends, many of which will derive from vernacular (often oral) traditions of communication and dissemination of knowledge (Hall, 1993). The preferred way to communicate the practice of PAR seems to be through the description of actual cases. A criticism from outside is that many of these lack the kind of detail that would enable a reader to comprehend fully and learn about the approach taken.

Further, in keeping with the emphasis on PAR as inquiry as empowerment, the actual methodologies that in orthodox research would be called research design, data gathering, data analysis, and so on take second place to the emergent processes of collaboration and dialogue that empower, motivate, increase self-esteem, and develop community solidarity. As de Roux (1991) puts it, the methodologies employed must at

> the rational level . . . be capable of releasing the people's pent-up knowledge, and in doing so liberate their hitherto stifled thoughts and voices, stimulating creativity and developing their analytical and critical capabilities. . . . [And] at the emotional level, the process [must] be capable of releasing feelings, of tearing down the participants' internal walls in order to free up energy for action. (p. 44)

Community meetings and events of various kinds are an important part of PAR, serving to identify issues, to reclaim a sense of community and emphasize the potential for liberation, to make sense of information collected, to reflect on progress of the project, and to develop the ability of the community to continue the PAR and developmental process. These meetings engage in a variety of activities that are in keeping with the culture of the community and might look out of place in an orthodox research project. Thus storytelling, sociodrama, plays and skits, puppets, song, drawing and painting, and other engaging activities encourage a social validation of "objective" data that cannot be obtained through the orthodox processes of survey and fieldwork. It is important for an oppressed group, which may be part of a culture of silence based on centuries of oppression, to find ways to tell and thus reclaim their own story (Salazar, 1991).

The process of participation and dialogue often starts with an intervention that has a formal objective of adult literacy or development of health care. Thus in a tribal village in India funds were originally provided for an adult education project. Despite many difficulties, not least of which was dealing with the "culture of silence" of the village, the educators were able to develop these classes as "a forum for open discussion on the socioeconomic position of the village and a place for beginning action to change it" (Singh, 1981, p. 164). The outcome of this was not only improved economic conditions (the villagers decided to build a road to the village, where no proper link with the wider world had existed), but also an enhanced sense of community self-determination and a social structure in which future development decisions might be made.

PAR may also use methodology that looks more "orthodox": The systematic gathering of information, for example, through survey techniques, and then making sense of it from the perspective of the community is often an important source of people's knowledge and empowerment (de Roux, 1991; Gaventa & Horton, 1981; Rahman, 1991; Tandon & Brown, 1981).

◆ Action Science and Action Inquiry

In his early work on action inquiry, Torbert (1981b) argued that

> research and action, even though analytically distinguishable, are inextrica-
> bly intertwined in practice. . . . Knowledge is always gained in action and
> for action. . . . From this starting point, to question the validity of social
> science is to question, not how to develop a *reflective* science *about* action,
> but how to develop genuinely well-informed action—how to conduct an
> *action science.* (p. 145)

Action science and action inquiry are forms of inquiry into practice; they are concerned with the development of effective action that may contribute to the transformation of organizations and communities toward greater effectiveness and greater justice (Torbert, 1991a). Action science is a body of work developed over the past two decades primarily by Argyris and Schön (1974, 1978; Argyris, Putnam, & Smith, 1985; Schön, 1983). Starting in part from this work, Torbert has emphasized some contrasting issues in his development of action inquiry, particularly with regard to power and leadership.

Theories of Action

Central to the action science perspective is the identification of the theories that actors use to guide their behavior; the claim is that it is possible to identify such theories and in broad terms to predict their consequences. A key distinction here is between espoused theories, which are those an individual claims to follow, and theories-in-use that can be inferred from action; these two may be consistent or inconsistent, and the actor may or may not be aware of any inconsistency. Theories-in-use may be made explicit by reflection on action (Argyris et al., 1985, pp. 81-83).

One of the major difficulties of action science rests in the defensiveness of human beings, their ability to produce self-fulfilling and self-sealing systems of action and justification, often with patterns of escalating error

(Argyris et al., 1985, p. 61). These difficulties are compounded by the requirement to reflect not only on the action strategy being employed, but also on the "governing variables" (Argyris et al., 1985, p. 84), the assumptions that lie behind and inform the action strategy. Thus the critical distinction also made by Argyris and Schön (1974) between single-loop and double-loop learning, *double-loop learning* referring to the capacity of individuals to reflect on and amend not only their action strategies, but also the governing variables behind those strategies.

Argyris and his colleagues have identified two theories of action that illustrate these issues. Model I is a defensive theory that limits action science, commonplace in Western institutions; Model II is a normative theory that promotes a spirit of open inquiry.

The governing variables of Model I are (a) to achieve the purpose as the actor defines it; (b) to win, not to lose; (c) to suppress negative feelings; and (d) to emphasize rationality. This theory of action gives rise to defensive and controlling behavior that limits and cuts short possibilities for inquiry and learning. There is little public testing of ideas, and behavior is fixed in a self-sealing conventional pattern leading to decreased effectiveness.

In contrast to Model I, the "normative perspective that guides the action scientist" is found in Model II, the governing variables of which include (a) valid information, (b) free and informed choice, and (c) internal commitment. These are "the features of the alternative worlds that action science seeks to create" (Argyris et al., 1985, p. 98). These very different governing variables lead to behavioral strategies that actively seek information and increased participation from others, and thus lead to greater effectiveness.

Torbert's articulation of action inquiry builds on the work of Argyris and his colleagues, but also departs from it in significant ways. Action *science* focuses on the implicit cognitive models of practitioners and on their actual verbal actions. Action *inquiry,* although it addresses these, in addition addresses outcomes (measured empirically) and the quality of one's own attention (monitored by meditative exercises as one acts). Further, action inquiry addresses the question of how to transform organizations and communities into collaborative, self-reflective communities of inquiry.

Torbert argues that for an individual, community, or organization to practice action inquiry, that person, community, or organization requires valid knowledge of four "territories" of human experience: first, knowledge about the system's own *purposes*—an intuitive or spiritual knowledge of what goals are worthy of pursuit and what demands attention at any point in time (and thus also the knowledge of when another purpose becomes more important); second, knowledge about its *strategy,* an intellectual or cognitive knowledge of the theories underlying its choices; third, a knowledge of the *behavioral* choices open to it—essentially a practical knowledge, resting on an awareness of oneself and on interpersonal skill; and finally, knowledge of the *outside world,* in particular an empirical knowledge of the consequences of its behavior. Thus:

> The vision of action inquiry is an attention that spans and integrates the four territories of human experience. This attention is what sees, embraces, and corrects incongruities among mission, strategy, operations, and outcomes. It is the source of the "true sanity of natural awareness of the whole." (Torbert, 1991a, p. 219)

For Torbert (1991a), action inquiry is "a kind of scientific inquiry that is conducted in everyday life." Action inquiry differs from orthodox science in that it is concerned with "primary" data encountered "on-line" and "in the midst of perception and action" and only secondarily with recorded information. Action inquiry is "consciousness in the midst of action" (p. 221).

Now, as Torbert (1976) points out, "the discipline and rigor involved in this sort of research is formidable"; he suggests that a person must undergo what appears to be an unimaginable scale of self-development before becoming capable of relationally valid action (p. 167). In exploring this issue of personal development further, Torbert draws on the ancient tradition of search for an integrative quality of awareness and on modern theories of ego development, particularly the work of Loevinger (1976) and Kegan (1980) (see Table 10.1).

From these theories we can see that only toward the *later* stages of development is the person "aware that there are alternative frames, that perceptions, including one's own, are always framed by assumptions, and that such assumptions can be tested and transformed" (Torbert, 1989, p. 86). Thus it is not until the stage Torbert calls the *strategist* does behavior that can be characterized as collaborative inquiry appear: Earlier stages are characterized by what he calls "mystery-mastery" behavior, which is similar to Argyris's Model I. Collaborative inquiry involves the individual practitioner in continually reflecting on his or her own behavior-in-action while

275

TABLE 10.1 Governing Frames at Successive Developmental Stages

Stage	Torbert	Kegan	Loevinger	Governing Frame	Focus of Awareness
1	impulsive	impulsive	impulsive	impulse rules reflexes	
2	opportunist	imperial	opportunistic	needs, interests rule impulses	outside world, effects
3	diplomat	interpersonal	conformist	expectations rule interests	socially expected behavior
4	technician	(transition)	(transition)	internal craft logic rules expectations	internal logic, thought
5	achiever	institutional	conscientious	system success in environment rules craft logics	interplay of plan, practice, and effect
6	strategist	(transition)	autonomous	principle rules system	synthetic theory of system environment development over time
7	magician	(transition)	(transition)	process (interplay of principle/action) awareness rules principle	interplay of awareness, thought, action, and outside world in eternal now
8	ironist	interindividual	integrated	intersystem development awareness rules process	interplay of self and other systems in Kairatic history

SOURCE: Torbert (1989,, 1991a).

simultaneously behaving in a fashion that invites other members of the community to do the same (and is thus similar to Argyris's Model II).

For the organization or community, collaborative inquiry involves explicit shared reflection about the collective dream and mission, open rather than masked interpersonal relations, systematic evaluation and feedback of collective and individual performance, and direct facing and creative resolution of those paradoxes that otherwise become polarized conflicts (Torbert, 1987, p. 128).

In his later writing, Torbert (1991a, n.d.) emphasizes that transformational leadership and the exercise of transforming power are essential if organizational cultures characterized by mystery-mastery or Model I processes are to change into communities of inquiry characterized by collaborative inquiry or Model II. He suggests there are four types of social power:

unilateral power, diplomatic power, rational power, and transforming power. These are based on discussions of Hobbes, Rousseau, Kant, and Rawls, respectively. Organizations will not change through the exercise of unilateral leadership or through abdication of leadership. Rather, they require the power of balance, a subtle, ironic, at times diabolical, certainly paradoxical, exercise of all four types of power. Torbert uses Gandhi as one example of a transformational leader quite willing to act unilaterally and to break all codes of acceptable behavior when he viewed it to be in the service of his people.

But even when using power unilaterally, transforming leadership invites cooperation and mutuality from others. It is based on an effort to be aware of the present moment in all its fullness, recognizing that such an effort can never be completely successful. Transforming power is not just open to feedback, but is actively vulnerable in seeking challenge and contradiction, seeking out ways in which its exercise is blind and unaware. Transforming power is particularly sensitive to the timeliness of behavior, and to the analogical, metaphorical quality of action. And the intent of transforming power is to empower all those who come within its reach, including those who oppose its influence. Torbert's (1991a, n.d.) recent work provides many examples of the quest for the exercise of such transforming power.

The Practice of Action Science and Action Inquiry

The purpose of both practices is to engage with one's own action and with others in a self-reflective way, so that all become more aware of their behavior and of its underlying theories. Both practices base their work on the "raw" data of accounts and recordings of practice (usually in the form of "talk") gathered by the actors themselves, and both encourage public testing of one's own perceptions and the use of action experiments to test new theories of action and to develop new skills. One of the key skills in this process is to find ways of sidestepping one's own and others' defensive responses to the painful process of self-reflection.

Both Argyris and his colleagues and Torbert explore in detail the behavioral skills needed for this. Argyris, pointing to the extreme difficulties of discovering mistakes in action, suggests seven heuristic rules for the action scientist (Argyris et al., 1985, pp. 258-261). Similarly, Torbert identifies four dimensions of conversation—framing, advocacy, illustration,

277

and inquiry—that correspond to the four territories of experience—purpose, strategy, behavior, and the outside world. In *framing,* the speaker names assumptions that bound the conversation, the "name of the game," the purpose of speaking; in *advocacy,* a particular path of action is argued for explicitly; in *illustration,* the advocacy is grounded in a concrete example or colorful story; and in *inquiry,* the listeners are explicitly invited to respond.

Torbert argues that confusion and the misuse of power result when these four parts of speech are left tacit, and asserts that a person practicing action inquiry will, as well as developing a span of attention across the four territories of consciousness, cultivate a form of speech that explicitly includes these four aspects of conversation. The process of self-study in action is a way of cultivating this span of awareness and behavioral flexibility (Torbert, 1991a, 1991b; Torbert & Fisher, 1992).

◆ Co-Operative Inquiry, Participatory Action Research, and Action Inquiry: A Comparison

These three approaches to participative research start from different ideological perspectives, draw on different intellectual traditions, and emphasize different aspects of practice. Yet together they stand in marked contrast to orthodox social research. To date they have to a very large extent been self-contained traditions, with little constructive interchange of ideas and practice, so a comparison can be expected to show what they might learn from each other and ways in which they may be complementary in practice. (I have resisted the temptation to compare the three in a chart or diagram because I feel that this might lead the reader to see comparisons in a more robust way than intended.)

Ontology

The ontological position of all participative approaches to inquiry is well expressed by Paulo Freire (1982):

> The concrete reality for many social scientists is a list of particular facts that they would like to capture; for example, the presence or absence of water, problems concerning erosion in the area. For me, the concrete reality is something more than isolated facts. In my view, thinking dialectically, the

278

concrete reality consists not only of concrete facts and (physical) things, but also includes the ways in which the people involved with these facts perceive them. Thus in the last analysis, for me, the concrete reality is the connection between subjectivity and objectivity, never objectivity isolated from subjectivity. (p. 30)

This is close to a relativist ontology (Guba, 1990). In some important senses we choose our reality and our knowing of it—individually and collectively; therefore, valid human inquiry essentially requires full participation in the creation of personal and social knowings:

We have to learn to think dialectically, to view reality as a process, always emerging through a self-contradictory development, always becoming; knowing this reality is neither subjective nor objective, it is both wholly independent of me and wholly dependent on me. (Reason & Rowan, 1981, p. 241)

As methods of *action* inquiry, practitioners of all three would emphasize that these constructions of reality become manifest not just through the "mind," but through the *reflective action* of persons and communities. They draw on many sources: on Dewey's (1929) criticism of the traditional separation of knowledge and action, on MacMurray's (1957) argument for the primacy of action over reflection, on Habermas's (1972) articulation of a critical science serving emancipatory interests, on Maxwell's (1984) proposal for a philosophy of wisdom based on offering solutions to practical human concerns, on Skolimowski's (1992) argument that the process of living is a process of knowing. PAR would emphasize the collective aspect of this, pointing to ways in which the reality of oppressed people is colonized by an alien reality, whereas Torbert (1991a) would emphasize the intensely personal in his quest for living inquiry.

Knowledge arises in and for action. The interest, as Argyris and his colleagues point out, is not in developing an applied science, but in a genuine science of action. All three forms of inquiry emphasize the systematic testing of theory in live-action contexts.

The implication of this epistemology of action is that the primary outcome of all these forms of inquiry is a change in the lived experience of those involved in the inquiry. Participants are empowered to define their world in the service of what they see as worthwhile interests, and as a consequence they change their world in significant ways, through action—

building a road to their village, developing a new form of holistic medical practice—and through experience—developing a sense of empowerment and competence. The articulation of the new forms of knowledge in lectures, articles, and books is a secondary outcome.

Epistemology

The three approaches unite to emphasize the fundamental importance of experiential knowing. Thus for co-operative inquiry experience is the "touchstone" of the method, involving a "fundamental phenomenological discrimination of persons in relation to their world" (Heron, 1981a, p. 158; 1992); for PAR it is "through the actual experience of something that we intuitively apprehend its essence; we feel, enjoy and understand it as reality" (Fals-Borda & Rahman, 1991, p. 4); and the vision of action inquiry is of an interpenetrating consciousness of living inquiry (Torbert, 1991a, p. 258). Thus all three approaches hold strongly the vision that people can learn to be self-reflexive about their world and their action within it. The notions of praxis, critical subjectivity, double-loop learning, and interpenetrating consciousness are very close.

All three approaches articulate an extended epistemology: For the co-operative inquiry this involves an interplay of experiential, presentational, propositional, and practical knowledge; for PAR it involves the reclaiming of three broad ways of knowing—thinking, feeling, and acting (Tandon, 1989); and for action inquiry it is an attention that interpenetrates the territories of intuitive purposes, intellectual strategy, behavioral expression, and the outside world. All three perspectives embrace the idea that experiential knowing arises through participation with others.

With this emphasis on experiential knowing comes the need to explore the question of subjectivity. The co-operative inquiry perspective is that research is always personal, political, and spiritual; knowledge is always from a perspective and for a purpose. The co-operative inquiry method— the cycling and recycling through phases of action and reflection, and the application of validity procedures—is the discipline through which the co-inquirers are able to *critically see through* their subjectivity. They are able to articulate the perspective they are taking and begin to see through the distortions that arise through the bias of their personal and class position. Thus the process of inquiry must also always involve the personal development of the co-inquirers as they move from being relatively unreflexively subjective toward a position of critical subjectivity (Reason & Marshall, 1987; Reason & Rowan, 1981, chap. 10).

The PAR perspective provides us in addition with understanding of how ideology and epistemology, knowledge and power, are bound up together. If an inquiry is primarily engaged in service of a dominant class it will not need to dialogue with people: it is not interested in their reality, but rather in imposing on them a dominant reality. On the other hand, if an inquiry is engaged in the service of the development of people, it will necessarily engage with them in dialogue. This points us in the direction of the possibility of a "real popular science" (Fals-Borda, 1981, 1982).

I have been asked by the editors of this volume to comment on the relationship between the epistemology of participative approaches to inquiry and postmodern and poststructural perspectives. These, as I understand them, argue that we cannot sensibly speak of raw, lived experience because experience can be accessed only through the discourse or text through which it is expressed, and that there are multiple shifting discourses, all determined through the social context. Thus any attempt at an experiential knowing is impossible from the start because we can do no more than interpret our experience through existing categories of thought, all of which lie open to radical deconstruction.

I have two problems with this perspective. First, the argument for experiential knowing is that of a radical phenomenology: Our primal experience of the world, if we will only open ourselves to it, is present prior to culture (Heron, 1992). To be sure, our experience is deeply influenced by our discourse, but we can learn to bracket off that discourse and approach experience more directly. We can do this through mindfulness disciplines (meditation, T'ai Chi, Gurdjief work [Torbert, n.d.], Alexander Technique, and so on), through consciousness-raising, and through systematic engagement with the cycles of action and reflection that are a central part of participative and action inquiry methods.

My second problem is that the poststructural perspective, certainly in its extreme form, is overintellectualized and thus both nihilistic and oppressive. Voices are just voices; they have no claim to truth, so the search for voice is seen as being the search for any old voice. And given current power relations on the planet, the first voices likely to be "deconstructed" are those of people already oppressed, the voices of the poor, of women, but also the voices of the body and of the earth itself. Spretnak (1992) argues that the excesses of philosophical deconstructionism are as life denying as scientism, and points out that the erasure of the body is first and foremost the erasure of the female body.

Participative, action-oriented approaches to inquiry work to move beyond this overintellectualized approach and to ground knowing and action literally in the body of experience—"coming to our senses," as Berman (1989) puts it.

Data

It is interesting to note that the three approaches place different emphases on what is to be taken as "data," the recording of experience for the purpose of reflection. At the more conservative end, Argyris's version of action science relies almost entirely on formally recorded reports of conversations. Torbert's version of action inquiry includes as data a whole range of personal experience and idiosyncratic expression, and, although primarily verbal, reaches toward what he terms the "meditatively postverbal" (personal communication, 1992). Co-operative inquiry relies primarily on rational verbal reports of experience, but is branching out into imaginative storytelling (Reason & Hawkins, 1988) and metaphor (Cunningham, 1984).

Toward the other end of the spectrum, PAR wholeheartedly embraces a whole range of expressive forms, including song, dance, and theater, as well as more orthodox forms of data. This expressive activity in PAR not only enriches the inquiry, but provides a means through which ordinary people may experience and validate the data being used. If we take Heron's admonition to take expressive forms of knowing seriously and learn from the example of PAR, we may see much richer, more colorful, and more intense forms of inquiry in the future.

Attitudes Toward Leadership

In celebrating the common people's knowledge, and in emphasizing the role of participation and self-direction in development, the perspective of PAR is radically egalitarian. Rahman (1991, p. 20) argues that movements for social change are normally led by intellectuals who are in a position to provide leadership not because of any particular aptitude but because they are privileged by their economic and social status. He points to the many dangers of relying on an elite leadership for social transformation: the dangers of inflated egos; the fragility of commitment in the face of attractive temptations; the problems of the growth in size of the elite class as a movement grows and the danger of attracting new adherents holding altogether different commitments; and, finally, the self-perpetuating character of the institutions created to provide leadership. He argues that "democracy . . . is a necessity for revolutionary development" because it gives "freedom to take initiatives" (p. 22).

Yet, paradoxically, many PAR projects would not occur without the initiative of someone with time, skill, and commitment, someone who will almost inevitably be a member of a privileged and educated group. PAR appears to sit uneasily with this. Salazar (1991) points out how both participatory researchers and those with whom they aspire to work are in Colombian society part of a "long chain of transmission of authoritarian traits," and that outsiders are prone to "see what should be done" and maybe rush in without full participation. Thus "authoritarian attitudes (even unconsciously) may lead to actions which reproduce current domination patterns" (p. 56). On the other hand, Brown (1993) and his colleagues have established training programs for leaders of nongovernmental organizations doing innovative work in developing countries.

It is interesting to contrast this wary attitude toward leadership with Torbert's (1991a) argument that transformational leadership and the skilled exercise of the power of balance is *essential* for the development of social systems toward greater justice and effectiveness. Heron (1989) similarly argues for what he terms "distress-free charismatic authority" in group facilitation, which he sees as involving an ever-changing balance among three modes: hierarchy and the exercise of legitimate authority; the peer principle and the sharing of power with a group; and the autonomy principle, which respects the freedom of each person to exercise his or her own judgment.

Although we may accept that persons are fundamentally self-directing and celebrate the common people's altruism and ability to cooperate, we must also recognize that in Northern and Southern societies alike many of the groups who might benefit from participative inquiry are alienated from the processes of knowledge creation and may be part of a "culture of silence" (Singh, 1981; Whitmore, 1994). It is arguable that a practice that emphasizes participation demands an understanding of enlightened leadership. Thus co-operative inquiry is an emergent process that participants are first led through, amend and develop in the light of their experience, and finally embrace as their own. Action inquiry includes the construction of "liberating structures" (Torbert, 1991a, chap. 5) that paradoxically demand the exercise of freedom. PAR requires sustained authentic dialogue between intellectuals and the people they wish to serve.

In all this there is a tension between the ideal—and the rhetoric—of participation and the practical demands for effective leadership. This tension, this living paradox, we have to live with, to find creative resolution moment to moment.

These questions of leadership draw our attention to the process of training—both the training of initiating facilitators and "animators" and the training of participants. There is a whole range of skills required for participative research, skills that are very different from those of orthodox research, and that include personal skills of self-awareness and self-reflexiveness, facilitative skills in interpersonal and group settings, political skills, intellectual skills, and data management skills. For discussions on training for leadership in PAR, see de Oliveira (1982); D'Abreo (1981); PRIA (1982, 1987a, 1987b); Bobo, Kendall, and Max (1991); Highlander Center (1989); Brown (1993); and Fals-Borda (1988). For work addressing training for leadership in action sciences and action inquiry, see Argyris et al. (1985, chaps. 9-12), Schön (1983), Torbert (1981a, 1991a, 1991b), and Krim (1988); for co-operative inquiry, see especially Heron (1989).

A Mutual Critique of the Three Approaches

While accepting that the three methodologies are in some sense cousins in a family of participative research, it is useful to look from one to the others in a friendly and supportive critique. Thus co-operative inquiry appears from the perspective of PAR to overemphasize the psychological at the expense of the political, the microprocesses of small group behavior at the expense of the wider political processes that define reality. And from the perspective of action inquiry it can be seen as lacking a robust theory of action and of the exercise of power.

From the perspective of co-operative inquiry the writings on PAR appear to romanticize the goodness and democratic tendencies of the common people, and to ignore the ways in which all groups may be destructive and distort their experience. Reports on PAR projects often appear to be long on ideology and short on systematic practice. From the perspective of action inquiry, PAR, in emphasizing the importance of sharing power, fails

284

to consider seriously the ways in which leaders of democratic movements must develop personally and learn to exercise transforming power.

Finally, action inquiry may appear from the other two perspectives to be advocating an updated version of a Western and masculine "rugged individualism," to be elitist in its emphasis on the later stages of ego development, and to ignore the contribution of common people in both the small group and the wider collective.

A Possible Integration

What, then, are the major strengths of each approach and how might they be integrated? The PAR strategy of developing knowledge through empowering dialogue initially between an animator and a community of people appears to be most appropriate when the inquiry involves a relatively large number of people who are initially disempowered. PAR also draws our attention to the political issues concerning ownership of knowledge, and to the need to create communities of people who are capable of continuing the PAR process. We see this process at work in the underprivileged rural and urban settings in Southern countries, and as Gaventa (1991) points out, it is also appropriate in Northern countries, particularly as the gap between rich and poor grows wider.

Co-operative inquiry is a strategy more likely to be successful with a group of people who experience themselves as relatively empowered and who wish to explore and develop their practice together. Thus it is a form of inquiry appropriate for smaller groups of professionals—for example, doctors, teachers, or managers—who wish to explore and develop their practice systematically. It is also a process through which a group of disempowered people may join together to explore their world, although initially such a group may be more dependent on an initiating facilitator in the manner of PAR.

Action inquiry draws our attention to the particular individual skills required for valid inquiry with others. It confronts us with the need to cultivate a wide-ranging and subtle attention; it suggests that we can develop such an attention only as we move toward the later stages of ego development; and it offers methods for the detailed examination of our purposes, theories, and behavior, and the consequences of these for our world. Torbert suggests that, in a sense, action inquiry is a discipline relevant to those most deeply committed to participative approaches to

285

inquiry, persons who wish to play leadership roles in cultivating this process with others and who wish to inquire about their actual effects as they do so (personal communication, 1992).

One might say that PAR serves the community, co-operative inquiry the group, and action inquiry the individual practitioner. But this is clearly a gross oversimplification, because each of the triad is fully dependent on the others. It would seem that a PAR project would be strengthened if the animators met together as a co-operative inquiry group to reflect on their practice; a co-operative inquiry would be helped if the members cultivated the interpenetrating attention advocated by action inquiry.

Let me then speculate about how these three processes might come together in one project. Imagine a group of people concerned with changing some aspect of their world—it might be a group of PAR animators engaged in developmental work in rural villages, or a group of teachers exploring education as liberation in London or New York, or a group of health care professionals wishing to work in a more holistic and person-centered fashion. Members of such a group would meet together as a co-operative inquiry group, defining their common area of interest and moving through cycles of action and reflection, meeting regularly to review progress.

In their work with a wider group of people—the villagers, the students, the patients—they would engage in the developmental dialogue of PAR. They would work to gain entry and trust in a community, help that community define its needs, and engage in all the processes of PAR discussed above. This might mean that a particular project becomes the focus of this aspect of their work—a developmental process in a village, a self-help or healing group with patients.

At the same time, they would scrutinize their individual practices through action inquiry, keeping comprehensive records of their experiences and behaviors, reviewing these in detail, engaging in experiments in action, and so on. Of course, these PAR and action inquiry processes would also become the subjects for mutual reflection in the co-operative inquiry group, which would probably lead to creative new ways of engaging in the wider group involved in PAR, so the whole process would knit together as one whole.

In view of the complementarity of these three approaches to research with people, it is curious that so far they have developed in separate communities with little cross-fertilization of ideas. It is my hope that this chapter will provide a stimulus for some future dialogue.

◆ References

Argyris, C., Putnam, R., & Smith, M. C. (1985). *Action science: Concepts, methods, and skills for research and intervention.* San Francisco: Jossey-Bass.

Argyris, C., & Schön, D. (1974). *Theory in practice: Increasing professional effectiveness.* San Francisco: Jossey-Bass.

Argyris, C., & Schön, D. (1978). *Organizational learning.* Reading, MA: Addison-Wesley.

Baring, A., & Cashford, J. (1991). *The myth of the goddess: Evolution of an image.* London: Viking.

Bateson, G. (1972a). The logical categories of learning and communication. In G. Bateson, *Steps to an ecology of mind.* San Francisco: Chandler.

Bateson, G. (1972b). *Steps to an ecology of mind.* San Francisco: Chandler.

Berman, M. (1989). *Coming to our senses: Body and spirit in the hidden history of the West.* New York: Simon & Schuster.

Bobo, K., Kendall, J., & Max, S. (1991). *Organizing for social change.* New Market, TN: Highlander Center.

Brown, L. D. (1993). Participatory action research for social change: Collective reflections with Asian nongovernmental development organizations. In M. Elden & R. Chisholm (Eds.), Varieties of action research [Special issue]. *Human Relations, 46,* 249-273.

Cancian, F. M., & Armstead, C. (1992). Participatory research. In E. F. Borgatta & M. Borgatta (Eds.), *Encyclopedia of sociology* (Vol. 3). New York: Macmillan.

Cancian, F. M., & Armstead, C. (1993). Bibliography on participatory research. *Collaborative Inquiry, 9.*

Cohen, A. B., Greenwood, D. J., & Harkavay, I. (1992). Social research for social change: Varieties of participatory action research. *Collaborative Inquiry, 7,* 2-8.

Cooperrider, D. L., & Srivastva, S. (1987). Appreciative inquiry in organizational life. In W. Pasmore & R. Woodman (Eds.), *Research in organizational change and development* (Vol. 1, pp. 129-169). Greenwich, CT: JAI.

Cunningham, I. (1984). *Teaching styles in learner centred management development programmes.* Unpublished doctoral dissertation, Lancaster University.

D'Abreo, D. A. (1981). Training for participatory evaluation. In W. Fernandes & R. Tandon (Eds.), *Participatory research and evaluation: Experiments in research as a process of liberation.* New Delhi: Indian Social Institute.

de Oliveira, R. D. (1982). The militant observer: A sociological alternative. In B. Hall, A. Gillette, & R. Tandon (Eds.), *Creating knowledge: A monopoly? Participatory research in development.* New Delhi: Society for Participatory Research in Asia.

de Roux, G. I. (1991). Together against the computer. In O. Fals-Borda & M. A. Rahman (Eds.), *Action and knowledge: Breaking the monopoly with participatory action research.* New York: Intermediate Technology/Apex.

De Venney-Tiernan, M., Goldband, A., Rackham, L., & Reilly, N. (1994). Creating collaborative relationships in a co-operative inquiry group. In P. Reason (Ed.), *Participation in human inquiry* (pp. 120-137). London: Sage.

Devereaux, G. (1967). *From anxiety to method in the behavioural sciences.* The Hague: Mouton.

Dewey, J. (1929). *The quest for certainty.* New York: Minton, Balch.

Elden, M., & Chisholm, R. (Eds.). (1993). Varieties of action research [Special issue]. *Human Relations, 46*(2).

Fals-Borda, O. (1981). Science and the common people. *Journal of Social Studies, 11,* 1-21.

Fals-Borda, O. (1982). Participatory research and rural social change. *Journal of Rural Cooperation, 10,* 25-40.

Fals-Borda, O. (1988). *Knowledge and people's power: Lessons with peasants in Nicaragua, Mexico and Colombia.* New Delhi: Indian Social Institute.

Fals-Borda, O., & Rahman, M. A. (Eds.). (1991). *Action and knowledge: Breaking the monopoly with participatory action research.* New York: Intermediate Technology/Apex.

Fernandes, W., & Tandon, R. (Eds.). (1981). *Participatory research and evaluation: Experiments in research as a process of liberation.* New Delhi: Indian Social Institute.

Fox, M. (1991). *Creation spirituality: Liberating gifts for the peoples of the earth.* New York: HarperCollins.

Freire, P. (1970). *Pedagogy of the oppressed.* New York: Herder & Herder.

Freire, P. (1982). Creating alternative research methods: Learning to do it by doing it. In B. Hall, A. Gillette, & R. Tandon (Eds.), *Creating knowledge: A monopoly? Participatory research in development.* New Delhi: Society for Participatory Research in Asia.

Gaventa, J. (1991). Toward a knowledge democracy. In O. Fals-Borda & M. A. Rahman (Eds.), *Action and knowledge: Breaking the monopoly with participatory action research.* New York: Intermediate Technology/Apex.

Gaventa, J., & Horton, B. (1981). A citizen's research project in Appalachia. *Convergence, 14,* 30-40.

Greenwood, D. J., Whyte, W. F., & Harkavay I. (1993). Participatory action research as process and as goal. In M. Elden & R. Chisholm (Eds.), Varieties of action research. *Human Relations, 46,* 175-192.

Guba, E. G. (Ed.). (1990). *The paradigm dialog.* Newbury Park, CA: Sage.

Habermas, J. (1972). *Knowledge and human interests; Theory and practice; Communication and the evolution of society* (J. J. Shapiro, Trans.). London: Heinemann.

Hall, B., Gillette., A., & Tandon, R. (Eds.). (1982). *Creating knowledge: A monopoly? Participatory research in development.* New Delhi: Society for Participatory Research in Asia.

Hall, B. (1992, December). Letter to the editor. *Collaborative Inquiry, 8.*

Hall, B. (1993). Participatory research. In *International encyclopedia of education.* London: Pergamon.

Heron, J. (1971). *Experience and method: An inquiry into the concept of experiential research.* Surrey, UK: University of Surrey, Human Potential Research Project.

Heron, J. (1977). *Catharsis in human development.* Surrey, UK: University of Surrey, Human Potential Research Project.

Heron, J. (1981a). Experiential research methodology. In P. Reason & J. Rowan (Eds.), *Human inquiry: A sourcebook of new paradigm research.* Chichester, UK: John Wiley.

Heron, J. (1981b). Philosophical basis for a new paradigm. In P. Reason & J. Rowan (Eds.), *Human inquiry: A sourcebook of new paradigm research.* Chichester, UK: John Wiley.

Heron, J. (1988). Validity in co-operative inquiry. In P. Reason (Ed.), *Human inquiry in action.* London: Sage.

Heron, J. (1989). *The facilitator's handbook.* London: Kogan Page.

Heron, J. (1992). *Feeling and personhood: Psychology in another key.* London: Sage.

Highlander Center. (1989). *Highlander: An approach to education presented through a collection of writings.* New Market, TN: Author. (Available from Highlander Center, 159 Highlander Way, New Market, TN 37820, USA)

Kegan, R. (1980). *The evolving self.* Cambridge, MA: Harvard University Press.

Keller, E. F. (1985). *Reflections on gender and science.* New Haven, CT: Yale University Press.

Krim, R. (1988). Managing to learn: Action inquiry in city hall. In P. Reason (Ed.), *Human inquiry in action.* London: Sage.

Lichtenstein, B. M. (1988). Feminist epistemology: A thematic review. *Thesis Eleven, 21,* 140-151.

Loevinger, J. (1976). *Ego development.* San Francisco: Jossey-Bass.

MacMurray, J. (1957). *The self as agent.* London: Faber & Faber.

Maslow, A. (1968). *Toward a psychology of being.* New York: Van Nostrand.

Maturana, H., & Varela, F. (1986). *The tree of knowledge: A new look at the biological roots of human understanding.* Boston: New Science Library.

Maxwell, N. (1984). *From knowledge to wisdom: A revolution in the aims and methods of science.* Oxford: Basil Blackwell.

Naess, A. (1989). *Ecology, community and lifestyle.* Cambridge: Cambridge University Press.

Plant, J. (Ed.). (1989). *Healing the wounds: The promise of ecofeminism.* Philadelphia: New Society.

PRIA. (1982). *Participatory training for rural development.* New Delhi: Society for Participatory Research in Asia.

PRIA. (1987a). *Participatory training for adult educators.* New Delhi: Society for Participatory Research in Asia.

PRIA. (1987b). *Training of trainers: A manual for participatory training methodology in development.* New Delhi: Society for Participatory Research in Asia.

PRIA. (n.d.). [Brochure]. (Available from the Society for Participatory Research in Asia, 42 Tughlakabad Institutional Area, New Delhi-62, India)

Quantz, R. A. (1992). On critical ethnography (with some postmodern considerations). In M. D. LeCompte, W. L. Millroy, & J. Preissle (Eds.), *The handbook of qualitative research in education* (pp. 447-505). New York: Academic Press.

Rahman, M. A. (1991). Glimpses of the "other Africa." In O. Fals-Borda & M. A. Rahman (Eds.), *Action and knowledge: Breaking the monopoly with participatory action research.* New York: Intermediate Technology/Apex.

Randall, R., & Southgate, J. (1980). *Co-operative and community group dynamics . . . or your meetings needn't be so appalling.* London: Barefoot.

Reason, P. (Ed.). (1988). *Human inquiry in action.* London: Sage.

Reason, P. (Ed.). (1994). *Participation in human inquiry.* London: Sage.

Reason, P., & Hawkins, P. (1988). Inquiry through storytelling. In P. Reason (Ed.), *Human inquiry in action.* London: Sage.

Reason, P., & Heron, J. (1986). Research with people: The paradigm of co-operative experiential inquiry. *Person Centred Review, 1,* 456-475.

Reason, P., & Marshall, J. (1987). Research as personal process. In D. Boud & V. Griffin (Eds.), *Appreciating adults learning: From the learner's perspective*. London: Kogan Page.

Reason, P., & Rowan, J. (Eds.). (1981). *Human inquiry: A sourcebook of new paradigm research*. Chichester, UK: John Wiley.

Reinharz, S. (1992). *Feminist methods in social research*. New York: Oxford University Press.

Rogers, C. (1961). *On becoming a person*. London: Constable.

Rogers, C. (1969). *Freedom to learn*. New York: Charles Merrill

Rowan, J. (1976). *Ordinary ecstasy: Humanistic psychology in action*. London: Routledge & Kegan Paul.

Salazar, M. C. (1991). Young laborers in Bogota: Breaking authoritarian ramparts. In O. Fals-Borda & M. A. Rahman (Eds.), *Action and knowledge: Breaking the monopoly with participatory action research*. New York: Intermediate Technology/Apex.

Schön, D. A. (1983). *The reflective practitioner: How professionals think in action*. New York: Basic Books.

Schwartz, P., & Ogilvy, J. (1980). *The emergent paradigm: Changing patterns of thought and belief* (Analytical Report No. 7, Values and Lifestyles Program). Menlo Park, CA: SRI International.

Singh, M. (1981). Literacy to development: The growth of a tribal village. In W. Fernandes & R. Tandon (Eds.), *Participatory research and evaluation: Experiments in research as a process of liberation*. New Delhi: Indian Social Institute.

Skolimowski, H. (1992). *Living philosophy: Eco-philosophy as a tree of life*. London: Arkana.

Spretnak, C. (1992). *States of grace: The recovery of meaning in the postmodern age*. New York: Harper.

Srivastva, S., Obert, S. L., & Neilson, E. (1977). Organizational analysis through group processes: A theoretical perspective. In C. L. Cooper (Ed.), *Organizational development in the UK and USA*. London: Macmillan.

Stull, D. D., & Schensul, J. (1987). *Collaborative research and social change: Applied anthropology in action*. Boulder, CO: Westview.

Tandon, R. (1982). A critique of monopolistic research. In B. Hall, A. Gillette, & R. Tandon (Eds.), *Creating knowledge: A monopoly? Participatory research in development*. New Delhi: Society for Participatory Research in Asia.

Tandon, R. (1989). Participatory research and social transformation. *Convergence, 21*(2/3), 5-15.

Tandon, R., & Brown, L. D. (1981). Organization building for rural development: An experiment in India. *Journal of Applied Behavioural Science, 17,* 172-189.

Torbert, W. R. (1976). *Creating a community of inquiry: Conflict, collaboration, transformation*. New York: John Wiley.

Torbert, W. R. (1981a). Empirical, behavioural, theoretical and attentional skills necessary for collaborative inquiry. In P. Reason & J. Rowan (Eds.), *Human inquiry: A sourcebook of new paradigm research*. Chichester, UK: John Wiley.

Torbert, W. R. (1981b). Why educational research has been so uneducational: The case for a new model of social science based on collaborative inquiry. In P. Reason & J. Rowan

(Eds.), *Human inquiry: A sourcebook of new paradigm research.* Chichester, UK: John Wiley.

Torbert, W. R. (1987). *Managing the corporate dream: Restructuring for long-term success.* Homewood, IL: Dow Jones-Irwin.

Torbert, W. R. (1989). Leading organizational transformation. In W. Pasmore & R. Woodman (Eds.), *Research in organizational change and development* (Vol. 3, pp. 83-116). Greenwich, CT: JAI.

Torbert, W. R. (1991a). *The power of balance: Transforming self, society, and scientific inquiry.* Newbury Park, CA: Sage.

Torbert, W. R. (1991b). Teaching action inquiry. *Collaborative Inquiry, 5.*

Torbert, W. R. (n.d.). *Leadership and the spirit of inquiry.* Unpublished manuscript.

Torbert, W. R., & Fisher, D. (1992). Autobiographical awareness as a catalyst for managerial and organizational development. *Journal of Management Education and Development, 23*(3), 184-198.

Traylen, H. (1989). *Health visiting practice: An exploration into the nature of the health visitor's relationship with their clients.* Unpublished master's dissertation, University of Bath, School of Management.

Traylen, H. (1994). Confronting hidden agendas: Co-operative inquiry with health visitors. In P. Reason (Ed.), *Participation in human inquiry* (pp. 59-81). London: Sage.

Whitaker, D., Archer, L., & Greve, S. (1990). *Research, practice and service delivery: The contribution of research by practitioners.* London: Central Council for Education and Training in Social Work.

Whitmore, E. (1994). To tell the truth: Working with oppressive groups in participatory approaches to inquiry. In P. Reason (Ed.), *Participation in human inquiry* (pp. 82-98). London: Sage.

Whyte, W. F. (Ed.). (1991). *Participatory action research.* Newbury Park, CA: Sage.

Whyte, W. F. (1992). Note on concept clarification in research methodology. *Collaborative Inquiry, 8,* 5-6.

11

Clinical Research

William L. Miller & Benjamin F. Crabtree

◆ Conversing at the Wall

Melissa belongs to the clan of one-breasted women (T. T. Williams, 1991) and lives amidst a Yankee New England landscape of walls. Poor, frightened, and 32 years old, she knows the breast cancer is spreading. Her life, composed of memories, children, career, lovers, and anticipated hopes, appears shredded; she fears no one is listening. Her doctors hide their fears and lose their empathy behind liver enzyme tests and offers of experimental chemotherapy clinical trial protocols. They feel tired, overregulated, and inadequate in the face of death but conceal their emotions behind a wall of professional arrogance. Melissa is administered a survey, which measures social support, locus of control, and risk exposure, by epidemiologists who fear loss of funding to the richly endowed laboratory across the street. There, experimental work on gene transfer techniques continues even as the investigators grouse about the annoying scratches of soft data epidemiologists, politicians, and feminists. Both groups of researchers hide behind their walls of objectivity and measurement. Meanwhile, a local social scientist listens to Melissa's story, observes the landscape of separation and domination, and then retreats behind an academic wall of jargon and disciplinary tradition. Terrified, angry, and confused, Melissa suffers more losses behind her own private wall.

This is the clinical research space we have witnessed—many conversations behind walls, but increased suffering in the clinical world. In this chapter, we imagine a clinical research space where Melissa, her doctors, and the researchers meet and seek transformation. We imagine a conversation at the walls (Brueggemann, 1991)—at the place where the walls meet clinical reality. This volume celebrates the qualitative research community's conversation behind the wall—the internal discourse about who we are and what we do, and about the faith and hope for our own transformation that is engendered there. Clinical biomedical research is currently dominated by positivism and a patriarchal bias that has ignored the qualitative and critical conversation. Fortunately, calls have begun for a shift away from a strictly positivist position, opening the way for greater methodological diversity, including the use of qualitative research methods (e.g., Freymann, 1989; McWhinney, 1986, 1989; Waitzkin, 1991). Patients and clinicians have usually been left out of all research conversations.[1] This chapter is about translation—about conversation at the walls. At the walls separating clinician from patient, qualitative from quantitative, academy from practice, very different ways or cultures of knowing can meet and converse. The clinical questions are the common ground (Taylor, 1993). It is at the walls where, in a language understandable by the existing clinical world, a space for more expansive imagination is created, tools for listening and seeing are shared, and transforming stories are enacted.

The understanding of clinical research presented in this chapter arises from the nexus of applied anthropology and the practice of primary health care. Both authors have joint appointments in family medicine and anthropology; we are on both sides of several walls. Our social science roots were fed by the development of clinically applied anthropology (Chrisman, 1977; Chrisman & Maretzki, 1982; Fabrega, 1976, 1979; Foster, 1974; Foster & Anderson, 1978; Polgar, 1962) in the 1970s, nurtured by the later work of Kleinman (1988, 1992; Kleinman, Eisenberg, & Good, 1978), Good and Good (1981), Lock (1982, 1986), Pelto and Pelto (1990), and Young (1982a, 1982b), and currently challenged by the poststructuralist debate (Burawoy et al., 1991; Clifford & Marcus, 1986; Jackson, 1989). One of us (WLM) has a busy urban family practice, and both of us actively participate in the politics and discourse of academic biomedicine and academic social science. The biomedical influence, with its perceived therapeutic imperative, steers toward pragmatic interventions and the desire for explicitness in information gathering and decision making and highlights the appeal of positivism and technology. The actual practice of patient care reveals the uncertainty and particularity (McWhinney, 1989) of clinical praxis and turns one toward storytelling, relationship, and interpretation. Trying to publish storied knowledge in biomedical journals exposes the realities of power and domination. The juxtapositions of seeing patients and teaching anthropology graduate students, medical students, and family practice residents focus the need to integrate teaching, practice, and research and locates a common ground for conversation—the clinical experience and the questions that arise there.

The guiding premise of this chapter is that the questions emerging from clinical experience frame conversation and determine research design (Brewer & Hunter, 1989; Diers, 1979; Miller & Crabtree, 1992). Clinical researchers have at least six discernible research styles available: experimental, survey, documentary-historical, field (qualitative), philosophical, and action/participatory (Lather, 1991; see also Reason, Chapter 10, this volume). The clinical research space needs to be open to all of these possible sources and types of knowledge. Thus this chapter is structured around the following three goals: creating an open research space that celebrates qualitative and critical approaches to the clinical world; providing the tools necessary for discovering and confirming clinical stories and knowledge within this space; and identifying and describing the means for sharing the stories and knowledge. The emphasis is on the clinical text of Western biomedicine and the particular subtext of the patient-physician clinical encounter, because of our own location in that place, but the discussion is easily transferred to other clinical contexts, such as nursing care, education, and organizational management (see also Berg & Smith, 1988; Sapsford & Abbott, 1992; Schein, 1987).

◆ Creating a Space

The clinic is a public sanctuary for the voicing of trouble and dispensation of relief.2 Each clinic participant crafts meaning out of the "facts" and "feelings" inherent in each clinical encounter and seeks to weave a comforting cloth of support. Clinical participants rarely study themselves in their clinical context and thus fail to challenge their own situated knowledge(s) and empower their own transformation. This requires bringing qualitative methods to the clinical experience, an experience where people appear unhappy.

"My back! I can't go on this way!" exclaims Liz, 34, single, high school educated, Hispanic, and mother of two preschool children, when Dr. George Ford, a primary care physician, enters the clinical space. He immediately pursues diagnosing the "disease" producing her pain. Unable to identify pathology, he concludes it is "only a strain" and hurriedly recommends bed rest, moist heat, and analgesics. Liz, unable to stay bed bound in an apartment with a 1-year-old and a 3-year-old, experiences worsening pain. Over the next year, the pain remains and finally results in surgery, chronic pain, disability, and permanent loss of employment. Elizabeth Ramirez's self-concept as Hispanic, woman, parent, employee, and citizen is hopelessly bedridden. George, confused and unhappy, continues seeing his patients.

This is the real world of clinical practice, involving intentions, meanings, intersubjectivity, values, personal knowledge, and ethics. Yet, most published clinical research consists of observational epidemiology (Feinstein, 1985; Kelsey, Thompson, & Evans, 1986; Kleinbaum, Kupper, & Morgenstern, 1982; Sackett, 1991) and clinical trial designs (Meinert, 1986; Pocock, 1983). These studies involve separating the variables of interest from their local, everyday milieus, entering them into a controlled research environment, and then trying to fit the results back into the original context. For example, Dr. Ford is aware of randomized trials demonstrating clinical efficacy for short-term bed rest in patients with back pain (Deyo, Diehl, & Rosenthal, 1986; Wiesel, Cuckler, DeLuca, et al., 1980), but he encounters difficulty when applying this information to the particular back pain and disability experienced by Ms. Ramirez.

Qualitative researchers have seen and heard the story and suffering of Liz and George, but it has been retold in a language that patients and clinicians do not understand (e.g., Fisher, 1986; Fisher & Todd, 1983; Lazarus, 1988; Mishler, 1984; West, 1984; G. Williams, 1984). Neither clinicians nor patients know the language of "ethnomethodology," "hermeneutics," "phenomenology," "semiotics," or "interpretive interactionism." Most qualitative clinical research is published in a language and in places that benefit researchers and not the patients and practitioners. Qualitative researchers have asked that clinicians join, listen to, and speak the "voice of the lifeworld" (Mishler, 1984). We ask clinical qualitative researchers to do the same.

The dominant biomedical world and the small qualitative research community both tend to maintain methodological and academic rigidity. Bringing clinical researchers to their walls is not easy. The strategy we advocate for creating a space assumes that change is more experience based than rational and that clinical participants must actively try methods if they are to adopt them. Thus we emphasize clinical participants' answering their own questions, using methods appropriate for those questions.

The dominant biomedical paradigm is rooted in a patriarchal positivism; *control through rationality* is the overriding theme. Deborah Gordon (1988) identifies the following seven basic premises of the biomedical model:

1. scientific rationality
2. emphasis on individual autonomy, rather than on family or community
3. the body as a biochemical machine, with emphasis on physiochemical data and objective, numerical measurement
4. mind/body dualism
5. diseases as entities
6. emphasis on the "visual"
7. reductionism and the seeking of universals

The characteristics of the clinical medical world that follow from this model include the following:

1. male centeredness
2. physician centeredness
3. specialist orientation
4. emphasis on credentials
5. high value on memory
6. a process orientation, with emphasis on technology, ritual, and therapeutic activism
7. division of the clinical space into "front" (receptionists, billing clerks, and office managers) and "back" (doctors, nurses, and phlebotomists)
8. the definition, importance, and sanctity of "medical time"
9. emphasis on patient satisfaction
10. reverence for the privacy of the doctor-patient relationship (Helman, 1990; Pfifferling, 1981; Stein, 1990)

These are the assumptions, values, and beliefs that characterize the dominant voice of the medical clinic and that currently define the boundaries of clinical research.

We propose that clinical researchers investigate questions emerging from the clinical experience, pay attention to and reveal any underlying values and assumptions, and direct the results toward clinical participants. This refocuses the gaze of clinical research onto the clinical experience and redefines its boundaries as the answer to three questions: Whose question is it? Are hidden assumptions of the clinical world revealed? For whom are the research results intended (i.e., who is the stakeholder or audience)? Patients and providers are invited to explore their own and/or each other's questions and concerns with whatever methods are necessary. Clinical researchers share ownership of the research with clinical participants, thus undermining the patriarchal bias of the dominant paradigm and opening its assumptions to investigation. This is the situated knowledge, the "somewhere in particular" (Haraway, 1991, p. 196), where space is created to find a larger, more inclusive vision of clinical research.

What are some of the clinically grounded questions that can serve as windows for opening imagination at the walls? Clinicians and patients seeking *support* in the health care setting confront three fundamental questions of clinical praxis: What is going on with my *body*? What is happening with my *life*? Who has what *power*? Each of these questions has *physical/behavioral, cultural/historical, social/emotional,* and *spiritual* ramifications. For example, from the story of Dr. Ford and Ms. Ramirez, there are body questions about support. Are anti-inflammatory medications more effective than simple analgesics? How many patients perceive side effects from anti-inflammatory medications? What is the lived experience and meaning of back pain for patients and clinicians? There are questions concerning the support of one's life or biography. Do explanatory models of back pain relate to rehabilitation outcome? How does one's self-concept relate to back pain? What are patients' and clinicians' hopes, despairs, fears, and insecurities concerning back pain? How does past experience connect to the immediate experience of back pain? There are questions of power about how people are supported. What is happening when patients with back pain present to clinicians in different organizational contexts of care? What patterns exist in these different settings? Who influences whom? How is the patient or clinician's power undermined or enhanced? Many of these questions are adequately addressed only if qualitative methods enter into the clinical research space.

◆ Providing the Tools for Multimethod Clinical Research

Research Design

Design decisions begin with the question. A fundamental tenet of the proposed vision of clinical research is that *the question and clinical context are primary; methods must adjust to the clinical setting and the clinical question*. Clinical researchers should remain free to mix and match methods as driven by particular clinically based questions. Interpretive social science has traditionally feared mixed methods because this usually has meant treating qualitative as only a method subservient to the positivist paradigm or materialistic inquiry. We not only imagine a clinical research space where qualitative methods are empowered and constructivist and critical paradigms accepted, but note that it already exists (see the examples to follow).

If the question about one's body, one's life, or power concerns "how many," "how much," "how often," "what size," or numerically measurable associations among phenomena, then a survey research style using the designs and methods of observational epidemiology is appropriate. If the question asks "if _____, then _____," or "is _____ more effective than _____," then an experimental style is reasonable. Many questions about body, life, and power, however, concern experience, meaning, patterns, relationships, and values; these questions refer to knowledge as story. Who will support Liz and George? How are treatments embodied by Ms. Ramirez into her life story (see Johnson, 1987; Kirmayer, 1992; Martin, 1987)? How do insurance practices and workers' compensation laws constrain the possibilities of Liz and George's lived story? These questions weave the concerns of body, life, and power into a holistic narrative and call for the designs and methods of the qualitative clinical researcher.

In attempting to evaluate the physical/behavioral, conceptual/historical, social/emotional, and spiritual features relevant to a particular clinical question, multiple paradigms (see the chapters in Part II of this volume) and methods are necessary. In some studies, the aims of the research and the research question can be clearly addressed using a single research method. This *single method design* may be either qualitative or quantitative. For example, an important question for helping Dr. Ford and Ms. Ramirez get past their misunderstandings is, How do patients and physicians understand pain? As this question asks for qualitative description (What

298

meanings/practices occur in lived experience?), a field study using open-ended in-depth interviews is an appropriate approach. Such a clinical study was done and reported by a family physician/psychologist research team who observed and interviewed 28 family practice residents using a grounded interpretive investigation to facilitate understanding what happens when residents encounter dying patients (Dozor & Addison, 1992).

The research design often requires both qualitative and quantitative approaches (Stange & Zyzanski, 1989). There are at least four different formats in which qualitative and quantitative methods are integrated within a multimethod approach: concurrent design, nested design, sequential design, and combination design. Each of these is illustrated with examples from the story of Ms. Ramirez and Dr. Ford and from the clinical research literature. We have found these formats helpful in explaining qualitative research to traditional, more quantitatively oriented, clinical researchers.

Concurrent design. In some circumstances it is helpful if two independent studies are conducted concurrently on the same study population and the results then converged (e.g., Chesla, 1992; Fielding & Fielding, 1986). For example, clinical trials are enhanced if the researchers simultaneously conduct interpretive studies to help them understand the clinical trial process and to help explain why an intervention does or does not work. Dr. Ford might want to know, Is an anti-inflammatory medication more effective than a simple analgesic in hastening patients' return to work? This prescription-testing question suggests a randomized clinical trial. But Dr. Ford also wants to know about the context and process of the trial (What is going on here? How does it work?) so he can better understand how to apply the results to Ms. Ramirez's particular situation. A concurrent field study can address these additional concerns. As an illustration, Willms (1991) has reported on the qualitative portion of a "concurrent design" based on a clinical trial of a smoking intervention (Wilson, Taylor, Gilbert, et al., 1988).

Nested design. Qualitative and quantitative methods can also be directly integrated within a single research study. In order to avoid Type III error (i.e., solving the wrong problem), quantitative studies need to incorporate qualitative methods to help identify and operationalize key variables. Dr. Ford may puzzle, Do themes in patients' back pain narratives serve as prognostic indicators for predicting rehabilitation outcomes? The overall question seeks statistical explanation generation (Does variable x relate to other variables?), but the key variable, "themes in patient narratives," requires identification (What is important here?). Dr. Ford can answer both questions by simultaneously collecting and analyzing pain narratives to measure the key independent variables within the context of a prospective epidemiological study design, thus nesting field methods within a survey style. For example, Borkan, Quirk, and Sullivan (1991) used a "nested design" in which the injury narratives from elderly hip fracture patients became key measurements for an epidemiological study looking at hip fracture rehabilitation outcome.

Sequential design. For many research questions, it is useful for the results of one study to inform another. This is the context in which epidemiologists most easily grasp the significance of qualitative methods. They recognize the importance of using field methods for identifying and describing key variables before developing measurement instruments for hypothesis testing. The reverse can also be true. Dr. Ford theorizes there is a relationship between low self-esteem and the likelihood of back pain becoming chronic. Then he wonders, What is the experience of back pain in patients with reported feelings of low self-esteem? This theory-testing question requires that a survey method be used to identify a sampling frame of patients with back pain and low self-esteem for subsequent qualitative investigation. Snadden and Brown (1991) used such a "sequential design," in which a questionnaire measuring attitudes concerning asthma was used to identify respondents reporting high levels of stigma, who were then interviewed using interpretive research methods.

Combination design. Some questions seek to grasp the rich complexity of context and thus require some combination of the above design options. Ethnographers and evaluation researchers commonly use such case study design (Lincoln & Guba, 1985; Merriam, 1988; Patton, 1990; Pelto & Pelto, 1978; Yin, 1989). Dr. Ford overhears Dr. Anne Jefferson commenting on how much she enjoys caring for patients with back pain. Dr. Ford asks himself, How is the experience of clinicians and patients around the presentation of back pain shaped by the organizational context of care? In order to answer this question, he designs a comparative ethnographic study of his and Dr. Jefferson's practices. The study includes sequential design using field methods to identify patterns followed by survey techniques to confirm the findings, and the study uses a single-method design involving record review. Using a "combination design" within a heuristic framework, Miller (1992) included semistructured ethnoscience interviews, key informant interviews, and participant observation to understand how practicing family physicians manage their daily practices.

The clinical research space, created by focusing on the questions arising from the clinical experience, opens many possibilities for using the full range of qualitative methods. The challenge is to translate qualitative collection and analysis methods into clear, jargon-free language without sacrificing the methods' integrity rooted in the disciplinary conversations behind the wall. The next two subsections, on collection and analysis, present one translation for discussing qualitative methods at the wall of clinical research.

Collection Strategies

A full range of qualitative data collection approaches is presented in the chapters in Part IV of this volume. The research questions uncovered by Dr. Ford and Ms. Ramirez highlight the diversity of designs and methods required of the multimethod clinical researcher. To address questions about individual pain experience and the important themes in a person's pain stories, the investigators are best served by an open-ended, individual in-depth interview collection strategy. Data for addressing the question about the group of patients with low self-esteem and back pain, however, are more efficiently collected using focus group interviews. Participant observation, on the other hand, is preferred for exploring the process and behavior occurring during the clinical trial investigating the efficacy of anti-inflammatory medication.

Clinical researchers need a full inventory of qualitative collection methods so they can choose a culturally and developmentally appropriate communication tool for the topic of interest (Briggs, 1986). This often-overlooked guideline for choosing collection strategies is especially important in the clinical setting, where it can help avoid doing harm to research participants. For example, if Ms. Ramirez prefers sharing her personal experience of battering and back pain as a third-person, "this friend I know" story in small, informal groups, then becoming a participant in those groups is more sensitive and appropriate than using probing individual in-depth interviews. The latter can have profound effects on participants by exposing intense pain and shame without the social and cultural resources readily available for support. This concern is all the more imperative given that institutional review boards at most medical institutions do not see qualitative designs as "real" research and thus almost automatically give them expedited approval.

Qualitative clinical researchers must carefully consider sampling strategies before beginning data collection. Traditional clinical investigators assume this means some type of randomization protocol. The notion of small size, purposeful, or information-rich sampling strikes them as anecdotal and not trustworthy. How can one make any generalizations? they ask. The conversation is continued by distinguishing among clinicians' different ways of knowing and by staying focused on the question. Clinicians readily admit to using clinical experience, the notion of "typicality," and intuition along with probability-based studies in their clinical work. Which of these ways of knowing they use predominantly depends on the question and the quality and richness of their knowledge. Information-rich sampling options are more easily grasped when explained in this context. Kuzel (1992) and Patton (1990) have written excellent summaries of the many sampling strategies available to help qualitative clinical researchers decide what, how, and how many.

Analysis Strategies

Qualitative analysis is much more complex and potentially confusing than data collection and has not been well translated for clinical audiences. Fortunately, Renata Tesch (1990) has recently presented one of the first systematic and explicit overviews of qualitative analysis with a focus on computer applications. She identifies the following three core steps common to nearly all qualitative analysis methods: developing an organizing system, segmenting the data, and making connections. In earlier work, we have identified "four idealized analytic styles" based on these core steps: immersion/crystallization, editing, template, and quasi-statistical (see Figure 11.1) (Miller & Crabtree, 1992). Lumping the many diverse qualitative analysis traditions into these four categories simplifies the language without losing the core meaning; qualitative analysis is made more accessible to biomedical clinicians and patients.

In immersion/crystallization, the three core steps are collapsed into an extended period of intuition-rich immersion within the text (Moustakas, 1990; Stein, 1990). It is the interpreter, as an editor, who serves as the organizing system in the editing style (Addison, 1992; Crabtree & Miller, 1992a; McCracken, 1988; Strauss & Corbin, 1990; Willms, Best, Taylor,

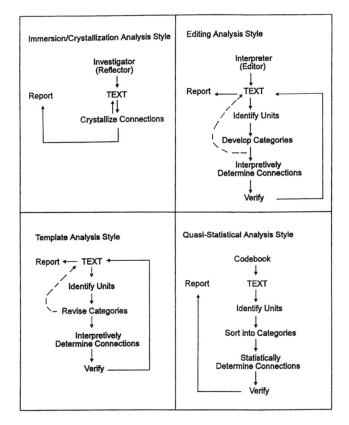

Figure 11.1. Diagrammatic Representation of Different Analysis Styles
SOURCE: Crabtree and Miller (1992b).

et al., 1990), whereas an open-ended template or codebook is the organizing system for template analysis (Crabtree & Miller, 1992b; Miles & Huberman, 1984; Spradley, 1979, 1980). A more detailed codebook is used in quasi-statistical analysis (Weber, 1985). Each style represents a different relationship between the analyst and the text.

How does one pick which analysis style to use for a particular research topic? Figure 11.2 presents an analysis space that includes a horizontal continuum of the four analysis styles representing the distance the analyst is from the actual text. This continuum reflects the structural rigidity of the organizing system. The vertical continuum represents the use of a specific analysis filter through which the text material is perceived. Some

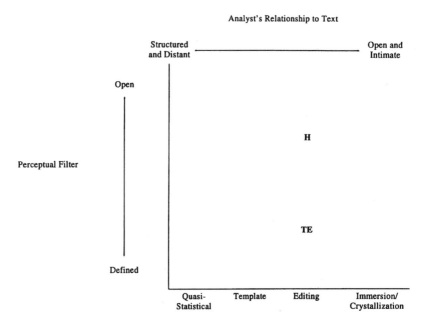

Figure 11.2. The Analytic Space: Diagrammatic Representation of Two Continua for Creating a Qualitative Analysis Strategy

of these filters are very specific and explicitly limit what can be perceived in the text given the particular style used, whereas other filters are very porous and leave the analyst open to much more of the text-as-it-is. For example, traditional ethnography (TE), which uses the outline of cultural materials (Murdock, Ford, Hudson, et al., 1950) as its perceptual filter and thus has a carefully defined screen, is low in the space but within the editing style (see Crabtree & Miller, 1991, 1992a), which is on the more open spectrum of distance from text. Hermeneutics (H), through the process of bracketing, seeks to open the analyst to maximum experience within an editing-style relationship, and thus uses a more open perceptual filter (Addison, 1992; Allen & Jenson, 1990).

The analysis space, similar to the understanding of naturalistic inquiry presented by Willems and Rausch (1969), is used to design the analysis approach. First, the researcher must examine the question and aims of the research. If the goal is exploration, discovery, or seeking to understand the experience of others, the analyst must use an analytic method that keeps him or her more open and intimate with the text. If the goal is theory testing, however, an approach involving more structure and distance from the text is desirable. A second consideration is the amount of knowledge already in hand about the subject or question of interest. If there is much existing literature, especially qualitative literature, then more structure and distance is beneficial. If theory is very explicit and well established in the area of inquiry, then using an approach with a more defined filter is helpful. A third consideration is design coherence with the data collection technique. For example, observational data, already filtered by a note taker, might be analyzed better using methods with a more defined perceptual filter, whereas analysis methods with a less defined filter are preferable with in-depth interview data.

Finally, the operating paradigm affects the researcher's approach to analysis. Materialistic inquiry calls for a more structured relationship with the text and a more clearly defined perceptual filter, because control, prediction, and consistency are valued. Constructivist inquiry, on the other hand, is iterative, and the analysis approach often changes through the collection/analysis cycles and needs to remain open to emergent experience and design.

The analytic approach chosen is usually a compromise among the factors noted above. One of the research examples from the story of Dr. Ford and Ms. Ramirez helps illustrate this choice process. Dr. Ford used a survey to identify patients with low self-esteem and back pain and then conducted focus group interviews with these patients, seeking to answer the question, What is the experience of back pain in patients reporting feelings of low self-esteem? As the question explores what is happening in patients' narrative lives, the operating paradigm is constructivist inquiry. Collection and analysis are done iteratively. The goal of exploration, the absence of significant literature about the question, and the use of interviews argue for a style that is unstructured, fosters intimate contact with the text, and minimizes perceptual filtering in the initial analysis of the first focus group transcripts and field notes. An immersion/crystallization style or a very open editing style (such as hermeneutics) with no explicit perceptual screen is thus appropriate. The analysis of subsequent focus group transcripts may shift to a more explicit editing or template style depending on the specifics of the emerging understanding. When the analysis nears completion, the research process shifts to decisions about telling the story.

◆ Telling the Stories

Where to Tell the Stories

Qualitative clinical research is now being discussed and tried within primary care internal medicine and family medicine because specific efforts were made to translate and introduce qualitative research in workshops within professional meetings, through newsletters, and through methods publications emphasizing clinical usefulness.[3] Developing networks with leaders in primary care research was prioritized. This was facilitated by qualitative researchers demonstrating skill in dominant paradigm methods (e.g., Crabtree, Gelfand, Miller, et al., 1992), and by a multimethod or mixed-method emphasis arguing for the additive and not exclusionary value of qualitative approaches to questions (e.g., Miller, Crabtree, & Yanoshik, 1991).

Qualitative clinical research is now appearing in clinical journals, especially in the field of primary care. *Qualitative Health Research* and *Culture, Medicine, and Psychiatry* are bridge-building publications with an almost exclusive emphasis on qualitative clinical research. All of the primary care journals now have reviewers trained in qualitative research, and all have published examples of qualitative studies. *Family Medicine* focuses on methodology and education-related studies. The *Archives of Family Practice, Family Practice, Journal of the American Board of Family Practice, Journal of Family Practice, Journal of General Internal Medicine,* and *Nurse Practitioner* all emphasize research of direct clinical relevance. The *Family Practice Research Journal* is specifically targeted for the novice researcher. The next step is to establish means of communicating results with the patient population.

How to Tell the Stories

There are some specific writing strategies that will facilitate communication of and receptivity to qualitative clinical research (Richardson, 1990; Wolcott, 1990). The most important is avoiding jargon and keeping language simple and concrete. The use of typologies and continua as rhetorical frames is helpful because these initially appear rational and measurable, qualities valued by traditional clinical researchers. Interpretive aspects can be maintained through the emphasis of cultural/historical and/or inductive construction and grounding in lived clinical experience. It is also useful for researchers to communicate either in the biomedically dominant visual mode—through tables, charts, diagrams, and data matrices—or in the clinically familiar narrative mode of case reports.

The dominant audience for clinical research perceives the issues of "validity," "reliability," and "generalizability" as scientific fundamentalist dogma resulting in heightened concerns about *bias*. Daly and McDonald (1992) recently published an account of a collaborative, multimethod study of the impact of echocardiography on patients' perceptions of self. Their story describes how difficult it can be to have a conversation at the wall: "The biggest problem was that physicians saw qualitative research methods as . . . prone to bias. Highly structured methods of analyzing qualitative data were effectively used . . . and are probably necessary for 'covering one's back' in multidisciplinary teams" (p. 416). The strategies Daly and McDonald present affirm a need for qualitative researchers to translate their wisdom from behind the wall and engage in conversations at the wall. But we believe it is *not* necessary to "cover one's back" and possibly sacrifice the integrity of qualitative approaches.

Developing a common language does not need to mean being co-opted by the dominant frames of discourse and having to use a language of analogy, such as *transferability* is analogous to *generalizability*. We are seeking a conversation at the wall where the unique strengths of each can be applied to the many questions arising out of the clinical experience. The prevailing mode of discourse for qualitative clinical researchers no longer needs to be one of justification (Kahn, 1993). Perception and subjectivity or "bias" are essential data and a crucial part of the knowledge generated by qualitative research. Local context and the human story, of which each individual and community story is a reflection, are primary goals of qualitative research, and not "generalizability." The methodological guidelines for quantitative methods are not relevant for qualitative clinical researchers. The rules of evidence for qualitative clinical research are addressed by Richardson in Chapter 12, Volume 3 of this series, but can be translated for clinical audiences in the form of telling methodologically, rhetorically, and clinically convincing stories.

Methodologically convincing stories answer the question, How was the research designed and done? It is important to make explicit how and why the research design, sampling strategies, and data collection and analysis techniques fit the question and research context, as discussed earlier. It is helpful to mention when the research design is cross-sectional, prospective, case control, or similar to some other one from observational epidemiology (Ward, 1993). Specific techniques, such as triangulation, member checking, and searching for disconfirming evidence (Kuzel & Like, 1991), should also be addressed when applicable.

Relationship is essential to the clinical experience. Kahn (1993) has proposed that a language of relationship be used to judge the methodological adequacy of clinical qualitative research. A methodologically convincing story addresses three different relationships. The investigator's *relationship with informants* is noted, with emphasis on how each influenced the other during the research process. The *relationship with the data* is described, in a way that is certain to comment on the circularity or iterative aspects of the research experience. Finally, the *relationship with the readers* is defined, such that the researcher's authorial intent is clear.

A *rhetorically convincing story* answers the question, How believable is this text? The audience is drawn into the story and begins imagining that the story is about them. When this occurs, the conclusions make more sense for the reader. The language and style of writing need to be familiar to the audience. Some of the quotations and observations selected to illustrate interpretations also need to reflect the readers' experiences and/or values. A rhetorically convincing story assures the reader that the author has walked in their shoes. Bunge (1961) reviews some of the features that characterize a believable story.

A *clinically convincing story* answers the question, Does this study make clinical sense? A story is clinically convincing if it successfully answers the three questions defining the clinical research space. The *question* must matter to clinical participants and the results specifically address that question. This usually means attention is directed to the pragmatic intervention and policy focus of the clinical world. The *audience* or stakeholder is also a clinical participant for whom the results matter, and this is obvious in the text. Finally, the manuscript reveals *assumptions* about the physical/behavioral, social/emotional, cultural/historical, or spiritual aspects of clinical participants' bodies, lives, and/or power.

Qualitative clinical research is convincing if the methods are appropriate for the question and the investigator's relationships with informants, data, and audience are clearly addressed; if the audience recognizes itself in the findings; and if the question and results matter to clinical participants. All of these criteria are more easily satisfied if a collaborative team does the research. When this team includes clinical participants, a community of discourse is created where conversations at the walls can begin (see Denz-Penhey & Murdoch, 1993).

◆ Summary

There are many clinical worlds. Each of them is a place where support is sought and power invoked. The clinical world and people's need for support occur in nursing, primary health care, specialized medical care, administration and management, education, social work, family therapy, mental health, public health, engineering, and law. In each of these worlds there are questions emerging from practice. These are the questions, the settings, and the participants for doing qualitative clinical research. This is where the conversation starts. The research is judged by the clinical difference it makes.

People continue to meet in clinics hoping to weave a comforting cloth of support, but the created relationships and patterns are now more varied, more confusing, and often too expensive. Concerns about access and cost do matter, but they are not adequately addressed without facing the abusive and dismembering experience of being a woman in the medical clinic, the pervasive delegitimation of patient experience, the clinicians' increasing sense of helpless imprisonment, and the mounting problems, discontinuities, and cultural conflicts within local communities. Knowing the probabilities is not enough and is often inappropriate. The stories' uniqueness and context are also essential threads in the fabric. Without them our bodies and lives remain fragmented and power is imposed. Melissa remains isolated within the clan of one-breasted women. She, and we, need the breadth of qualitative research. Qualitative clinical researchers must move from behind their walls, engage the clinical experience and its questions, and practice humility and fidelity within a community of discourse at the walls. This is a dangerous, but exciting, conversation, because it promises that no one can stay the same. Clinical research can heal by transforming into praxis. A recently published qualitative clinical study concludes, "The response of the general practitioner to the results was the recognition that he and his patients were operating on different levels of knowledge concerning their problem. As one who regarded himself as a champion of these patients and the legitimacy of their illness, this came as something of a shock" (Denz-Penhey & Murdoch, 1993, p. 17). As he was changed, so can we all be changed. In time, all walls crumble, power shifts, and healing begins.

◆ Notes

1. The word *patient* derives from the Latin word *patiens,* meaning "to suffer," and from the Latin words *paene,* "almost," and *penuria,* "need." People seek clinicians because they have need and are suffering. They are no longer complete; they lack adequate support. People come to clinicians because they do not perceive themselves as equal and/or whole. They are "patients" in need of movement toward wholeness.

2. The word *clinic* derives from the Greek words *klinikos,* meaning "of a bed," and *klinein,* "to lean, recline." From this sense, *a clinic is a physical and social place for those in need of support* (this support can be medical, managerial, educational, legal, economic, religious, nursing, social, psychological, or some combination of these). This understanding defines clinic as a bounded text for research.

3. The professional meetings include those of the Primary Care Research Methods and Statistics Conference, the North American Primary Care Research Group, the Society of General Internal Medicine, and the Society for the Teachers of Family Medicine. The newsletters are the *Interpreter* and *Medical Encounter,* and the methods publications are represented by the Sage Publications book series, *Research Methods for Primary Care.*

◆ References

Addison, R. B. (1992). Grounded hermeneutic research. In B. F. Crabtree & W. L. Miller (Eds.), *Doing qualitative research* (pp. 110-124). Newbury Park, CA: Sage.

Allen, M. N., & Jenson, L. (1990). Hermeneutical inquiry: Meaning and scope. *Western Journal of Nursing Research, 12,* 241-253.

Berg, D. N., & Smith, K. K. (Eds.). (1988). *The self in social inquiry: Researching methods.* Newbury Park, CA: Sage.

Borkan, J. M., Quirk, M., & Sullivan, M. (1991). Finding meaning after the fall: Injury narratives from elderly hip fracture patients. *Social Science and Medicine, 33,* 947-957.

Brewer, J., & Hunter, A. (1989). *Multimethod research: A synthesis of styles.* Newbury Park, CA: Sage.

Briggs, C. (1986). *Learning to ask.* Cambridge: Cambridge University Press.

Brueggemann, W. (1991). *Interpretation and obedience: From faithful reading to faithful living.* Minneapolis: Fortress.

Bunge, M. (1961). The weight of simplicity in the construction and assaying of scientific theories. *Philosophy of Science, 28,* 120-149.

Burawoy, M., Burton, A., Ferguson, A. A., Fox, K. J., Gamson, J., Gartrell, N., Hurst, L., Kurzman, C., Salzinger, L., Schiffman, J., & Ui, S. (Eds.). (1991). *Ethnography unbound: Power and resistance in the modern metropolis.* Berkeley: University of California Press.

Chesla, C. A. (1992). When qualitative and quantitative findings do not converge. *Western Journal of Nursing Research, 14,* 681-685.

Chrisman, N. J. (1977). The health seeking process: An approach to the natural history of illness. *Culture, Medicine, and Psychiatry, 1,* 351-377.

Chrisman, N. J., & Maretzki, T. W. (Eds.). (1982). *Clinically applied anthropology: Anthropologists in health science settings.* Boston: D. Reidel.

Clifford, J., & Marcus, G. E. (Eds.). (1986). *Writing culture: The poetics and politics of ethnography.* Berkeley: University of California Press.

Crabtree, B. F., Gelfand, A. E., Miller, W. L., et al. (1992). Categorical data analysis in primary care research: Log-linear models. *Family Medicine, 24,* 145-151.

Crabtree, B. F., & Miller, W. L. (1991). A qualitative approach to primary care research: The long interview. *Family Medicine, 23,* 145-151.

Crabtree, B. F., & Miller, W. L. (1992a). The analysis of narratives from a long interview. In M. Stewart, F. Tudiver, M. Bass, et al. (Eds.), *Tools for primary care research* (pp. 209-220). Newbury Park, CA: Sage.

Crabtree, B. F., & Miller, W. L. (1992b). A template approach to text analysis: Developing and using codebooks. In B. F. Crabtree & W. L. Miller (Eds.), *Doing qualitative research* (pp. 93-109). Newbury Park, CA: Sage.

Daly, J., & McDonald, I. (1992). Covering your back: Strategies for qualitative research in clinical settings. *Qualitative Health Research, 2,* 416-438.

Denz-Penhey, H., & Murdoch, J. C. (1993). Service delivery for people with chronic fatigue syndrome: A pilot action research study. *Family Practice, 10,* 14-18.

Deyo, R. A., Diehl, A. K., & Rosenthal, M. (1986). How many days of bedrest for acute low back pain? A randomized clinical trial. *New England Journal of Medicine, 315,* 1064-1070.

Diers, D. (1979). *Research in nursing practice.* Philadelphia: J. B. Lippincott.

Dozor, R. B., & Addison, R. B. (1992). Toward a good death: An interpretive investigation of family practice residents' practices with dying patients. *Family Medicine, 24,* 538-543.

Fabrega, H., Jr. (1976). The function of medical care systems: A logical analysis. *Perspectives in Biology and Medicine, 20,* 108-119.

Fabrega, H., Jr. (1979). The ethnography of illness. *Social Science and Medicine, 13,* 565-575.

Feinstein, A. R. (1985). *Clinical epidemiology: The architecture of clinical research.* Philadelphia: W. B. Saunders.

Fielding, N. G., & Fielding, J. L. (1986). *Linking data.* Beverly Hills, CA: Sage.

Fisher, S. (1986). *In the patient's best interest: Women and the politics of medical decisions.* New Brunswick, NJ: Rutgers University Press.

Fisher, S., & Todd, A. D. (Eds.). (1983). *The social organization of doctor-patient communication.* Washington, DC: Center for Applied Linguistics.

Foster, G. M. (1974). Medical anthropology: Some contrasts with medical sociology. *Medical Anthropology Newsletter, 6,* 1-6.

Foster, G. M., & Anderson, B. G. (1978). *Medical anthropology.* New York: John Wiley.

Freymann, J. G. (1989). The public's health care paradigm is shifting: Medicine must swing with it. *Journal of General Internal Medicine, 4*, 313-319.

Good, B. J., & Good, M. D. (1981). The meaning of symptoms: A cultural hermeneutic model for clinical practice. In L. Eisenberg & A. M. Kleinman (Eds.), *The relevance of social science for medicine* (pp. 165-196). Boston: D. Reidel.

Gordon, D. (1988). Tenacious assumptions in Western medicine. In M. Lock & D. Gordon (Eds.), *Biomedicine examined* (pp. 19-56). Boston: D. Reidel.

Haraway, D. J. (1991). *Simians, cyborgs and women: The reinvention of nature.* London: Routledge.

Helman, C. G. (1990). *Culture, health and illness.* Boston: Butterworth-Heinemann.

Jackson, M. (1989). *Paths toward a clearing: Radical empiricism and ethnographic inquiry.* Bloomington: Indiana University Press.

Johnson, M. (1987). *The body in the mind.* Chicago: University of Chicago Press.

Kahn, D. L. (1993). Ways of discussing validity in qualitative nursing research. *Western Journal of Nursing Research, 15*, 122-126.

Kelsey, J. L., Thompson, W. D., & Evans, A. S. (1986). *Methods in observational epidemiology.* New York: Oxford University Press.

Kirmayer, L. J. (1992). The body's insistence on meaning: Metaphor as presentation and representation in illness experience. *Medical Anthropology Quarterly, 6*, 323-346.

Kleinbaum, D. G., Kupper, L. L., & Morgenstern, H. (1982). *Epidemiologic research: Principles and quantitative methods.* Belmont, CA: Lifetime Learning.

Kleinman, A. M. (1992). Local worlds of suffering: An interpersonal focus for ethnographies of illness experience. *Qualitative Health Research, 2*, 127-134.

Kleinman, A. M. (1988). *The illness narratives: Suffering, healing, and the human condition.* New York: Basic Books.

Kleinman, A. M., Eisenberg, L., & Good, B. (1978). Culture, illness, and care: Clinical lessons from anthropologic and cross-cultural research. *Annals of Internal Medicine, 88*, 251-258.

Kuzel, A. J. (1992). Sampling in qualitative inquiry. In B. F. Crabtree & W. L. Miller (Eds.), *Doing qualitative research* (pp. 31-44). Newbury Park, CA: Sage.

Kuzel, A. J., & Like, R. C. (1991). Standards of trustworthiness for qualitative studies in primary care. In P. G. Norton, M. Stewart, F. Tudiver, M. J. Bass, & E. V. Dunn (Eds.), *Primary care research: Traditional and innovative approaches* (pp. 138-158). Newbury Park, CA: Sage.

Lather, P. (1991). *Getting smart: Feminist research and pedagogy with/in the postmodern.* New York: Routledge.

Lazarus, E. S. (1988). Theoretical considerations for the study of the doctor-patient relationship: Implications of a perinatal study. *Medical Anthropology Quarterly, 2*, 34-58.

Lincoln, Y. S., & Guba, E. G. (1985). *Naturalistic inquiry.* Newbury Park, CA: Sage.

Lock, M. (1982). On revealing the hidden curriculum. *Medical Anthropology Quarterly, 14*, 19-21.

Lock, M. (1986). The anthropological study of the American medical system: Center and periphery. *Social Science and Medicine, 22*, 931-932.

Martin, E. (1987). *The woman in the body: A cultural analysis of reproduction.* Boston: Beacon.

McCracken, G. (1988). *The long interview.* Newbury Park, CA: Sage.

McWhinney, I. R. (1986). Are we on the brink of a major transformation of clinical method? *Canadian Medical Association Journal, 135,* 873-878.

McWhinney, I. R. (1989). An acquaintance with particulars. *Family Medicine, 21,* 296-298.

Meinert, C. L. (1986). *Clinical trials: Design, conduct, and analysis.* New York: Oxford University Press.

Merriam, S. B. (1988). *Case study research in education.* San Francisco: Jossey-Bass.

Miles, M. B., & Huberman, A. M. (1984). *Qualitative data analysis: A sourcebook of new methods.* Beverly Hills, CA: Sage.

Miller, W. L. (1992). Routine, ceremony, or drama: An exploratory field study of the primary care clinical encounter. *Journal of Family Practice, 34,* 289-296.

Miller, W. L., & Crabtree, B. F. (1992). Primary care research: A multimethod typology and qualitative roadmap. In B. F. Crabtree & W. L. Miller (Eds.), *Doing qualitative research* (pp. 3-28). Newbury Park, CA: Sage.

Miller, W. L., Crabtree, B. F., & Yanoshik, M. K. (1991). Expanding the boundaries of family medicine research. *Family Medicine, 23,* 425-426.

Mishler, E. G. (1984). *The discourse of medicine: Dialectics of medical interviews.* Norwood, NJ: Ablex.

Moustakas, C. (1990). *Heuristic research: Design, methodology, and applications.* Newbury Park, CA: Sage.

Murdock, G. P., Ford, C. S., Hudson, A. E., et al. (1950). *Outline of cultural materials* (3rd ed.). New Haven, CT: Human Relations Area Files.

Patton, M. Q. (1990). *Qualitative evaluation and research methods* (2nd ed.). Newbury Park, CA: Sage.

Pelto, P. J., & Pelto, G. H. (1978). *Anthropological research: The structure of inquiry* (2nd ed.). New York: Cambridge University Press.

Pelto, P. J., & Pelto, G. H. (1990). Field methods in medical anthropology. In T. M. Johnson & C. F. Sargent (Eds.), *Medical anthropology: Contemporary theory and method* (pp. 269-297). New York: Praeger.

Pfifferling, J. H. (1981). A cultural prescription for medicocentrism. In L. Eisenberg & A. M. Kleinman (Eds.), *The relevance of social science for medicine* (pp. 197-222). Boston: D. Reidel.

Pocock, S. J. (1983). *Clinical trials: A practical approach.* New York: John Wiley.

Polgar, S. (1962). Health and human behavior: Areas of interest common to the social and medical sciences. *Current Anthropology, 3,* 159-205.

Richardson, L. (1990). *Writing strategies: Reaching diverse audiences.* Newbury Park, CA: Sage.

Sackett, D. L. (1991). *Clinical epidemiology: A basic science for clinical medicine* (2nd ed.). Boston: Little, Brown.

Sapsford, R., & Abbott, P. (1992). *Research methods for nurses and the caring professions.* Bristol, PA: Open University Press.

Schein, E. H. (1987). *The clinical perspective in fieldwork.* Newbury Park, CA: Sage.

Snadden, D., & Brown, J. B. (1991). Asthma and stigma. *Family Practice, 8,* 329-335.

Spradley, J. P. (1979). *The ethnographic interview.* New York: Holt, Rinehart & Winston.

Spradley, J. P. (1980). *Participant observation.* New York: Holt, Rinehart & Winston.

Stange, K. C., & Zyzanski, S. J. (1989). Integrating qualitative and quantitative research methods. *Family Medicine, 21,* 448-451.

Stein, H. F. (1990). *American medicine as culture.* Boulder, CO: Westview.

Strauss, A. L., & Corbin, J. (1990). *Basics of qualitative research: Grounded theory procedures and techniques.* Newbury Park, CA: Sage.

Taylor B. (1993). Phenomenology: One way to understand nursing practice. *International Journal of Nursing Studies, 30,* 171-179.

Tesch, R. (1990). *Qualitative research: Analysis types and software tools.* New York: Falmer.

Waitzkin, H. (1991). *The politics of medical encounters: How patients and doctors deal with social problems.* New Haven, CT: Yale University Press.

Ward, M. M. (1993). Study design in qualitative research: A guide to assessing quality. *Journal of General Internal Medicine, 8,* 107-109.

Weber, R. P. (1985). *Basic content analysis.* Beverly Hills, CA: Sage.

West, C. (1984). *Routine complications: Troubles with talk between doctors and patients.* Bloomington: Indiana University Press.

Wiesel, S. W., Cuckler, J. M., DeLuca, F., et al. (1980). Acute low back pain: An objective analysis of conservative therapy. *Spine, 5,* 324-330.

Willems, E. P., & Rausch, H. L. (1969). *Naturalistic viewpoints in psychological research.* New York: Holt, Rinehart & Winston.

Williams, G. (1984). The genesis of chronic illness: Narrative re-construction. *Sociology of Health and Illness, 6,* 175-200.

Williams, T. T. (1991). *Refuge: An unnatural history of family and place.* New York: Pantheon.

Willms, D. G. (1991). A new stage, a new life: Individual success in quitting smoking. *Social Science and Medicine, 33,* 1365-1371.

Willms, D. G., Best, J. A., Taylor, D. W., et al. (1990). A systematic approach for using qualitative methods in primary prevention research. *Medical Anthropology Quarterly, 4,* 391-409.

Wilson, D. M. C., Taylor, D. W., Gilbert, J. R., et al. (1988). A randomized trial of a family physician intervention for smoking cessation. *Journal of the American Medical Association, 260,* 1570-1574.

Wolcott, H. F. (1990). *Writing up qualitative research.* Newbury Park, CA: Sage.

Yin, R. K. (1989). *Case study research: Design and methods* (2nd ed.). Newbury Park, CA: Sage.

Young, A. (1982a). The anthropologies of illness and sickness. In B. Siegel, A. Beals, & S. Tyler (Eds.), *Annual review of anthropology* (Vol. 11, pp. 257-285). Palo Alto, CA: Annual Reviews.

Young, A. (1982b). When rational men fall sick: An inquiry into some assumptions made by medical anthropologists. *Culture, Medicine, and Psychiatry, 5,* 317-335.

Suggested Readings

◆ Chapter 1

Behar, R. (1996). *The vulnerable observer: Anthropology that breaks your heart*. Boston: Beacon.

Behar, R., & Gordon, D. A. (Eds.). (1996). *Women writing culture*. Berkeley: University of California Press.

Olson, G. A., & and Olson, E. (Eds.). (1995). *Women writing culture* (foreword by Donna Haraway; afterword by Henry A. Giroux). Albany: State University of New York Press.

◆ Chapter 2

Berg, B. L. (1995). *Qualitative research methods for the social sciences*. Boston: Allyn & Bacon.

Creswell, J. W. (1994). *Research design: Qualitative and quantitative approaches*. Thousand Oaks, CA: Sage.

Kvale, S. (1996). *Interviews: An introduction to qualitative research interviewing*. Thousand Oaks, CA: Sage.

Marshall, C., & Rossman, G. B. (1989). *Designing qualitative research*. Newbury Park, CA: Sage.

Maxwell, J. A. (1996). *Qualitative research design: An interactive approach*. Thousand Oaks, CA: Sage.

Strauss, A. L., & Corbin, J. (Eds.). (1997). *Grounded theory in practice*. Thousand Oaks, CA: Sage.

◆ Chapter 3

Agar, M. H. (1996). *The professional stranger*. San Diego, CA: Academic Press.

Annells, M. (1996). Grounded theory method: Philosophical perspectives, paradigm of inquiry, and postmodernism. *Qualitative Health Research, 6,* 379-393.

Creswell, J. W. (1997). *Qualitative inquiry and research design*. Thousand Oaks, CA: Sage.

Maxwell, J. A. (1996). *Qualitative research design: An interactive approach*. Thousand Oaks, CA: Sage.

Miller, G., & Dingwall, R. (Eds.). (1997). *Context and method in qualitative research*. Thousand Oaks, CA: Sage.

Morse, J. M. (Ed.). (1992). *Qualitative health research*. Newbury Park, CA: Sage.

Morse, J. M. (Ed.). (1994). *Critical issues in qualitative research methods*. Thousand Oaks, CA: Sage.

Morse, J. M., & Field, P. A. (1997). *Principles of qualitative methods*. Thousand Oaks, CA: Sage.

Silverman, D. (Ed.). (1997). *Qualitative research: Theory, method, and practice*. Thousand Oaks, CA: Sage.

◆ Chapter 4

Hamel, J. (1993). *Case study methods*. Newbury Park, CA: Sage.

Stake, R. E. (1995). *The art of case study research*. Thousand Oaks, CA: Sage.

Yin, R. K. (1994). *Case study research: Design and methods* (3rd ed.). Thousand Oaks, CA: Sage.

◆ Chapter 5

Atkinson, P. A. (1990). *The ethnographic imagination: Textual constructions of reality*. London: Routledge.

Atkinson, P. A. (1992). *Understanding ethnographic texts*. Newbury Park, CA: Sage.

Becker, H. S. (1970). *Sociological work: Method and substance*. New Brunswick, NJ: Transaction.

Burgess, R. G. (Ed.). (1982). *Field research: A source book and field manual*. London: Allen & Unwin.

Clifford, J., & Marcus, G. E. (Eds.). (1986). *Writing culture: The poetics and politics of ethnography*. Berkeley: University of California Press.

Coffey, A., & Atkinson, P. A. (1996). *Making sense of qualitative data*. Thousand Oaks, CA: Sage.

Delamont, S. (1992). *Fieldwork in educational settings*. London: Falmer.

Emerson, R. M., Fretz, R. I., & Shaw, L. L. (1995). *Writing ethnographic field notes*. Chicago: University of Chicago Press.

Hammersley, M. (1992). *What's wrong with ethnography? Methodological explorations*. London: Routledge.

Hammersley, M. (1998). *Reading ethnography: A critical guide* (2nd ed.). London: Longman.

Hammersley, M., & Atkinson, P. (1995). *Ethnography: Principles in practice* (2nd ed.). London: Routledge.

Lofland, J., & Lofland, L. (1995). *Analyzing social settings* (3rd ed.). Belmont, CA: Wadsworth.

McCall, G. J., & Simmons, J. L. (Eds.). (1969). *Issues in participant observation*. Reading, MA: Addison-Wesley.

Sanjek, R. (Ed.). (1990). *Fieldnotes: The makings of anthropology*. Ithaca, NY: Cornell University Press.

Van Maanen, J. (1988). *Tales of the field: On writing ethnography*. Chicago: University of Chicago Press.

◆ Chapter 6

Berger, P. L., & Luckmann, T. (1967). *The social construction of reality: A treatise in the sociology of knowledge*. Garden City, NY: Doubleday.

Garfinkel, H. (1967). *Studies in ethnomethodology*. Englewood Cliffs, NJ: Prentice Hall.

Gubrium, J. F. (1992). *Out of control: Family therapy and domestic disorder*. Newbury Park, CA: Sage.

Gubrium, J. F., & Holstein, J. A. (1997). *The new language of qualitative method*. New York: Oxford University Press.

Heritage, J. (1984). *Garfinkel and ethnomethodology*. Cambridge: Polity.

Holstein, J. A. (1993). *Court-ordered insanity: Interpretive practices and involuntary commitment*. Hawthorne, NY: Aldine de Gruyter.

Pollner, M. (1987). *Mundane reason: Reality in everyday and sociological discourse*. Cambridge: Cambridge University Press.

Schutz, A. (1970). *On phenomenology and social relations*. Chicago: University of Chicago Press.

Silverman, D. (Ed.). (1997). *Qualitative research: Theory, method, and practice*. Thousand Oaks, CA: Sage.

Smith, D. (1987). *The everyday world as problematic*. Boston: Northeastern University Press.

◆ Chapter 7

Glaser, B. G. (Ed.). (1994). *More grounded theory methodology: A reader*. Mill Valley, CA: Sociology Press.

Strauss, A. L., & Corbin, J. (Eds.). (1997). *Grounded theory in practice*. Thousand Oaks, CA: Sage.

◆ Chapter 8

Bell, S., & Yalom, M. (Eds.). (1990). *Revealing lives: Autobiography, biography, and gender*. Albany: State University of New York Press.

Broughton, T. L., & Anderson, L. (Eds.). (1997). *Women's lives/women's times: New essays on auto/biography.* Albany: State University of New York Press.

Crossan, J. (1991). *The historical Jesus: The life of a Mediterranean Jewish peasant.* New York: HarperCollins.

Crossan, J. (1994). *Jesus: A revolutionary biography.* New York: HarperCollins.

Fast, H. (1990). *Being red.* Boston: Houghton Mifflin.

Kridel, C., Bullough, R., Jr., & Shaker, P. (Eds.). (1996). *Teachers and mentors: Profiles of distinguished twentieth-century professors of education.* New York: Garland.

Polakow, V. (1994). *Lives on the edge: Single mothers and their children in the other America.* Chicago: University of Chicago Press.

Stone, I. (1957). The biographical novel. In I. Stone, J. O'Hara, & M. Kantor, *Three views of the novel.* Washington, DC: Library of Congress.

Stone, I. (1961). *The agony and the ecstasy.* New York: Doubleday.

Vasari, G. (1967). *Lives of the most eminent painters.* New York: Heritage. (Original work published 1568)

◆ Chapter 9

Jenkins, K. (Ed.). (1997). *The postmodern history reader.* New York: Routledge.

◆ Chapter 10

Carr, W., & Kemmis, S. (1986). *Becoming critical: Education, knowledge and action research.* London: Falmer.

Fisher, D., & Torbert, W. J. (1995). *Personal and organizational transformations: The true challenge of continual quality improvement.* London: McGraw-Hill.

Heron, J. (1996). *Co-operative inquiry: Research into the human condition.* London: Sage.

Heron, J., & Reason, P. (in press). A participatory inquiry paradigm. *Qualitative Inquiry.*

Reason, P., & Heron, J. (1996). *A layperson's guide to co-operative inquiry* [On-line]. University of Bath, Centre for Action Research in Professional Practice. Available: http://www.bath.ac.uk/carpp/LAYGUIDE.html

Reason, P., & Lincoln, Y. S. (Eds.). (1996). Quality in human inquiry [Special issue]. *Qualitative Inquiry, 2*(1).

Selener, D. (1997). *Participatory action research and social change.* Ithaca, NY: Cornell Participatory Action Research Network.

Skolimowski, H. (1995). *The participatory mind.* London: Arkana.

Toulmin, S., & Gustavsen, B. (1996). *Beyond theory: Changing organizations through participation.* Amsterdam: John Benjamins.

Wadsworth, Y. (1993). *Do it yourself social research.* Melbourne: Victoria Council of Social Service, Melbourne Family Care Organization.

Journals

Convergence Ottawa: International Council for Adult Education Concepts and Transformation, published by John Benjamins, Amsterdam

Systemic Practice and Action Research, published by Plenum, London

Institutional Development (Innovations in Civil Society), published by the Society for Participatory Research in Asia, New Delhi

◆ Chapter 11

Britten, N. (1995). Qualitative interviews in medical research. *British Medical Journal, 311,* 251-253.

Crabtree, B. F., Yanoshik, K., Miller, W. L., & O'Connor, P. (1993). Selecting individual or group interviews. In D. Morgan (Ed.), *Successful focus groups.* Newbury Park, CA: Sage.

Creswell, J. W. (1997). *Qualitative inquiry and research design.* Thousand Oaks, CA: Sage.

Elder, N., & Miller, W. L. (1995). Reading and evaluating qualitative research studies. *Journal of Family Practice, 41,* 279-285.

Griffiths, F. (Ed.). (1996). Exploring qualitative research in general practice. *Family Practice, 13*(Suppl.), S1-S30.

Kai, J. (1996). What worries parents when their preschool children are acutely ill, and why: A qualitative study. *British Medical Journal, 313,* 983-986.

Keen, J., & Packwood, T. (1995). Case study evaluation. *British Medical Journal, 311,* 444-446.

Kuzel, A., Engel, J., Addison, R., & Bogdewic, S. (1994). Desirable features of qualitative research. *Family Practice Research Journal, 14,* 369-378.

Mays, N., & Pope, C. (1995). Observational methods in health care settings. *British Medical Journal, 311,* 182-184.

McVea, K., Crabtree, B. F., Medder, J., Susman, J., et al. (1996). An ounce of prevention? Evaluation of the "Put Prevention in Practice" program. *Journal of Family Practice, 43,* 361-369.

Miller, W. L., Yanoshik, K., Crabtree, B. F., & Reymond, W. (1994). Patients, family physicians, and pain: Visions for interview narratives. *Family Medicine, 26*(3).

Pope, C., & Mays, N. (1995). Reaching the parts other methods cannot reach: An introduction to qualitative methods in health and health services research. *British Medical Journal, 311,* 42-45.

Stange, K. C., Miller, W. L., Crabtree, B. F., & Zyzanski, S. J. (1994). Multimethod research: Approaches for integrating qualitative and quantitative methods. *Journal of General Internal Medicine, 9,* 278-282.

Name Index

Subject Index

About the Authors

Paul Atkinson is Professor of Sociology and Head of the School of Social and Administrative Studies at the University of Wales, Cardiff. His past research has included ethnographic work on medical education, industrial training for unemployed school leavers, and the everyday work of hematologists. He is currently directing research on the work of discovery among a group of medical geneticists and, with Sara Delamont and Odette Parry, on the academic socialization of doctoral students in the natural and social sciences. He took his B.A. in social anthropology at Cambridge and his Ph.D. at Edinburgh. His current methodological interests include work on the rhetoric of ethnography and the use of various computing strategies for qualitative data analysis. His books include *The Clinical Experience* (1981), *Language, Structure and Reproduction* (1985), *The Ethnographic Imagination* (1990), *Understanding Ethnographic Texts* (1992), and, with Martyn Hammersley, *Ethnography: Principles in Practice* (1983). A second edition of the last of these is currently in preparation. A monograph on medical talk and medical work, based on fieldwork with hematologists, is also forthcoming.

Juliet Corbin is a Lecturer at the School of Nursing, San Jose State University, San Jose, California, and Research Associate, Department of Social and Behavioral Sciences, University of California, San Francisco. She is coauthor, with Anselm Strauss, of *Basics of Qualitative Research* (1990), as well as coauthor of the research monograph *Unending Work and Care*

(1988) and of the policy book *Shaping a New Health Care System* (1988). She has also authored or coauthored a number of research and methodological papers, including an important theoretical work titled "A Trajectory Model for Reorganizing the Health Care System." She is currently researching the role of the body in action and writing up a fieldwork study about the flow of work in hospitals.

Benjamin F. Crabtree, Ph.D., is a medical anthropologist in the Department of Family Medicine, University of Nebraska Medical Center, where he is Professor and Director of Research. He has contributed numerous articles and chapters on both qualitative and quantitative methods, covering topics ranging from time series analysis and log-linear models to in-depth interviews and qualitative analysis strategies. He is coeditor of *Doing Qualitative Research* and *Exploring Collaborative Research* and is currently working on a book on comparative case studies. In his current work, he is using case study designs to model primary care practices as nonlinear complex adaptive systems. His work has been published in such journals as the *Journal of Clinical Epidemiology, Public Health Reports, Journal of Family Practice,* and *Family Medicine.*

Norman K. Denzin is Distinguished Professor of Communications, College of Communications scholar, and Professor of Sociology and Humanities at the University of Illinois, Urbana-Champaign. He is the author of numerous books, including *The Cinematic Society, Images of Postmodern Society, The Research Act, Interpretive Interactionism, Hollywood Shot by Shot, Symbolic Interactionism and Cultural Studies, The Recovering Alcoholic,* and *The Alcoholic Self,* which won the Cooley Award from the Society for the Study of Symbolic Interaction in 1988. He is editor of *Studies in Symbolic Interaction: A Research Annual, Cultural Studies,* and *Sociological Quarterly.* He is coeditor of the *Handbook of Qualitative Research* and of *Qualitative Inquiry.* In 1997, he won the George Herbert Mead Award from the Society for the Study of Symbolic Interaction. This award recognizes lifetime contributions to the study of human behavior.

Jaber F. Gubrium is Professor in the Department of Sociology at the University of Florida. He has conducted research on the social organization of care in diverse treatment settings, from nursing homes and physical rehabilitation to counseling centers and family therapy. His continuing fieldwork on the organizational embeddedness of social forms serves as a basis for the formulation of a sociology of description. He is the editor of the *Journal of Aging Studies* and author of *Living and Dying at Murray Manor* (1975), *Oldtimers and Alzheimer's* (1986), *Analyzing Field Reality* (1988), *The Mosaic of Care* (1991), *Out of Control* (1992), and *Speaking of Life* (1993). He is also coauthor, with James Holstein, of *What Is Family?* (1990) and *Constructing the Life Course* (1994).

Martyn Hammersley is Professor of Educational and Social Research, School of Education, The Open University, Milton Keynes, United Kingdom. He was educated in sociology at the London School of Economics and the University of Manchester. His main areas of research have been in the sociology of education and social research methodology. He has written many articles in these fields, and his books include *Ethnography: Principles in Practice* (with Paul Atkinson; 1983), *The Dilemma of Qualitative Method* (1989), *Reading Ethnographic Research* (1991), *What's Wrong With Ethnography?* (1992), and *The Politics of Social Research* (1995).

James A. Holstein is Professor of Sociology at Marquette University. His research brings an ethnomethodologically informed constructionist perspective to a variety of topics, including mental illness, social problems, family, the life course, and dispute processing. His recent publications include *Court-Ordered Insanity* (1993) and *What Is Family?* (1990) and *Constructing the Life Course* (1993), coauthored with Jaber Gubrium. He and Gale Miller have recently coedited *Reconsidering Social Constructionism* and *Constructionist Controversies,* and they also coedit the research annual *Perspectives on Social Problems.* He and Jaber Gubrium have recently published two texts on qualitative inquiry: *The Active Interview* (1995) and *The New Language of Qualitative Method* (1997).

Valerie J. Janesick, Ph.D., is Professor of Educational Leadership and Policy, Florida International University, in Miami and Fort Lauderdale, Florida. She teaches classes in qualitative research methods, action research, curriculum theory, curriculum planning and evaluation, and developing intercultural awareness in education. Her work in international curriculum development and on international perspectives and cultural use of languages in the education setting has enabled her to travel widely. She is also writing about integrating the arts and humanities into qualitative research projects. Previous to her current appointment, she has taught qualitative research methods at the State University of New York, Albany; Gallaudet University; and the University of Kansas. Her work has been published in *Curriculum Inquiry, Anthropology and Education Quarterly,* and various education journals. She has just completed a book for Sage Publications titled *Stretching Exercises for Qualitative Researchers* and is looking forward to her next projects, which include a text on ethics and the qualitative researcher, a text on curriculum and qualitative inquiry, and classes in Irish step dancing.

Yvonna S. Lincoln is Professor of Higher Education and Head of the Department of Educational Administration at Texas A&M University. She has an Ed.D. from Indiana University and previously taught at the University of Kansas and Vanderbilt University. She is a specialist in higher education research, organizational analysis, program evaluation, and alternative paradigm research. Her work has been published in such well-received books as *Fourth Generation Evaluation, Naturalistic Inquiry, Effective Evaluation* (all coauthored with Egon Guba), and *Organizational Theory and Inquiry,* as well as in a host of papers and conference presentations. She has been honored with awards for her research from the American Evaluation Association, Division J (Postsecondary and Higher Education) of the American Educational Research Association, and the Association for Institutional Research. She has served as President of the American Evaluation Association and as Vice President of Division J of the American Educational Research Association, and has been keynote speaker at more than a dozen conferences.

William L. Miller, M.D., M.A., a family physician anthropologist, is currently Vice Chair and Program Director in the Department of Family Medicine at Lehigh Valley Hospital in Allentown, Pennsylvania. He is active in an effort to make qualitative research more accessible to health care researchers. He has contributed book chapters and articles detailing step-by-step applications of qualitative methods, including the book *Doing Qualitative Research,* which he coedited. His research interests center on the role of the patient-physician relationship in health care, on physician and patient understanding of pain and pain management, and on hypertension. In his current work, he is using case study designs to model primary care practices as nonlinear complex adaptive systems.

Janice M. Morse (R.N., Ph.D. [anthropology], Ph.D. [nursing], FAAN) is a Professor in the Faculty of Nursing and Director of the International Institute of Qualitative Methodology at the University of Alberta and Adjunct Professor in the School of Nursing at Pennsylvania State University. She has an interest in developing qualitative methods and has published on both basic and advanced methods. Her books include *Qualitative Research Methods for Health Professionals* (with Peggy Anne Field; second edition, 1995), *Qualitative Health Research* (1992), *Qualitative Nursing Research: A Contemporary Dialogue* (revised edition, 1991), *Critical Issues in Qualitative Research Methods* (1994), and *Completing a Qualitative Project* (1997). She is the editor of *Qualitative Health Research,* an interdisciplinary, bimonthly journal concerned with qualitative methods and research. She is currently funded by the National Institutes of Health to conduct a qualitative study to explore the use and meaning of comfort in nursing.

Peter Reason is Director of the Centre for Action Research in Professional Practice at the University of Bath, which offers a postgraduate program in action research and a master's degree in responsibility and business practice. His major academic work has been to contribute to the development of a participatory worldview and associated approaches to inquiry, and in particular to the theory and practice of cooperative inquiry. He has applied this particularly in medical and complementary medical fields. His current interests include the further development of this method and its application to personal and organizational learning, radical shifts in epistemology and consciousness, professional and managerial practice as inquiry, education as liberation, and high-quality postconventional personal behavior. He is coeditor of *Human Inquiry: A Sourcebook of New Paradigm Research* (with John Rowan; 1981) and editor of *Human Inquiry in Action* (1988) and *Participation in Human Inquiry* (1994). He is also coeditor, with Yvonna S. Lincoln, of a special issue of *Qualitative Inquiry* titled "Quality in Human Inquiry," and has authored book chapters and journal articles on cooperative inquiry and the participative worldview.

Louis M. Smith is Professor of Education, Washington University, St. Louis, where he has taught for 38 years. He was trained at Oberlin College and the University of Minnesota and has held positions at the University of Minnesota Psychoeducational Clinic, the St. Paul Public Schools, and Cemrel, Inc. Through a mix of sabbaticals, fellowships, and smaller conferences, he has been fortunate to spend considerable time in New Zealand, Australia, Israel, and the United Kingdom. In the midst of all this, he and his colleagues have written half a dozen books and an array of articles and final reports.

Robert E. Stake is Professor of Education and Director of the Center for Instructional Research and Curriculum Evaluation at the University of Illinois at Urbana-Champaign. A specialist in the evaluation of educational programs, he was trained at Princeton University in psychology, and has taught at the University of Nebraska as well as having visiting appointments at universities in four countries. Among the honors that have been accorded him are the highest offices of two divisions of the American Educational Research Association and Fulbright fellowships to Sweden and Brazil. He is the author of *Quieting Reform,* a metaevaluation study of an urban youth program called Cities-in-Schools; *Evaluating the Arts in Education; Case Studies in Science Education* (with Jack Easley); *Evaluating Curriculum* (with Steven Kemmis); and *Custom and Cherishing: The Arts in Elementary Schools* (with Liora Bresler and Linda Mabry).

Anselm Strauss (December 18, 1916–September 5, 1996) was Emeritus Professor, Department of Social and Behavioral Sciences, University of California, San Francisco. He coauthored, with Barney Glaser, *The Discovery of Grounded Theory* (1967), the foundational first book on this methodology, and also authored *Qualitative Analysis for Social Scientists* (1987) and (with Juliet Corbin) *Basics of Qualitative Research* (1990). He and his coworkers published many research monographs, including *Psychiatric Ideologies and Institutions* (1964), *Awareness of Dying* (1965), *Time for Dying* (1968), and *The Social Organization of Medical Work* (1985). His theoretical writings include *Mirrors and Masks* (1958), *Negotiations* (1978), and *Continual Permutations of Action* (1993). A *Festschrift* edited by David Maines, titled *Social Organization and Social Processes* (1991), contains papers by ex-students and collegial friends that reflect his writings and teaching. He was a visiting professor at various foreign universities, including the University of Paris and Cambridge University, and is known for both his theoretical and research writing.

Gaye Tuchman is Professor of Sociology at the University of Connecticut, where she also serves on the graduate faculty of communication sciences.

Her books include *Making News: A Study in the Construction of Reality* (1978) and (with Nina Fortin) *Edging Women Out: Victorian Novelists, Publishers, and Social Change* (1989). The 1990, 1991, and 1992 Distinguished Publication Committee of the American Sociological Association cited *Edging Women Out* as one of the 10 best books of the past three years. In the academic year 1994-1995, she served as President of the Eastern Sociological Society.